MARK

Jesus Christ, Love in Action

A COMMENTARY BY
PRACTICAL CHRISTIANITY FOUNDATION
L. L. SPEER, FOUNDER

GREEN KEY BOOKS

HOLIDAY, FLORIDA

MARK: JESUS CHRIST, LOVE IN ACTION

©2004 by the Practical Christianity Foundation. All Rights Reserved.

International Standard Book Number: 1932587454

Cover Art: The Resource Agency, Franklin, Tennessee
Production and prepress: JJ Graphics/Impact Productions

Printed in the United States of America

All scriptural references, unless otherwise noted, are quoted from GOD'S WORD® Translation. ©1995 by God's Word to the Nations. Used by permission.

Scripture quotations marked (KJV) are taken from The Holy Bible, King James Version.
Scripture quotations marked (NKJV) are taken from The Holy Bible, New King James Version. ©1979, 1980, 1982 by Thomas Nelson, Inc. Used by permission. All rights reserved.

For information:
Green Key Books
2514 Aloha Place
Holiday, Florida 34691
www.greenkeybooks.com

Library of Congress Cataloging-in-Publication Data available on request.

CONTENTS

PREFACE

From the conception of the Practical Christianity Foundation, it has been the goal of the organization to convey the truth in Scripture through verse-by-verse devotional studies such as this one. As part of that goal, we agree in an attempt neither to prove nor disprove any traditional or alternative interpretations, beliefs, or doctrines, but rather to allow the Holy Spirit to reveal the truth contained within the Scriptures. Any interpretations relating to ambiguous passages that are not directly and specifically verifiable by other scriptural references are simply presented in what we believe to be the most likely intention of the message based upon those things that we are specifically told. In those instances, our conclusions are noted as interpretive, and such analyses should not be understood as doctrinal positions that we are attempting to champion.

This study is divided into sections, usually between six and eight verses, and each section concludes with a "Notes/Applications" passage, which draws practical insight from the related verses that can be applied to contemporary Christian living. The intent is that the reader will complete one section per day, will gain a greater understanding of the verses within that passage, and will daily be challenged toward a deeper commitment to our Lord and Savior

Jesus Christ. Also included at certain points within the text are "Dig Deeper" boxes, which are intended to assist readers who desire to invest additional time to study topics that relate to the section in which these boxes appear. Our prayer is that this study will impact the lives of all believers, regardless of age, ethnicity, or education.

Each of PCF's original projects is a collaborative effort of many writers, content editors, grammatical editors, transcribers, researchers, readers, and other contributors, and as such, we present them only as products of the Practical Christianity Foundation as a whole. These works are not for the recognition or acclamation of any particular individual but are written simply as a means to uphold and fulfill the greater purpose of our Mission Statement, which is "to exalt the Holy Name of God Almighty by declaring the redemptive message of His Son, the Lord Jesus Christ, to the lost global community and equipping the greater Christian community through the communication of the Holy Word of God in its entirety through every appropriate means available."

Practical Christianity Foundation
Value Statements

1. We value the Holy Name of God and will strive to exalt Him through godly living, committed service, and effective communication. *"As long as you live, you, your children, and your grandchildren must fear the Lord your God. All of you must obey all his laws and commands that I'm giving you, and you will live a long time"* (Deuteronomy 6:2).

2. We value the redemptive work of the Lord Jesus Christ for a lost world and will strive to communicate His redemptive message to the global community. *"Then Jesus said to them, 'So wherever you go in the world, tell everyone the Good News'"* (Mark 16:15).

3. We value the Holy Word of God and will strive to communicate it in its entirety. *"16Every Scripture passage is inspired by God. All of them are useful for teaching, pointing out errors, correcting people, and training them for a life that has God's approval. 17They equip God's servants so that they are completely prepared to do good things"* (2 Timothy 3:16–17).

4. We value spiritual growth in God's people and will strive to enhance that process through the effective communication of God's Holy Word, encouraging them to be lovers of the truth. *"But grow in the good will and knowledge of our Lord and Savior Jesus Christ. Glory belongs to him now and for that eternal day! Amen"* (2 Peter 3:18).

5. We value the equipping ministry of the church of the Lord Jesus Christ and will strive to provide resources for that ministry by the communication of God's Holy Word through every appropriate means available. *"11He also gave apostles, prophets, missionaries, as well as pastors and teachers as gifts to his church. 12Their purpose is to prepare God's people to serve and to build up the body of Christ"* (Ephesians 4:11–12).

INTRODUCTION

The Gospel of Mark was written about A.D. 57–59 by a Jewish disciple of the Christian faith, the same "John Mark" mentioned at least ten times in the New Testament. John was his Hebrew name, and Mark was his Gentile name.[1] All of the early church fathers ascribe this gospel to a young man who was not one of the twelve apostles but was a disciple of Paul and later of Peter. He is often referred to as the interpreter of Peter's teaching, and Peter apparently gave Mark his stamp of approval for the use of these teachings among the early churches.[2]

Mark accompanied his cousin Barnabas on Paul's first missionary journey. Paul became displeased with Mark because he chose to return home to Jerusalem, so Paul took Silas and Barnabas took Mark for their later missionary adventures. Paul apparently reconciled with Mark since he later referred to him with affection *(2 Timothy 4:11–12)*.

According to early church history, Mark later traveled with Peter and was most likely nearby when Peter was crucified in Rome. After Peter's death, Mark traveled to Alexandria in Egypt, where he founded and established a prominent church. After only a few years,

John Mark suffered a martyr's death by being dragged through the streets of Alexandria.

The style of the text generates drama. The sentences are relatively short with numerous action verbs, marking the text with a sense of urgency. For example, Mark uses the word *immediately* and its synonyms forty-one times in sixteen chapters. He emphasizes Jesus' actions more than His teachings. He recounts only one lengthy discourse by Jesus, and the rest of the book recaps brief encounters with relatively little discussion.

In this gospel, one does not witness a meek and mild Jesus. Rather, the Son of Man is depicted as an energetic and tireless action hero, moving quickly from scene to scene, healing the sick, casting out demons, and confronting his opponents.

Since it appears that Mark was in Rome with Peter when this gospel was written, it is safe to assume that Roman Christians were his intended primary audience. There are times when Mark slows down to explain a Jewish custom so that the Gentile reader can understand the Jewish frame of reference, which accounts for the presence of the Roman method of calculation and the use of some Latin words in the text. Rather than confuse his Gentile readers, who would benefit little from the Jewish background and the Old Testament Scriptures, Mark instead jumps from one event to the next, revealing more and more physical evidence of Jesus' position as the Son of Man and Son of God. Therefore, even one who is unfamiliar with the Jewish heritage can still be convinced of God's plan to redeem lost humanity through the unique evidence portrayed in the life, death, and resurrection of Jesus, the Christ, God's Anointed One.

In Mark's haste to get to the core of Jesus' message, there is no account of His birth or His childhood. There are no "shepherds in the field" or "wise men from the East." The Gospel of Mark starts quickly with the ministry of John the Baptist, progresses directly to the ministry of Jesus, and concludes just as quickly with Jesus' statement following His resurrection to "go in the world [and] tell everyone the Good News," before He was received into heaven. There is possibly no other account of Jesus' life and ministry more dynamic and captivating than the gospel according to Mark.

MARK 1

Mark 1:1–8

1:1 *This is the beginning of the Good News about Jesus Christ, the Son of God.*

This short phrase typifies Mark's direct and concise style. This book is the Good News about Jesus Christ, the Son of God. The name *Christ*, Greek for "anointed one," is the same as the Old Testament word *Messiah*. When the word *Christ* is added to *Jesus*, we are reminded that Jesus, His God-given birth name, is indeed the Anointed One, His God-ordained position in history. This Promised One had been the hope of all the faithful throughout the Old Testament generations.

1:2 *The prophet Isaiah wrote, "I am sending my messenger ahead of you to prepare the way for you."*

Mark moves directly to Old Testament references that demonstrate the purpose of God from prior centuries. The Lord God previously stated through His prophets that one would come as a messenger, preparing the way for His Messiah: "'I'm going to send my messenger, and he will clear the way ahead of me. Then the Lord you are looking for will suddenly come to his temple. The messenger of the promise will come. He is the one you want,' says the Lord of Armies" *(Malachi 3:1)*.

This verse refers to Jesus as the fulfillment of Old Testament promises and positions the revelation of Jesus as God's Messiah in the center of all history. Jesus is the focal point of God's eternal purpose. Mark brings to his gospel the basic premise that past generations looked forward to this unique, overwhelming event. No other event in human history could equal the sacrifice of Jesus, God's Anointed One. Past believers looked forward with anticipation; future genera-tions will look back with joy and thanksgiving, but none of this was fulfilled until God sent His messenger to prepare the way.

1:3 *"A voice cries out in the desert: 'Prepare the way for the Lord! Make his paths straight!'"*

Quoting the prophet Isaiah, Mark employs a typical method of estab-lishing the validity of the recent historical events—that what had happened recently was foretold years earlier: "A voice cries out in the desert: 'Clear a way for the Lord. Make a straight highway in the wilderness for our God'" *(Isaiah 40:3)*. The Old Testament Scriptures unveil a logical, consistent development throughout the history of Israel that resulted in the fulfillment of prophecies concerning the Messiah. Isaiah simply states that preparations must be made for the visitation of the Lord. Historically, it was customary that any visit from the king would involve the cleaning and smoothing of the roads that he would follow on his journey. The Old Testament often portrays the promised Messiah as a great King, established by the Lord God Himself.

1:4 *John the Baptizer was in the desert telling people about a baptism of repentance for the forgiveness of sins.*

Mark proceeds directly to the ministry of a man named John, also known as "the Baptizer," who was the fulfillment of Old Testament prophecies. God ordained him to prepare the way of the Lord. John and Jesus were related through their mothers, Elizabeth and Mary: "Elizabeth, your relative, is six months pregnant with a son in her old age. People said she couldn't have a child" *(Luke 1:36)*.

John was born to Elizabeth and Zechariah following an extraordinary promise. Elizabeth and Zechariah were an elderly couple, who, though childless, remained faithful to God. As a priest, Zechariah served one week every six months in the temple in Jerusalem. While Zechariah was serving his assigned time as priest, the Lord's angel visited him and promised him a son. Zechariah laughed because Elizabeth was too old to bear children. Because he laughed at the word of the Lord's messenger, Zechariah was immediately struck mute. When he returned home to his wife, she became pregnant. Nevertheless, Zechariah was unable to speak until Elizabeth gave birth to John, their only child *(Luke 1:5–64)*.

John's divine commission was to prepare the way of the Lord by warning the people of Israel to repent of their sins. They were God's chosen people, soon to receive the promised Messiah. John performed his baptisms in the wilderness. His message was comprised of repentance for the remission of sins, a remarkable deviation from the typical Jewish understanding of the day because it called for individuals to repent of their sins. The people of Israel still considered their nation to be God's chosen people, yet this specific, direct message, in typical prophetic fashion, rebuked them for their sinful ways and urged them to return to the Lord.

1:5 *All Judea and all the people of Jerusalem went to him. As they confessed their sins, he baptized them in the Jordan River.*

John's ministry impacted the entire region. It appears that a multitude of people from Jerusalem and the surrounding area gravitated to his message. Evidently, the hearts of the people were sensitive to this new prophet and his message of individual repentance for sins, so they responded. They confessed their sins and, as a sign of their repentance, were baptized by John. Ultimately, the entire region was being prepared for the coming Anointed One.

1:6 *John was dressed in clothes made from camel's hair. He wore a leather belt around his waist and ate locusts and wild honey.*

The manner in which Mark describes John's physical appearance brings to mind the style of other Old Testament prophets. John looked like a wild man living off the land. Following the fashion of the prophet, he wore a rough camel-hair tunic, which demonstrated the austerity of his lifestyle. He also wore a leather belt or girdle. As the son of a priest, he was entitled to the garments ascribed to his priestly heritage; however, John refused such outward show, preferring instead to be clothed in the garment of a prophet. He was clothed much like Elijah, the great prophet of the Lord during the time of Ahab:

> [7]*The king asked them, "What was the man like who told you this?"*
>
> [8]*They replied, "He was hairy and had a leather belt around his waist."*
>
> *"That's Elijah from Tishbe," the king answered. (2 Kings 1:7–8)*

John was likely aware of this similarity, because Jesus later confirmed that John the Baptist was His forerunner and had come in the spirit of Elijah.

John did not preach his message of repentance in the towns and villages of the region. He lived the austere, separated life of the prophet in the wilderness, untouched by worldly enticements. To hear his message, people had to travel to him.

1:7 *He announced, "The one who comes after me is more powerful than I. I am not worthy to bend down and untie his sandal straps.*

John could be considered the last of the Old Testament prophets since the message of "repentance for the forgiveness of sins" was the declarative element of his ministry *(verse 4)*. However, there was also a predictive component, focusing on a person who would soon appear on the scene of Israel's history. John clarified that this one would be much more powerful than he was. When questioned about it, John gave a distinct answer.

> *27John answered, "People can't receive anything unless it has been given to them from heaven. 28You are witnesses that I said, 'I'm not the Messiah, but I've been sent ahead of him.'*
>
> *29"The groom is the person to whom the bride belongs. The best man, who stands and listens to him, is overjoyed when the groom speaks. This is the joy that I feel. 30He must increase in importance, while I must decrease in importance." (John 3:27–30)*

1:8 *I have baptized you with water, but he will baptize you with the Holy Spirit."*

John explained the difference between his ministry and the ministry of the one Who would follow him. John's ministry was primarily symbolic yet essential. He baptized with water, signifying the fact that the individual must repent of his sins. In contrast, He Who would follow John would have a ministry of substance and power. John could talk about the message, but this one would consummate the message by the baptism of the Holy Spirit. John was speaking of the Lord Jesus Christ, Who would remove the stain of sin itself.

Notes/Applications

As we begin this journey through the Gospel of Mark, it is important to note how the author clearly and logically establishes the authority of Jesus Christ. By understanding the Old Testament prophecies about Christ, the fulfillment of those prophecies, and the message of the one on Whom all Scripture centers, we are led into a journey of faith that is as relevant for us today as it was for those who heeded the voice of John the Baptizer crying "out in the desert." In essence, John was proclaiming, "Get ready! He's coming! The one you've heard about from childhood, the one you've been waiting for all your life, is coming soon!"

Hearing a message like that, wouldn't we be stirred to excitement—or at least curiosity? Mark records that people journeyed out of their way (into the desert) to hear what this wild-looking man had to say, but John did not mince words. Along with the thrilling news that the Messiah's arrival was imminent, he told people to repent of their sins and be baptized as an outward sign of their inward cleansing. God asks no less of us today.

The events recorded in the Gospel of Mark unfold like scenes in a centuries-old drama. However, now the lead character is about to take the stage, securing the triumphant outcome of the story. That story began with the fall of mankind and culminates with God's eternal plan to bring His rebellious creation back to Him. While opening our eyes to the reality of the human dilemma—mired in sin and callous disregard for the Creator—Mark shows us God's solution to that dilemma in the person of Jesus, the Son of God.

Jesus' ministry was destined to eclipse the ministry of John the Baptizer, and John knew it. That is why John said he was not worthy to untie the sandal strap of the one who was coming when he pronounced in verse eight, "I have baptized you with water, but he will baptize you with the Holy Spirit." As Christians, we, too, can aspire to no higher calling than to be a "forerunner" in pointing the lost to Christ the Lord.

Mark 1:9–15

1:9 *At that time Jesus came from Nazareth in Galilee and was baptized by John in the Jordan River.*

Of all of the people coming to John from the surrounding area, Mark focuses on a particular person, Jesus from Nazareth in Galilee. Nazareth, located about twenty miles southwest of the Sea of Galilee, was the hometown where Jesus lived and learned His trade as a carpenter from Joseph, Mary's husband. At the age of thirty, it was time for Jesus to leave home to embark upon the ministry for which He had been sent.

Jesus traveled southward toward the Jordan River at the northern end of the Dead Sea, and there he met John. The three other gospel accounts give more detail about this event. John knew that Jesus was the one about Whom he had prophesied. The Gospel of Matthew records that John at first refused Jesus' request for baptism and asked instead to be baptized by Jesus: "But John tried to stop him and said, 'I need to be baptized by you. Why are you coming to me?'" *(Matthew 3:14)*. After all, John had declared that the one Who followed him would be the greater. Should the servant baptize his master or the prophet baptize the person Who fulfills his prophecy? Should a man baptize his Lord? But Jesus insisted upon this symbolic demonstration of submission to God, and John, therefore, baptized Jesus in the Jordan River:

> [13]*Then Jesus appeared. He came from Galilee to the Jordan River to be baptized by John.* [14]*But John tried to stop him and said, 'I need to be baptized by you. Why are you coming to me?'*
>
> [15]*Jesus answered him, "This is the way it has to be now. This is the proper way to do everything that God requires of us."*
> (Matthew 3:13–15)

1:10 *As Jesus came out of the water, he saw heaven split open and the Spirit coming down to him as a dove.*

As Jesus emerged from the river, the heavens opened, and the Spirit of God, appearing in the form of a dove, descended upon the Son of God. The baptism itself did not appear remarkable, but the event began to take on special meaning immediately following the baptism.

1:11 *A voice from heaven said, "You are my Son, whom I love. I am pleased with you."*

A voice from heaven, that of God the Father, made a clear declaration: Jesus was God's Son, in Whom He was well pleased. At this spectacular event, the Almighty God publicly identified Jesus as His Son. This continues to provide irrefutable evidence, spoken by the tongue of God Himself, of Jesus' divine nature. *"The Father and I are one"* (John 10:30).

1:12–13 *[12]At once the Spirit brought him into the desert, [13]where he was tempted by Satan for 40 days. He was there with the wild animals, and the angels took care of him.*

Events quickly intensified. As soon as Jesus came out of the water, the Spirit drove Him into the desert to be tempted. The exact location of the desert remains uncertain. The importance of the passage surely relies more on Christ's isolation and handling of the temptation than on the region in which the temptation occurred.

In the desert, Jesus lived with wild beasts for forty days. While His physical circumstances were challenging, the spiritual circumstances were far more compelling. Just after the Father had declared that Jesus was indeed His Son, the Holy Spirit drove Jesus into a situation where He was tempted by Satan for forty days.

This passage records a pivotal moment for all of history. The two ancient enemies go head to head in confrontation. Jesus, God in the flesh, won this epic confrontation as He was sustained and supported by God's angels. Matthew's detailed gospel account shows that Jesus met each of the three temptations with the armor of the

Word of God when He responded to Satan by saying, "Scripture says" *(Matthew 4:1–11)*.

This is the ultimate reality. This battle between Jesus and Satan refers to only one of the many battles that ensue in this spiritual warfare. Ultimately, this battle plays out in the heart and soul of every individual born into this world. Everything that we as human beings think or believe or think we believe determines our position in this battle, and everything we do in the surroundings of our earthly reality is overshadowed by the awesome, eternal struggle going on around us *(Ephesians 6:12)*. Man's keenest observation throughout his lifetime demonstrates that he is totally unaware, totally oblivious to this truth and this ultimate reality. Sadly, such ignorance will lead him to perdition apart from the Holy Spirit's intervention.

DIG DEEPER: *Satan*

Before the creation of man, Satan led a major revolt against Almighty God *(Isaiah 14:9–14)*. Since then, a vast war has been waged over the hearts and souls of all men. Satan hates God, hates mankind, and especially hates the Son of God through Whom he is destined to perish. Satan will win some battles—he will surely capture a large part of God's creation—but ultimately, he will lose the war, and Christ will claim the victory *(Revelation 20:1–15)*!

1:14 *After John had been put in prison, Jesus went to Galilee and told people the Good News of God.*

Some time after Jesus' temptation in the wilderness, John was imprisoned for his ministry. Too many people were being influenced by his message, so it appeared necessary to silence him. However, after the attempt to silence God's message through John, Jesus commenced His public ministry in Galilee, the region of Palestine where He lived.

1:15 *He said, "The time has come, and the kingdom of God is near. Change the way you think and act, and believe the Good News."*

The phrase "has come" as used in this verse implies that all of history pointed to this particular period of time, and now the anticipated time had arrived. John the Baptizer and other prophets pointed to some future event, some future person. Jesus' message was clear: The promised time was now here!

Jesus also stated that the kingdom of God was "near." The people of Jesus' era daily experienced life under the domination of a king. For unnumbered centuries, they had lived under monarchies. The Jewish people in particular lived under monarchies from the time of Saul. Many times, the Jewish monarchies were overthrown by "heathen" nations, and the people suffered terribly under the yoke of foreign domination. Their one hope, their one light at the end of a long, dark tunnel was the promise of a Messiah, Who would restore the kingdom to Israel. Consequently, when Jesus preached that this promised kingdom was at hand, the people became excited at the prospect of their deliverance.

But there was a twist to Jesus' message. The operative word of Jesus' message was *repent*. The Greek word μετάνοια (metanoia) means "a change of mind that results in a change of behavior and lifestyle."[1] In English, there is a strong negative connotation suggesting contrition, but in Greek, the statement has a strong positive component indicating a change that reaches deep into the core of one's being. While the word implies a change of mind, it goes much deeper into the very soul of man.

The wonderful part of Jesus' message is the fact that it is *Good News*. The word *gospel* means "good news." Jesus' message was clear:

• The time is now
• The kingdom of God has arrived
• Repent
• Believe in the gospel

Notes/Applications

Every follower of Christ faces times of temptation, whether physical, emotional, or spiritual. In those moments when we feel most vulnerable, we would do well to follow the example of Jesus, Who went into the "desert" before us and won the battle with the enemy not by brute force, but by refusing to succumb to Satan's tactics.

As this gospel account develops, a clear depiction of the person and character of Jesus Christ emerges. From what we have read so far, we have learned that Jesus is:

• The one prophesied by Old Testament writings
• The one prophesied by John the Baptizer
• The one ordained by God Himself
• The one Who conquers Satan's temptations
• The one Who declares the good news of salvation to the world

If the witness of Mark, Peter's disciple, is true, then we, too, are faced with the eternal God in the person of Jesus, His Son. What we do with this encounter will affect the rest of our earthly lives as well as our eternal destinies. We can ignore the Good News and discount this witness, but doing so means that we will lead a life centered on personal, human endeavors with all of the weaknesses inherent to our nature. If we choose this path, we make this brief, earthly existence our final authority. King Solomon, the wisest man who ever lived, ultimately determined that such a self-centered life left him empty with a sense of worthlessness.

> [10]If something appealed to me, I did it. I allowed myself to have any pleasure I wanted, since I found pleasure in my work. This was my reward for all my hard work.
>
> [11]But when I turned to look at all that I had accomplished and all the hard work I had put into it, I saw that it was all pointless. It was like trying to catch the wind. I gained nothing from any of my accomplishments under the sun. (Ecclesiastes 2:10–11)

Conversely, the person who is moved by the gospel accounts must confront the claims of the eternal Creator. What will we do with the reality of Jesus Christ? If we follow Him, we can spend the rest of our earthly lives enjoined with our Lord in the battle for the souls of those around us, centering our lives upon the ultimate reality fought on the stage of human existence as we team up with God in preparing hearts for the age to come. Again, what will we do with Jesus?

Mark 1:16–20

1:16 *As he was going along the Sea of Galilee, he saw Simon and his brother Andrew. They were throwing a net into the sea because they were fishermen.*

Early in His ministry, Jesus began choosing His disciples. He had traveled from the desert west of Jericho toward Galilee in the north, and as He walked by the Sea of Galilee, He saw two brothers fishing. We learn from the Gospel of John that these two men were likely disciples of John the Baptizer when Jesus called them.

1:17 *Jesus said to them, "Come, follow me! I will teach you how to catch people instead of fish."*

Jesus was not offering Simon and Andrew a simple invitation. He commanded them to follow Him. In addition, He indicated the position that they would occupy by heeding His command. By using imagery relating to the occupation of fishing, Jesus spoke to these men in terms they could understand. He intended to make Simon and Andrew fishers of people. By using some unforeseen method, they would be equipped to cast their net into the sea of humanity and retrieve people from it.

1:18 *They immediately left their nets and followed him.*

Simon and Andrew immediately abandoned their fishing expedition. Jesus did not involve them in a long discourse explaining Who He was, making them a job offer, and then sealing it with a written agreement. The simple command to follow required a response. Jesus' words drew them from their homes and occupations without their knowing where that road led.

1:19 *As Jesus went on a little farther, he saw James and John, the sons of Zebedee. They were in a boat preparing their nets to go fishing.*

A little farther along the Sea of Galilee, the scene repeats itself with two other brothers, James and John, the sons of Zebedee. In this case, however, they were not actually fishing but repairing their nets. The Gospel of Luke informs us that these two men were partners with Simon and Andrew: "James and John, who were Zebedee's sons and Simon's partners, were also amazed. Jesus told Simon, 'Don't be afraid. From now on you will catch people instead of fish'" *(Luke 5:10)*.

1:20 *He immediately called them, and they left their father Zebedee and the hired men in the boat and followed Jesus.*

Again, immediately, without delay or discussion, these two brothers responded in the same way that Simon and Andrew had. In this case, however, the men's father, Zebedee, was present. We can imagine him shouting at his sons to get back to work, but this verse does not indicate that such an altercation occurred or that the sons found themselves torn between duty to their father and their need to respond to the command of Jesus, Whom they probably knew of through the witness of John the Baptizer.

Notes/Applications

The command of Jesus to follow after Him demanded a response. The disciples Jesus called, all of whom had "day jobs," responded immediately and followed Him. In fact, this entire passage in Mark is flooded with a sense of urgency and intensity.

Few people respond to the call of Jesus with such immediate commitment. Instead, we offer a host of reasons why we cannot follow Him right now. Yes, we mean to follow Him—we really do intend to walk the straight and narrow someday—but the timing is not right. In other gospel accounts, Jesus told parables indicating that, even in His own time, not everyone responded to Him in the same way these simple fishermen did.

> [59]*He told another man, "Follow me!"*
>
> *But the man said, "Sir, first let me go to bury my father."*
>
> [60]*But Jesus told him, "Let the dead bury their own dead. You must go everywhere and tell about the kingdom of God."*
>
> [61]*Another said, "I'll follow you, sir, but first let me tell my family goodbye."*
>
> [62]*Jesus said to him, "Whoever starts to plow and looks back is not fit for the kingdom of God." (Luke 9:59–62)*

Some of us follow the example of these humble fishermen and readily follow Him. Others of us must go through agonizing times before we readily submit to the one Who died to save us, and many never do follow Him.

What holds us back from the call of God? Are we too busy to bother, or does the volume of our busy lives drown out His voice? Perhaps, we make a start but easily get diverted, back into the same rut of self-dependency in which we have resided.

The sense of urgency Jesus imparted to the fishermen is all too real for us today as well.

> [24]*Therefore, everyone who hears what I say and obeys it will be like a wise person who built a house on rock. [25]Rain poured, and floods came. Winds blew and beat against that house. But it did not collapse, because its foundation was on rock.*
>
> [26]*Everyone who hears what I say but doesn't obey it will be like a foolish person who built a house on sand. [27]Rain poured, and floods came. Winds blew and struck that house. It collapsed, and the result was a total disaster. (Matthew 7:24–27)*

Jesus' parable of a wealthy farmer chillingly makes the point.

> [16]*A rich man had land that produced good crops. [17]He thought, "What should I do? I don't have enough room to store my crops." [18]He said, "I know what I'll do. I'll tear down my barns and build bigger ones so that I can store all my grain and goods in them. [19]Then I'll say to myself, 'You've stored up a lot of good things for years to come. Take life easy, eat, drink, and enjoy yourself.'"*

[20]But God said to him, "You fool! I will demand your life from you tonight! Now who will get what you've accumulated?" [21]That's how it is when a person has material riches but is not rich in his relationship with God. (Luke 12:16–21)

Let us not wait for calamity to strike before answering God's call. He has a thrilling destiny in store for everyone who takes Him at His word: "Come, follow Me!"

Mark 1:21-28

1:21 *Then they went to Capernaum. On the next day of worship, Jesus went into the synagogue and began to teach.*

Jesus, with His four willing disciples, traveled to Capernaum, very near the north shore of the Sea of Galilee. We do not know when they arrived in this Galilean city, but we do know that He immediately entered the synagogue on the Sabbath.

It was not unusual for a Jewish man to enter the synagogue on the Sabbath. It was unusual that Jesus entered the synagogue and assumed the position of teacher or, in the Hebrew, "rabbi." Throughout biblical literature and the writings of the early church fathers, we have no indication that Jesus had been trained as a rabbi. He was certainly reared in the Jewish tradition and at an early age showed His thorough knowledge and understanding of the Scriptures. At the age of twelve, He sat with the teachers and amazed them with His understanding: "⁴⁶Three days later, they found him in the temple courtyard. He was sitting among the teachers, listening to them, and asking them questions. ⁴⁷His understanding and his answers stunned everyone who heard him" (*Luke 2:46-47*). However, for someone to enter the synagogue and assume the position of rabbi would be offensive to the Jewish mind, particularly to the ruling scribe or rabbi.

1:22 *The people were amazed at his teachings. Unlike their scribes, he taught them with authority.*

Apparently, when Jesus began to teach, the people accepted Him as their rabbi, and they marveled at His teaching. He taught them with authority, unlike the scribes and Pharisees. Of course, recalling Mark's opening statement that Jesus Christ is the Son of God, we know that He could address His audience with authority because He knew the answers to their questions.

On the other hand, the scribes based their teaching on a discussion of Scripture by using an argumentative style, which led to much debate on what a certain word or phrase meant. More often than not, no conclusions were drawn, so traditionally, the people attending synagogue left with little learning or no understanding of the passage discussed. In contrast, Jesus taught with full wisdom and understanding of the truth, providing firm conclusions to the meaning of the Holy Scriptures.

1:23 *At that time there was a man in the synagogue who was controlled by an evil spirit. He shouted,*

A man in the audience had an "evil spirit." Although this man might have exhibited strange behavior, the community allowed him to participate in the life of the synagogue. It is hard to understand the reason for his inclusion in the community, for the Greek word used to describe him, ἀκαθάρτῳ (akathartow), really means that he was ceremonially unclean.[2] Thus, he should have been considered unacceptably defiled according to Jewish law. Perhaps, others were unaware of his condition. In other contexts, this word implies a strong moral component, likely referring to sexual impurity. It could be argued that this man did not exhibit strange behaviors but had a secret lifestyle that went unnoticed in the congregation, which would account for his participation in their congregational life. However, as we will read, this man's problem ran much deeper.

1:24 *"What do you want with us, Jesus from Nazareth? Have you come to destroy us? I know who you are—the Holy One of God!"*

The man blurted out a derogatory statement against Jesus. It is possible that some in the congregation agreed with this declaration. After all, Jesus was not an ordained rabbi and might have been perceived as an imposter. Since His teaching was radically different from that of the other scribes, some might have seen Him as a threat to centuries of Jewish tradition.

Nevertheless, the final part of the declaration, "I know who You are—the Holy One of God," identified this teacher as God's Anointed, the Messiah. What was this? This man first challenged Jesus' self-assumed position and then declared Him to be the Messiah. Even the demon(s) recognized Jesus for Who He was. By this time, many of the observers probably saw the man as deranged.

1:25 *Jesus ordered the spirit, "Keep quiet, and come out of him!"*

We do not know if Jesus even raised His voice in response to this outcry. The Greek word for "keep quiet" is ἐπετίμησεν (epetimasen), which denotes an imperative command.[3] This is the same word used in Luke 8:24 when Jesus calmed the stormy sea. Jesus did not chastise or argue with this unclean spirit. He simply commanded the spirit to be quiet and to depart from the man.

1:26 *The evil spirit threw the man into convulsions and came out of him with a loud shriek.*

Up to this point, it is likely that many simply observed this altercation between Jesus and a member of their congregation with some trepidation. It appeared as though the man were in control of his faculties; he had simply challenged Jesus. However, when Jesus commanded the spirit to leave the man, the spirit caused the man to have a convulsion. Now, it became evident to the congregation that he was not in charge. When Jesus spoke, the spirit cried out with a loud voice and left the man.

1:27 *Everyone was stunned. They said to each other, "What is this? This is a new teaching that has authority behind it! He gives orders to evil spirits, and they obey him."*

First, the congregation was astonished by Jesus' teaching because of His authoritative method of discussing the Hebrew Scriptures. Now, they were even more amazed because He not only spoke with authority, but He also acted with authority. Even demons obeyed this rabbi's commands because no "evil spirit" can withstand the command of Jesus.

The congregation now had clear evidence that this rabbi could be compared with no other. Their mouths hung open in amazement because of the expulsion of the evil spirit. Jesus had earned the right to teach and to be called Rabbi.

1:28 *The news about him spread quickly throughout the surrounding region of Galilee.*

Even the most casual observers would remember such an experience for the rest of their lives. With so many people talking about this extraordinary event, without doubt, people in the nearby regions knew about it within a few hours. As we will see, by the end of the day, Jesus rose from relative obscurity to public acclamation.

Notes/Applications

If we could travel back in time and sit among this congregation, what would our reaction have been? An unknown teacher, trailed by a band of equally unknown men, sat down in the local synagogue and began teaching, and surprisingly, the words He uttered had the authoritative ring of truth. Not only that, but when He commanded an evil spirit to depart from someone, His power and authority were unmistakable.

We have all noticed how quickly a good story flies through town. This event was no different. In fact, the interplay of supernatural powers heightened interest to a feverish pitch. Jesus caused such a stir that "the news about him spread quickly throughout the surrounding region of Galilee" *(verse 28)*. It was one thing to hear about a man rumored to be the Son of God. It was quite another to see His divine authority in action. Suddenly, theory gave way to reality, and individuals were faced with a call of eternal magnitude: to believe or not to believe in the Son of God.

It may seem odd that Jesus was so low-key in commanding the demon to depart, but remember He had the right to be. Just as a horse may act up with a novice rider but promptly obey once its master rules the reins, the evil spirit recognized the Lord of heaven and earth. He had to flee at Jesus' command. This is further proof of the unseen battle waged for human souls, the ancient clash between good and evil. However, as the apostle Paul wrote to the church in Rome, those who align themselves with Jesus Christ are in the hands of a loving, all-powerful God and need not fear.

> [31]*If God is for us, who can be against us? . . . * [35]*What will separate us from the love Christ has for us? Can trouble, distress, persecution, hunger, nakedness, danger, or violent death separate us from his love? . . .*
>
> [37]*The one who loves us gives us an overwhelming victory in all these difficulties.* [38]*I am convinced that nothing can ever separate us from God's love which Christ Jesus our Lord shows us. We can't be separated by death or life, by angels or rulers, by anything in the present or anything in the future, by forces* [39]*or powers in the world above or in the world below, or by anything else in creation.* (Romans 8:31, 35, 37–39)

Such assurance gives us the courage to face each new day, as well as the "fiery darts" Satan aims in our direction.

Mark 1:29–34

1:29 *After they left the synagogue, they went directly to the house of Simon and Andrew. James and John went with them.*

Again, the action that is so unique to Mark's gospel is evident. Jesus and His disciples did not take a leisurely walk after the dramatic events in the synagogue. They went directly to the house of Simon and Andrew.

1:30 *Simon's mother-in-law was in bed with a fever. The first thing they did was to tell Jesus about her.*

Simon's mother-in-law suffered from a fever that kept her bedridden. Having just witnessed the expulsion of the evil spirit, these disciples were beginning to understand they were following someone with unusual power. If He could cast out a demon, might He not be able to help Peter's mother-in-law recover from a fever? The disciples sought help from Jesus right away.

1:31 *Jesus went to her, took her hand, and helped her get up. The fever went away, and she prepared a meal for them.*

Jesus approached the woman, took her hand, and raised her up. In the process of being lifted by Jesus' helping hand, she was immediately healed. The fever left. Her strength returned, and she felt well enough to provide some food for them. The disciples must have been further convinced of Jesus' authority. In just a few hours, they had seen Him cast out a demon (spiritual warfare) and heal this woman of a fever (physical healing). His authority extended over both the spiritual and physical realms.

1:32 *In the evening, when the sun had set, people brought to him everyone who was sick and those possessed by demons.*

On the same day, at dusk, Jesus was surrounded by a host of people that were sick and demon-possessed. Those who did not attend the synagogue service or who had attended synagogues in other nearby towns were now aware of this rabbi Who commanded their attention. Jesus quickly emerged as the central figure in Galilee. This day belonged to Jesus of Nazareth.

1:33 *The whole city had gathered at his door.*

The congregation from the synagogue swelled to include the entire populace of Capernaum. Everybody gathered at the door of Simon's home to catch a glimpse of this new teacher and to witness His next move.

1:34 *He cured many who were sick with various diseases and forced many demons out of people. However, he would not allow the demons to speak. After all, they knew who he was.*

What did Jesus do when confronted with this overwhelming attention? Quietly but firmly, He touched them, spoke to them, healed them, and cast out their demons. The crowd desired entertainment just as we do today, but Jesus gave them much more. The people needed Him. He answered their need not with words but with actions that proved themselves in the results.

Curiously, as the demons were cast out, Jesus commanded them to be silent because "they knew who he was." The implications of this statement are both positive and negative. The statement implies that these demons, the angels of His archenemy, Satan, knew Jesus. They recognized Him as the Messiah, God's Anointed. In contrast, the crowd did not really know Whom they watched. They saw Him but did not know Him. Were they chasing after a prophet, a healer, or an amazing magician? The crowd comprised people of a sinful nature and blinded by fleshly existence. They perceived only the events—this one healed of a fever, another restored to sanity after the demon was exorcised, and another restored to strength—yet they did not see the eternal, spiritual struggle taking place on their very doorstep.

Jesus commanded the demons to be silent because they were not to reveal to the crowd the identity of the one Who had cast them out. Although we are not told why, we could conclude that Jesus followed the Word of God recorded in Isaiah when the Lord God commanded the prophet: "Make these people close-minded. Plug their ears. Shut their eyes. Otherwise, they may see with their eyes, hear with their ears, understand with their minds, and return and be healed" *(Isaiah 6:10)*. Whatever God's reason, the people did not comprehend the reality of what took place, and they were not supposed to know.

Notes/Applications

As a result of the events in the synagogue, the rumor mill had really done its work, and Jesus' fame spread like a brush fire throughout the region. The crowds flocked to see the show. They could not wait to be a part of the action. Evidently, they craved entertainment just as our modern culture does today. Why else would we pay exorbitant fees for sporting events, concerts, theme parks, and other forms of entertainment? Certainly, people chase after false "gods" to fill a void deep in their souls.

In this passage, the crowd chased after Jesus, the true God. Despite their cheerful shouts and excited whispers, they did not know Who Jesus was, and they did not understand the implications of what they observed. He was the answer to their needs, known and unknown, yet they did not understand Who He was. What a sobering thought. The crowd watched miracles that defied spiritual and physical laws but remained clueless.

Is it possible that we, too, can chase after false gods? Of course. But is it also possible that we chase after Jesus and never really know Who He is? Unfortunately, this also can be true. We may see infinite outward manifestations of Jesus' divinity but never draw into the reality of the eternal God. In another gospel account, Jesus revealed to the people who witnessed the miraculous feeding of five thousand that He alone could fill the void in their spirits.

³²*Jesus said to them, "I can guarantee this truth: Moses didn't give you bread from heaven, but my Father gives you the true bread from heaven. ³³God's bread is the man who comes from heaven and gives life to the world."*

³⁴*They said to him, "Sir, give us this bread all the time."*

³⁵*Jesus told them, "I am the bread of life. Whoever comes to me will never become hungry, and whoever believes in me will never become thirsty. ³⁶I've told you that you have seen me. However, you don't believe in me. ³⁷Everyone whom the Father gives me will come to me. I will never turn away anyone who comes to me. ³⁸I haven't come from heaven to do what I want to do. I've come to do what the one who sent me wants me to do. ³⁹The one who sent me doesn't want me to lose any of those he gave me. He wants me to bring them back to life on the last day. ⁴⁰My Father wants all those who see the Son and believe in him to have eternal life. He wants me to bring them back to life on the last day." (John 6:32–40)*

Why settle for the shallow diversions of popular culture when we can have a thrilling life adventure with the one true God?

Mark 1:35–39

1:35 *In the morning, long before sunrise, Jesus went to a place where he could be alone to pray.*

One can imagine that Simon's home was busy until late on that Sabbath. Nevertheless, Jesus rose before daybreak and left Simon's home to find a quiet, deserted place. He was alone, just as He was when tempted by Satan in the desert. He longed to be alone to communicate with His Father.

1:36 *Simon and his friends searched for him.*

Simon and his companions had not gotten up with Jesus, so they did not know where He had gone. Other Bible versions simply indicate that Simon and the other disciples looked for Jesus.[4]

1:37 *When they found him, they told him, "Everyone is looking for you."*

"Everyone is looking for you" might seem to be a generalization, but it was likely the truth. The people hoped that the events that began on that Sabbath in Capernaum, especially those of the previous night, would continue into this new day. Word spread quickly, and people everywhere desired to find Him and be healed by Him. They wanted what Jesus could do for them.

1:38 *Jesus said to them, "Let's go somewhere else, to the small towns that are nearby. I have to spread the Good News in them also. This is why I have come."*

Jesus had another objective. After only one day in Capernaum, He intended to go into the surrounding towns of Galilee and preach. The message would be the same: "The kingdom of God is near. Change the way you think and act, and believe the Good News" (*verse 15*). He had a clear understanding of His mission because He was ordained not by the Jewish community but by God the Father to preach this Good News.

1:39 *So he went to spread the Good News in the synagogues all over Galilee, and he forced demons out of people.*

Fulfilling His purpose, Jesus repeated the Capernaum scene in the other towns throughout Galilee. He performed this task in the synagogues, the holy center of the Jewish community. We know from the other gospels that He was an itinerant preacher, teaching in many places, but the synagogues were the primary place where He delivered His message of the kingdom of God. In many instances, He continued to demonstrate His authority over the spiritual realm by casting out demons from those who were possessed.

Notes/Applications

In the midst of His ministry, Jesus sought to be alone. He needed times of solitude to speak to His heavenly Father. What close, loving relationship can maintain its vitality without times of being together? It is only natural to desire time alone with the ones we love. Imagine a marriage in which spouses saw one another only a few times a year. Fellowship is the cement that keeps a bond tight.

This passage offers a stark contrast to our present age. Many of us work hard all day long and then rush out to be surrounded by people—sometimes even crowds of people. We drop into bed at night only to awaken the next day and repeat the cycle. We never have time—or take the time—to be alone. We never clear our schedules long enough to enjoy the presence of our Father.

Jesus knew Who He was, and He intimately knew His heavenly Father. Because of this closeness, He yearned to pray in solitude. Do we really know who we are, let alone Who Jesus is? Maybe our blinded humanity prevents us from facing the reality of who we are. When confronted with our own mortality and our hopelessness in doing anything about it, we simply ignore it by staying busy, fooling ourselves into thinking we are "making the most of life." In the light of eternity and the one Who transcends all time and space, we find that we are fools who have spent our entire lives chasing nothing more than empty, foolish dreams.

Jesus, however, daily invites us to refresh our spirits. *"When you pray, go to your room and close the door. Pray privately to your Father who is with you. Your Father sees what you do in private. He will reward you"* (Matthew 6:6). Every believer needs these times of recharging that only come from intimacy with God. The one Who promised the woman at the well a draft of living water will also fill our cups to overflowing: *"*[13]*Jesus answered her, 'Everyone who drinks this water will become thirsty again.* [14]*But those who drink the water that I will give them will never become thirsty again. In fact, the water I will give them will become in them a spring that gushes up to eternal life'* " (John 4:13–14). But we must first meet Him one-on-one at the well.

Mark 1:40–45

1:40 *Then a man with a serious skin disease came to him. The man fell to his knees and begged Jesus, "If you're willing, you can make me clean."*

Jesus preached the message of the kingdom of God to all the towns of Galilee. During this time, a leper came to Jesus on bended knee and asked to be made clean. We sense an intensity in this man's request because Mark used words and phrases connoting urgency. This man was not silently asking; he was crying out loud, begging to be made clean. However, even in his distress, he realized that Jesus would only cleanse him if Jesus were willing.

This man had leprosy, the most feared disease in that time. There was a strong correlation between leprosy, the physical illness, and sin, the spiritual illness. Throughout Old Testament accounts, if someone contracted leprosy, people believed it occurred because he had sinned. The leper was virtually quarantined from the rest of the community. This horrible disease resulted in the rotting of one's flesh. It was also a horrible disease emotionally because the leper was separated from all community life and from the comforts of home and family. The sense of desolation and hopelessness must have been overwhelming, so we can imagine this man's anguish as he begged to be cleansed and returned to his family.

1:41 *Jesus felt sorry for him, reached out, touched him, and said, "I'm willing. So be clean!"*

This is the first occurrence in Mark's gospel in which we see an emotion tied to Jesus' behavior. Everything before this time has been action filled. Now, as this man cried out to Jesus for cleansing, Jesus was notably moved with compassion. Seeing this man's physical and emotional anguish, Jesus stretched out His hand and touched him. In so doing, Jesus addressed both issues of the man's request: 1) to

"If you're willing," He said, "I'm willing"; and, 2) to "You can make me clean," He responded, "Be clean."

What a wonderful response to this man's anguish! Jesus was willing to cleanse this man and restore him to health. Contrary to the quarantine prescribed by the Mosaic Law, Jesus compassionately reached out and physically touched the leper.

1:42 *Immediately, his skin disease went away, and he was clean.*

As soon as Jesus spoke the words, "So be clean," the man was healed and became completely clean. The leprosy did not leave him in one hour or in ten minutes. It left him immediately.

It is interesting to note that the Greek word for "cleanse," καTηαριζo (katharizo), from which we have the English word *catharsis*, involves both physical and ceremonial cleansing.[5] The same word is used throughout this passage. When the leper asked to be made clean, he requested a return to cleanliness. When Jesus responded, a prefix was added to the word, indicating that Jesus commanded the man's leprosy to be "cleaned out," specifically to be cleaned thoroughly or to be scrubbed until thoroughly clean. No trace of the disease was left. Jesus' words provided thorough reprieve from the consequences of the disease.

1:43 *Jesus sent him away at once and warned him,*

This verse reveals a second emotion of Jesus, a stern, authoritative component to His personality. Jesus had compassion on the man and healed him. He then issued a strict warning, showing both His love and authority. In the person of Jesus, the Son of God, these particular emotions are not contradictory.

1:44 *"Don't tell anyone about this! Instead, show yourself to the priest. Then offer the sacrifices which Moses commanded as proof to people that you are clean."*

Jesus warned the healed man not to tell anyone about what had happened. This warning restated the same command He had given to the demon that He called forth from the man in the synagogue.

The second part of the warning refers to the Law of Moses (*Leviticus 14*). If a person was healed from the disease of leprosy, he was to show himself to the priest and receive a clean bill of health so that he could return to the life of the community and to his family. Usually, the priest issued an offering on the person's behalf in gratitude for the healing. Even though Jesus proclaimed Himself to be the fulfillment of the Law and the Prophets, He did not circumvent the procedure of the Law.

1:45 *When the man left, he began to talk freely. He spread his story so widely that Jesus could no longer enter any city openly. Instead, he stayed in places where he could be alone. But people still kept coming to him from everywhere.*

What an amazing verse! The man did not obey Jesus' stern warning. The first thing he did was broadcast to everyone that he was healed. He disregarded Jesus' warning. In contrast to this man's disobedience, the demon in verse twenty-six obeyed Jesus' command to keep silent. The demon obeyed, and the man disobeyed. Why did this happen? Is it because the demons are profoundly cognizant of the person of Jesus, but man is not (*James 2:19*)? Was it possible for this man to be healed of this horrible disease yet remain unaware of the person Who had healed him? This account exemplifies how man functions when faced with spiritual warfare. He sees the events but is only dimly aware of their significance. This man acknowledged Jesus as the healer, the magician, and the spectacular person, but he did not know Him.

The result of this disobedience? Jesus was swamped with demands on His time and energy and, therefore, could no longer enter the city and proclaim the gospel of the kingdom of God. He then left the city and escaped to the outlying areas. This man's disobedience impacted Jesus' plan to enter the towns of Galilee and to preach to all. Now, the message became clouded with the personality of the one healed rather than the Healer. Now, the message was no longer available to everyone in the city but only to those who were willing to go out into the outlying area and search for Jesus.

Notes/Applications

In this section, we glimpse the heart of God as Jesus was moved with compassion on behalf of the leper. Many of us grew up with an image of God as a stern judge, eager to invoke His wrath and punish His wayward creation. While Scripture clarifies that God is the righteous Judge of everything in heaven and on earth *(Psalm 7:11, 98:9; Deuteronomy 32:36; Romans 2:16)*, we see through the actions of Jesus that even His judgment coexists with the endless reservoir of love He has for us: "I correct and discipline everyone I love" *(Revelation 3:19)*. His every thought and inclination toward us is compelled by love: "God has shown us his love by sending his only Son into the world so that we could have life through him" *(1 John 4:9)*.

From the previous section, we learned from Jesus' example that we need quiet time alone with our Father. Now, in light of such a loving but righteous Lord, a second principle is revealed: we also need to obey Him. Both components contradict everything our sinful human nature dictates as reasonable. Certainly, this is what happened to the leper after Jesus healed him. Though warned to keep quiet, the man told everyone he encountered. His disobedience seems like a small thing to us, but look what it cost Jesus. He could no longer minister openly in the city and was, therefore, forced into the deserted places. But His message and miracles were so powerful that people still came "from everywhere" to witness the man from Galilee.

Have we neglected quiet time with the Lord, thereby hindering His guidance? Have we willingly disobeyed what He has impressed upon us to do? What impact has our disobedience had on the cause of Christ?

Jesus' Journeys: Chapter One

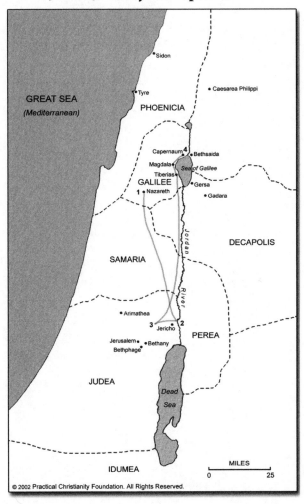

1. Jesus left His home in Nazareth.

2. Jesus was baptized by John the Baptist in the Jordan River.

3. Jesus endured temptation by Satan in the desert near Jericho.

4. Jesus returned to Capernaum, taught in the synagogue, cast out a demon, and dealt with the gathering crowds.

MARK 2

Mark 2:1–7

2:1 *Several days later Jesus came back to Capernaum. The report went out that he was home.*

After a brief journey into the surrounding towns of Galilee, where He preached, healed, and cast out demons, Jesus returned to Capernaum, which served as "headquarters" for His early Galilean ministry. Jesus was apparently able to return to Simon's house with little fanfare. However, that respite did not last long. The word spread that this rabbi had returned.

2:2 *Many people had gathered. There was no room left, even in front of the door. Jesus was speaking God's word to them.*

Again, people gathered at Simon's door. The crowd grew larger still, all of them anxious to catch a glimpse of this teacher Whose remarkable deeds had captured the attention of everyone in the region. Somehow, Jesus found a spot from which He could address the crowd.

Mark emphasizes the actions of Jesus—where Jesus went and the related healings that occurred. While Mark does not dwell on the content of Jesus' message, we can be sure that it again centered on the theme stated in Mark 1:15: "The time has come, and the kingdom of God is near. Change the way you think and act, and believe the Good News."

2:3 *Four men came to him carrying a paralyzed man.*

Four men arrived on this scene, carrying a paralyzed man. This man was apparently a quadriplegic, paralyzed in all of his extremities. Consequently, he was totally dependent upon the good will of those four men, who carried him to this Healer, hoping to find relief from his infirmity.

2:4 *Since they could not bring him to Jesus because of the crowd, they made an opening in the roof over the place where Jesus was. Then they lowered the cot on which the paralyzed man was lying.*

Most residences in this region had stairways to a flat roof constructed of lathe and tile[1] *(Luke 5:19)*. This architecture was pragmatic in the environs of Galilee. A family would sometimes sleep on the roof during the warmer season of the year. It is quite apparent that what was about to happen was no small task.

The crowd was so large that these men could not even come close to getting Jesus' attention, so these men, intent on their objective, carried the invalid to the roof. They then destroyed part of this structure by making a hole in it. The hole was substantial, large enough to lower the invalid on his bed without losing control. It was a brave and dangerous maneuver, not without risks. However, their focus was clear; they were determined to get this man to Jesus.

2:5 *When Jesus saw their faith, he said to the man, "Friend, your sins are forgiven."*

Simon might not have appreciated these men destroying the roof of his house, but Jesus was very impressed. Evidently, Jesus understood the intense focus of these men and that they would stop at nothing to help their friend, and He was pleased by their faith. As the paralytic lay before Him, Jesus simply said, "Friend, your sins are forgiven."

This is the first occasion in the Book of Mark in which Jesus addressed healing in relation to sin. Earlier, He had commanded a demon to leave a man, and then He cleansed the leper. This time, He did not address the physical symptom but the spiritual malady. We begin to see that this rabbi had authority over both the visible, physical symptoms of the diseases of mankind and the internal sin condition as well. Again, what was really happening? Was the paralytic's condition merely the result of a failure of his physical system? Or was this man's condition an example of the entire physical world's sin nature since the time of Adam?

2:6 *Some scribes were sitting there. They thought,*

The crowd consisted of a vast array of individuals from the entire spectrum of the Jewish society—the curious, the believing, the educated, the rich, and the poor. Some were wildly exuberant about this new rabbi. Others, however, were not. Among the skeptical were the scribes, who had devoted their lives to the study of the Law of Moses, to the Scriptures, and to the rabbinical tradition. They were intent on obeying the Word of the Lord God item by item and word for word. When these men observed what Jesus said to this man, their religiously trained minds began to work through all the Scriptures. They tried to understand what they had seen and heard through the eyes of their theological understanding.

2:7 *"Why does he talk this way? He's dishonoring God. Who besides God can forgive sins?"*

This verse reveals the scribes' theological understanding. The scribes, in their collective minds, questioned Jesus' authority to forgive sins and asked the rhetorical question: "Who besides God can forgive sins?" In their limited understanding, no human being had the power to forgive sins. Therefore, they concluded that Jesus spoke blasphemy and was usurping the power of God by taking on Himself the power to forgive sins. This rabbi, despite the good things He had done in healing people and casting out demons, had now stepped over the line because He had equated Himself with the Lord God Jehovah.

Notes/Applications

On this particular day in Capernaum, the wandering rabbi from Nazareth did something especially shocking when He told a paralyzed man that his sins were forgiven. From our comfortable vantage point with the benefit of hindsight and the four gospel accounts, we may be surprised at the scribes' reaction, but how different would our own response have been if we had lived in that time, steeped in tradition and schooled in Old Testament teaching? After all, no one but God could forgive sins.

Despite Jesus' growing reputation for shocking crowds and overturning traditions, we sense the people's growing confidence in Him. When Jesus healed the man with the evil spirit during His previous visit to Capernaum, spectators might have dismissed the miracle as some sort of psychological magic. However, on this occasion, four men brought to Jesus a man so incapacitated it would be impossible to deny the reality of a healing. The people watching this scene unfold must have approached the moment with mixed feelings. Was this feat beyond the reach of the unusual rabbi? Surely, though, a hopeful anticipation buzzed through the crowd that Jesus might make something happen. Therefore, when He opened His mouth to speak, His response, "Your sins are forgiven," baffled them.

When a watch stops, does the watchmaker fix the problem by moving the hands? No, the hands move properly only when the inner workings of the watch are in sync. Treating symptoms will never cure the problem. Likewise, on this occasion, Jesus addressed not the symptom but the inner workings of the paralyzed man—his sin nature. *"As a face is reflected in water, so a person is reflected by his heart"* (Proverbs 27:19).

We get the impression that Jesus, on this and earlier occasions when He commanded the demon to depart or the leper to be cleansed, was really commanding the inner workings of the individual's condition.

Do the hands of our "clocks" seem out of sync? Is something holding us back from total commitment to Him? If so, this story from the Gospel of Mark demonstrates what we need to do—submit our hearts to the Master's restoration and allow Him to make us whole again. *"A person's soul is the Lord's lamp. It searches his entire innermost being"* (Proverbs 20:27).

Mark 2:8-12

2:8 *At once, Jesus knew inwardly what they were thinking. He asked them, "Why do you have these thoughts?*

It is evident from this verse that the scribes did not confer openly. In their collective minds, they believed that He had just spoken blasphemy against the High God. Jesus, containing in His essence the very nature of God, read their minds. In so doing, Jesus brought the conflict brewing in their hearts out into the open. These learned men must have been astonished when Jesus voiced the intent and content of their thoughts.

2:9 *Is it easier to say to this paralyzed man, 'Your sins are forgiven,' or to say, 'Get up, pick up your cot, and walk'?*

Jesus placed a question before the scribes. The answer, of course, was obvious. It really was not a question of the spoken word at all. Rather, it was the authority behind the words that really mattered. If Jesus' ministry up to this point was conveyed by the power of His speech without any results confirming His power and authority, He would not have attracted the tremendous crowds. He would have been perceived as just another false prophet. Jesus' words meant something. When He spoke, the results were immediate, and they were observable. This summarizes Mark's message throughout this gospel. There is authority in the teachings of Jesus, and this authority is confirmed by ensuing results. There is observable evidence that Jesus is indeed the Son of the living God.

2:10 *I want you to know that the Son of Man has authority on earth to forgive sins." Then he said to the paralyzed man,*

Jesus challenged the scribes' unspoken skepticism. He identified Himself as the Son of Man, a term relatively familiar to the Jewish mind. While acknowledging His humanity through the use of the term, He was about to reveal His corresponding position as the

Son of God. He bridged the gap of their understanding from what they could accept (Son of Man) to what they ultimately could not accept (Son of God). It was a most appropriate opportunity to introduce Himself as the Son of Man, though the theology of the term extended beyond that which had been developed by their understanding of the term. Jesus acknowledged that claiming the power to forgive sins was easy, but it was another matter altogether to provide evidence that physically demonstrated this authority. Jesus did not tell the scribes that their conclusions were wrong. In fact, they were right, and it was time to back up His words with action.

> **DIG DEEPER:** *Son of Man*
>
> In the Book of Mark, the Lord Jesus is referred to, either by narrative description or self-designation, as the "Son of Man" only fourteen times. Unlike the title "Son of God," which denotes the glory of His deity, the title "Son of Man" reveals the human element of His existence—the person of God that would suffer, die, and live again as a sacrifice for the sins of the world (*Matthew 8:20; 17:9–12; Luke 9:22; 22:69; 24:7*).

2:11 *"I'm telling you to get up, pick up your cot, and go home!"*

Having plainly established His authority as the Son of Man, Jesus addressed the man by instructing him to take up his bed and return to his home. It is hard to imagine the unparalleled joy of this man and his four friends. They had come in expectant faith, and they were rewarded.

2:12 *The man got up, immediately picked up his cot, and walked away while everyone watched. Everyone was amazed and praised God, saying, "We have never seen anything like this."*

This man, who had been paralyzed, now got up. He picked up his own bed without the aid of his four friends and walked home in front of numerous witnesses. The people were absolutely amazed.

Here was a man they had known for years as a hopeless paralytic. Now, he walked. This was no magic trick, no psychological healing. This was the knitting of bone and muscle and nervous system into an integrated, operating, whole person. Furthermore, it occurred immediately. They glorified God because it had to be the work of God Himself! Astounded, the crowd declared the uniqueness of this event. They had never seen anything like this. They had never met anyone like this.

Notes/Applications

In this passage, we begin to see Jesus in a different light. So much of current thought, literature, and cinema portray Jesus as a passive prophet—"gentle Jesus, meek and mild." Mark, on the contrary, depicts a very bold, straightforward Jesus Who declared His identity to the crowd of people.

Jesus discerned the doubts simmering in the scribes' hearts before they could even verbalize them. He sees into our hearts as well and reads the doubts, hopes, confusions, and aspirations unique to every individual:

> *23Examine me, O God, and know my mind.*
> *Test me, and know my thoughts.*
> *24See whether I am on an evil path.*
> *Then lead me on the everlasting path. (Psalm 139:23–24)*

The knowledge that God sees into human hearts is both com-forting and disturbing. What will He see when He looks into our hearts? Will He find a genuine seeker, although, perhaps, plagued by doubts now and then but still pressing forward in the faith journey? Or will He discover a heart that wants to believe—even wants to obey—but too easily turns aside to the temptations of this age?

> *9Don't you know that wicked people won't inherit the kingdom of God? Stop deceiving yourselves! People who continue to commit sexual sins, who worship false gods, those who commit adultery, homosexuals, 10or thieves, those who are greedy or drunk, who use*

abusive language, or who rob people will not inherit the kingdom of God. ⁱⁱThat's what some of you were! But you have been washed and made holy, and you have received God's approval in the name of the Lord Jesus Christ and in the Spirit of our God. (1 Corinthians 6:9–11)

Once Jesus declared to the crowd Who He was, the burden of belief was on their heads. The same is true for us. Why then are we intimidated not to share this clear message with those around us who so desperately need the Good News? May God give us the boldness to live lives that declare the saving grace of Jesus Christ. St. Francis of Assisi said it well: "Preach the gospel at all times; if necessary, use words."

Mark 2:13–17

2:13 *Jesus went to the seashore again. Large crowds came to him, and he taught them.*

Jesus withdrew from the crowds at Simon's house. The entire circumstance must have been charged with emotional energy, leaving Jesus tired. He needed to withdraw and have some time alone. Although the absence of Mark's favorite word, *immediately*, might lead us to conclude that this event did not occur directly after healing the paralytic, it is likely that it followed soon thereafter.

Regardless of the time factor, we see that Jesus withdrew to the Sea of Galilee. However, He did not get an opportunity to rest. The crowd pursued Him, and again, He stopped and taught them.

2:14 *When Jesus was leaving, he saw Levi, son of Alphaeus, sitting in a tax office. Jesus said to him, "Follow me!" So Levi got up and followed him.*

Apparently, Jesus concluded His discourse with the crowd and began walking along the shore. As Jesus had called Simon and Andrew while they fished, He simply looked at Levi, a tax collector sitting in the tax office, and said to him, "Follow Me!" There was no lengthy interview, nor are we told of Levi's qualifications. Once Jesus called him, Levi left his tax office and followed Jesus.

We wonder about the physical qualities and magnetism of Jesus. What commanded the attention of the person He addressed? Did He speak quietly? Did He speak firmly? What was His body language? Was it His face? His eyes? The tone of His voice? Who can explain how Jesus could address a perfect stranger in such a way that he would leave his life's occupation, walk away, and attach himself to the one Who had called him? Certainly, His teachings and deeds were extraordinary, but was He also extraordinary in His appearance—the way He looked and the way He conducted Himself? Whatever His appearance, the result was remarkable. Levi rose and followed Jesus. Jesus alone knew the reasons for His invitation to Levi, also known as Matthew, one of the chosen twelve apostles.

2:15 *Later Jesus was having dinner at Levi's house. Many tax collectors and sinners who were followers of Jesus were eating with him and his disciples.*

Shortly afterward, Jesus and His disciples, along with many others, gathered at Levi's house for a meal. Apparently, the social standing of those eating at Levi's table were "tax collectors and sinners."

In this context, the word *sinners* does not mean that those who did not attend the meal were not sinners. It is describing a certain social level of these people as seen through the eyes of the scribes and the Pharisees. These were common people not counted among the religious elite. Sitting with these common folk were tax collectors.

What an unlikely alliance had been forged. Tax collectors were held in contempt because they had traded their Jewish heritage to be an official in the hated Roman hierarchy. As tax collectors, they achieved some degree of wealth compared to their Jewish counterparts. They gained their wealth by charging the common man with the Roman tax and then adding a sum for the cost of collection. Tax collectors were intensely disliked, yet there they were, sitting at a meal with Jesus and His disciples.

2:16 *When the scribes who were Pharisees saw him eating with sinners and tax collectors, they asked his disciples, "Why does he eat with tax collectors and sinners?"*

When the scribes and Pharisees saw this unusual occurrence, they wondered about this rabbi's judgment. He had established Himself with considerable authority throughout the region of Galilee. He taught with authority. He commanded demons to leave. He healed lepers. He even forgave sins. His authority was without question. However, His judgment was now under scrutiny. There He sat, visiting a tax collector and eating a meal with Levi's colleagues and a bunch of sinners. After He had established Himself as an authoritative rabbi, why would He not prefer to dine with the religious elite—the scribes and the Pharisees?

It is obvious that the scribes and Pharisees were not included in this group sharing a meal with Jesus. In fact, it would have been considered religiously unclean for them to do so. If they had been invited, they would have declined the invitation. Wouldn't Jesus have been wise to make some small gesture of kindness toward these recognized religious leaders? Why did Jesus avoid their friendship? After all, they represented a powerful religious and political constituency. Did they not deserve some credit for their religious fervor?

2:17 *When Jesus heard that, he said to them, "Healthy people don't need a doctor; those who are sick do. I've come to call sinners, not people who think they have God's approval."*

Jesus heard their question and understood their concern. He explained His reason for separating Himself from those who chose to appear as God's emissaries. He directly informed them that His purpose was to bring the reality of His Father's message to those who recognized their spiritual deadness. If the scribes and Pharisees were so convinced of their righteous living before Almighty God, it would be difficult to convince them of their desperate need for forgiveness. Jesus made no effort to court their respect or companionship, for they were self-righteous hypocrites. Their religious fervor was motivated by social standing and acceptance—totally external. Jesus' message remained the same as it was in the beginning: repent. Therefore, Jesus aligned Himself with the common man—the one who would repent and follow Him, who would admit his need for repentance, and who would seek fellowship with Jesus. This person desired to sit and dine with Jesus.

When Jesus said to the paralytic, "Friend, your sins are forgiven," He drove a wedge between Himself and the religious elite of His day. They could not understand, and they certainly did not condone His alleged blasphemy. Jesus further offended their dignity and their self-importance by aligning Himself with the lower strata of society and, in effect, telling these religious zealots that He preferred the company of sinners.

Notes/Applications

Once again, Jesus rocked the boat by "doing the wrong thing" and "hanging around the wrong people," and as a result, the scribes and Pharisees were outraged by His behavior. We can imagine how they shook their heads and even tore their clothes at His "blasphemous" behavior. Why was Jesus' behavior considered blasphemous? Because He did not act the way righteous people were supposed to act if they wanted to remain in the good graces of the religious leaders.

Like the Jewish scribes, many people today come to Jesus with religious, even "Christian" backgrounds. They approach Jesus carrying the banner of their self-righteous importance but forgetting the very first word of the gospel message: repent.

Even though we may approach Jesus with a truly broken and contrite heart, we struggle to avoid self-righteousness in dealing with others. Have we forgotten what Jesus saved us from?

> *²He pulled me out of a horrible pit,*
> *out of the mud and clay.*
> *He set my feet on a rock*
> *and made my steps secure.*
> *³He placed a new song in my mouth,*
> *a song of praise to our God. (Psalm 40:2–3)*

Jesus displayed the heart of the Father, eager to include the broken, outcast members of society, but we, too, often behave like the Pharisees. "Look at me. Jesus saved me. I'm a good person. Don't you want to be like me?"

In contrast, grace and a profound humility mark the believer who is spiritually mature. Such a person understands the precious, fragile beginning of faith and gently leads others to the feet of Christ. May we never try to usurp Jesus' place and implicate ourselves into the message of salvation. "*8God saved you through faith as an act of kindness. You had nothing to do with it. Being saved is a gift from God. 9It's not the result of anything you've done, so no one can brag about it. 10God has made us what we are. He has created us in Christ Jesus to live lives filled with good works that he has prepared for us to do*" (Ephesians 2:8–10).

Mark 2:18–22

2:18 *John's disciples and the Pharisees were fasting. Some people came to Jesus and said to him, "Why do John's disciples and the Pharisees' disciples fast, but your disciples don't?"*

While Jesus dined with tax collectors and sinners, the disciples of John and those of the Pharisees refrained from eating because they had been fasting. Fasting was a regular part of the Pharisees' religious observance. Apparently, the disciples of John the Baptizer followed this observance as well, though Jesus' disciples did not. After John's disciples had been baptized in the Jordan under a message of repentance, they must have returned to following the traditions of the religious leaders of the day. We know from other gospel narratives that the Pharisees publicly fasted so that others could see what "good" people they were *(Matthew 6:16–18)*. Whatever the reasons, we can conclude that the Pharisees considered fasting as evidence of their commitment to religious tradition. Therefore, John the Baptizer's disciples joined with the Pharisees and came to Jesus to inquire about the differences in their religious traditions and behaviors.

2:19 *Jesus replied, "Can wedding guests fast while the groom is still with them? As long as they have the groom with them, they cannot fast.*

Jesus freely answered their question, though it certainly must have seemed a very strange response. True, it was unthinkable that a wedding guest would fast or mourn in the presence of the groom, but what did that have to do with their question? They certainly were aware of the feasts associated with wedding celebrations but could not understand the implication that Jesus posed.

Jesus' answer, within the context of weddings, made sense. No one would ever think of fasting when the groom was celebrating his union with his bride. This was a time of great happiness, a time for celebrating the joys of life. Fasting, on the other hand, was a time for quiet reflection and withdrawal from the normal routines of life. The messianic significance of this statement would not become apparent until some time later.[2]

2:20 *But the time will come when the groom will be taken away from them. Then they will fast.*

Again, Jesus stated the obvious and the not so obvious. It would be more appropriate to fast after the wedding celebration. Under ordinary circumstances, the groom would take his bride into his home, and the exuberant celebration would end. Life in the community and for the new couple would return to more ordinary routines. This was the obvious understanding of Jesus' reply, but what did Jesus mean by the statement "when the groom will be taken away"? Evidently, this statement implied that the groom would not take his bride home and start a family. It seems as though the groom would not be acting under his own volition but that some undisclosed event or person would remove him. What could this possibly mean to those who had asked the reasons why Jesus' disciples did not fast? This answer could not possibly be comprehended then, but it would become clear at the end of Jesus' earthly ministry when a time for mourning and fasting would come.

2:21 *"No one patches an old coat with a new piece of cloth that will shrink. Otherwise, the new patch will shrink and rip away some of the old cloth, and the tear will become worse.*

As Jesus continued His explanation, it seems that He avoided any further discussion of fasting. Instead, He proceeded to give a lesson on tailoring, a subject that everyone could relate to because it was an integral part of their daily lives. Everyone knew that a person could not sew a new piece of cloth into an old garment to make a repair. When the repaired garment was washed, the new piece of cloth would shrink and actually worsen the tear that it was intended to mend.

2:22 *People don't pour new wine into old wineskins. If they do, the wine will make the skins burst, and both the wine and the skins will be ruined. Rather, new wine is to be poured into fresh skins."*

Was Jesus avoiding a genuine conversation with the Pharisees and John the Baptizer's disciples? Using a similar analogy equally familiar to His audience, Jesus continued by discussing the containers used with new wine. Because the fermenting process expanded the contents of a container, it was advisable to put new wine into new wineskins. Older wineskins would have become brittle over time, whereas new wineskins were able to expand with the pressures produced in the fermenting process.

Just as a wedding party celebrates the joys of a new marriage, new cloth cannot be sewn into an old garment, and new wine cannot be contained in old wineskins. The imagery conveys a joyful, growing, stretching event that bursts the older conventions of traditional culture. The stale traditions of the Pharisees could not contain the birth of Christ's kingdom, which produced excitement in the great crowds that witnessed so many healings. Nothing could suppress the wonder at the moment when they heard Jesus tell the paralytic that his sins were forgiven. It would be difficult to put on the face of mourning and fasting when all around there was nothing but cause to celebrate and rejoice.

Notes/Applications

If any doubt lingered regarding Jesus' reputation for strange talk and even stranger ways, Jesus' conversation with the disciples of John and the Pharisees clinched it. We can almost hear those present saying, "Come again?" Asked a perfectly normal question, Jesus replied with three cryptic answers—metaphors about weddings, unshrunk cloth, and wine. Was this man for real?

Of course, we understand this passage not through the eyes and ears of those present but with the full gospel narrative implanted in our minds. Jesus was speaking figuratively about Himself. He is indeed the Groom. *"When the end comes, the kingdom of heaven will be like ten bridesmaids. They took their oil lamps and went to meet the groom"* (Matthew 25:1). *"Let us rejoice, be happy, and give him glory because it's time for the marriage of the lamb. His bride has made herself ready"* (Revelation 19:7).

Jesus was telling the people that while He was in their presence—the Son of God walking the earth in human flesh—it was surely a time of wonder and enchantment, a time of joy and celebration. He knew the day would come when He would be taken from them through His death on the cross, resurrection, and ascension in order to fulfill God's plan for salvation.

True to the metaphor, Jesus the Groom sealed our opportunity to unite in a sacred covenant with the holy God. History tells the story of how His message literally tore apart Jewish traditions by challenging the complacent, ritualistic, dead religiosity of the religious elite. It even tore apart the Roman empire generations later. No human "wineskin" could contain the volatility that resulted from Jesus' revolutionary message when the words of that message became flesh-and-blood reality on the cross.

Sometimes, we, too, may pose our questions while reading the Bible or hearing the still, small voice of His Spirit in our hearts. However, we can be assured that our Groom has our ultimate good in mind even when we do not understand the details: "We know that all things work together for the good of those who love God—those whom he has called according to his plan " *(Romans 8:28)*. God's part in our unfolding drama is to guide us; our part is simply to follow and to obey.

Mark 2:23-28

2:23 *Once on a day of worship Jesus was going through the grainfields. As the disciples walked along, they began to pick the heads of grain.*

On another Sabbath day, Jesus and His disciples walked through someone's grainfields. As they walked, the disciples plucked the seeds of grain for the purpose of eating them as permitted by Mosaic Law: "If you go into your neighbor's grain field, you may pick grain by hand. But never use a sickle to cut your neighbor's grain" (*Deuteronomy 23:25*). The Law was intended to provide immediate nourishment for the traveler. The traveler was restricted to his immediate need and was, therefore, not permitted to harvest grain for future use.

2:24 *The Pharisees asked him, "Look! Why are your disciples doing something that is not permitted on the day of worship?"*

The Pharisees disagreed with Jesus' and the disciples' interpretation of the Law. The Sabbath was sacred, so no work was permitted on this day that was set aside for rest. However, the Pharisees had long before distorted the Law and used it as an instrument to oppress the people of God. They considered themselves the sole interpreters of the Law, and they rendered harvesting the seeds of grain on the Sabbath as a labor that was not allowed: "You may work six days, but on the seventh day you must not work. Even during the time of plowing or harvesting you must not work on this day" (*Exodus 34:21*).

2:25 *Jesus asked them, "Haven't you ever read what David did when he and his men were in need and were hungry?*

Notice that the Pharisees questioned Jesus but not His disciples. Although the disciples were the offending party, their leader was held responsible for the actions of His followers. It was His responsibility to maintain the integrity of the Law of Moses among His students.

Jesus did not reprimand His disciples. Rather, He defended their behavior, reminding the Pharisees of an incident in their Old Testament history when David, the king of Israel's glory days, fled from the anger of Saul, his king:

> *¹David went to the priest Ahimelech at Nob. Ahimelech was trembling as he went to meet David. "Why are you alone?" he asked David. "Why is no one with you?"*
>
> *²"The king ordered me to do something," David answered the priest Ahimelech, "and he told me, 'No one must know anything about this mission I'm sending you on and about the orders I've given you. I've stationed my young men at a certain place.'" ³David added, "Now, what do you have to eat? Give me five loaves of bread or whatever you can find."*
>
> *⁴"I don't have any ordinary bread," the chief priest answered David. "But there is holy bread for the young men if they haven't had sexual intercourse today."*
>
> *⁵David answered the priest, "Of course women have been kept away from us as usual when we go on a mission. The young men's bodies are kept holy even on ordinary campaigns. How much more then will their bodies be holy today?"*
>
> *⁶So the priest gave him holy bread because he only had the bread of the presence which had been taken from the Lord's presence and replaced with warm bread that day. (1 Samuel 21:1–6)*

2:26 ***Haven't you ever read how he went into the house of God when Abiathar was chief priest and ate the bread of the presence? He had no right to eat those loaves. Only the priests have that right. Haven't you ever read how he also gave some of it to his men?"***

Jesus paraphrased the story that had been handed down through the Scriptures to generations of the Jewish faithful. David ate the showbread, which was used ceremoniously in temple worship. Eating the showbread was expressly forbidden in the Law of Moses. After this bread had served its ceremonial purpose, only the priests were allowed to eat it. What makes the story more confusing is the fact that David obtained the bread on the premise of a lie. He told the high priest that he was on a special mission for Saul, the king, when, in fact, he was running from Saul. This did not justify the lie, but it is evident that God often works His purpose despite our disobedience to His Law.

There appears to be a textual discrepancy in this passage. Jesus stated that this incident took place in the days of Abiathar. The Old Testament passage quoted from 1 Samuel specifically says that this incident took place during the term of Ahimelech. Some scholars explain this usage by referring to a common rabbinical practice of identifying a certain section of the Old Testament Scriptures by referring to the most prominent personage of that period.[3] Ahimelech occupied the office of high priest for a very short time while his son Abiathar rose to great prominence during David's reign. Since Abiathar was renowned and Ahimelech could barely be remembered, Jesus apparently used the more commonly known name of Abiathar so that the reference could be more easily found.

2:27 *Then he added, "The day of worship was made for people, not people for the day of worship.*

Jesus enunciated a basic principle that the Pharisees completely misunderstood and misinterpreted. He spoke of the Sabbath in the passive voice. The inference is that God, the Creator, made the Sabbath for man's benefit. God provided this special day so that man could rest from his labor and reflect on the greater purpose for which he was made *(Genesis 2:2–3)*. It was not intended that adherence to the Sabbath should become so strict and regulated that man would ultimately lose the anticipated benefits of the law's purpose.

2:28 *For this reason the Son of Man has authority over the day of worship."*

The conclusion of this debate serves as another example of Jesus' divine position. If God created the Sabbath to benefit man, God is the one Who has acted upon His creation. When Jesus then informed His listeners that He, the Son of Man, was Lord of the Sabbath, He was telling them that He is in unity with the Father.

This chapter opens with Jesus pronouncing forgiveness of sin on a crippled man. He claimed a position equal with God. The chapter concludes with a similar claim by Jesus. He is the Lord of the Sabbath. He is one with the Creator. The Pharisees in their anger only exposed their hypocrisy and false claims as the arbiters of God's Law.

With these subtle yet forceful reminders, Jesus slowly revealed His identity to all who followed Him—His disciples, the crowds, and His enemies. The following passage also confirms the absolute reality of Jesus' identity as Lord of the Sabbath. He answers to no man. He controls all events, even those defying the traditional interpretations of Sabbath rules.

Notes/Applications

Was man made for the divinely decreed Sabbath rest, or was the Sabbath rest made for man? This could begin to sound like a chicken-or-egg query if Jesus had not flatly stated the answer. To the disciples' relief, He told the Pharisees that the Sabbath was made for man and not the other way around. As Lord of the Sabbath, He saw fit to allow His hungry followers to refresh themselves with food, no matter what day of the week it was.

Isn't it good to know we serve a practical God? Unlike the Pharisees, who unnecessarily split hairs over matters of the Law, Jesus always drove straight to the heart of the Law, fulfilling its true meaning. He took the complexity of the Mosaic Law and reduced it to two simple commandments: Love the Lord your God with all your heart, soul, mind, and strength, and love your neighbor as you love yourself *(Mark 12:30–31).*

Jesus again demonstrated two great lessons relating to His identity and His relationship to the Father. Twice in this chapter He declared His unity, His oneness, with the Father. He made it clear that no discord exists between them. What the Father purposes, the Son fulfills. Therefore, we must conclude that the Father and the Son are one. God forgives sin; Jesus is ordained by His eternal office to forgive sin. God is the Creator and Overseer of the Sabbath; Jesus is the Lord of the Sabbath.

The second lesson gleaned is that this "oneness" makes Jesus the Sovereign of all history. That means He is also the Sovereign over our lives. As the gospel account continues, Jesus will draw consciously and resolutely closer to the cross. Even His own hand-picked disciples had trouble grasping the reality of His identity. They certainly saw Him as a man of great and unusual power, but did they see Him as their sovereign Lord? Do we?

Jesus understood the Father's heart and willingly moved toward His own death. He knew that He was the only sacrifice capable of reconciling mankind to a right relationship with God. That is why He is referred to as the Lamb of God.

> *⁹Then they sang a new song,*
> > *"You deserve to take the scroll and open the seals on it,*
> > > *because you were slaughtered.*
> > *You bought people with your blood to be God's own.*
> > > *They are from every tribe, language, people, and*
> > > *nation.. . .*
> *¹²In a loud voice they were singing,*
> > *"The lamb who was slain deserves to receive*
> > > *power, wealth, wisdom, strength, honor, glory, and*
> > > *praise." (Revelation 5:9,12)*

As we go about our daily lives, it is easy to forget that the physical realm in which we dwell is temporary—it's passing away. True reality lies beyond the door of death in the realm where each of us is inevitably headed. Do our daily choices point us in the direction of an eternity with God? Have we dismissed the gentle tugging of the Spirit? Have we reduced our religion to rules rather than sought relationship with our God?

MARK 3

Mark 3:1-6

3:1 *Jesus went into a synagogue again. A man who had a paralyzed hand was there.*

During the previous account of the confrontation with the Pharisees, Jesus' answers did not satisfy the Pharisees when they questioned Him about giving His disciples approval to pluck grain on the Sabbath. Jesus' answers did not fit their traditionally accepted interpretations.

After their discussion on the moral rightness of plucking grain on the Sabbath, Jesus entered the synagogue. An entourage followed Him—His disciples, the Pharisees, and the curious onlookers. There, Jesus saw a man with a paralyzed hand.

It is important to note that the synagogue was the place where Jesus did much of His teaching. We often think of Him by the Sea of Galilee or on a mountainside. However, up to this point in Mark, Jesus spent much of His time in the synagogue, the center of Jewish community life. His authority to teach in this special place had been established by His miraculous works, but His acceptance was apparently limited to the general congregation. Jesus still had His critics who sought opportunity to discredit this popular new rabbi.

3:2 *The people were watching Jesus closely. They wanted to see whether he would heal the man on the day of worship so that they could accuse him of doing something wrong.*

From the previous passage and the description in the following verses, we know that the phrase "the people" clearly refers to the Pharisees. In the previous dialogue, the Pharisees were dissatisfied with Jesus' responses. He had repeatedly challenged their religious thinking, so tempers were frayed by this point.

They watched Jesus closely to see if He would continue pushing beyond their accepted limits. If Jesus healed this man on the Sabbath, He was definitely breaking the Law of Moses as interpreted in the Jewish rabbinical tradition. It was permissible to intervene in another's circumstance or even in an animal's circumstance if there was an immediate threat to life, but a crippled hand did not qualify as a life-threatening circumstance. The healing of this man's hand could wait until after the Sabbath. After all, this man had suffered from this condition for a long time.

Apparently, the Pharisees were no longer content with simply observing this new rabbi. He had pushed them too far. They now watched His every move with the intention of gaining evidence that could be used to destroy Him. Jesus had drawn the line in the sand. He stood on one side with the Pharisees on the other. They would never cross that line to accept Jesus. They were now His accusers, and they sought to destroy Him.

3:3 *So he told the man with the paralyzed hand, "Stand in the center of the synagogue."*

Jesus addressed the man by instructing him to step into the center of the synagogue. This man may not have appealed to Jesus to heal him as we have seen in other passages. Perhaps, he was simply attending the synagogue along with the rest of the people, but Jesus asked him to take center stage. Just as Jesus perceived what was in the Pharisees' hearts in the earlier passage, He was very much aware of the current climate. He knew that the stakes in this drama had been raised and that their animosity had been kindled. They certainly did not wish Him well. In fact, they wished Him harm.

In the Greek text, the command to "stand in the center" or "step forward" can literally be translated "rise into the middle." This depicts a man sitting on the sidelines. He had a paralyzed hand but did not appear to want any part in this controversy. Nevertheless, Jesus summoned him into the middle of the debate.

3:4 *Then he asked them, "Is it right to do good or to do evil on the day of worship, to give a person back his health or to let him die?" But they were silent.*

Jesus stood in the synagogue, surrounded by friend and foe. There, next to the man with the paralyzed hand, He addressed the Pharisees by posing a layered question. Which was better—to do good or evil, to save life or to kill? Of course, this particular viewpoint could be applied to any day of the week. Jesus asked the question, but the Pharisees remained silent. The manner in which Jesus asked the question made it difficult for them to respond. If they said, "Yes! Of course, it is better to do good," they were endorsing Jesus' action. If they said, "No," they were saying that it is permissible to do evil and to kill. Obviously, they were caught in a trap. They certainly did not intend to endorse the ministry of this new rabbi, but they also could not oppose His action either. Their silence must have been deafening as it exposed their hypocrisy.

3:5 *Jesus was angry as he looked around at them. He was deeply hurt because their minds were closed. Then he told the man, "Hold out your hand." The man held it out, and his hand became normal again.*

Jesus knew very well that the Pharisees could not answer His question without making fools of themselves. He knew the intent of their hearts and that they sought evidence to accuse Him of failing to obey the Law of Moses. As Jesus looked at the Pharisees, He was angry. Was He angry because He knew their motives or because He hated them? His anger was triggered by His distress over the Pharisees' willful blindness of the evidence that they had witnessed with their very eyes. Their hearts were calloused with pride and hypocrisy.

Throughout this gospel, Jesus ministered publicly. He did not cultivate a secret message for a chosen few. His message was openly delivered to everyone able to hear His voice and observe the authority with which He resolved mankind's maladies. The disciples saw exactly the same events as the Pharisees did, yet they came to totally opposite conclusions. The disciples accepted Him as an unusual rabbi Whose actions confirmed His words, whereas the Pharisees labeled Him as an imposter and blasphemer.

Jesus told the man to stretch out his hand. When the man obeyed, his hand was restored to the strength of his other hand. Jesus did not say to a demon, "Come out of him." He did not say, "Be cleansed," or even, "Friend, your sins are forgiven." In fact, Jesus never addressed the problem. He simply instructed the man to stretch out his hand, and the restoration was already complete.

3:6 *The Pharisees left, and with Herod's followers they immediately plotted to kill Jesus.*

The Pharisees were furious. Rather than rejoice in someone made whole, they left the scene and immediately conspired with Herod's people. This rabbi had defied the religious system that had rewarded the scribes and Pharisees with lofty positions of status and respect. They were esteemed for the power they held and were considered holy men of God. Jesus had exposed their prideful intentions, and the Pharisees were afraid of losing their standing. Better to align themselves with their hated enemies, the Herodians, than to acknowledge the ministry of this rabbi.

From this point on, they plotted for a way to kill Jesus. Some translations use the word *destroy* instead of *kill*. We can be sure that the Pharisees wanted to destroy His reputation and to break His hold on the people. They wanted to expose Him as a fraud—just another false prophet appearing on the scene of Jewish life.

Notes/Applications

The die was cast. There was no turning back. The religious leaders of the day were prepared to plot against one of their own people to destroy Him and cut off His ministry. They would not stop until they saw their mission completed.

Sadly, we often see this very scenario played out in the church today. Jesus told His followers to expect persecution by the world, but when criticism or harsh actions originate in the house of God, we feel the sting of rejection, shock, anger, and sadness. Jesus, in His humanity, must have felt these emotions, too, but He knew His ultimate mission and determined to carry it out. Jesus came to bring hope and salvation to the "lost sheep" of Israel and, ultimately, to the entire world.

How do we respond when religious leaders or those we respect act in a hurtful manner? What do we do when we see Christians "shoot their wounded" rather than help them back to their feet? Are we the ones "pulling the trigger" against our Christian family? The apostle Paul instructed the new believers at Ephesus to be devoted to Christ and to one another: "[20]You are built on the foundation of the apostles and prophets. Christ Jesus himself is the cornerstone. [21]In him all the parts of the building fit together and grow into a holy temple in the Lord. [22]Through him you, also, are being built in the Spirit together with others into a place where God lives" *(Ephesians 2:20–22)*.

As believers, we have been built on the foundation of Christ, so Paul's admonition holds true for us as well. Being "rooted and grounded in love," we are encouraged to "know the love of Christ which passes knowledge" *(Ephesians 3:17,19, NKJV)* and to extend that patient love to our Christian family members when they experience spiritual challenges and become disillusioned.

> *4Love is patient. Love is kind. Love isn't jealous. It doesn't sing its own praises. It isn't arrogant. 5It isn't rude. It doesn't think about itself. It isn't irritable. It doesn't keep track of wrongs. 6It isn't happy when injustice is done, but it is happy with the truth. 7Love never stops being patient, never stops believing, never stops hoping, never gives up.*
>
> *8Love never comes to an end. There is the gift of speaking what God has revealed, but it will no longer be used. There is the gift of speaking in other languages, but it will stop by itself. There is the gift of knowledge, but it will no longer be used.* (1 Corinthians 13:4–8)

When we are rejected by those who claim to serve God, we must remind ourselves of this passage in the Gospel of Mark. Jesus, the Son of God, demonstrated to the world that He was the very essence of God Himself. Some followed Him without reservation, while others could not see past their own agenda. Our encouragement today lies in the sure knowledge that God knows those who are His. Jesus Himself intercedes on our behalf, and not everyone belongs to Him. In the midst of this assurance, we realize that we very well could suffer the same consequences Jesus endured, but that is a small price for being a child of His, redeemed with the precious blood of Christ.

Mark 3:7–12

3:7–8 *⁷Jesus left with his disciples for the Sea of Galilee. A large crowd from Galilee, Judea, ⁸Jerusalem, Idumea, and from across the Jordan River, and from around Tyre and Sidon followed him. They came to him because they had heard about everything he was doing.*

Jesus and His disciples left the synagogue confrontation with the Pharisees and returned to the Sea of Galilee. A new scene opens before us as a "large crowd" from beyond the region of Galilee and Capernaum gathered around Jesus. The multitude probably numbered in the thousands.

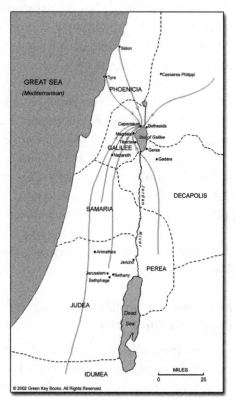

These people came from all over the region, even from as far as Judea and Idumea. Why did this huge number of people seek this rabbi? Because they were hearing of the miracles He was doing, such as healing the sick, curing lepers, making the lame to walk, and casting out demons. Not only that, but when Jesus cast out a demon and restored a man who had an evil spirit, the crowds experienced the excitement generated by the teaching of this young rabbi—teaching that was confirmed by action.

3:9 *Jesus told his disciples to have a boat ready so that the crowd would not crush him.*

The Son of God made logistical preparations to protect Himself by instructing the disciples to have a small boat ready. The press of the crowd was so great that He literally prepared an escape route. If it became too dangerous, He could board the boat and push off from shore to separate Himself from the crowd.

The crowds traveled from great distances, some from as far as seventy-five miles or more. Whatever lives they left behind, however long and arduous their journey, and whatever the demands of the unknown conditions once they arrived, they were willing to forsake everything and endure anything to catch a glimpse of this renowned teacher. The Jewish people, subdued and ruled by foreign nations since Nebuchadnezzar had taken Jerusalem in 586 B.C., were desperate. This special person had captured their imagination and hopes. Could this be the Messiah? Could this be God's Anointed, the fulfillment of all the prophetic visions? The general populace swarmed like bees around Jesus.

3:10 *He had cured so many that everyone with a disease rushed up to him in order to touch him.*

These people attempted an amazing thing. If they could just touch Him, they might be restored to health. They were not disappointed. Just to touch the teacher was health and wholeness. He set them free from their sicknesses. What could the Pharisees be thinking when faced with such an abundance of evidence?

3:11 *Whenever people with evil spirits saw him, they would fall down in front of him and shout, "You are the Son of God!"*

Jesus continued His ministry, casting out demons from those so afflicted by setting them free from their spiritual slavery. In response, the demons' only reaction was to recognize the source of this healing power and readily acknowledge Jesus as the Son of God.

At this time in Jesus' ministry, three primary groups were confronted with the reality of the Son of God. First, there were those who were captivated by His words and His deeds. These were by far the largest group. They saw a unique individual walking among them with grace and humility and Who was not seeking the company of the rich or powerful. He taught them with authority, confirmed by extraordinary deeds. Second, there were those such as the scribes and the Pharisees who looked for the opportunity to destroy His ministry. They could not possibly accept this blasphemer. They observed the same authoritative teachings and the same spectacular events, but their conclusions were exactly the opposite. Jesus had trespassed the bounds of all Jewish propriety, so He had to be silenced. Last, there were the demons that Jesus called forth from their victims. These were the only beings that clearly saw Jesus as the Son of the Most High God. Strangely, the two human sides of this triangle were either clouded in their perceptions or totally opposed to Jesus. The demons, servants of Jesus' archenemy Satan, understood perfectly the opposition they faced, and they acknowledged His lordship. Only the demons were without the cloud of mankind's sinful nature. They knew their days were numbered.

3:12 *He gave them orders not to tell people who he was.*

For the moment, Jesus wanted things to continue as they were. The demons knew His true identity, but He directed them to keep quiet because He did not yet want the entire world to know and acknowledge Him. Why allow mankind to struggle under the cloud of self-directed sinfulness? If He would have revealed His identity, the crowds would no longer have struggled with doubts, questions, and failures generated from their own feeble conditions. And yet, had He not already done so by the indisputable evidence of His actions?

Notes/Applications

This passage leaves us with a looming question. Why did Jesus warn the evil spirits not to tell people Who He was? Our human reasoning would assume that the sooner the world knew the Son of God the better. Why the big secret? Why the wait? Almighty God has His own timetable. He knew what He was doing, and so did Jesus, Who always followed His Father's bidding.

In the fullness of time, which turned out to be very soon, Jesus unveiled Himself for mankind to ponder, to accept, or to reject. Once confronted with the reality of the Son of God, each of us faces sobering questions. What will we do with Him? Will we follow Jesus or continue to make our own way in the world?

We also confront frustrating questions of timing. When God does not answer our prayers according to our expectations, what is our reaction? Do we continue to trust Him and wait for His perfect timing, or do we take matters into our own hands?

> [8]"My thoughts are not your thoughts,
>   and my ways are not your ways," declares the Lord.
> [9]"Just as the heavens are higher than the earth,
>   so my ways are higher than your ways,
>   and my thoughts are higher than your thoughts."
>   (Isaiah 55:8–9)

> Surrender yourself to the Lord, and wait patiently for him.
>   Do not be preoccupied with an evildoer, who succeeds in his
>   way when he carries out his schemes. (Psalm 37:7)

Just as this passage demonstrates, the eye of man is clouded with his sin nature. Jesus Himself spoke of man's difficulty to perceive the ways of God. This was certainly the case for the scribes and Pharisees and continues to be for those who want the rewards of Christianity without its inherent requirement of dying to self. *"²⁴Then Jesus said to his disciples, 'Those who want to come with me must say no to the things they want, pick up their crosses, and follow me. ²⁵Those who want to save their lives will lose them. But those who lose their lives for me will find them. ²⁶What good will it do for people to win the whole world and lose their lives? Or what will a person give in exchange for life?' "* (Matthew 16:24–26).

Mark 3:13–19

3:13 *Jesus went up a mountain, called those whom he wanted, and they came to him.*

The scene quickly changed as Jesus again sought some relief from the crowds that His ministry had attracted. However, this retreat had the particular purpose of calling some apart for a special ministry. At this time, Jesus summoned a chosen group of people specifically selected from the rest of the crowd. Why? Simply because He wanted them. Just as in the previous accounts in which Jesus called some fishermen to follow Him, these people also came to Him without hesitation. This call was not an invitation but an inviolable summons.

3:14–15 *¹⁴He appointed twelve whom he called apostles. They were to accompany him and to be sent out by him to spread the Good News. ¹⁵They also had the authority to force demons out of people.*

The Greek word for *appointed* is derived from the verb "to make." This particular usage of the word, however, implies a stronger, more intensive action. We can safely conclude that these individuals were specifically separated from the rest of the people for a special purpose. They were selected from the people because Jesus wanted them to be with Him. This choice was not some arbitrary move at establishing friendships. Rather, they were appointed for a specific task—"to be sent out by him to spread the Good News." He intended that these twelve men go out in His name to preach the same message that He proclaimed: "The time has come, and the kingdom of God is near. Change the way you think and act, and believe the Good News" (*Mark 1:15*).

This verse has another word common to the Christian's vocabulary. The word *send* comes from the Greek word ἀποστέλλη (apostellay), which is the verb form of the word for "apostle." Out of the crowd that followed Jesus, these individuals comprised the inner circle—chosen, appointed, and sent.

Spreading the Good News has been a primary focus of the Christian church ever since Jesus walked on the earth. It was the command that He gave His disciples, the primary mission of the Twelve. It is the crux of the Great Commission. It conveys all that the Lord intended, declaring the method by which the gospel of Jesus Christ is made known. It is the method by which the believer proclaims Jesus' message to the world.

The demons alone clearly indicated that Jesus was the Son of God. Jesus commanded the demons to refrain from exposing His true identity. Those people that followed Jesus, who hung on His every word amazed at the spectacular deeds that He performed, knew He was sent by God but only dimly understood Who He was. However, Jesus placed the responsibility for the open declaration of His message squarely on these imperfect, human vessels flawed by their sinful nature. God empowered imperfect men to convey His perfect message.

Just as Jesus had healed many from all sorts of illnesses and cast out demons from those possessed, these twelve would have the same power from God. This particular gift of healing and casting out demons was given to the Twelve without reservation: "Jesus called his twelve disciples and gave them authority to force evil spirits out of people and to cure every disease and sickness" *(Matthew 10:1)*.

3:16 *He appointed these twelve: Simon (whom Jesus named Peter),*

Mark names the Twelve, who were chosen by Jesus for this special ministry. First, there was Simon, whom Jesus had called from his labor of fishing to become a fisher of men. Jesus gave Simon a special second name of *Peter,* meaning "Rock." This name indicated Jesus' special purpose for Simon and the role that he was to play in the years ahead.

3:17 *James and his brother John (Zebedee's sons whom Jesus named Boanerges, which means "Thunderbolts"),*

There were also the brothers James and John, who were the sons of Zebedee. Jesus also had a special name for these two fishermen. The word *Boanerges* is an Aramaic word. While this was the regional language, Greek was the more universal language, spoken throughout the Middle East. *Boanerges* means "Thunderbolts," sometimes translated as "Sons of Thunder," denoting rage and destruction. Jesus obviously observed these two brothers and chose them for the task He had planned for them, partially due to their personality traits, which included their fiery temperaments. They were a zealous and aggressive pair unlike the "meek and mild" stereotype generally associated with Jesus and His disciples.

3:18–19 *¹⁸Andrew, Philip, Bartholomew, Matthew, Thomas, James (son of Alphaeus), Thaddaeus, Simon the Zealot, ¹⁹and Judas Iscariot (who later betrayed Jesus).*

Mark then identified each of the remaining chosen twelve by name. The last disciple he identified was Judas Iscariot, who ultimately betrayed Jesus. He was included in Jesus' inner circle and was privileged to hear the private teaching that was theirs alone to hear. He certainly participated in the public ministry of Jesus as well, yet his single identification was as the one "who later betrayed Jesus."

Was the choice of Judas Iscariot evidence of fallibility in Jesus? Why would He choose this man? Could this one, Who authenticated His ministry with so many miracles, possibly make a mistake like this? Judas was chosen precisely because he would be the one to betray Jesus. In His sober words about discipleship, Jesus said, "I chose all twelve of you. Yet, one of you is a devil" *(John 6:70)*. At the Last Supper, as the Twelve discussed the coming events, Jesus was not surprised that Judas had already made arrangements to sell his Master to the religious leaders of the Sanhedrin. Jesus just commanded Judas to perform the task quickly. When we read

Mark 14:16–21 along with this verse, we begin to understand that none of this was mere chance but was the clearly defined plan of God the Father.

Notes/Applications

Though He was the Son of God, divinity in the flesh, Jesus was also a man. Like us, He desired close friends with which to share His life. This passage includes the famous calling of the Twelve—the men who would follow Jesus over the next three years and sit at His feet. They were friends, but they were also much more than that. These were the human vessels Jesus poured His "words of life" into, the ones directly charged with taking the gospel to the uttermost parts of the earth. They were given the awesome privilege of having the Son of God as their personal mentor to teach them, guide them, rebuke them when necessary, and equip them for preaching God's message of repentance.

On the surface, it appears that Jesus chose the Twelve for the individual characteristics He saw in them. However, in light of the entire scriptural narrative, we realize these men had a special place in history because they were chosen long before they were born. Jesus was no accidental rabbi. He was and is the intended Messiah, God's perfect sacrificial Lamb Who would redeem members of lost humanity, and these twelve men were destined to participate as an integral part of God's eternal plan.

As we contemplate the immensity of this grace and the plan conceived by God Himself, we must wonder where we fit. So many go through life without any concept of the reality of salvation. However, all who are redeemed share in the glory of Christ's redemption, having been called into this relationship according to the Father's good pleasure.

It is no accident that we find ourselves inside the fold of the Good Shepherd:

> *27My sheep respond to my voice, and I know who they are. They follow me, 28and I give them eternal life. They will never be lost,*

and no one will tear them away from me. ²⁹My Father, who gave them to me, is greater than everyone else, and no one can tear them away from my Father. ³⁰The Father and I are one" (John 10:27–30).

And to what purpose? To proclaim and live out the message. So much of Christian teaching leads us to believe that we are the ones who orchestrate our salvation. We somehow approach the throne of God's grace through our own merit. However, if we observe the Twelve, we realize that there was nothing extraordinary about these men.

> ²⁶*Brothers and sisters, consider what you were when God called you to be Christians. Not many of you were wise from a human point of view. You were not in powerful positions or in the upper social classes. ²⁷But God chose what the world considers nonsense to put wise people to shame. God chose what the world considers weak to put what is strong to shame. ²⁸God chose what the world considers ordinary and what it despises—what it considers to be nothing—in order to destroy what it considers to be something. ²⁹As a result, no one can brag in God's presence.* (1 Corinthians 1:26–29)

If we believe that any eternal merit exists in our lives as a result of our good works or good intentions, we are deceived and do not appreciate the fact that we are His people simply because of what He has accomplished in and through us. We must not cheapen our salvation by imposing our personal merit upon it. Salvation is rich beyond our wildest dreams because of the great plan of the eternal God and Creator as revealed in the death and resurrection of His Son, Jesus Christ our Lord.

So many people float through life without a sense of destiny, a purpose energizing their daily living with meaning. Once we respond to the call of Christ, we realize He was the "missing piece" all along—the only one who can give our lives a sense of mission that transcends the here and now. As the twelve disciples were charged, we, too, are called to spread the Good News of God's grace to everyone who will listen. Jesus chose the Twelve simply because it fulfilled the Father's plan. He called us to Himself for the same reason. What will we do with so great a salvation?

Mark 3:20–30

3:20 *Then Jesus went home. Another crowd gathered so that Jesus and his disciples could not even eat.*

The multitude now converged on the house that Jesus and the disciples had entered. This crowd so persisted in its attempts to see and touch Jesus that the Twelve could not even eat. We do not know the precise circumstances of this event. Was it the press of the crowd that prevented them from sitting down anywhere in the house to eat, or was it simply the fact that there was so much demand for Jesus' time that He did not have the opportunity to eat?

3:21 *When his family heard about it, they went to get him. They said, "He's out of his mind!"*

Although this verse indicates that Jesus' family "went to get him," their motive remains unclear. However, those around Jesus observed Him to be "out of his mind." It would be understandable that a constant, ongoing schedule enduring for several days would result in extreme exhaustion. Even with this condition, Jesus did not take time to rest or to eat. He rode the wave of human desperation that rippled through this crowd of lost, sick, and searching people. With need that was so great, how could the Son of Man turn away to rest or eat?

3:22 *The scribes who had come from Jerusalem said, "Beelzebul is in him," and "He forces demons out of people with the help of the ruler of demons."*

Earlier, we observed that Jesus initiated the dialogue with the scribes and Pharisees. In Mark 2:6–12, He understood what they were thinking. He grasped the error of their thinking and challenged them to rethink their centuries-old teachings. This was impossible for them to do because their minds and hearts were closed to the truth He represented. Their ultimate responsibility was to guard the traditions of the rabbis and their enviable social position in the Jewish community. They were, after all, the religious elite.

Now, the scribes did not simply watch the behavior of this new teacher. They sought to ensnare Him "so that they could accuse him of doing something wrong" *(verse 2)*. The scribes took the offensive, and Jesus faced their vocal opposition and their full attack on His person and ministry. No longer were the scribes simply going to observe and question Him. They were now intent on attacking this unruly and rebellious rabbi. They came from Jerusalem, the Holy City, David's city, and accused Jesus of being possessed not by ordinary demons but by Beelzebul, Satan himself.[1]

The scribes applied rabbinical logic that resulted in erroneous conclusions. Jesus had proved to be a blasphemer by the unforgivable act of pronouncing a man's sins forgiven. A blasphemer could not operate under the will of the Holy God of Israel. Therefore, according to the Pharisees and scribes, Jesus was not the emissary of the Lord God but of Satan. The scribes did not argue that Jesus was not able to cast out demons. Their logic acknowledged that demons were undoubtedly cast out of those persons. In fact, they had seen Jesus do so on several occasions. Their conclusion, therefore, was that Jesus must have been under the influence of Satan himself, and under that influence as Satan's emissary, Jesus could direct the behavior of the lesser demons.

With this logical conclusion firmly embedded in their thinking, the religious elite believed that it was their holy responsibility to inform the crowds not to believe this man. In addition, they believed that they had a holy obligation to warn the general populace of the dangers of this man. From their well-informed, holy rabbinical tradition, they saw Jesus as a menace to society.

3:23 *Jesus called them together and used this illustration: "How can Satan force out Satan?"*

This time, Jesus did not publicly confront their accusations. He quietly called them aside for a personal dialogue about the conclusions they had drawn. Again, we have not been privileged to hear the teachings of Jesus as He addressed the crowds. We are only told of His conversations with His detractors. On this occasion, Jesus answered the logic of the rabbinical teaching with a godly logic, which was incisive and irrefutable.

If Jesus were indeed possessed by Beelzebul, it would be totally illogical that He should cast out Satan's messengers, his demons. After all, Satan's primary goal is to create confusion and to thwart the purposes of God. If a lesser demon had managed to infiltrate a person's thinking and behavior, he had been successful in damaging that soul in its search for truth found only in the living and holy God of Israel. Why would Satan then remove his lesser counterpart and clear a man's line of understanding, thereby opening that man to the possibilities that existed when he understood the reality of the living God?

3:24 *If a kingdom is divided against itself, that kingdom cannot last.*

Jesus repeated the logic of the previous verse on a more practical level. What is true for Satan in his cosmic, unending struggle against the Lord God Who made him is also true for any earthly kingdom. If it is divided and its energies are diffused in internal strife, that kingdom will surely crumble.

3:25 *And if a household is divided against itself, that household will not last.*

Again, Jesus repeated the logic on a more personal level. If a person did not understand how a kingdom operated, he would understand how a home operated. The home that lives in constant conflict among its own members will fail. It will not be able to withstand all of the external forces brought to bear on the sanctity of that home.

Jesus made every effort to ensure the understanding of the scribes that had traveled from Jerusalem to Capernaum, a distance of nearly seventy miles. They needed to understand the flaw in their earthly logic. Yes, it is true that Satan controls the behavior of his lesser emissaries, but it would be unreasonable to conclude that Satan would rise up against his own demons in order to achieve some unseen goal perceived by this rabbi, Jesus.

3:26 *So if Satan rebels against himself and is divided, he cannot last. That will be the end of him.*

Clearly, if Satan were the source of Christ's miracles, it would be completely counterproductive. Satan would be creating an operating mechanism that resulted in his own destruction. Was it really logical that this would be Satan's ultimate purpose, that he would be interested in his own demise? The logic of the scribes was truly preposterous, running counter to the very nature of Satan's purpose. "A *thief comes to steal, kill, and destroy*" (John 10:10).

3:27 *"No one can go into a strong man's house and steal his property. First he must tie up the strong man. Then he can go through the strong man's house and steal his property.*

Jesus further advanced the common-sense logic of His argument against the scribes. He did so on a personal level that everyone who heard Him could understand. Jesus contended that when someone entered a strong man's house in order to steal his goods, the man would make some attempt to defend his household. He would attack the intruder and defend the integrity of his home. Therefore, the intruder would first have to disable the man so that the homeowner would be unable to resist the intruder's actions. Then, the intruder could obtain full access to the entire house.

Rather than support Satan and his legions, Jesus described Himself as an intruder Who had broken into the normal routine of Satan's household.[2] Previously, following His baptism, Jesus overcame the power of Satan and vanquished any temptation the adversary threw at Him. When Jesus entered humanity, He represented the means by which Satan would finally be conquered. He entered the world of sin, Satan's household, and demonstrated His authority and His power over His eternal adversary by casting out Satan's lesser emissaries when He found them in possession of a poor human soul.

> I will make you and the woman hostile toward each other.
> I will make your descendants
>   and her descendant hostile toward each other.
> He will crush your head,
>   and you will bruise his heel. (Genesis 3:15)

> The God of peace will quickly crush Satan under your feet. (Romans 16:20)

3:28–29 ²⁸**"I can guarantee this truth: People will be forgiven for any sin or curse. ²⁹But whoever curses the Holy Spirit will never be forgiven. He is guilty of an everlasting sin."**

Remember the scene. Jesus quietly argued His point to these scribes from Jerusalem. He understood their viewpoint and their line of reasoning that brought them to such an erroneous conclusion. He also saw the fallacy of their argument, and most of all, Jesus sadly recognized that in their spiritual blindness they would never understand their error. Therefore, Jesus concluded with a very sobering admonition.

God's great forgiveness can forgive anything and everything that poor, blind, stumbling men may conceive or do, including the sin of blasphemy or ridiculing God the Father. But, in all of God's great, unquenchable mercy, there is one unforgivable sin: blasphemy against the Holy Spirit. This sin occurs when the work of the Holy Spirit is attributed to Satan and his dominion.[3] Jesus claimed that everything that He had said and done to this point was accomplished by the power of the Spirit of God. His foregoing discussion removed any other conclusion than that Jesus was the Son of God. By God's power alone, He had spoken with authority, healed all sorts of sicknesses, and cast out demons. If the scribes who had heard His words and seen His deeds could not conclude that these miracles originated from the Holy Spirit, they stood in danger of eternal condemnation.

This was a very solemn occasion. With quiet urgency, Jesus pressed these scribes from Jerusalem concerning the fallacy of their reasoning, presenting them with the validity of His own logic. This may have been the last time Jesus spoke to them in such a quiet, persuasive manner without the pressure of the crowds and the related need to maintain their personal dignity. Jesus warned them that His message should be accepted simply by virtue of the evidence of His teaching, His deeds, and His truth.

3:30 *Jesus said this because the scribes had said that he had an evil spirit.*

The scribes contended that Jesus exorcised demons by the power of Satan: "Many of them said, 'He's possessed by a demon! He's crazy! Why do you listen to him?' " *(John 10:20)*. In essence, they declared that the authority of Satan had accomplished all of the wonderful things that Jesus had done. If this was their final conclusion, they were then subject to eternal judgment because of their unbelief. Considering Jesus' argument, only one conclusion fit the facts. Jesus was the Son of God as evidenced in His teaching and His deeds. Any other conclusion was irrational, the product of a mind blinded by Satan.

Notes/Applications

Jesus' memorable conversation with the scribes from Jerusalem depicts the great chasm that exists between those who believe in the Son of God and those who do not. It seems inconceivable that anyone could deny that Jesus was Who He claimed to be after they were confronted with such a great body of evidence. Sadly, people did then, and they still do today.

This chasm between believers and unbelievers on earth is evident in their dialogue, their deeds, and their very lives, and exists into eternity. Believers can certainly understand unbelievers. Like them, we once walked in the darkness of our own self-direction until the Spirit of the living God illuminated the error of our ways. However, unbelievers can never understand the direction and focus of believers. They have never experienced the release from sin nor the enlightenment of the mind that comes when the Spirit's witness overwhelms them. "³So if the Good News that we tell others is covered with a veil, it is hidden from those who are dying. ⁴The god of this world has blinded the minds of those who don't believe. As a result, they don't see the light of the Good News about Christ's glory. It is Christ who is God's image" (*2 Corinthians 4:3–4*). There will continue to exist a dynamic tension between belief and unbelief.

Countless men and women live with doom hanging over their hearts because they willfully reject Jesus the Christ. They may very well transfer their rejection to us as believers, but we must be mobilized by compassion to accept such challenges, petitioning God for their rescue from an eternal finality of hopeless separation from Him.

> ²⁹*What do you think a person who shows no respect for the Son of God deserves? That person looks at the blood of the promise (the blood that made him holy) as no different from other people's blood, and he insults the Spirit that God gave us out of his kindness. He deserves a much worse punishment. . . . ³¹Falling into the hands of the living God is a terrifying thing"* (*Hebrews 10:29, 31*).

Mark 3:31–35

3:31 *Then his mother and his brothers arrived. They stood outside and sent someone to ask him to come out.*

When Jesus' mother and brothers observed the press of the crowds around Him and the fact that He had no time to rest or eat, they said that He was "out of His mind" *(verse 21)*. Now, His brothers and His mother came requesting to see Him. The size of the crowd made it difficult for them to get to Him, so they sent a message stating that they wanted to see Him. The rumors they had heard must have caused them some concern for His well being.

3:32 *The crowd sitting around Jesus told him, "Your mother and your brothers are outside looking for you."*

The message, passed on to Jesus through the crowd, conveyed that His mother and brothers wanted to see Him. It seems as though the crowd sympathized with this request by a concerned mother. In context, it appears that they wanted Jesus to know His family's request and expected that He would see them because family was of primary importance in the Jewish mind. It would be considered disrespectful for Jesus not to respond to the request of His mother and brothers.

3:33 *He replied to them, "Who is my mother, and who are my brothers?"*

Then, Jesus did the unthinkable. He challenged the thinking of virtually everyone in the crowd. Jesus did not answer His mother's request. Instead, He posed a question that must have stopped everyone in their tracks. Certainly, He knew His mother and brothers. He wanted the people to consider this earthly relationship in the context of His person as the Son of God.

3:34 *Then looking at those who sat in a circle around him, he said, "Look, here are my mother and my brothers.*

A moment of silence hung in the air as Jesus quietly surveyed those around Him. He gave them a chance to reflect on His question. He was also giving them a chance to settle down since His question probably caused quite a stir. As His eyes traveled over the crowd and looked into the eyes of His followers, Jesus said, "Here are My mother and My brothers!" The people must have gasped in shock. They all knew His mother and His brothers. They also knew that *they* were not His mother and brothers, yet Jesus said that they were.

This teacher Whom they had followed was becoming more perplexing every day. He had taught them with authority. He had performed spectacular miracles before their very eyes. They had waited with eager anticipation on His every word. Now, He claimed that they were His family. It seems obvious that the people who followed Him were still learning, still needing to understand His message. Jesus constantly challenged their understanding by exhorting them to look at the world from His perspective as the Son of God.

3:35 *Whoever does what God wants is my brother and sister and mother."*

Jesus finally explained. He had just presented the crowd with a perplexing question that made Him appear out of touch with His surroundings. Maybe He was out of His mind. From the earthly perspective, He certainly demonstrated some strange behavior.

However, Christ's explanation clarified everything. He was not talking about His earthly ties or relationships. He spoke as the Son of God. Anyone and everyone who obeyed the will of God was related to Him. They were as close as the relationship between a mother and son or the closest of brothers.

Notes/Applications

In contrast with the earlier passage that was frightening in its finality, this heartwarming passage offers an analogy of the relationship believers have with Jesus Christ. After astonishing the crowd with an odd question, Jesus answered His question by indicating just how close we can be to Him. We can be as close as His mother and His brothers.

The earlier debate with the scribes had the clinical tone of a courtroom defense—refuting lies with logic. Apparently, the scribes had left the scene, so Jesus was left surrounded by hungry souls who ardently sought Him. In this intimate setting, He taught them what it was like to be His follower. To their surprise, Jesus likened it to being His brothers and sisters, members of the same family who share a bond of love and familiarity.

The term *brother* implies the strongest possible bond—that of flesh and blood. John Newton, beloved hymnist, captures a glimpse of our blessed kinship with Christ and expresses the song of our hearts:

Poor, weak and worthless though I am
I have a rich almighty Friend;
Jesus, the Savior, is His Name;
He freely loves, and without end.

He ransomed me from hell with blood,
And by His power my foes controlled;
He found me wandering far from God,
And brought me to His chosen fold.
He cheers my heart, my wants supplies,
And says that I shall shortly be,
Enthroned with Him above the skies;
O what a Friend is Christ to me!

But, ah! my inmost spirit mourns;
And well my eyes with tears may swim,
To think of my perverse returns:
I've been a faithless friend to Him.

Often my gracious Friend I grieve,
Neglect, distrust, and disobey;
And often Satan's lies believe
Sooner than all my Friend can say.

He bids me always freely come,
And promises whate'er I ask:
But I am straitened, cold and dumb,
And count my privilege a task

Before the world that hates His course,
My treach'rous heart has throbbed with shame;
Loath to forego the worlds applause,
I hardly dare avow His Name.

Sure, were I not most vile and base,
I could not thus my Friend requite!
And were not He the God of grace,
He'd frown and spurn me from His sight.[4]

Mark 4:1–9

4:1 *Jesus began to teach again by the Sea of Galilee. A very large crowd gathered around him, so he got into a boat and sat in it. The boat was in the water while the entire crowd lined the shore.*

For the first time in the Gospel of Mark, we experience the teaching of Jesus directed toward those who appear to be His sincere followers. In our previous discussions, we learned the teachings of Jesus as a result of His confrontations with the scribes and the Pharisees. Now, at last, we are brought into the experience of His followers.

Jesus returned to the sea, one of His favorite spots. The multitude was so great that there was not enough room for everybody. Previously, Jesus had a boat prepared in case the crowd grew too large *(Mark 3:9)*. Now, Jesus entered the boat, sat down, and taught the multitude. Thanks to Mark's excellent word picture, we see the scene unfold as we join the crowd on land. Our attention is drawn to Jesus sitting in a small boat on the Sea of Galilee.

4:2 *He used stories as illustrations to teach them many things. While he was teaching them, he said,*

Jesus taught them many things, some of which are recorded in Mark's gospel, but Mark does not relate all of His teachings. In the Gospel of John, we read that the total accumulation of Jesus' teachings is immeasurable *(John 21:25)*.

Jesus typically taught the crowd by using parables. The word *parable*, a direct transliteration of the Greek word παραβολαισ (parabowlais), might today be called an "illustration." Jesus taught the crowd using illustrations that drew on familiar, common experiences. He stated the obvious, that which everyone knew to be true, but buried in the parable was a deeper meaning that related the illustration to an eternal truth. Many people understood the obvious analogy, but only a few perceived the eternal truth that Jesus taught them.

4:3 *"Listen! A farmer went to plant a seed.*

Jesus started with the instruction, "Listen!" The Greek verb is in the imperative, meaning that Jesus commanded the crowd to pay attention. What followed was a story about a farmer who sowed his seed on the land. Since many in the crowd were likely from an agricultural background, they could well relate to such a story.

4:4 *Some seeds were planted along the road, and birds came and devoured them.*

Long before the first seed was sown, much time and effort was spent preparing the soil. The field was plowed to bring fresh soil to the top. The big clumps of earth were broken into a smoother mixture of soil. All preparations were made to enhance an optimum yield.

When the time came to sow the seed, the farmer knew that much seed would be spread on the ground. There would never be one hundred percent yield because some seed did not fall on the soil that was prepared to receive the seed. Some would fall on the hardened earth surrounding the prepared soil. That seed simply lay on top of the hard ground, making it available to hungry birds, which ate the exposed seeds.

4:5 *Other seeds were planted on rocky ground, where there wasn't much soil. The plants sprouted quickly because the soil wasn't deep.*

At the side of the field remained some areas that had not been prepared and were quite full of stones. Generally, these areas were hard and lacked depth. When the seed fell on this type of earth, it might have germinated and pushed its roots down into the shallow soil. It would not take long for this seed to sprout because it was not deeply planted.

4:6 *When the sun came up, they were scorched. They didn't have any roots, so they withered.*

Just as it did not take long for this seed to sprout, it also quickly disappeared because the root structure was restricted as a result of the shallow soil. Consequently, when the sun reached its peak, the earth baked, and the seedling disappeared. It was deprived of the moisture that would have been provided from a deeper root structure and could not maintain its strength.

4:7 *Other seeds were planted among thornbushes. The thornbushes grew up and choked them, and they didn't produce anything.*

On the perimeter of the prepared soil grew thorns. These thornbushes had a much deeper root structure and had apparently been growing for a long time. As the weeds developed, their roots sucked precious moisture and nutrients from the new seed and literally choked the life from the seeds. The seed may have sprouted and started growing, but inevitably, the thorns won this battle.

4:8 *But other seeds were planted on good ground, sprouted, and produced thirty, sixty, or one hundred times as much as was planted."*

However, the seed that fell "on good ground," on soil properly cultivated, sprouted vigorously and grew to full maturity. In its mature stage, this seed would bear fruit, exceedingly multiplying the simple little seed that was originally planted. This seed was profitable to the sower because there was a reward to show for all his hard work.

4:9 *He added, "Let the person who has ears listen!"*

This simple story of the sower drew to a close. Jesus had really said nothing new. He had not helped anyone to improve his farming technique. The people knew everything He had just told them. Why would the crowd grow to such unmanageable proportions just to hear someone tell them something they already knew? Would it not be far better to be at home planting the seed for one's own gain? Would it not be more profitable to be fishing in the sea than listening to someone tell stories about the obvious?

Just then, Jesus issued a summation requiring special attention. At the beginning, He said, "Listen!" Now, Jesus admonished, "Let the person who has ears listen!" We have all been sitting in this crowd and have heard everything He said. Of course, we have ears. Of course, we heard His message. What more did He want us to understand from this message?

Notes/Applications
If we close our eyes and see the picture unfold around us, we can almost become another member of this crowd gathered around Jesus by the sea. Anticipation would grow as the rabbi from Nazareth spoke, but would we be somewhat disappointed by such a simple message about a farmer sowing seed on the earth?

Obviously, Jesus emphasized the extreme significance of His message to His listeners. Twice, He urged them to listen. Apparently,

Jesus spoke about much more than farming, but His meaning was not readily understood by the crowd. The scribes tried to understand Jesus' teaching through their own frame of reference, and the people depicted in this passage also struggled to gain insight, wanting desperately to understand His words.

Like those gathered at the sea that day, we must listen with our hearts to hear what the Son of God is saying to us. How do we hear Him when He does not stand before us in physical form? We hear Him through communing with the Holy Spirit, through praying, through studying the Word, and through allowing His truth, principles, and insights to take root in our hearts and minds. Through His Holy Spirit, these teachings will be cultivated like seed sown in soil and brought to mind as we go about our day. *"Help me understand your guiding principles so that I may reflect on your miracles"* (Psalm 119:27). *"*[35]*You were shown these things so that you would know that the Lord is God. There is no other god.* [36]*He let you hear his voice from heaven so that he could instruct you. He showed you his great fire on earth, and you heard him speak from the column of fire"* (Deuteronomy 4:35–36). Making Jesus our frame of reference as the source of all truth, we can "live out loud" the message He conveyed to mankind.

Mark 4:10–20

4:10 *When he was alone with his followers and the twelve apostles, they asked him about the stories.*

In the preceding section, Jesus gave the illustration of a farmer sowing seed, a subject most of those gathered knew from personal experience. There was a level at which everyone observed what Jesus taught. However, there was a deeper message based on Jesus' identity as the Son of God.

Now, Jesus, alone with the Twelve and some other followers, was queried about this illustration. Evidently, the disciples, too, searched for the real message. They had heard the same thing as everyone else but attained no better understanding.

It is possible to read some deeper meaning and render an interpretation that could be substantiated by the content of the message. However, in this passage Jesus issued His interpretation. This is an important principle for all Bible study. We must always look for the message to be interpreted by the context itself and by other related passages as we draw on the resources of the Bible itself. Failure to do so leads to conclusions from personal experience and not from the mind and heart of God. Such conclusions are usually erroneous and often lead to misinterpretation. Many cults have started in this manner. Even our Christian perspectives may be tainted, and the message may fail to deliver the impact that God intended. We might end up like the scribes and the Pharisees, defending man's interpretation and totally losing sight of Jesus, God's Anointed Redeemer.

4:11 *Jesus replied to them, "The mystery about the kingdom of God has been given directly to you. To those on the outside, it is given in stories:*

Previously noted were three groups that encountered this rabbi: the scribes and Pharisees, the followers, and the demons. Through

Mark's gospel and Peter's witness, we now share in a fourth group, called the Twelve.

Since Mark was Peter's disciple, we are privileged to have a record of Jesus' explanation of the parable. We have the great opportunity to participate not only in the experience of the thousands of people who followed Jesus but in the experience of the chosen Twelve. When we join them in this privileged, intimate conversation with their Lord, we share the experience of Jesus' inner circle. Jesus told them something wonderful. They had been given the opportunity of knowing the mystery of God's kingdom. They would not only know the mystery of this life but the mystery of God's own heart as well.

Jesus further explained to them that those "on the outside" would only be taught about the kingdom in parables. This verse shows that even those who follow Jesus are divided into two groups, the chosen and those on the outside. It is a life-changing experience to be among the inner circle of God's chosen. The reality of this world's fragile existence is that "many are called, but few chosen" (*Matthew 20:16, NKJV*).

4:12 *'They see clearly but don't perceive. They hear clearly but don't understand. They never return to me and are never forgiven.' "*

This verse reveals a hard and difficult truth. It is a statement that grinds our preconceived notions about God into nothing. It grates on our sensibilities and our sensitivities and flies in opposition to everything we believe about a "loving, forgiving God." It is offensive to our human ways of thinking.

Jesus declared His explanation, His reasons, for teaching the masses in parables. In this verse, Jesus paraphrased the words of Isaiah the prophet.

> [9]*And he said, "Go and tell these people,*
> *'No matter how closely you listen, you'll never understand.*
> *No matter how closely you look, you'll never see.'*

> [10]*Make these people close-minded.*
> *Plug their ears.*
>> *Shut their eyes.*
>> *Otherwise, they may see with their eyes,*
> *hear with their ears,*
> *understand with their minds,*
>> *and return and be healed."* (Isaiah 6:9–10)

During Isaiah's time, God issued this order to His chosen messenger so that the wrath of God would visit the rebellious and wicked nation that had defied His rule and transgressed His Law. Isaiah knew at the very beginning of his ministry that he was doomed to fail, even though he was faithful to the message God had given him.

Jesus endorsed Isaiah's words. The reason He spoke to the crowds in parables was unthinkable. He intended for them to continue in their sin-blinded ways so that they would perish in their sins. This seemingly benign teaching about a farmer sowing seed now began to take on some ominous undertones.

4:13 *Jesus asked them, "Don't you understand this story? How, then, will you understand any of the stories I use as illustrations?*

Jesus then questioned His followers. This parable was relatively simple. Could it be true that His closest followers, maybe even the chosen Twelve, did not understand this simple lesson on the reality of God's world? If they had such difficulty understanding this basic illustration, how would they understand the other parables that He had taught to the crowds and that He intended to continue using to teach them? The Twelve needed to be led step-by-step through an explanation of this illustration so that they could rightly comprehend His message. Even the Twelve required being led from the blindness of their sin nature into the correct understanding of Jesus and the message that He brought to the lost world.

4:14 *"The farmer plants the word.*

Jesus patiently and carefully began His explanation. The seed represents the word from God. The familiar Greek word λόγοσ (logos) is used here, but it should not be understood in the same manner as the apostle John used it in his gospel account *(John 1:1, 14)*. In this context, *word* carries the meaning of "message." The sower gave forth the message, and we know that from the beginning of this gospel, Jesus Himself preached the message, "The kingdom of God is near. Change the way you think and act, and believe the Good News" *(Mark 1:15)*.

4:15 *Some people are like seeds that were planted along the road. Whenever they hear the word, Satan comes at once and takes away the word that was planted in them.*

Some seed fell by the wayside. The message was told to some who heard it yet immediately withdrew from it. The message was sown "in their hearts," but Satan never gave it a chance to sprout and flourish, so it was destroyed almost as soon as it was received.

4:16–17 *[16]Other people are like seeds that were planted on rocky ground. Whenever they hear the word, they accept it at once with joy. [17]But they don't develop any roots. They last for a short time. When suffering or persecution comes along because of the word, they immediately fall from faith.*

Some seed fell upon hard, rocky soil. The people represented by this soil heard the message and were immediately overjoyed to receive it. It appears that they accepted the message without much thought. They based their decision to receive the word primarily on the impulse of the moment. Consequently, they were swept along on the tide of their own emotion.

As a result, these individuals would not possess much depth and their commitment would be short-lived. They mistakenly believed that everything would always be pleasant and enjoyable. Their decision consisted of euphoric emotion based on an expectation of personal benefit. However, when adversity came and things did not go right, the shallowness of their conviction was exposed. In contrast, the reality of the Christian experience has demonstrated on numerous occasions that with faith comes persecution and trial.

4:18–19 *¹⁸Other people are like seeds planted among thornbushes. They hear the word, ¹⁹but the worries of life, the deceitful pleasures of riches, and the desires for other things take over. They choke the word so that it can't produce anything.*

Some seed fell among the thorns. Weeds constantly threaten the farmer's crop. In fact, whatever the crop, the farmer must battle with the weeds if the crop is to yield a harvest.

Jesus defined three of these weeds: 1) "the worries of life," 2) "the deceitful pleasures of riches," and 3) "the desires for other things." This definition probably requires little comment, primarily because we recognize these realities in our own lives.

Who of us is not concerned with the worries of life? Who of us does not struggle with budgeting our income and providing for our families? These are essential to our human existence, but they must never supplant our reliance upon the Lord's provision.

Who of us is not concerned with the deceitful pleasures of riches? No matter where we are on the financial spectrum, we always need a little more. We spend our entire lives trying to improve our financial situation, yet Jesus cautioned that this constant chase after riches is destructive. Our lust for wealth and our greed will consume our very souls in the end. *"¹⁵Don't love the world and what it offers. Those who love the world don't have the Father's love in them"* (1 John 2:15). Who of us is not concerned with the accumulation of more things? We want more not because we need it but because we are captives of the concept that material possessions provide happiness, security, and social position *(Matthew 6:31–33)*.

4:20 *Others are like seeds planted on good ground. They hear the word, accept it, and produce crops—thirty, sixty, or one hundred times as much as was planted."*

Finally, the message was heard by some referred to as "good ground." On such good soil, the message sprouted, grew, matured, and yielded fruit. The primary purpose of sowing the seed was that it might bear fruit. The "word" in these people was the living, growing, dynamic Word of God. Nothing choked its growth. Their focus and direction remained clear.

It is important to recognize that all of the seeds did not yield equal production. However, the amount of fruit produced is not the issue here. It is simply that when the word is sown in good ground it will bear fruit.

Notes/Applications

Jesus explained the deeper meaning of the parable of the sower. As we listen along with the small group gathered with the Twelve, a terrible sense of foreboding overwhelms us. Jesus predicted a grim future for the masses. Moreover, He said that what awaited them was not redemption but judgment.

Could this be true? Did the Son of God deny the crowd the information they needed? Why didn't He declare to the crowd the truth about His identity so that many might be saved?

Apparently, Jesus, as Isaiah before Him, declared a message that confounded the hearers rather than clarified any anomalies. Jesus proclaimed a message to the nations, but He did not remove the scales from the eyes of those who remained in darkness as the result of centuries of sinful, willful rebellion against God.

The Gospel of John describes Jesus as "the Lamb of God who takes away the sin of the world" (*John 1:29*), but despite Jesus' centrality in Scripture and in the saga of human history, it is the work of the Holy Spirit to guide men into understanding and redemption. It is the work of the Holy Spirit to prepare the soil of a person's corrupt soul for the planting of the seed that leads to redemption and a life of fruitful service to God. Jesus Himself defined, as well as confirmed, this work of the Spirit in the Gospel of John.

> [16]*I will ask the Father, and he will give you another helper who will be with you forever.* [17]*That helper is the Spirit of Truth. The world cannot accept him, because it doesn't see or know him. You know him, because he lives with you and will be in you.* . . .
>
> [26]*However, the helper, the Holy Spirit, whom the Father will send in my name, will teach you everything. He will remind you of everything that I have ever told you.* (John 14:16–17, 26)

Anyone who clings to the truth of Scripture and calls upon Christ as Lord and Savior has the assurance of salvation. In this, we know the seed of the Word has been sown on good soil in our hearts. Each of us stumbles from time to time along our spiritual journey, but God promises to complete the work He began in us by bringing the seed to full fruition: "I'm convinced that God, who began this good work in you, will carry it through to completion on the day of Christ Jesus" *(Philippians 1:6).*

Mark 4:21–25

4:21 *Jesus said to them, "Does anyone bring a lamp into a room to put it under a basket or under a bed? Isn't it put on a lamp stand?*

Jesus continued speaking to the Twelve. As in the parable of the sower, Jesus gave another common illustration. He reminded them that a lamp is designed to dispel the darkness. No one would light a lamp and then cover it so that it could not fulfill the purpose for which it was designed. Rather, the lamp would be placed high "on a lamp stand" in order to spread its illumination as far as possible.

> *[14]You are light for the world. A city cannot be hidden when it is located on a hill. [15]No one lights a lamp and puts it under a basket. Instead, everyone who lights a lamp puts it on a lamp stand. Then its light shines on everyone in the house. [16]In the same way let your light shine in front of people. Then they will see the good that you do and praise your Father in heaven. (Matthew 5:14–16)*

4:22 *There is nothing hidden that will not be revealed. There is nothing kept secret that will not come to light.*

Jesus taught the Twelve the true purpose of the message. Previously, He stated that He spoke to the crowds in parables so that they would not fully understand. Now, Jesus began to develop a complimentary theme in a paradoxical tone. He had not come to preach a message that would be hidden forever but one that would soon be broadcast. The tense of the verbs used here implies that this was always the intention. There was no divine conspiracy to send Jesus into the world and then forever conceal His identity from the world.

At this time, Jesus taught in parables, and His message was obscured by the very simplicity of His illustrations (2 Corinthians 4:3–4). However, the purpose of the message would not remain hidden forever. It would soon be plain for all whose eyes He opened.

4:23 *Let the person who has ears listen!"*

Again, Jesus admonished His chosen Twelve, and those of us called to be His disciples, to listen carefully to Him. Jesus was speaking of more than the physical act of hearing. He was urging us to listen with the ears of our hearts and to understand the message that would bring us light. *"We are his servants because the same God who said that light should shine out of darkness has given us light. For that reason we bring to light the knowledge about God's glory which shines from Christ's face"* (2 Corinthians 4:6).

4:24 *He went on to say, "Pay attention to what you're listening to! Knowledge will be measured out to you by the measure of attention you give. This is the way knowledge increases.*

Jesus expanded His admonition of hearing to include the responsibility of applying the precepts of His message. He warned His listeners to approach understanding with care. This verse implies that the degree of our understanding is directly proportional to the effort put into listening. It would be pointless to listen to the teacher only to disregard His teaching.

4:25 *Those who understand these mysteries will be given more knowledge. However, some people don't understand these mysteries. Even what they understand will be taken away from them."*

Jesus further intensified the impact of His admonition. Those who heeded that which they heard would be entrusted with greater spiritual understanding. However, the opposite also held true. Those who forsook Christ's message would forfeit what little understanding they did possess.

This verse affirms the parable of the sower: "[16]Other people are like seeds that were planted on rocky ground. Whenever they hear the word, they accept it at once with joy. [17]But they don't develop any roots. They last for a short time. When suffering or persecution comes along because of the word, they immediately fall from faith"

(Mark 4:16–17). Apparently, some relationship exists between our response in understanding and the degree of understanding that we receive. As we focus on Jesus and perceive more of His message, we grow in our understanding of the truth.

Notes/Applications

If there were ever any encouragement for the Christian to apply himself to the study of God's Word, this passage is it. Jesus told those gathered around Him that anyone having spiritual understanding would be given even more understanding. He was, in essence, saying, "Do you grasp the truths I am telling you? If so, rejoice, for you will understand even more of what I have to teach you."

The apostle Paul exhorted Timothy, his "son" in the Lord, to become an expert, living testament: "Do your best to present yourself to God as a tried-and-true worker who isn't ashamed to teach the word of truth correctly" *(2 Timothy 2:15). "¹⁶Every Scripture passage is inspired by God. All of them are useful for teaching, pointing out errors, correcting people, and training them for a life that has God's approval. ¹⁷They equip God's servants so that they are completely prepared to do good things"* (2 Timothy 3:16–17).

Jesus' admonition in Mark 4:21–25 is far more stringent than Paul's. Paul exhorted Timothy in a church environment that probably had little opposition, and Timothy had proven himself to be an apt pupil. Jesus, on the other hand, chided His disciples who did not yet comprehend or who barely perceived the message He so passionately wanted them to understand.

Jesus' admonition addressed both sides of the coin. If we seek, we will find. If we listen, we will hear. If we seek to understand, understanding will be given to us. Conversely, if we do not seek, we will not find. If we do not listen, we will not hear. If we do not understand, the little bit of understanding we have will be taken away.

The most important thing to note in this passage is that spiritual understanding is a gift. What we learn about Jesus in the context of human philosophy is simple knowledge. After all, the scribes and

Pharisees had seen and heard Jesus, yet they were more interested in maintaining their status quo than in really understanding this rabbi. They learned about Jesus, but they failed to accept His significance. The mystery of the kingdom of God is given only to those who yearn to understand. We who are committed to following Jesus are God's remnant of faithful followers in this age, so let us ask ourselves: Are we diligently applying ourselves to the study of His Word?

Mark 4:26–34

4:26–27 *²⁶Jesus said, "The kingdom of God is like a man who scatters seeds on the ground. ²⁷He sleeps at night and is awake during the day. The seeds sprout and grow, although the man doesn't know how.*

Jesus continued His discourse on the kingdom of God. In the earlier sower parable, the points of focus were the ground upon which the seed fell and, more specifically, how the ground received the seed. These verses, however, draw attention to the man who had sown the seed. After planting the seed and without any further labor on the man's part, the seed sprouted and grew.

The man did not make this happen. He simply served as the agent who placed the seed in the ground. The sower performed his task even though he was utterly incapable of understanding the mystery in the seed. He did not understand the nutritional requirements of that seed. He merely served as the means by which the seed came into contact with the fertile soil. Nevertheless, the seed broke through the earth and began to grow, and the mystery of that transformation remained outside the man's understanding.

4:28 *The ground produces grain by itself. First the green blade appears, then the head, then the head full of grain.*

Jesus, the Master Teacher, again stated the obvious to His hearers. They knew that, once planted, the seed would naturally produce a crop and provide food for the person who had sown it. "The ground produces grain by itself" shows that it did so without human intervention. The Greek word is αὐτομάτη (automatay), from which we get the word *automatic*. God alone would complete the work. In fact, when man attempts to intervene in the affairs of the kingdom, there is increased likelihood of disruption rather than growth.

4:29 *As soon as the grain is ready, he cuts it with a sickle, because harvest time has come."*

At the appointed time, once the grain ripened, the man set himself about the task of reaping the reward of the harvest, all of which had been produced outside the realm of his control.

4:30 *Jesus asked, "How can we show what the kingdom of God is like? To what can we compare it?*

Without any interpretation of the preceding parable, Jesus continued to explain the essence of the kingdom of God. He had already told two parables in which the subject of farming served as an analogy. In both of these, the subject was an intimate part of their everyday life. How could it be any easier to understand?

It is wise to remember Jesus' comments when He explained the parable of the sower to His disciples and to recall that his simple message was for those He chose to follow Him. The very parables that helped His disciples understand had the dual purpose of making it difficult for others to grasp the meaning.

4:31 *It's like a mustard seed planted in the ground. The mustard seed is one of the smallest seeds on earth.*

In this parable, our attention is directed to a mustard seed, the smallest of seeds. Jesus chose this particular seed because of its size to illustrate further how the kingdom of God works.

4:32 *However, when planted, it comes up and becomes taller than all the garden plants. It grows such large branches that birds can nest in its shade."*

The resulting plant would tower in comparison to the tiny seed from which it came. As a part of the natural order of God's creation, the mustard plant would become a home for birds that would build their nests and raise their young in the shade of its branches.

4:33 *Jesus spoke God's word to them using many illustrations like these. In this way people could understand what he taught.*

This verse further confirms the great number of parables that Jesus must have told. Jesus employed this teaching method throughout His earthly ministry. Mark notes that Jesus spoke to the people using parables so the "people could understand what he taught." Perhaps the listeners experienced some sort of emotional overload. Was Jesus' message so intense that it was necessary for people to have some time to assimilate His teaching? What was so hard to understand about a sower sowing seed or the growth of that seed or a mustard seed? These were common, everyday occurrences, yet it appears that Jesus had to deliver the "food" of the kingdom at some measured pace so that the people had time to digest it.

4:34 *He did not speak to them without using an illustration. But when he was alone with his disciples, he explained everything to them.*

We are again reminded that Jesus avoided any method of speaking to the people other than by parable. Even these simple teachings were difficult for the crowds to understand, but in private Jesus explained the parables' meanings to the Twelve.

Mark could be perceived as the purveyor of the cryptic message. In the earlier chapters, he tells us that Jesus taught the crowds, but the only way we learn His message is through His adversarial conversations with His opponents. Now, the opposite holds true. Mark retells these kingdom parables and, except for the first one, does not explain them. Only the Twelve benefited from Christ's illumination of the mysteries shared with the masses.

Notes/Applications

It is easy to discuss the interpretation of Jesus' earlier parable when Jesus Himself did the interpreting. However, we do not have that luxury in this passage, nor can we go to the other gospels to see if they shed light on this particular parable, because it is unique to the Gospel of Mark.

Some believe that this is a parable about evangelism, urging the Christian to swing the sickle and harvest the seed that is fully grown and ready. Others see it as an analogy of how the Word grows inside a believer—growing to full maturity until the time when the Son of Man swings the sickle and receives the fruit of His followers' labors. Though either of these two interpretations could be argued using this text, Jesus clearly explained that the parable depicts what the kingdom of God is like.

This parable focused on the growth process rather than the condition of the soil. Perhaps the first parable of the sower is spoken from God's perspective, showing His full knowledge of the process by which the seed grows in varying soils of the human heart, whereas the second parable demonstrates the growth of the kingdom of God from man's perspective. The seed is sown. How it sprouts and grows, we do not know, but we can be sure that it does grow. We can be certain that it bears fruit. Nevertheless, the process of growth is beyond our ability to control or understand. It rests in God's hands. We share the Good News not because others' salvation depends on us. We witness out of obedience and leave the results to Him.

We cannot make things happen but must trust God to work out every detail as we seek His guidance: "We know that all things work together for the good of those who love God—those whom he has called according to his plan" *(Romans 8:28)*.

Mark 4:35–41

4:35 *That evening, Jesus said to his disciples, "Let's cross to the other side."*

Evidently, Jesus presented these kingdom parables in one day. At the end of the day, He again sought to escape the pressure of the crowd. He now desired silence and rest. Remember that Jesus had been in a small boat as He taught the crowd. Now, He instructed His disciples to push off and cross to the other side of the Sea of Galilee.

4:36 *Leaving the crowd, they took Jesus along in a boat just as he was. Other boats were with him.*

Jesus sought rest from the crowd, but even with this maneuver, a small flotilla of boats followed along with Him. There was no relief from the sensation-hungry crowd. They were determined to follow Him no matter where He went or what method of transportation He used.

From this translation, it appears that Jesus simply got tired and left the crowd sitting on the shoreline. The Greek text used to describe the separation of Jesus from the crowd means to "send away."[1] It is good to note that Jesus was very aware of the emotions of the crowd. Therefore, He did not leave them sitting by the shore but dismissed them, thus bringing closure to an exciting day.

As tired as He was, Jesus allowed a small group of boats to accompany Him across the sea. Some of His disciples were accomplished fisherman, and this was their home territory. Since Jesus was already in the boat, they simply hoisted anchor and set sail.

4:37 *A violent windstorm came up. The waves were breaking into the boat so that it was quickly filling up.*

It is not uncommon for sudden squalls to arise on the Sea of Galilee. The configuration of the surrounding terrain can create treacherous conditions, the hills and valleys functioning as wind tunnels capable of quickly funneling normal winds into a whirling tempest.[2]

4:38 *But he was sleeping on a cushion in the back of the boat. So they woke him up and said to him, "Teacher, don't you care that we're going to die?"*

Jesus, exhausted from the day's efforts, slept despite the storm. He was perfectly at rest, both physically, on a pillow in the back of the boat, and spiritually, knowing that all things remained in His hands.

However, the fishermen who earlier took charge of this voyage were deathly afraid. This was out of their control. Certainly, as seasoned fishermen familiar with this body of water, they had been in storms before, but this must have been one exceptional storm if it so frightened these veterans. The group of boats following them were also facing the peril of this angry storm.

The disciples woke Jesus by calling out, "Teacher!" Whatever their perception of Jesus at this time, they knew Him as Teacher. For everything He said and did, they understood little more than that He was their teacher and that He possessed unusual wisdom and power.

4:39 *Then he got up, ordered the wind to stop, and said to the sea, "Be still, absolutely still!" The wind stopped blowing, and the sea became very calm.*

Jesus awoke to the disciples' fear and to the howling storm, the source of their fear. He responded first by addressing the problem. He rebuked the wind and stilled the sea. The Greek word is πεφίμωσο (pefimowso), which was the same command He spoke when He rebuked the demon to "keep quiet, and come out of him" (Mark 1:25). This did not simply mean for the demon to be silent, but that Jesus muzzled it. Jesus now also essentially "muzzled" the sea.

Could it be that these veteran fishermen were frightened out of their wits by a simple storm? Probably not, since they had survived on this sea through many storms. Could it be that these seasoned fishermen were terrorized by a sea that had gone wild beyond anything in their experience? Could it be that the storm was generated by demons?[3] Such a storm would have been great cause for alarm no matter how experienced they were. No wonder they feared for their lives, yet with one word from Jesus, the winds ceased and the sea grew calm.

4:40 *He asked them, "Why are you such cowards? Don't you have any faith yet?"*

Jesus then directed His attention from the source of the disciples' fear toward the fearful ones themselves. Jesus was disappointed with His chosen disciples. They had been with Him and had seen Him perform various miracles that defied human explanation. He had just spent the entire day with them discussing the parables of the kingdom. If they really comprehended the identity of this teacher, they did not need to be afraid. They should have known that, as the Son of God, He was always in control. In the midst of the most terrible storm they had ever seen, they should have experienced calm assurances concerning their physical safety.

4:41 *They were overcome with fear and asked each other, "Who is this man? Even the wind and the sea obey him!"*

The sea grew calm. The winds died. All was peaceful. Their lives were spared, but Jesus had rebuked them for their lack of faith. The result? A new fear greater than their fear of the rolling sea. How could this be? After witnessing Jesus silence the winds and the sea, they became more frightened than before.

How amazing that the disciples were now afraid of the one Who had saved their lives! This provides ample evidence of their lack of comprehension of Who Jesus was or the scope of His authority.

After everything they had witnessed, they had not yet grasped that they had been chosen by the Creator of all, Who has total authority over His creation. Those participating in this voyage would never be the same because they had seen the power of Almighty God in the person of Jesus Christ *(John 1:1–3).*

Notes/Applications

When Jesus arose to face the storm, He did something so extraordinary it frightened the disciples more than the churning sea had moments before. He commanded the elements to be still, and they obeyed.

Until this point, Jesus' followers knew Him as a teacher. They knew Him as a healer, yet they still perceived Him to be merely a great man. Only the demons had acknowledged Him as the Son of God, yet when Jesus calmed the sea, there could be no more doubt. Forgiving sins was an internal, spiritual matter. Stopping a raging storm and calming the violent waves was a tangible, physical matter, verifiable by hard evidence. Here was a feat that lay solely within the realm of the Creator's power. Realizing just Who was in the boat with them, the disciples grew afraid of the one Who had saved them.

The scriptural record shows this to be a consistent response of human beings when they encounter the living God. From Genesis to Revelation, we witness humans trembling and falling on their faces in God's presence. When the suffering Job demanded an explanation from God, surely Job must have quaked in his sandals *(Job 40:6–7).* After God interrogated him, Job answered meekly,

> *³You said, "Who is this that belittles my advice*
> *without having any knowledge about it?"*
> *Yes, I have stated things I didn't understand,*
> *things too mysterious for me to know. . . .*
> *⁵I had heard about you with my own ears,*
> *but now I have seen you with my own eyes.*

> ⁶*That is why I take back what I said,*
>   *and I sit in dust and ashes to show that I am sorry. (Job 42:3, 5–6)*

As fallible humans ourselves, we can sympathize with the disciples' fear, yet still, Jesus chastised them for their lack of faith. The Son of God was gradually stretching the faith of these simple men just as He stretches our faith day by day through the circumstances of our lives. No one prefers hard times, yet God assures us that these times of spiritual testing serve a purpose of maturing us in the faith: "²My brothers and sisters, be very happy when you are tested in different ways. ³You know that such testing of your faith produces endurance. ⁴Endure until your testing is over. Then you will be mature and complete, and you won't need anything" *(James 1:2–4)*. Like the disciples caught in a surging sea, we grow stronger "faith muscles" not in merely talking about the things of God but in the laboratory of real life, and in the process, we grow more in sync with the captain of our souls.

MARK 5

Mark 5:1–5

5:1 *They arrived in the territory of the Gerasenes on the other side of the Sea of Galilee.*

After narrowly escaping death on the stormy sea and being frightened even more by the actions of their teacher, the disciples finally arrived at their destination on the opposite shore of the Sea of Galilee. They came to a part of the country where the inhabitants were known as Gerasenes. Ancient manuscripts and modern translations differ in the identification of these people as either Gadarenes or Gerasenes, though both refer to the same general region.[1] Others attribute the difference to the location of the town of Gersa within the greater region of Gadara.[2] Little is known about this region, which makes it difficult to locate on a map. Only a general region on the eastern shore of the Galilean sea is typically identified as Gadara. Because of the herd of swine being raised in this area (as we will see later), we might conclude that Gadara was inhabited mostly by Gentiles since Jews considered the pig to be an unclean animal.

5:2 *As Jesus stepped out of the boat, a man came out of the tombs and met him. The man was controlled by an evil spirit*

No sooner did Jesus arrive on the shore than a demon-possessed man approached Him. The man, not Jesus, initiated this encounter. This particular man was obviously an outcast. Unlike the demon-possessed man in the synagogue in chapter one, this man was not permitted among the rest of his community. Evidently, his behavior was too bizarre and threatening to allow him to mingle with others.

Matthew's account of this event records two men confronting Jesus at the shore *(Matthew 8:28)*. However, Mark's mention of only one man does not contradict Matthew's account since Mark does not necessarily restrict the presence to only one cave dweller but likely mentions the one most fiercely affected with demon possession.[3]

5:3 *and lived among the tombs. No one could restrain him any longer, not even with a chain.*

An excessively violent spirit freely reigned over this man's faculties. His behavior made him a reproach to society. He could not be bound even when chains were used instead of conventional rope.

5:4 *He had often been chained hand and foot. However, he snapped the chains off his hands and broke the chains from his feet. No one could control him.*

Other area inhabitants had attempted to control this man, and despite the use of metal chains, he always managed to break free. The Greek word for *control* is the same as that used for harnessing a wild animal. This man, under the influence of demons, possessed superhuman strength. His neighbors greatly feared him and had long ago given up hope that he could ever return to a normal life.

5:5 *Night and day he was among the tombs and on the mountainsides screaming and cutting himself with stones.*

Apparently, the man's frenzy drove him to self-mutilation. That was no comfort to those who could hear his eerie wailing throughout the night as he was driven to harm himself. This man must have been the source of much grief and annoyance.

The solution would seem to lie in the capture and control of this maniac. However, as we discovered earlier, this was impossible because of his superior strength. He was a long-term problem with no solution in sight.

Notes/Applications
This chilling passage portrays Jesus facing yet another situation that could not be handled by human strength or ingenuity. The demon-possessed man raged beyond the control of others. Even chains proved worthless in the face of his superhuman strength. As an outcast from society, he was banished to live among the tombs where he howled day and night and cut himself with stones.

Weary from the crowd's demands, Jesus arrived in the region where the man lived, and immediately, the demoniac ran to meet Him. Being the Son of God gave Jesus a high profile in the spirit realm where the fallen angels knew Him by name and frequently cried out, agitated in His presence.

Like those who unsuccessfully attempted to subdue the powers of Satan displayed in this madman, we, too, are helpless against Satan's might apart from the greater power and authority of the Lord Jesus Christ. We must be aware of the reality that evil forces are constantly combating God's angels beyond the veil of this present, temporal world: "This is not a wrestling match against a human opponent. We are wrestling with rulers, authorities, the powers who govern this world of darkness, and spiritual forces that control evil in the heavenly world" *(Ephesians 6:12)*. How do we defy the strength of these unseen opponents? The Almighty empowers us with "the armor that God supplies. In this way you can take a stand against the devil's strategies" *(Ephesians 6:11)*. This figurative armor comprises the belt of truth, the breastplate of righteousness, the shoes of the gospel of peace, the shield of faith, the helmet of salvation and the sword of the Spirit, which is the Word of God—our only offensive weapon in spiritual warfare *(Ephesians 6:14–17)*.

Like the Gadarenes, we must recognize our own futility in opposing the adversary. The battle is not ours but the Lord's, and even at His "weakest" moments *(Mark 4:38)*, His strength and authority are immeasurably superior to the mightiest efforts of Satan and his demons. Say to God, "How awe-inspiring are your deeds! Your power is so great that your enemies will cringe in front of you" *(Psalm 66:3)*.

Mark 5:6–13

5:6 *The man saw Jesus at a distance. So he ran to Jesus, bowed down in front of him,*

The man watched the boats arrive on the shore, and once he saw Jesus step onto the shore, he bolted for Him. When he neared Jesus, he fell on the ground. As in the other instances of demon possession, the demons instantly recognized and acknowledged Jesus' position, power, and authority *(Mark 3:11)*.

5:7 *and shouted, "Why are you bothering me now, Jesus, Son of the Most High God? Swear to God that you won't torture me."*

In his usual shrieking cry, the demon acknowledged the true identity of the man that the others called Rabbi. To this point, Jesus had performed spectacular healings and other miracles, which openly demonstrated that He was the Son of God.

That the demon recognized clearly the identity of the Son of the Most High God does not mean that he loved Jesus or that he wanted to be near Jesus. Demons are, after all, antagonists of the Almighty God in the cosmic struggle between Christ and His arch-enemy, Satan, the great deceiver of the human race. Rather, the demon made one plea to Jesus: "Swear to God that you won't torture me." He demonstrated a wonderful example of two things that man had yet to do: 1) acknowledge the absolutely unique position that Jesus holds in all of history; and 2) acknowledge his own position within the scope of that history. The demon realized that he could not resist the word that Jesus would speak to him because he also recognized Jesus' supremacy and knew that Jesus would not simply ignore the situation. By His very nature, Christ would confront the circumstances head-on.

5:8 *He shouted this because Jesus said, "You evil spirit, come out of the man."*

Jesus spoke the words to set the man free from the power of the demon. In chapter one, Jesus ordered the spirit to "keep quiet" to show His power over the unclean spirit possessing the man in the synagogue. Here, Jesus simply told the spirit to "come out!"

5:9 *Jesus asked him, "What is your name?" He told Jesus, "My name is Legion [Six Thousand], because there are many of us."*

After Jesus had issued the command that destroyed the power of this demon over the man, He then asked the demon to identify himself.

The demon replied that his name was Legion, because the man was possessed not by one but by many demons. As a common reference of the time, a Roman legion consisted of six thousand soldiers.[4] Although we are not told exactly how many demons possessed the man, we can safely conclude that there was a great number.

5:10 *He begged Jesus not to send them out of the territory.*

The demon recognized that his time was up and that he could not withstand the authority of the Son of the Most High God. Therefore, he urgently pled with Jesus not to banish them from the region.

5:11–12 *¹¹A large herd of pigs was feeding on a mountainside nearby. ¹²The demons begged him, "Send us into the pigs! Let us enter them!"*

As He looked around the area, Jesus observed a herd of swine nearby. The demons also saw the herd and begged Jesus to send them into the swine, that they might enter them. Without becoming too engrossed in the theology of demons and demon-possession, we know that humans can be demon-possessed. However, we see here that animals can also be possessed by demons.

5:13 *Jesus let them do this. The evil spirits came out of the man and went into the pigs. The herd of about two thousand pigs rushed down the cliff into the sea and drowned.*

The conversation between Jesus and Legion ended. Jesus immediately gave the demons permission to enter the herd of swine. Under Legion's influence, the entire herd of about two thousand pigs ran in a wild, violent stampede headlong into the sea and drowned. Though many commentators speculate as to why Jesus might allow the demons' request and why Jesus would so needlessly destroy an entire herd of pigs, we must yield to the sovereignty of God in these matters.[5] At the very least, we are amazed at both the severity of Legion's possession and the enormity of God's deliverance.

Notes/Applications
Without exception, Jesus knew His enemies and drew them into open battle in front of several witnesses. Also, without exception, Jesus' enemies knew Him and were profoundly aware of His identity as the Son of God. The text says that Legion ran up and worshiped Jesus—not out of love but by virtue of Jesus' authority. The very presence of the Son of God antagonized the evil spirits.

Contrast this with most people, even many Christians, who go about their lives oblivious to the unseen battle raging all around us for the souls of men and women. As we survey the misery of the human race and recoil in horror at headline events, it seems that demons are still rampant in our world. In light of a world that teeters on the brink of madness and feeds on the tragedy of human despair and disbelief, we have only one refuge. It remains the same for believers today as it did for His intimate companions then. Our refuge is Jesus Christ, the Son of Almighty God, who keeps these demons at bay. In His power, we have soundness of mind, clarity of thought, and a precious salvation that preserves us despite the forces seeking to consume us. *"A thief comes to steal, kill, and destroy. But I came so that my sheep will have life and so that they will have everything they need"* (John 10:10).

Mark 5:14–20

5:14 *Those who took care of the pigs ran away. In the city and countryside they reported everything that had happened. So the people came to see what had happened.*

The people responsible for the herd of swine fled. Imagine what ran through their minds: "We are going to lose our jobs. We are going to be thrown into prison. Our boss may have us killed. No one will believe this story. We watched with our own eyes and cannot believe it ourselves!" Only the terror in their eyes could have made anyone believe their story. With terror and panic, they told everyone how the swine plunged into the sea. Their terror astounded the hearers, and many came to the seaside to confirm the story.

5:15 *They came to Jesus and saw the man who had been possessed by the legion of demons. The man was sitting there dressed and in his right mind. The people were frightened.*

What did they see when they arrived? They saw Jesus and the man they knew too well. But here sat this maniac, whom they had tried to shackle with chains on many occasions, sitting with his clothes on and quietly talking as though he were perfectly sane. He no longer screamed and cut himself with stones. The change was unmistakable.

The resultant emotion was one of fear because there was no way to explain such a dramatic change. Their solution had been to try to bind the madman and control his fits, though they were unsuccessful because of his superhuman strength. Jesus' solution was to set him free from the bondage of the demonic power that had controlled him. The result was a man restored in every respect. Naturally, the people were terrified because this was beyond explanation.

5:16 *Those who saw this told what had happened to the demon-possessed man and the pigs.*

Not only did the Twelve witness what happened to this wild man, but so, too, did the swine herders. Together, they recalled in detail the deliverance of the man, the violent pleadings of Legion, and the destruction of the swine.

5:17 *Then the people began to beg Jesus to leave their territory.*

After hearing the story, the Gadarenes concluded that Jesus should leave the region. This must have been a difficult decision, and there might have been some debate about it. Here was this madman now whole and in his right mind. He would never again be a threat to their children. His shrieking would no longer haunt their night dreams. On the other hand, they had lost two thousand pigs. Such economic loss would take years to recover. They did not know what to make of all that had transpired or of the one Who had caused the mayhem, so they begged Jesus to leave the area. Their fear of the one Who was able to cast out demons was even greater than their fear of the one who had been possessed by demons.

5:18 *As Jesus stepped into the boat, the man who had been demon-possessed begged him, "Let me stay with you."*

Quietly and without argument, Jesus got into the boat to leave. The former madman of the Gadarenes was a fortunate man. He pled with Jesus for the opportunity to accompany Him from that day forward. The word translated as "begged" is the same word used to describe the pleadings of Legion. The man earnestly implored Jesus, Who had set him free from so terrible a bondage.

5:19 *But Jesus would not allow it. Instead, he told the man, "Go home to your family, and tell them how much the Lord has done for you and how merciful he has been to you."*

Jesus denied the man's request. Rather, He directed him to return to his family and friends and to proclaim what the Lord had done for him. Jesus described His action as a demonstration of His compassion.

As participants of this story through the eyes of Mark, we are thrilled at the restoration of this man. We are moved by his plea to accompany Jesus. What a wonderful request! The man responded with a grateful heart and sought to demonstrate his love by traveling with Jesus. Why did Jesus deny this poor, tortured soul who had been set free the dearest desire of his heart? We are not privileged to know the mind of God, but there was a task the man could accomplish. In a land inhabited by Gentiles, Jesus commissioned him to testify about the great things the Lord had done for him. He was a Gentile with a powerful, personal message to be shared among his Gentile neighbors.

5:20 *So the man left. He began to tell how much Jesus had done for him in the Ten Cities. Everyone was amazed.*

The man departed, apparently happy and willing to do what Jesus had instructed. He proclaimed his message to the entire region of the Ten Cities, or Decapolis, which lay east of the Sea of Galilee and the Jordan River. The man's testimony awed the crowds. Just as everyone had been aware of this wild man living in the tombs and caves, screaming and shrieking in his misery, they were now amazed as they heard him tell how he had encountered Jesus, the Christ, and how he had been set free.

Notes/Applications

Perhaps, at first reading, Jesus' refusal to allow the man to accompany Him strikes us as unusual. Somehow, it seems ungracious of Jesus to deny a desperate man such a sincere request, but once again, we must trust that God's ways are higher than our ways. We cannot fathom His intents and purposes, but we can rest in the knowledge that His ways are perfect. God had ordained a unique ministry for this healed soul. Scripture does not tell us how many people came to salvation through this man's testimony, but it is easy to imagine a great number. In the light of eternity, it was probably more expedient for the man to remain in his region and tell his neighbors "how much Jesus had done for him" than for him to follow Jesus on His travels.

Perhaps we find ourselves at a crossroads facing a difficult choice. Human wisdom may point us toward one route, but the still small voice of the Spirit calls us to tread down another. *"⁵If any of you needs wisdom to know what you should do, you should ask God, and he will give it to you. God is generous to everyone and doesn't find fault with them. ⁶When you ask for something, don't have any doubts. A person who has doubts is like a wave that is blown by the wind and tossed by the sea"* (James 1:5–6). Such truth challenges our shallow faith. We desire to keep control of our lives, and in the end, we forfeit opportunities to prove what God will do for those who give everything to Him.

Just as Jesus left the crowd, crossed the storm-tossed sea, and confronted demons to redeem one tormented soul, He crosses the centuries of time eternal and searches the tombs of our dead existence to set us free from our own demons. What better evidence of His divine appointment do we need? What greater expression of His loving faithfulness? We can learn a valuable lesson from this redeemed man. He wanted the exciting mission of accompanying Jesus but was satisfied and willing to assume the position for which Christ had prepared him. Are we so willing?

Mark 5:21–34

5:21 *Jesus again crossed to the other side of the Sea of Galilee in a boat. A large crowd gathered around him by the seashore.*

Jesus returned to a scene only slightly different from the one He left the evening before. The crowds gathered, awaiting His return. Jesus remained by the sea because the size of the crowd restricted His ability to walk freely.

5:22 *A synagogue leader named Jairus also arrived. When he saw Jesus, he quickly bowed down in front of him.*

In view of the numerous incidents in which the religious leaders opposed Jesus, we easily assume that they all were His enemies. However, this was obviously not the case.

Jairus, a ruler of the synagogue, came to Jesus and fell at His feet. This verse does not imply that Jairus inwardly worshiped Jesus but only that he outwardly gestured with deferential obeisance as he made his request to Jesus.

5:23 *He begged Jesus, "My little daughter is dying. Come, lay your hands on her so that she may get well and live."*

Prostrate before Jesus, Jairus presented his request. He was aware that Jesus had healed many people. If there was any hope of saving his beloved daughter, whom he deeply loved, Jesus was that hope. His daughter was not mildly ill; she was dying. The best medical help available in that day could not stop her steady decline toward death, so Jairus asked Jesus to come to his home and to lay His hands on her so that she would be healed.

5:24 *Jesus went with the man. A huge crowd followed Jesus and pressed him on every side.*

Jesus left the relative safety near the sea and followed Jairus toward his home. He could barely maneuver through the crowd because of its enormous size.

5:25–26 *²⁵In the crowd was a woman who had been suffering from chronic bleeding for twelve years. ²⁶Although she had been under the care of many doctors and had spent all her money, she had not been helped at all. Actually, she had become worse.*

While Jesus followed Jairus, another need pressed upon Him. In the clutches of the crowd, seemingly unnoticed, was a woman who had endured a gynecological condition for twelve years. It is interesting to note that she had suffered not only from the condition but also specifically at the hands of physicians. Although she spent everything, the doctors had failed to help her, and her condition steadily deteriorated.

Sadly, this condition made the woman ceremonially unclean. According to Mosaic Law, any woman so afflicted was a social outcast. She could not associate with the rest of the Jewish community because she was considered spiritually impure.

> *²⁵If a woman has a discharge of blood for many days other than her monthly period, she is unclean. If her period lasts longer than usual, she will be unclean as long as she has a discharge. It is like her period. ²⁶As long as she has a discharge, any bed she lies on or anything she sits on is unclean. It is like her period. ²⁷Those who touch these things are unclean and must wash their clothes and their bodies. They will be unclean until evening.* (Leviticus 15:25–27)

Consequently, not only was this woman worsening physically, but she carried with her the emotional shame of being shunned from her community.

5:27 *Since she had heard about Jesus, she came from behind in the crowd and touched his clothes.*

Like so many in that region, she had heard the amazing stories about this new rabbi. His reputation for healing and casting out demons was unparalleled in Jewish history, so she fought the crowd to get close enough to touch Jesus' garment. This was no small task since the throng literally pressed Jesus on all sides. Nevertheless, she somehow managed to reach Jesus and touch His clothing. *"He had cured so many that everyone with a disease rushed up to him in order to touch him"* (Mark 3:10).

5:28 *She said, "If I can just touch his clothes, I'll get well."*

This woman firmly believed she would be healed if she could just touch Jesus' garment. She did not need Him to say anything to her. She did not need His touch in return. She had no doubt.

5:29 *Her bleeding stopped immediately. She felt cured from her illness.*

When she did finally touch Jesus, she was immediately healed. After twelve years of affliction and after spending all of her earthly wealth to no avail, she experienced instant and complete healing. She felt the health and vitality flow through her body. This did not take an hour or even five minutes. Jesus' healing power was instantaneous.

5:30 *At that moment Jesus felt power had gone out of him. He turned around in the crowd and asked, "Who touched my clothes?"*

Jesus became instantly aware that someone had touched Him. In the midst of the pushing, shoving, and jostling of the crowd, this event was intensely private and personal. It occurred between the woman and Jesus. He knew He had been touched because He felt the power flowing from Him to heal her. Therefore, Jesus turned around and asked, "Who touched My clothes?"

5:31 *His disciples said to him, "How can you ask, 'Who touched me,' when you see the crowd pressing you on all sides?"*

His disciples were incredulous. Obviously, with everyone pushing against Him on all sides, He had been touched numerous times. How ridiculous for Jesus to ask such a question! However, they only perceived the external situation. They did not see the private event that occurred between these two individuals, the healer and the healed one. They did not yet realize that Jesus had answered the need of yet another broken and despairing soul.

5:32 *But he kept looking around to see the woman who had done this.*

Jesus ignored the disciples' inane question. He looked beyond the skeptical faces surrounding Him to find the woman. He wanted to meet this person and to speak to her.

5:33 *The woman trembled with fear. She knew what had happened to her. So she quickly bowed in front of him and told him the whole truth.*

The woman knew she was healed, but she also knew that she had broken the Mosaic Law by forcing herself through the crowd toward Jesus. Those individuals responsible for maintaining the ceremonial cleanliness of their community would have been infuriated by her actions, so she could expect their angry response and anticipate punishment. Shaking with fear, she fell down before Jesus and told Him the whole truth. She threw herself at His mercy. She had been totally restored to health and wholeness, yet she now feared for her safety because she had transgressed the religious traditions.

5:34 *Jesus told her, "Daughter, your faith has made you well. Go in peace! Be cured from your illness."*

Jesus did not respond with anger or judgment. He behaved in such a way as to render the Jewish tradition suspect when it addressed the well being of an individual. He reached down to this woman, lifted her up, and spoke a wonderful word of healing. He called her *daughter*, marking the only recorded occasion where Jesus used this term. He then declared that her faith had made her well. There was no magic in His cloak. Many others touched Him this day and did not experience such healing. Rather, it was her faith in the one Whom she sought. The faith that compelled her to touch the Master's cloak restored her to health. In this newfound faith, she entered a special relationship with Jesus, and Jesus assured her that her affliction was removed. She would no longer physically or emotionally suffer from this condition.

Notes/Applications

What a tremendous story of faith and healing! This woman, an outcast to her own friends and family, exemplified undeterred faith in the Son of God. What a contrast to our own anemic search for relief from the miseries of this world!

Even as Christians, we find our response to Jesus to be somewhat lukewarm. We neglect private time in communion with the Lord through prayer and Bible study. We often attend church with a begrudging sense of duty. We serve our church family with hesitant commitment. We contribute to the needs of God's community with a jaundiced eye, holding back the bulk of our resources for our personal enjoyment. Are we fearful of a committed, focused searching that could result in the touch of the Savior and render us as fanatics or that could require us to reorganize the kingdoms we have built for ourselves?

> ²⁴*Therefore, everyone who hears what I say and obeys it will be like a wise person who built a house on rock.* ²⁵*Rain poured, and floods came. Winds blew and beat against that house. But it did not collapse, because its foundation was on rock.*
>
> ²⁶*Everyone who hears what I say but doesn't obey it will be like a foolish person who built a house on sand.* ²⁷*Rain poured, and*

floods came. Winds blew and struck that house. It collapsed, and the result was a total disaster. (Matthew 7:24–27)

Let us take our example from this woman who was willing to be shamed publicly in order to touch the Son of God. When she did, He rewarded her faith and persistence by making her whole. *"I trust you, O my God. Do not let me be put to shame. Do not let my enemies triumph over me"* (Psalm 25:2).

Mark 5:35–43

5:35 *While Jesus was still speaking to her, some people came from the synagogue leader's home. They told the synagogue leader, "Your daughter has died. Why bother the teacher anymore?"*

While Jesus spoke with the woman, some of Jairus' servants came to inform him that his daughter had died. Can we imagine the emotions that flowed through this ruler of the synagogue? He had begged Jesus to come and heal his daughter, and Jesus had responded by making His way through the crowd toward Jairus' home. Then, this unclean woman had interfered with Jesus and slowed His progress. If Jesus had not been detained, Jairus' daughter might not have died. The news was devastating, and Jairus could have blamed this woman for delaying Jesus' response to the need of his daughter.

It is clear from the servants that the time for healing had passed. There was no need for Jesus to trouble Himself about Jairus' daughter. They referred to Jesus as "Teacher," which was probably what Jairus called Him. The servants evidently believed that the situation had gone beyond the scope of this teacher's authority. The girl was dead.

5:36 *When Jesus overheard what they said, he told the synagogue leader, "Don't be afraid! Just believe."*

Jesus overheard the servants' conversation with Jairus. He knew the hopeless feelings coursing through Jairus' mind. Perhaps He also sensed some anger because too much time had been taken with this woman after she had been healed. Turning to this ruler of the synagogue, Jesus made an astounding statement: "Don't be afraid! Just believe." Jairus might have been thinking, *Jesus, if you heard my servants, then you know that my daughter has died. It is too late to believe!*

5:37 *Jesus allowed no one to go with him except Peter and the two brothers James and John.*

Jesus did not wait for Jairus' response. He commanded everyone to remain behind and took with Him only Peter, James, and John. Within the group of the chosen Twelve, there was a special place for these three men. No more crowds. No other disciples. Only the four of them went with this distraught father to see his daughter.

5:38 *When they came to the home of the synagogue leader, Jesus saw a noisy crowd there. People were crying and sobbing loudly.*

When they arrived, the mourning had already begun. In the Jewish culture, loud wailing was expected as a part of the mourning process.[6] We do not know how long it took to get to Jairus' home, but it might have been a considerable amount of time. Certainly, enough time had elapsed for the girl to be declared dead and for the grief and mourning to begin.

5:39 *When he came into the house, he asked them, "Why are you making so much noise and crying? The child isn't dead. She's just sleeping."*

Jesus entered the house and admonished them for all of the noise. The Greek word for *noise* could be translated "uproar." There was certainly much noise from those so distraught over the loss of the child. Jesus then made an astounding statement: "The child isn't dead. She's just sleeping." He had just entered the house, so He had not yet seen the young girl before making this remarkable diagnosis.

5:40 *They laughed at him. So he made all of them go outside. Then he took the child's father, mother, and his three disciples and went to the child.*

Jesus' statement was laughable. This rabbi was good. He was spectacular. He had done some fantastic things, but this declaration seemed ridiculous. He came into the house and, without even seeing the girl, proclaimed that she was only sleeping. This was simply too much to believe. Who did He think He was?

Jesus did not defend His statement or argue with anyone. He demonstrated His authority by sending them outside. Jesus then quietly took Jairus and his wife with the three disciples. Together, they entered the child's room where she lay dead before them.

5:41 *Jesus took the child's hand and said to her, "Talitha, koum!" which means, "Little girl, I'm telling you to get up!"*

Jesus held the child's hand and spoke to her a couple of simple Aramaic words, "Talitha, koum," which means, "Little girl, I'm telling you to get up." Inconceivable! Incomprehensible! She was dead, yet He was speaking to her as though she might actually hear Him!

5:42 *The girl got up at once and started to walk. (She was twelve years old.) They were astonished.*

Before their eyes, the unthinkable happened. The girl got up and walked—a twelve year old restored to life by "the resurrection and the life" *(John 11:25, NKJV)*. Six people had entered that room and had observed the girl lying there. It is easy to understand their absolute amazement when she got up and walked. Everyone in that room witnessed an event that superceded anything in the human experience.

5:43 *Jesus ordered them not to let anyone know about this. He also told them to give the little girl something to eat.*

The five people who accompanied Jesus as He tended to the girl were instructed not to reveal what had taken place. In addition, He urged them to get her some food to eat. As far as the people outside the room were concerned, Jesus' conclusion had been correct. She was "just sleeping," but the five people knew the truth. This girl who had been dead was now alive. Even death fell under the authority of this teacher. Surely, He was the Son of God!

Notes/Applications

The scribes and Pharisees had been angry when Jesus forgave the sins of the paralytic. In their thinking, He had overstepped the boundaries of Jewish law and tradition by doing something only God could do. When Jesus calmed the sea, He again did something that only God could do. His disciples cowered in fear of the one Who commanded the winds and the seas. Now, Jesus, in front of five witnesses, did something else that only God could do when He raised Jairus' daughter from the dead.

Day by day, miracle by miracle, Jesus demonstrated to the unbelieving crowds that He was indeed the Son of God. No one else could do the things He did. The witness of their eyes told the people that this was no ordinary man—could He really be the promised Messiah? The burden to believe or not to believe was on them, as it is for each member of the human race.

What will we do with the reality of the Son of God, Who gave His life to save us and knows each of us by name?

> [20]Therefore, we are Christ's representatives, and through us God is calling you. We beg you on behalf of Christ to become reunited with God. [21]God had Christ, who was sinless, take our sin so that we might receive God's approval through him.
>
> [1]Since we are God's coworkers, we urge you not to let God's kindness be wasted on you. [2]God says,
>
> "At the right time I heard you.
> On the day of salvation I helped you."
>
> Listen, now is God's acceptable time! Now is the day of salvation! (2 Corinthians 5:20–6:2)

Jesus' Journeys: Chapters Four and Five

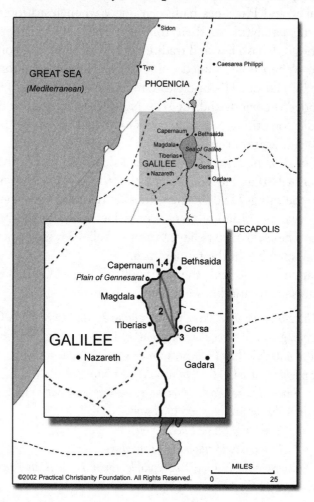

©2002 Practical Christianity Foundation. All Rights Reserved.

1. Jesus left Capernaum in chapter four.

2. Jesus muzzled the storm that frightened the disciples.

3. Jesus cast out Legion, and the swine plunged into the sea.

4. Jesus returned to Capernaum, where he healed the woman with an issue of blood and raised Jairus' daughter.

Mark 6:1–6

6:1 *Jesus left that place and went to his hometown. His disciples followed him.*

Jesus and His disciples left the area where Jairus' daughter had just been raised from the dead. This may have been Capernaum, which served as Jesus' headquarters during His early Galilean ministry. He went from there to the area around Nazareth, the place where He had been reared by Mary and Joseph.

6:2 *When the day of worship came, he began to teach in the synagogue. He amazed many who heard him. They asked, "Where did this man get these ideas? Who gave him this kind of wisdom and the ability to do such great miracles?*

Jesus entered the synagogue and assumed the position of the rabbi by sitting down and teaching the congregation. Many among the congregation were probably even childhood acquaintances. The congregation was flabbergasted by His teachings because Jesus had not been trained in the rabbinical tradition. Nevertheless, He sat in their synagogue, teaching them with profound wisdom about things they had never heard. Although His reputation as a healer was well known, they did not understand the source of His teachings or miracles. According to Luke's account, Jesus used this occasion to declare Himself as the fulfillment of Isaiah's prophecy (*Luke 4:16–21*).

6:3 *Isn't this the carpenter, the son of Mary, and the brother of James, Joseph, Judas, and Simon? Aren't his sisters here with us?" So they took offense at him.*

This is the only biblical reference where Jesus is referred to as a carpenter. It is likely that before entering into public ministry, Jesus made His living by following in the vocation of His earthly father (*Matthew 13:55*). Imagine the beautiful masterpieces crafted by the one Who created the very trees!

Jesus' words and actions raised many questions from the people. How would a carpenter know these things? They knew Jesus very well. He was the son of Mary. His brothers and sisters probably were among the congregation. They could not believe what was taking place in their synagogue, and they were greatly offended.

The Greek word σκανδαλίζω (scandalidzo), transliterated in this verse as "offended," gives us our English word *scandal*. The congregation was scandalized by its perception of Who He was in light of their familiarity with His background. They knew that Mary became pregnant before she was married to Joseph, so to them, Jesus was Mary's illegitimate son. How dare someone with His background have the audacity to sit in the place of the rabbi! He certainly taught with unusual wisdom, and He was able to do marvelous things. But how dare this illegitimate son try to legitimize Himself as their long-awaited Messiah!

6:4 *But Jesus told them, "The only place a prophet isn't honored is in his hometown, among his relatives, and in his own house."*

Jesus responded to the people's harsh judgment with a very simple statement. A prophet, especially among the Jewish community, was always revered and respected. They honored a prophet and generally accepted his message. However, in his home territory, a prophet was too well-known. Memories of childhood immaturity were too easily recalled and often hindered acceptance of adulthood significance. In Jesus' case, His brothers and sisters would have also been profoundly aware of the many comments they had heard about Jesus. They themselves probably considered Him only their half brother. It must have been quite a struggle for them to believe that their mother had not committed adultery prior to her marriage. Could her implausible explanation actually be true? For Jesus, the isolation and accusations of His childhood resurfaced and posed a barrier to His ministry in His own hometown.

6:5 *He couldn't work any miracles there except to lay his hands on a few sick people and cure them.*

As a result, Jesus' message and ministry were rejected. In truth, Jesus Himself was rejected. The congregation could not accept the message or the works if they came from the hands and heart of Mary's Son. Consequently, Jesus limited His works in Nazareth because of the hardness He recognized in their hearts. No crowds inundated His movements in Nazareth. He addressed only a few needs for healing—very few compared to His work in other Galilean territories.

6:6 *Their unbelief amazed him. Then Jesus went around the villages and taught.*

Jesus was amazed at their unbelief and animosity. He had come to them with the entire body of evidence of His divine authority. He had proved beyond doubt that He was God's Anointed, but they refused to accept Him.

Therefore, Jesus moved on. He left Nazareth and traveled to the surrounding area, continuing to teach those who would listen. Jesus did not try to convince the congregation of the validity of His ministry. If they could not accept Him on the basis of His mighty work, they would not accept Him. He proceeded instead to teach those who would respond.

Notes/Applications

The thrust of Mark's gospel account is that Jesus' actions validated His identity as the Son of God. Mark gives this summary statement in the first verse of the first chapter, yet despite the many actions that proved Jesus was the Son of God, the Lord saw little response from the people in His hometown of Nazareth. This is most likely because the community suspected His mother Mary to be an adulteress.

Before we hastily cast judgment on the unbelieving Nazarenes, let us examine ourselves. What causes doubt to spring up in our hearts? Have we not also witnessed God's amazing deeds in the lives of friends and loved ones and, perhaps, even in our own? Still, we often pray without truly believing, merely giving lip service to familiar words. Maybe we fret over finances, relationships, and other issues that Jesus commanded us to leave in His hands. *"[31]Don't ever worry and say, 'What are we going to eat?' or 'What are we going to drink?' or 'What are we going to wear?' [32]Everyone is concerned about these things, and your heavenly Father certainly knows you need all of them. [33]But first, be concerned about his kingdom and what has his approval. Then all these things will be provided for you"* (Matthew 6:31–33).

It would be nice if we could reach into the pages of biblical history and correct the Nazarenes' misconceptions about Jesus. Instead, we will have to settle for correcting our own hearts when they start to doubt. Did God promise something? Then He will do it. Does He keep His word? Always.

Mark 6:7–13

6:7 *He called the twelve apostles, sent them out two by two, and gave them authority over evil spirits.*

Jesus called the Twelve together. These disciples remained with Him every day since He had chosen them. They were aware of both His public teachings and of His private interpretations. Jesus now assigned them the task of sharing His ministry and equipped them with the authority to fulfill that task. They would share in the power of Jesus' ministry. Operationally, He sent them in groups of two, commissioned and equipped for their work in His name.

Their first assignment was a training ground for the future Great Commission that would be theirs for the rest of their lives. After Jesus rose from the dead and ascended in His glory to the heavens, these disciples would be empowered with the Holy Spirit, under Whose influence they would carry the gospel to the ends of the earth: "But you will receive power when the Holy Spirit comes to you. Then you will be my witnesses to testify about me in Jerusalem, throughout Judea and Samaria, and to the ends of the earth" *(Acts 1:8).*

6:8 *He instructed them to take nothing along on the trip except a walking stick. They were not to take any food, a traveling bag, or money in their pockets.*

They took with them only a staff—a walking stick similar to a shepherd's staff.[1] They were to take no food or money for their journey because their necessities would be provided as needed.

What a contrast to our business travels today and even our mission trips. We like to arrange things in advance. Our flights are scheduled. Our rental cars are reserved. Jesus' directive seems to make no sense. How could His men be expected to fulfill the objective of their commission without providing for the basic needs of their human existence?

6:9 *They could wear sandals but could not take along a change of clothes.*

Jesus directed them to wear sandals, for there was much ground to be covered. However, the disciples were not to pack even a second tunic because one would suffice.

A summary of Jesus' directions for their daily sustenance notes that the disciples were to take nothing extra. We can only surmise that Jesus intended for the disciples to depend on Him. He wanted them to understand that God was their resource in whatever endeavor they undertook, so they were commanded to embark upon this ministry without any personal funds or provisions. The result would be a valuable lesson in faith.

6:10 *He told them, "Whenever you go into a home, stay there until you're ready to leave that place.*

Jesus provided the disciples further instruction. Whenever they entered a town, they were to locate a household that could function as their headquarters and then remain there until the time came for them to leave that town.

How would the disciples know where to go? How would they know which people would be their hosts? The answer is that they knew nothing in advance. Jesus knew they would be cared for and that the loving Father would provide for all their needs.

6:11 *Wherever people don't welcome you or listen to you, leave and shake the dust from your feet as a warning to them."*

Jesus then outlined the spirit in which to conduct this ministry. Apparently, when the disciples entered a city, they were to follow Jesus' example—to preach, to heal, and to cast out demons. Jesus knew that their ministries would not attract everyone. He Himself had just experienced personal rejection in His own hometown of Nazareth.

Therefore, Jesus instructed His disciples to perform the task of the ministry and not to be concerned about the reception of their efforts. If received, they should rejoice and accept the hospitality. If not received, they should "leave and shake the dust from your feet as a warning to them." In the Jewish culture of that day, it was customary for a Jew to shake the dust off his feet when leaving pagan territories to preserve and maintain the purity of his Jewish culture.[2] This was a symbolic gesture that reminded the Jew of his unique heritage and that he was one of God's chosen. It was also a sign that the pagan did not participate in the Jewish tradition. Jesus now used this cultural custom against the Jewish people. This expression would symbolize that the disciples were Jesus' chosen. If they were not accepted, those who rejected them would never be members of God's chosen people. Their Jewish race would not be enough; they would not be chosen by the Son of God Himself, Jesus the Christ.

Rejection of His chosen delegates was rejection of Jesus. There is nothing more that God offers humankind than to send His only Son with an urgent call to repent.

6:12 *So the apostles went and told people that they should turn to God and change the way they think and act.*

After Jesus' instructions, the disciples performed their assigned task of proclaiming the Good News. Repentance was the predominant theme of John the Baptizer's ministry. When Jesus began His ministry, He preached the same message to the people: "The time has come, and the kingdom of God is near. Change the way you think and act, and believe the Good News" *(Mark 1:15)*. This was the same message that Jesus now passed on to His disciples.

6:13 *They also forced many demons out of people and poured oil on many who were sick to cure them.*

Just like their teacher, the disciples' ministries were marked by miracles. They, too, cast out many demons and healed the sick. Jesus not only assigned them to this task, but He also empowered them to accomplish such remarkable deeds.

Notes/Applications

So many principles can be gleaned from this account of the disciples' ministry. We earnestly seek formulas to apply to our lives and churches, but we need to exercise caution in this endeavor. God's pattern for one circumstance and for one group of people may not be His chosen pattern for all situations. God engineers a distinct blueprint for each of our ministries, and those plans will almost certainly be carried out in different ways.

If we distill the message of this passage down to one phrase, it is that God provides for His own. A second, ancillary message is that we need not worry about the details, which is, of course, exactly what our human nature does. We fret over this decision and that one, where our next mortgage payment will come from, whether we should take that new job in a distant city, whom we should marry, and so forth.

> [25]*So I tell you to stop worrying about what you will eat, drink, or wear. Isn't life more than food and the body more than clothes?*
>
> [26]*Look at the birds. They don't plant, harvest, or gather the harvest into barns. Yet, your heavenly Father feeds them. Aren't you worth more than they?*
>
> [27]*Can any of you add a single hour to your life by worrying?* (Matthew 6:25–27)

Though we are not told, surely similar doubts reared in the minds of the disciples. We can almost hear them: *Take only a staff? Is He joking?* But, whatever their initial reaction, the disciples did as their Master bid them, and God blessed their ministry.

Whatever we struggle with today, the best course of action is simply to submit it to God. *"Turn all your anxiety over to God because he cares for you"* (1 Peter 5:7). We are to literally heave our burdens off of our shoulders onto another—the Son of God. Jesus used a similar metaphor when He told the crowd, "[28]Come to me, all who are tired from carrying heavy loads, and I will give you rest. [29]Place my yoke over your shoulders, and learn from me, because I am gentle and humble. Then you will find rest for yourselves [30]because my yoke is easy and my burden is light" (*Matthew 11:28–30*).

As we trust our futures to God, He assures us that we can find rest in Him. Our call of allegiance is to go, relinquishing our earthly concerns and letting Him handle the details.

Mark 6:14–23

6:14 *King Herod heard about Jesus, because Jesus' name had become well-known. Some people were saying, "John the Baptizer has come back to life. That's why he has the power to perform these miracles."*

Already Jesus' fame had spread far and wide. He was not just "the talk of the town" but "the talk of the land." Even King Herod was aware of Jesus because His "name had become well-known." Herod Antipas was the son of Herod the Great, who destroyed all of the male children two years of age or younger in the area of Bethlehem in a vain attempt to eliminate the possibility of a Jewish king coming to the throne.[3] He heard of one born "King of the Jews" through the wise men of the East, who had followed the star to Bethlehem and found Jesus nearly thirty years earlier *(Matthew 2:2)*. Now, his son, Herod Antipas, occupied the throne and ruled as king with the approval of Rome. In reality, Herod Antipas was tetrarch of Galilee.[4] He was a Jew that served at the pleasure of Rome. Being a loyal puppet king made him phenomenally wealthy and powerful compared to his countrymen, who detested him for his allegiance to Rome.

Because of Jesus' reputation, some people, including Herod, surmised that Jesus was John the Baptizer risen from the dead.

6:15 *Others said, "He is Elijah." Still others said, "He is a prophet like one of the other prophets."*

In typical Jewish fashion, there arose much conjecture as to the identity of this new prophet. Some thought He might be Elijah, an extraordinarily powerful prophet who never saw death but was taken by a whirlwind to heaven. Others thought Jesus might be the prophet promised in Deuteronomy. This prophet was to stand above all the prophets, one through whom God would speak directly: "So I will send them a prophet, an Israelite like you. I will put my words in his mouth. He will tell them everything I command him" *(Deuteronomy*

18:18). Some had previously asked John the Baptizer, "Are you the prophet?" *(John 1:21).* Jewish believers knew this prophet would be very special, but they did not necessarily know He would be the Messiah.

Others simply thought that Jesus resembled one of the prophets. He certainly behaved like a prophet. His message was apocalyptic when He cried to the crowds to repent. He taught the people with prophet-like authority. The people were amazed at His teaching. There were all those remarkable reports of many being healed, of many being freed from domination by demons, and even of some being brought back to life.

6:16 *But when Herod heard about it, he said, "I had John's head cut off, and he has come back to life!"*

Regardless of the opinions of others, Herod recognized that Jesus was one spectacular individual, Whose reputation required close scrutiny. He believed that Jesus was John the Baptizer, restored to life after the king had beheaded him. Perhaps Herod's interpretation was tinged with guilt for taking the life of the innocent man who had chastised him because of his adulterous relationship with Herodias, his brother's wife. Interestingly, Herod had no difficulty with the idea of a resurrection.

6:17 *Herod had sent men who had arrested John, tied him up, and put him in prison. Herod did that for Herodias, whom he had married. (She used to be his brother Philip's wife.)*

This portion of Mark's gospel flashes back to John the Baptizer's death. John had challenged the unlawful relationship between Herod and his wife Herodias. In truth, Herodias was the wife of Herod's brother, named Herod Philip. Herodias was the daughter of Aristobulus, another son of Herod the Great. She married Herod Philip, who was also a son of Herod the Great and, therefore, was her half uncle. After spending some time in that marriage, Herodias left Herod Philip and moved in with Herod Antipas, another half uncle. It was Herodias who requested that John the Baptizer be killed (*Matthew 14:3*).

6:18 *John had been telling Herod, "It's not right for you to be married to your brother's wife."*

John observed the immoral behavior of Herodias and Herod Antipas and declared the relationship unlawful. Furthermore, this arrangement morally opposed the Jewish law. As God's prophet, John listened to the voice of God's moral law and openly challenged the morally bankrupt relationship between the king and his niece.

6:19 *So Herodias held a grudge against John and wanted to kill him. But she wasn't allowed to do it*

It appears that Herod may have tolerated John's rantings, but his wife did not. She became infuriated by the prophet's declaration concerning her unlawful marriage. She was determined to do as she pleased in her sexual relationships, and she was not going to be challenged by some prophet. Her intentions were clear, but she lacked the power to enforce them.

6:20 *because Herod was afraid of John. Herod knew that John was a fair and holy man, so he protected him. When he listened to John, he would become very disturbed, and yet he liked to listen to him.*

Here we find a remarkable acknowledgment by Herod. He truly feared John the Baptizer and acknowledged that he was a "fair and holy man." He was impressed by John's message and by his moral behavior. Herod Antipas actually listened to John and defended his ministry. Although he imprisoned John in order to placate Herodias' anger, Herod protected John within the walls of the prison from any further actions against him.

6:21 *An opportunity finally came on Herod's birthday. Herod gave a dinner for his top officials, army officers, and the most important people of Galilee.*

On Herod's birthday, Herodias received a great opportunity to secure her wish. Herod prepared a great celebration and invited the members of his royal court and probably also the Roman operatives and Jewish leaders of the region. Many of "the most important people of Galilee" would have heard relatively accurate information about John the Baptizer and Jesus, both of whom stirred up the complacency of the Jewish populace.

6:22 *His daughter, that is, Herodias' daughter, came in and danced. Herod and his guests were delighted with her. The king told the girl, "Ask me for anything you want, and I'll give it to you."*

As a part of the entertainment, Herodias' daughter came and danced before the king and his entourage. She was most likely the daughter of Herod Philip. We know this from Josephus, a first-century Jewish historian, who also recorded her name as Salome.[5] From the tone of the passage, she was a sensual young woman. Her dance evoked the men of the audience to prurient thoughts. In fact, Herod was so enraptured by the young girl's sensual dancing that he offered her anything she wanted.

6:23 *He swore an oath to her: "I'll give you anything you ask for, up to half of my kingdom."*

The girl may have hesitated, so Herod further repeated his offer and swore an oath, making his offer legally binding. He offered the absurd amount of up to half his kingdom. Obviously, the celebration had gone to his head. The mixture of wine and lust made him crazy for this young girl. He was determined to have her and was willing to give anything to have her submit to his lustful desires.

Notes/Applications

Mark disclosed the unusual string of events surrounding John the Baptizer's death. A striking contrast arises between the Herod that protected John from Herodias' anger and the Herod who succumbed to the sensual dance of a young girl. His wife's anger did not faze this Jewish tetrarch, but the dancing of a teenage girl weakened his resolve.

John had been reared in a godly environment from his birth. In fact, he belonged to God before he was born.

> [13]*The angel said to him, "Don't be afraid, Zechariah! God has heard your prayer. Your wife Elizabeth will have a son, and you will name him John.* [14]*He will be your pride and joy, and many people will be glad that he was born.* [15]*As far as the Lord is concerned, he will be a great man. He will never drink wine or any other liquor. He will be filled with the Holy Spirit even before he is born.* [16]*He will bring many people in Israel back to the Lord their God.* [17]*He will go ahead of the Lord with the spirit and power that Elijah had. He will change parents' attitudes toward their children. He will change disobedient people so that they will accept the wisdom of those who have God's approval. In this way he will prepare the people for their Lord." (Luke 1:13–17)*

As a young man, John began a ministry of baptism and the preaching of repentance for sins. Herod Antipas regarded John as a "fair and holy man" and accepted much of his message with gladness. However, when John's commitment to preach against immorality put the spotlight on Herod's unlawful marriage, it earned John the undying hatred of Herod's wife and eventually cost him his life. Nevertheless, he remained faithful to the ministry and message God had called him to deliver.

As we contrast these two men, one of them embodies our own earthly quest for pleasure and luxury. Who among us does not secretly crave a life of ease? We revel in the thought of gaining more possessions, but when we obtain them, we are disappointed that they do not satisfy after all. A life of self-centeredness is tragic, for in the end, we lose our eternal souls. It is far better to seek the wisdom of a man like John the Baptizer, who lived in the wilderness and dined on locusts and honey yet was at peace with his Creator.

Mark 6:24–29

6:24 *So she went out and asked her mother, "What should I ask for?" Her mother said, "Ask for the head of John the Baptizer."*

After Herod swore his oath to the young girl, she sought the advice of her mother, Herodias. The girl could have gained instant wealth beyond her wildest dreams. She could have even replaced her mother as Herod's consort and gained power as well as riches. However, having the body of a young woman but the mind of a child, she asked her mother. This was the opportunity for which Herodias had awaited. Every other tactic had resulted in failure, but her daughter's dance had accomplished the intended goal. Without hesitation, she requested the head of John the Baptizer. What a picture of Herodias' greed and hatred!

6:25 *So the girl hurried back to the king with her request. She said, "I want you to give me the head of John the Baptizer on a platter at once."*

The young girl immediately ran to the king and demanded John the Baptist's head on a platter. In the Greek manuscripts, two different words describe the girl's answer.[6] The first indicates the speed with which she responded to her mother's request, and the second shows how she returned to the king with a sense of power and control. She wanted her request to be granted without delay. The fact that she asked for John's head "on a platter" indicates that she made her demands known before the entire court in the spirit of the festive occasion. Now Herod was trapped. He had protected John from the anger of his wife, but now, he could not escape her appalling request.

6:26 *The king deeply regretted his promise. But because of his oath and his guests, he didn't want to refuse her.*

Herod was dismayed at the girl's request. He could not believe that she did not ask for something more typical of a young girl's desires, yet he was trapped because he had sworn an oath in front of the entire court. Herod had no recourse in denying the girl's request. His sworn oath had been given—and declared publicly. The king's word was considered law, so Herod was now obligated to fulfill his stepdaughter's request.

6:27 *Immediately, the king sent a guard and ordered him to bring John's head. The guard cut off John's head in prison.*

The girl asked for John's head "at once." Therefore, Herod immediately issued the command. He who had protected John in the past, now fell under legal obligation to end his life because of a sensual infatuation with the young woman. The order was carried out, and John the Baptizer, forerunner of the Messiah and preacher of repentance, was dead. He was executed on the whim of a puppet king seduced by a young girl's dance.

6:28 *Then he brought the head on a platter and gave it to the girl, and the girl gave it to her mother.*

What a grisly scene unfolded! John's head was presented on a platter to the young girl. The girl, in turn, gave it to her mother.

The festive occasion of Herod's birthday quickly became a debacle of sensuality, permeated by the evil hatred incited by John's righteous condemnation of Herodias' unlawful marriage. The young girl was already a hardened woman. She apparently did not flinch as the executioner gave her the head of the Baptizer. Unfazed, she carried the gruesome exhibition to her mother, who likely rejoiced at the sight.

Intrigue and seduction had no bounds. It appears that no one in the scene raised a voice against such treachery. There was no reprieve, no sanctuary where the righteous could be safe. There was only the quick dispatch of political expediency. These were hard and cruel times. John the Baptizer was silenced, while Herodias and Herod continued in their unlawful and immoral relationship.

6:29 *When John's disciples heard about this, they came for his body and laid it in a tomb.*

John's followers heard of the terrible death of their mentor and teacher. They took John's body and buried it in a nearby tomb.

Notes/Applications

In the intensity of his lust and pride, Herod made an impulsive commitment, offering Herodias' daughter anything she wanted up to half of his kingdom. He was willing to grant the young seductress wealth beyond her wildest imagination, but at her mother's prompting, she requested to have John the Baptizer beheaded. Herod, seemingly prepared to hand over unfathomable wealth, was unprepared for such a morbid demand. However, the king had essentially sworn an oath before a group of witnesses and thereby had obligated himself to fulfill the girl's request, even though doing so deeply distressed him. *"A person without good sense closes a deal with a handshake. He guarantees a loan in the presence of his friend"* (Proverbs 17:18).

We could easily detest Herod's senseless and hasty pledge, especially since it had such severe consequences for John the Baptizer. But how many times do we, even as Christians, make commitments without considering the ramifications? How often have these commitments had responsibilities beyond what we anticipated? These commitments may not be sinful. In fact, they may very well be necessary causes, but does the Lord mean for us to invest in that particular ministry or activity? Once we make a pledge, in order to be considered a person of integrity we are bound by our word. However, when we find ourselves locked into a situation that we know is not God's will for us, the Lord has provided a course of action for righting ourselves with the other parties involved.

¹*My son,*
   if you guarantee a loan for your neighbor
     or pledge yourself for a stranger with a handshake,
       ²*you are trapped by the words of your own mouth,*
         caught by your own promise.
³*Do the following things, my son, so that you may free yourself,*
   because you have fallen into your neighbor's hands:
     Humble yourself,
       and pester your neighbor.
     ⁴*Don't let your eyes rest*
       or your eyelids close.
     ⁵*Free yourself like a gazelle from the hand of a hunter*
       and like a bird from the hand of a hunter.
     (Proverbs 6:1–5)

Hasty commitments have consequences. They impact our relationship with the Master and with our loved ones. Yielding to the Holy Spirit's discernment regarding the best allocation of our time, energy, and resources in this manner is not a one-time occurrence in our Christian journey. It is a daily exercise of seeking the Lord's direction and purpose in our lives. By waiting for God's prompting, we will spare ourselves the consequences of acting before we think. *"It is a trap for a person to say impulsively, 'This is a holy offering!' and later to have second thoughts about those vows"* (Proverbs 20:25).

Mark 6:30–36

6:30 *The apostles gathered around Jesus. They reported to him everything they had done and taught.*

After Mark's parenthetical description of John the Baptizer's death, we return to the apostles' adventures as they returned from their first missionary journeys. The apostles were full of enthusiasm as they conveyed the many things they had taught and the miracles they had performed to their teacher.

6:31 *So he said to them, "Let's go to a place where we can be alone to rest for a while." Many people were coming and going, and Jesus and the apostles didn't even have a chance to eat.*

Jesus recognized that His disciples were riding on a wave of euphoria after having seen His power through their ministry, but they were also exhausted and had not had time to eat. He invited them to come aside and "rest for a while." Again, we see Jesus as the strategic planner, considering some very human elements. Just as He had His disciples prepare a boat for His own escape from the crowd's pressure, He now gave His small group a time to rest and regenerate.

6:32 *So they went away in a boat to a place where they could be alone.*

Once again, this small group of men sought to distance themselves from the crowds. They found a remote place where they could withdraw and rest. The fishermen among them knew just the place where they could be alone with Jesus, a place where they could find solace on the water.

6:33 *But many people saw them leave and recognized them. The people ran from all the cities and arrived ahead of them.*

This huge crowd watched them get into the boat and leave. It seems that the crowds began to anticipate Jesus' next moves and knew where He and the disciples were headed. They were literally there to greet the disciples when they landed. Perhaps the boat traveled close enough to the shore that the crowds could follow by land on foot. The crowd would have to cross the small river feeding the Sea of Galilee from the north over the bridge at Chammath of Gadara.[7] In their eagerness to be with Jesus, they interrupted His plans for a brief retreat.

6:34 *When Jesus got out of the boat, he saw a large crowd and felt sorry for them. They were like sheep without a shepherd. So he spent a lot of time teaching them.*

Jesus saw the huge crowd as He left the boat and was moved with compassion for them because "they were like sheep without a shepherd." Such a description evokes mental images of people wandering aimlessly, desperately looking for someone to guide and direct them.

The crowd had steadily grown from the first day of Jesus' ministry. Undoubtedly, many of them chased after Jesus because of His miracles and personal magnetism. Most were not firmly anchored in His teachings, and they still did not really comprehend that He was the Son of God. Nevertheless, Jesus again began to teach them many things.

6:35–36 *[35]When it was late, his disciples came to him. They said, "No one lives around here, and it's already late. [36]Send the people to the closest farms and villages to buy themselves something to eat."*

This event took place in the countryside along the north shore of the Sea of Galilee, and the city of Bethsaida lay a couple of miles to the north. The crowd had been listening to Jesus' teaching for most of the day. As the end of the day neared, the disciples came to Jesus to remind him of two things: they were far removed from the towns, and nightfall was quickly approaching.

Apparently, the crowd had not eaten all day. So the disciples, concerned about physical nourishment, advised Jesus to send the crowd away so that they could buy some food in the surrounding villages.

Notes/Applications

Jesus, compassionately gazing out over the crowd who rushed to meet Him on the other side of the Sea of Galilee, gave us a powerful glimpse into the shepherd heart of God. *"I am the good shepherd. The good shepherd gives his life for the sheep"* (John 10:11). If Jesus was moved with compassion for this crowd, which hungered for His words, we know that God must look with tender compassion on us as well.

Though smelly and dumb, sheep are incredibly loyal to the one who leads them. They know their shepherd's voice and will only come when called by that particular shepherd. Similarly, a good shepherd grows to know each of his sheep by name and even by their individual bleating. The realization that his sheep are helpless in the face of danger makes the shepherd all the more vigilant as they graze.

A shepherd metaphor permeates the poetic writings of King David as he described the one true God.

> *¹The Lord is my shepherd.*
>> *I am never in need.*
>>> *²He makes me lie down in green pastures.*
>>> *He leads me beside peaceful waters.*
>>> *³He renews my soul.*
>>> *He guides me along the paths of righteousness*
>>>> *for the sake of his name.*
>> *⁴Even though I walk through the dark valley of death,*
>>> *because you are with me, I fear no harm.*
>>>> *Your rod and your staff give me courage.*
>> *⁵You prepare a banquet for me while my enemies watch.*
>> *You anoint my head with oil.*

> *My cup overflows.*
> *⁶Certainly, goodness and mercy will stay close*
>   *to me all the days of my life,*
> *and I will remain in the Lord's house for days without end.*
>   *(Psalm 23)*

Although Jesus sought much-needed rest, He placed the desire of the searching crowd above His personal need for peace and quiet. He is a righteous judge, but He is also a loving shepherd who faithfully cares for His sheep. What encumbrances are we allowing to draw our immediate attention away from the good shepherd's voice? *"I have wandered away like a lost lamb. Search for me, because I have never forgotten your commandments"* (Psalm 119:176). *"³ᵇHe calls his sheep by name and leads them out of the pen. ⁴After he has brought out all his sheep, he walks ahead of them. The sheep follow him because they recognize his voice. ⁵They won't follow a stranger. Instead, they will run away from a stranger because they don't recognize his voice"* (John 10:3–5).

Mark 6:37–44

6:37 *Jesus replied, "You give them something to eat." They said to him, "Should we go and spend about a year's wages on bread to feed them?"*

At the close of a busy day, the twelve disciples made Jesus aware of a food shortage. His response must have shocked them. Jesus agreed with His disciples that the people were hungry, but He disagreed about the way they should be fed. Rather than sending the people away to get food from the nearby villages, Jesus commanded His disciples to feed the crowd themselves.

Did He really expect the disciples to buy two hundred denarii (approximately eight months' wages for the average worker) worth of bread to feed this crowd? The disciples responded with amazed denial. This was a seemingly impossible assignment well beyond their limited resources.

Even though Jesus appeared to be asking the impossible from them, why did they respond in this way? These were the same chosen Twelve who had just returned from a successful preaching mission. They performed all sorts of extraordinary deeds that defied human experience. Their entire journey with this carpenter turned rabbi had been astounding. Nevertheless, they still did not yet comprehend Christ's authority and power over creation.

6:38 *He said to them, "How many loaves do you have? Go and see." When they found out, they told him, "Five loaves of bread and two fish."*

Jesus did not argue with His disciples. He instead inquired about what they did have. After checking through the crowd, they brought back a rather discouraging report: five loaves of bread and two fish. In a parallel account, Andrew observed, "But they won't go very far for so many people" (John 6:9). The job of feeding these people with so few resources appeared to them to be an impossible endeavor.

6:39 *Then he ordered all of them to sit down in groups on the green grass.*

Now that He had five loaves of bread and two fish, He commanded the disciples to make the people sit down in groups. Jesus was very direct and assertive. As we see throughout these chapters, Jesus taught and acted with authority, a hallmark of His ministry.

6:40 *They sat down in groups of hundreds and fifties.*

The crowd was arranged block by block or group by group.[8] This was a method by which the task could be managed because it was simpler to feed a group of fifty or a group of one hundred rather than the entire crowd as one single mass. Such a method of arrangement was typical in terms of Jewish government. In the Old Testament, the Hebrew military regiments were arranged in such a manner. In Exodus eighteen, Jethro, Moses' father-in-law, showed Moses how to govern by dividing the great number of the Hebrew people into groups of ten, fifty, one hundred, and one thousand.

While the disciples were overwhelmed by the task, Jesus used this basic method of organizing a crowd of people into manageable portions.

6:41 *After he took the five loaves and the two fish, he looked up to heaven and blessed the food. He broke the loaves apart and kept giving them to the disciples to give to the people. He also gave pieces of the two fish to everyone.*

Jesus took this meager supply of food and, looking up to heaven, blessed it. Then Jesus broke the loaves and dispersed them to His disciples. We cannot understand this miracle. It is too much for our finite minds to grasp. The tense of the Greek verb that is translated as "gave" reveals that Jesus kept on giving the bread to His disciples. This implies that the bread kept multiplying as Jesus dispensed the loaves. There seemed to be no limit to the amount of bread provided. The same happened with the two fish, which Jesus also divided among His followers.

6:42 *All of them ate as much as they wanted.*

Once the food was given to the groups of people, they ate and were filled. They did not leave hungry. It was Jewish custom to provide food for one's guests in such quantities that the guests never left the table hungry, and this custom held true in this remarkable circumstance as Jesus hosted the meal.

6:43 *When they picked up the leftover pieces, they filled twelve baskets with bread and fish.*

Whatever method Jesus used to multiply and distribute the food from only five loaves of bread and two fish is not known. But when the people could eat no more, the disciples took up twelve baskets full of the leftovers. Not only had He satisfied the need, but He had done so above and beyond what was necessary. Furthermore, the amount of leftovers far exceeded the provisions with which they began.

The customary statement of amazement does not follow this miracle as for so many others in the Book of Mark. Those closest to Jesus, His disciples, collected these twelve baskets and appeared unfazed by the quantity of leftovers. Is it possible that such a remarkable feat was not recognized by the crowds or by Jesus' own disciples? This miracle is special both in size and in the lack of recognition it received.

6:44 *There were 5,000 men who had eaten the bread.*

This fact is even more unbelievable considering the actual numbers of those fed. In typical Jewish fashion, Mark accounts only for the number of men in the crowd. Adding in the number of women and children present, the size of this crowd likely exceeded this given number by several thousand. What a miracle of Jesus' provision for hungry people gathered to hear His word!

Notes/Applications

Apparently, the disciples had already forgotten the events that marked their recent missionary travels. When Jesus placed the problem of feeding the crowd squarely on their shoulders, they did not face the task with faith but with cold logic. They knew they did not have enough money to buy food for so many, and therefore they saw no way to feed such a crowd.

However, Jesus quietly resolved the matter by multiplying the small portions of bread and fish. Mark does not tell us what the disciples' reaction was to this miracle. After the euphoria of a successful missionary journey, were they so preoccupied that they could not recognize a miracle before their eyes?

Despite the stressful situation, Jesus set about the task of making use of what He had and multiplying it for His glory. We experience this miracle for ourselves whenever we trust Him to take our broken lives and make something beautiful out of them. God does not need a surplus of gifts and talents in the ones He chooses to carry out His mission; in fact, He seems to seek out those bereft of outward qualifications: Moses had a speech impediment; Jacob was a braggart and a cheat; Gideon was a coward; David was the lowest of his family; some of the disciples were unlearned fishermen; and Matthew was a despised tax collector. *"But he told me: 'My kindness is all you need. My power is strongest when you are weak.' So I will brag even more about my weaknesses in order that Christ's power will live in me"* (2 Corinthians 12:9). How can we, as believers, be so wonderfully used by Jesus and yet remain so utterly blind that we cannot see that He is still at work within and among us?

Mark 6:45–56

6:45 *Jesus quickly made his disciples get into a boat and cross to Bethsaida ahead of him while he sent the people away.*

Feeding the large crowd of people probably took several hours. Since this started rather late in the day, it must have been near dusk when Jesus made His disciples get into their boat and head toward Bethsaida.

Again, we see the word *immediately*. In this case, there is an even greater sense of urgency as Jesus "made His disciples get into a boat." The Greek verb translated as "made" actually means that He compelled them to get moving. The reason for Jesus' urgent command is not given in Mark's gospel but in John's. There, we discover that after the people ate their fill, they conspired to make Jesus their political deliverer: "Jesus realized that the people intended to take him by force and make him king. So he returned to the mountain by himself" *(John 6:15)*.

They got into their boat and headed for Bethsaida. There is some confusion about this specific location. According to Luke's gospel, the crowd of five thousand had been fed in a deserted place in the region of Bethsaida. So, why would one try to reach Bethsaida by sea if he were already located so near it by land? From ancient histories and geographies, it has been surmised that Bethsaida Julius on the east side of the Jordan river extended to the west side of the river and was known as Bethsaida Galilee, which would pinpoint their destination near Capernaum,[9] which is mentioned in John's gospel: "[16]When evening came, his disciples went to the sea. [17a]They got into a boat and started to cross the sea to the city of Capernaum" *(John 6:16–17)*. We may conclude that Jesus sent the disciples away toward Bethsaida Galilee near Capernaum. In other words, the disciples were returning to the home base.

Meanwhile, Jesus remained behind to send the huge crowd of people away, which must have been quite a task. None of the disciples were present to observe just how Jesus handled this farewell, so the text is silent on the details. It is interesting to note that, facing the conspiracy of those who sought to make Him king, Jesus sent His disciples away and handled it Himself.

6:46 *After saying goodbye to them, he went up a mountain to pray.*

Finally, the crowd dispersed, and Jesus remained completely alone. The disciples were on the sea as commanded. Whenever Jesus was alone, He returned to His primary source of strength. He did not rest. He prayed.

Yes, Jesus, the Son of God, sought time alone to pray. He needed time to share His burdens with His Father. We observe another instance when God the Son spoke with God the Father. This remains an unanswerable mystery of the Christian faith that is observable but not understandable.

6:47 *When evening came, the boat was in the middle of the sea, and he was alone on the land.*

It was now dark, and the boat was at sea while Jesus remained on shore. One can almost sense the drama of this account. The "middle of the sea" did not mean the geographical center of the Sea of Galilee. Traveling to Capernaum, the disciples would have crossed the sea's northern edge, a relatively short distance.

6:48 *Jesus saw that they were in a lot of trouble as they rowed, because they were going against the wind. Between three and six o'clock in the morning, he came to them. He was walking on the sea. He wanted to pass by them.*

Jesus saw the disciples struggling against the wind. This storm was not as intense as the one they had previously experienced *(Mark 4:35–41)*. Yet it seems that the stormy north winds drove the disciples off course and made their voyage longer and more difficult than they anticipated.[10]

Jesus came to them "between three and six o'clock in the morning."[11] The disciples were emotionally and physically exhausted. They had left the shore at sunset, and a new day would soon dawn. Earlier, under Jesus' direction, they had searched for a place to rest when the huge multitude of people followed them. Because of the opposing north wind, they were unsuccessful in their efforts to span the short distance to Capernaum.

Jesus, seeing their struggle, walked on the water toward them and "wanted to pass by them." We may ask, "Why would He see their struggle and approach them only to pass by?" In the translation of this phrase, the word παρελθεῖν (parelthain) from the Greek text actually comprises a compound of two root words that could be translated "come alongside" or "come next to." In context, therefore, the phrase might be better understood, "he came to them. He was walking on the sea. He wanted to come alongside them." It would have been uncharacteristic for Jesus to recognize such a need only to turn His back and ignore the situation.

6:49 *When they saw him walking on the sea, they thought, "It's a ghost!" and they began to scream.*

The disciples caught sight of Jesus walking on the sea toward them. Certainly, anyone would be scared senseless to see someone walking on the surface of any body of water, and the disciples were no exception. They believed an apparition was approaching them on the water, and they cried out, literally howling in fear.

6:50 *All of them saw him and were terrified. Immediately, he said, "Calm down! It's me. Don't be afraid!"*

This was not the vision of only one or two disciples. They all saw Jesus approaching their boat, walking on the surface of the sea in the early hours of the morning. They were frightened beyond words and literally shaken up. Jesus, Who was always mindful of their emotions, immediately called to them saying, "Calm down!" He identified Himself to His disciples to alleviate their fear.

The Gospel of Matthew expounds on this incident. Peter asked Jesus to confirm His identity. Jesus did and invited Peter to come to Him. Peter walked toward Jesus at first but then, frightened by the violent storm around him, began to sink. Jesus reached out his hand, grasped Peter, and saved him from sinking. They entered the boat together, and the storm was immediately quieted (*Matthew 14:28–33*). Interestingly, Mark, the disciple of Peter, did not include this incident in his gospel.

6:51 *He got into the boat with them, and the wind stopped blowing. The disciples were astounded.*

Jesus came alongside and entered the boat. When He did so, the wind ceased. We do not read that Jesus issued any command to the wind, so He probably said nothing to the elements of nature. He spoke only to His disciples, encouraging them not to be afraid, and His very presence brought instant relief from the tempestuous winds.

In an earlier passage, Jesus slept soundly in a boat amid a stormy sea (*Mark 4*). After Jesus calmed the winds, the disciples were more frightened at Jesus' ability to control nature than they were of the storm. The same appears true during this event. Mark describes the disciples as "astounded." However, in this case, the fear and amazement appear even more intense. In this verse, Mark uses the word ἐξίσταντοω (existantow), expressing that they were nearly out of their minds. When Jesus got into the boat and the winds ceased, their emotions were virtually overloaded.

6:52 *(They didn't understand what had happened with the loaves of bread. Instead, their minds were closed.)*

Evidently, the disciples did not entirely understand the miraculous event that had occurred earlier in the day when Jesus took five loaves of bread and two fish and fed a crowd of more than five thousand. Right before their eyes, Jesus performed a miracle that defied all logical explanation. Still, the disciples did not grasp it because "their minds were closed." How could this be? Again, these men had just returned from a successful missionary journey. They had seen and done many wonderful things, yet somehow, they could not put it all together. Their minds could not link the Jesus Who called them with the Jesus Who taught with authority, raised Jairus' daughter from the dead, calmed the winds and sea, fed a multitude, and walked on water. No wonder they were beside themselves with fear and wonder. They simply could not comprehend the significance of what they had seen. But who hardened their hearts? Was it the work of Satan? Was it the work of God? There is much evidence throughout the Book of Mark demonstrating how truly blind humankind is to the things of God. The blindness of hearts stained with sin is virtually a walk in total darkness.

6:53 *They crossed the sea, came to shore at Gennesaret, and anchored there.*

The original destination was Capernaum. However, the wind drove the disciples farther southwest along the shore of the sea, and they landed at Gennesaret, a fertile region just south of Capernaum. In fact, the Sea of Galilee was sometimes called the Lake of Gennesaret.

The wind ceased as Jesus got into the boat. His presence resolved the disciples' immediate problem. However, Jesus did not correct the problem that they had already veered off course. He did not put them back on course but instead allowed them to proceed to another destination farther west.

6:54–55 *[54]As soon as they stepped out of the boat, the people recognized Jesus. [55]They ran all over the countryside and began to carry the sick on cots to any place where they heard he was.*

The disciples immediately found themselves back in the thick of the battle. They had no rest. They had spent the entire night rowing and had missed their destination. And if that wasn't discouraging, the crowd had once again followed Jesus and the disciples along the shore. As dawn broke and the boat anchored, the weary disciples emerged from the boat, already surrounded by the crowd. Their first thought must have been, *Oh, no! Not again!* Surely, their original hope must have been to dock the boat and to recover from their strenuous physical labor and their emotionally draining experience.

Nevertheless, upon Jesus' arrival, people ran throughout the area looking for the sick so that He could heal them. Wherever He traveled, people caring for their ill relatives and friends sought Jesus for His healing touch.

Again and again, Mark emphasizes Jesus' amazing activity and productivity. If He was not the Son of God but merely human, the schedule could have killed Him. He taught the crowds publicly and His disciples privately. He actively healed those brought to Him. He fed a crowd of more than five thousand people. He spent the night in conversation with His Father. In the early hours before dawn, He saw the disciples' struggle as they tried to row their boat against a contrary wind, and He again calmed the seas. Jesus had already gone for days on end with little or no sleep, and now He and His small band of men were immediately confronted with the demands of the seeking crowd.

6:56 *Whenever he would go into villages, cities, or farms, people would put their sick in the marketplaces. They begged him to let them touch the edge of his clothes. Everyone who touched his clothes was made well.*

In typical fashion, Mark summarizes the activities of Jesus and His disciples without reference to time or place. We have no idea how many people Jesus touched during this period or the number of people who got close enough to touch Him. The verse simply states that everyone who touched Him was made well. What a glorious experience—to touch the Master and be made whole!

Two observations from other gospel accounts should be noted. First, Jesus was so well received by the crowds in the region that they desired to make Him their king against His will: "Jesus realized that the people intended to take him by force and make him king. So he returned to the mountain by himself" (*John 6:15*). Second, the timing of these events occurred late in the second year of Jesus' public ministry, near the time of Passover (*John 2:13; 6:4*).

Notes/Applications

How dramatic the scene in which Jesus walked on water toward the disciples. We have seen artistic renderings of this historic event in children's Bible storybooks, and we read in Matthew's gospel about Peter's bold request: "Lord, if it is you, order me to come to you on the water" (*Matthew 14:28*). What we cannot imagine is the fear piercing these men's hearts as they saw what appeared to be a ghost approaching them, since no human being could walk on water.

We suppose that we would act differently if thrust into a similar situation, but most likely, we, too, would prove to be just as human as Jesus' chosen Twelve if He were to appear before us today.

Our world is a frightening place, but the Bible tells us: "[3b]Don't lose your courage! Don't be afraid or alarmed or tremble because of your enemies. [4]The Lord your God is going with you. He will fight for you against your enemies and give you victory" (*Deuteronomy 2:3–4*). We live in a world pockmarked by evil—child abductions, acts of terrorism, random shootings, road rage, and other senseless acts of violence. We long for the assurance the disciples experienced when their hearts trembled. Jesus' reply to the disciples is the same one He gives us when we are assailed by fears and doubts: "Calm down! It's me. Don't be afraid!"

Jesus' Journeys: Chapter Six

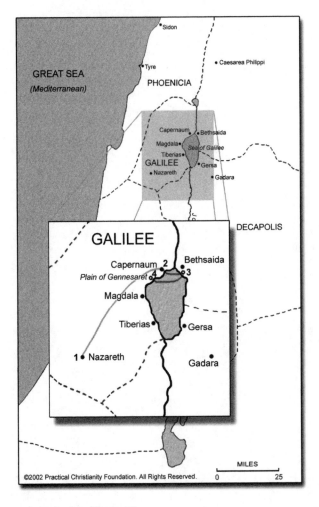

1. Jesus preached in Nazareth.

2. Jesus sent out the Twelve from Capernaum.

3. Jesus fed a crowd of more than five thousand near Bethsaida.

4. Jesus and His disciples anchored near Gennesaret where Jesus continued preaching and healing throughout Galilee.

Mark 7:1–5

7:1 *The Pharisees and some scribes who had come from Jerusalem gathered around Jesus.*

The Pharisees and the scribes were entrusted with the responsibility of maintaining the oral tradition of Jewish law from generation to generation. We can be sure that they did not walk the sixty to seventy miles from Jerusalem to the region of Galilee and Capernaum because of their desire to hear Jesus' teachings. They had already heard enough, and their anger against Jesus was kindled. They intended to trap Jesus into making a serious mistake in order to accuse Him and bring Him before the authorities so that He could be silenced (*Mark 3:6*). They would not tolerate this carpenter turned rabbi, Who presumed to teach them about the God of Abraham, Isaac, and Jacob. They believed they already knew all matters concerning the Law of Moses.

7:2 *They saw that some of his disciples were unclean because they ate without washing their hands.*

The religious elite believed they had seized proof of the teacher's total disregard for the laws of their ancestors when they found His disciples eating bread with unwashed hands. Some translations use the word *defiled*, which indicates that the Pharisees considered this a moral infraction of the law. Since they observed that Jesus' disciples did not follow their prescribed tradition, the Pharisees quickly noted the fault and concluded that Jesus' men could not possibly be considered righteous sons of Abraham.

7:3 *(The Pharisees, like all other Jewish people, don't eat unless they have properly washed their hands. They follow the traditions of their ancestors.*

Before eating, it was the custom of the Pharisees and other devout Jews to wash their hands, raise them, and allow the water to drip from their elbows.[1] They repeated this ritual several times to ensure that they would be eating with both clean hands and clean hearts. They earnestly desired to follow the traditions of their forefathers to the letter of the law and, thereby, gain some measure of righteousness. This practice had become a religious ritual, often repeated without thought. Secure in traditions such as this, these devout people believed they were honoring the law and, therefore, honoring the Lord. Even among other Jews, they considered themselves more righteous than the rest of God's chosen because of their strict adherence to such practices.

7:4 *When they come from the marketplace, they don't eat unless they have washed first. They have been taught to follow many other rules. For example, they must also wash their cups, jars, brass pots, and dinner tables.)*

With a further description, Mark continues to inform his Gentile readers of these Jewish traditions. These religious washings were observed in the washing of their hands before eating and also of the utensils used at the table. It was not a matter of simply washing dishes in a clearly prescribed manner. Nothing foreign would enter these righteous persons, who desired to remain pure before their God. Sadly, such righteousness and purity were largely ritualistic and did not provide true spiritual cleansing.

7:5 *The Pharisees and the scribes asked Jesus, "Why don't your disciples follow the traditions taught by our ancestors? They are unclean because they don't wash their hands before they eat!"*

The confrontation began. The challenge was laid before Jesus. After all, as the disciples' teacher and master, He was responsible for making sure that those who followed Him explicitly obeyed the traditions handed down from generation to generation. They challenged Jesus and not His disciples because it was He they hoped to trap.

Notes/Applications
The Talmud was the written result of generations of oral tradition passed down through the scribes and Pharisees. Within it, the law was defined and refined to specifics that make it virtually impossible to follow. For example, it contained 630 rules about the Sabbath alone—what was and was not lawful to do on this holy day.

To the Jews of Jesus' day, this summary of oral tradition, which dated back to the Babylonian captivity, had become equal to the Scriptures in importance. In fact, the interpretation of these traditions through generations of rabbinical teaching eventually superceded the authority of the law itself.

It was this tradition to which the Pharisees alluded when they confronted Jesus about His disciples' unwashed hands. It was also this tradition that Jesus challenged when He healed the man with the withered hand on the Sabbath. Since the Pharisees had elevated such tradition over the Scriptures, they hated Jesus because He continually confronted them with Scripture. He demonstrated the hostility of their spirits and despised their blind religiosity and fervent zeal.

To the scribes and Pharisees, obedience to tradition equaled righteousness. Jesus shocked the Jews of His day when He boiled the entire Law of Moses down to two commandments: Love the Lord your God with all your heart, soul, mind, and love others as you love yourself *(Matthew 22:37–39)*. Jesus was telling the pious religious leaders that without love for God and for others, religion is worthless.

> *¹³Do any of you have wisdom and insight? Show this by living the right way with the humility that comes from wisdom. ¹⁴But if you are bitterly jealous and filled with self-centered ambition, don't brag. Don't say that you are wise when it isn't true. ¹⁵That kind of wisdom doesn't come from above. It belongs to this world. It is self-centered and demonic. ¹⁶Wherever there is jealousy and rivalry, there is disorder and every kind of evil.*
>
> *¹⁷However, the wisdom that comes from above is first of all pure. Then it is peaceful, gentle, obedient, filled with mercy and good deeds, impartial, and sincere. ¹⁸A harvest that has God's approval comes from the peace planted by peacemakers. (James 3:13–18)*

Unlike the Pharisees, whose strict training made them proud, let us hope that our deliverance from the miry clay will make us humble vessels of God's love. *"He pulled me out of a horrible pit, out of the mud and clay. He set my feet on a rock and made my steps secure"* *(Psalm 40:2)*.

Mark 7:6–13

7:6–7 *⁶Jesus told them, "Isaiah was right when he prophesied about you hypocrites in Scripture: 'These people honor me with their lips, but their hearts are far from me. ⁷Their worship of me is pointless, because their teachings are rules made by humans.'*

Jesus exposed the falsehood of the scribes' and Pharisees' religious devotion. His words were blunt. He identified His opponents for what they truly were. Our English word *hypocrite* is a direct derivative of the Greek word ὑποκριτῶν (hypokriton). Essentially, a hypocrite's words do not coincide with his actions. This characterization by Jesus must have further angered these "righteous" Jews.

He did not address them in the heat of anger nor offer a personal analysis. Rather, He referred to the very Scriptures that the Pharisees claimed to hold in such high esteem. Jesus then quoted the prophet Isaiah and clearly defined His use of the term *hypocrite*:

> *The Lord says,*
> > *"These people worship me with their mouths*
> > *and honor me with their lips.*
> > > *But their hearts are far from me,*
> > > > *and their worship of me is based on rules*
> > > > *made by humans." (Isaiah 29:13)*

The outward display of commitment to Israel's God as demonstrated by the religious rituals was a facade. Any heartfelt love for the God Who had brought them out of Egypt and into the Promised Land was superficial. Their religious zeal erected a barrier between these self-proclaimed "holy men" and the God they claimed to worship.

As a result, the scribes' and Pharisees' worship was vain—empty, useless, hopeless, and futile. Since they had elevated the teaching of men to the point of religious worship, anything and everything they claimed was based on that hopeless foundation. There was no security, no hope, and no salvation to be found in their utterings. Only the repetitive demand to follow the rules, follow the rules, follow the rules. Those rules were created and maintained by the religious leaders with little regard to the Scriptures. They were man's perversions of God's ordinances. God brings light and life, whereas man brings darkness and death.

7:8 *"You abandon the commandments of God to follow human traditions."*

Not only had they failed to follow God's commands, the scribes and Pharisees had actually abandoned them. Having removed God from the center of their religious life, they replaced His commands with men's traditions. Jesus revealed the folly of their devotion, which was centered on ritualistic washings rather than on a genuine God-centered commitment. There is no reprieve, relief, or restoration when man focuses on himself rather than on his Creator.

7:9 *He added, "You have no trouble rejecting the commandments of God in order to keep your own traditions!*

Jesus then restated His argument in even stronger language. First, they laid aside the commandments of God. Now, they rejected them. Jesus had directly challenged these Pharisees. He had, in fact, judged their religious life and found it empty and useless. They had cast aside the Word of God for the rule of men.

Jesus' reprimand also confronted their self-image. Charging them with rejecting God's commands was tantamount to telling them that they were like the pagans that surrounded the Jewish nation or the Romans that ruled them.

7:10 *For example, Moses said, 'Honor your father and your mother' and 'Whoever curses father or mother must be put to death.'*

To prove His point, Jesus gave them an example that compared the true Mosaic Law to the oral tradition they followed: "Honor your father and your mother, so that you may live for a long time in the land the Lord your God is giving you" *(Exodus 20:12)*. Every Jewish child knew this instruction before he could read because this was the pinnacle of Jewish thought, next to the first commandment "to love the Lord your God." Jesus again quoted the Scriptures: "⁸Obey my laws, and live by them. I am the Lord who sets you apart as holy. ⁹Whoever curses his father or mother must be put to death. He has cursed his father or mother and deserves to die. *(Leviticus 20:8–9)*. The seriousness of the infraction was measured by the severity of the punishment required for those who failed to honor and revere their parents. Therefore, the penalty for adultery and the penalty for cursing one's parents were the same—death.

7:11–12 *"But you say, 'If a person tells his father or mother that whatever he might have used to help them is corban (that is, an offering to God), ¹²he no longer has to do anything for his father or mother.'*

Jesus then explained how their tradition had strayed from this simple command that came to their forefathers from God through His servant Moses. From the social aspects of this godly directive, children were to provide for their aging parents. It was generally understood that the child inherited his possessions from his parents while they were still alive so that the child could afford to provide for his parents in later years. Jewish tradition, however, had found a way around this strict requirement. The child could declare this material wealth to be corban, meaning it was "offered to God."[2] If possessions were dedicated to God, the child obviously could not use them to care for his parents.

Explanations differ between commentators regarding the implementation of this tradition. Some suggest that a child could merely declare the inheritance as corban, and that declaration itself sufficed.[3] Others insist that the Pharisees required that the corban be given in the temple, thereby enforcing the declaration of the profit to the Pharisees.[4] Either conclusion, however, affirms the Pharisees' wrongdoing for absolving people from their responsibility of caring for their parents as prescribed by the Mosaic Law.

7:13 *Because of your traditions you have destroyed the authority of God's word. And you do many other things like that."*

Therefore, the authority of God's Word fell secondary to the authority of tradition. The legal maneuvering of men within the Jewish tradition rendered God's commandment regarding the honor and care of one's parents as ineffective. Jesus further stated that there were numerous other examples where man's traditions trumped the commands of God. Indeed, these people were hypocrites.

Notes/Applications

The blunt, vivid language that Jesus used in this passage was a harsh but accurate judgment on the scribes and Pharisees. It is also God's judgment on anyone today who chooses a gospel other than the one founded on Jesus Christ, the absolute Truth.

Generation after generation has managed to dodge God's commandments, placing man's petty traditions at the pinnacle of worship. We twist, subvert, interpret, and misinterpret the Word of God so that it says what we want it to say. Nowhere in man's gospel is there room for Jesus as Lord and Savior. Nowhere is there room for mentioning His blood, atoning for our sins. After all, some believe that a blood sacrifice is too graphic, and sin is subject to perception. Such perverted theology will arrest our minds and paralyze our souls.

It is a fearful thing to feel the wrath of God. Did these scribes and Pharisees not sense a divine foreboding in the one Who condemned their piety and denounced the tradition they exalted to the status of Scripture? Are we ever so foolish as to flaunt the "things of God" yet through the witness of our lives deny that we know Him? *"So on the outside you look as though you have God's approval, but inside you are full of hypocrisy and lawlessness"* (Matthew 23:28).

Jesus' words are sobering for us all, so they bear repeating: "These people honor Me with their lips, but their hearts are far from Me" *(Mark 7:6)*.

Mark 7:14–23

7:14 *Then he called the crowd again and said to them, "Listen to me, all of you, and try to understand!*

Jesus had evidently spoken to the scribes and the Pharisees privately with only the disciples as witnesses. Now, however, He called for the crowd and asked for their attention as He told them something very important. This discourse was prompted by His discussion with the Pharisees concerning their religious traditions.

Now, Jesus asked for the multitude to listen carefully and understand a basic precept concerning faith. Unlike with the parable of the sower, Jesus wanted them to understand these teachings. This lesson was of such crucial significance that they dared not misunderstand lest they place their very souls in peril.

7:15 *Nothing that goes into a person from the outside can make him unclean. It's what comes out of a person that makes him unclean.*

We have learned of the great importance of ceremonial washing as defined by the scribes and the Pharisees. To them, it was imperative to wash every food vessel in a carefully prescribed method. It was even more important to follow the tradition of washing the hands so that the water dripped from the elbows. The primary purpose of these washings was to signify that nothing impure would enter their bodies. The religious elite were obsessed with the idea of bodily purity, thereby securing the worthy commendation of their God.

However, Jesus intended to set the record straight. He would show the crowd that such theological jargon was useless. Not only did it deny God the opportunity to speak through His Scriptures, it also set up man's law as supreme. In fact, it contradicted God's description of man's sinful nature.

Jesus explained that it was not those things that entered a man from the outside that caused his rottenness. The things that came out of a man were rooted in his inherent sinful nature.

7:16 *Let the person who has ears listen!"*

Jesus firmly admonished the crowd. They had better listen and understand the truth of His teachings. Understanding was not a matter of having ears to listen but of having an open heart to receive and obey the truth.

7:17 *When he had left the people and gone home, his disciples asked him about this illustration.*

Obviously, the disciples had once again missed the point. They heard what Jesus said, but they did not understand what He meant. Consequently, when the Twelve withdrew from the crowd along with Jesus, they asked Him to explain this statement.

7:18 *Jesus said to them, "Don't you understand? Don't you know that whatever goes into a person from the outside can't make him unclean?*

Jesus confronted His disciples' spiritual incompetence. They, like the crowd, failed to understand the point He had just made. Jesus had just informed the Pharisees and scribes that their religiosity was a total failure and that it provided no hope of redemption. Now, Jesus questioned whether His closest followers were religious failures like the Pharisees. Why could they not understand this simple message?

Jesus was saying that nothing that entered a man could hurt him. It could not make him ceremonially unclean. It would not make him impure. The washings commanded by the scribes and Pharisees were total folly, but these religious leaders did not understand this basic concept. If they did, they would have understood the futility of their oral traditions. Jesus sought to emphasize the true nature of this man-made tradition.

In the disciples' defense, they possibly felt torn between the rabbinical tradition, under which they were reared, and Jesus' teachings, which not only condemned those traditions but also taught things in direct contrast to them.

7:19 *It doesn't go into his thoughts but into his stomach and then into a toilet." (By saying this, Jesus declared all foods acceptable.)*

Jesus graphically explained that these washings did not cleanse the heart. The body is a wondrous work of God's creation. It processes the food that enters the stomach, takes what it needs, filters it, and uses it for sustaining life and health. What the body does not need, it eliminates. Therefore, eating food with unwashed hands, physically or ceremonially unwashed, could not make a man ceremonially unclean. It has no impact on his spiritual condition at all.

7:20 *He continued, "It's what comes out of a person that makes him unclean.*

Jesus pinpointed the issue. Man should not focus on what he takes in but on what he projects. "What comes out of a person," the outward display of his speech and actions, reflects his internal convictions, attitudes, and motives and reveals his spiritual position before God.

7:21–22 *²¹Evil thoughts, sexual sins, stealing, murder, ²²adultery, greed, wickedness, cheating, shameless lust, envy, cursing, arrogance, and foolishness come from within a person.*

Unrighteousness does not come from the stomach but from the heart. It originates from the very core of the person, the center of all thought and emotion: "The human mind is the most deceitful of all things. It is incurable. No one can understand how deceitful it is" (Jeremiah 17:9).

Jesus proceeded to identify some of the things that man does that amplify the uncleanness of his life. Evil thoughts are the conception of all evil deeds. Adulteries, cheating, and lust derive from man not as a by-product of his environment but as a mirror to his wicked soul.

7:23 *All these evils come from within and make a person unclean."*

These evils clearly demonstrate the heart condition of a person. Actions show beyond any doubt that such a man is unclean before God, his Maker. For this reason, Jesus explicitly attacked the foolishness of the Jewish oral traditions that emphasized the appearance of cleanliness and failed to deal with the reality of man's depravity. *"²⁷How horrible it will be for you, scribes and Pharisees! You hypocrites! You are like whitewashed graves that look beautiful on the outside but inside are full of dead people's bones and every kind of impurity. ²⁸So on the outside you look as though you have God's approval, but inside you are full of hypocrisy and lawlessness"* (Matthew 23:27–28). Broken and twisted lives result from such perversions. Lives are ended physically by man's violence, and lives are ended emotionally by sexual indiscretions:

> *¹⁹Now, the effects of the corrupt nature are obvious: illicit sex, perversion, promiscuity, ²⁰idolatry, drug use, hatred, rivalry, jealousy, angry outbursts, selfish ambition, conflict, factions, ²¹envy, drunkenness, wild partying, and similar things. I've told you in the past and I'm telling you again that people who do these kinds of things will not inherit the kingdom of God* (Galatians 5:19–21).

Notes/Applications

Jesus took issue with the falsehood engendered by the rabbinical teachings. He perceived the error of the Jewish tradition and attacked it with forceful language and logic.

God has always focused on the heart of man. We prefer to direct our focus on the outward things, but in God's economy, these things matter little: "But the Lord told Samuel, 'Don't look at his appearance or how tall he is, because I have rejected him. God does not see as humans see. Humans look at outward appearances, but the Lord looks into the heart' " (1 Samuel 16:7). Man is more comfortable hiding the evils of his heart behind a glowing exterior. He, therefore, cannot stand to be confronted by the holy God or by His Son. Jesus knew this about the Pharisees and sternly rebuked them. Hypocrisy is detestable in the eyes of God. How much more precious in His sight is the humble soul that cries out, "God, be merciful to me, a sinner!" *(Luke 18:13)*.

In the burning light of His truth, our facades crumble. All of our bravado is crushed beneath the Word of Truth, and we must acknowledge that we are truly unclean. When we acknowledge our true selves before Jesus, we must also confess our need to be cleansed, our need of a Lord and Savior, and rest assured that He is always ready to answer the cry of a heart truly longing for redemption. *"The Lord takes pleasure in his people. He crowns those who are oppressed with victory" (Psalm 149:4)*.

Mark 7:24–30

7:24 *Jesus left that place and went to the territory of Tyre. He didn't want anyone to know that he was staying in a house there. However, it couldn't be kept a secret.*

Similar to when Jesus entered the area of the Gesarenes in chapter five, He again traveled into Gentile territory. After a brief discussion about man's internal uncleanness, He rose and went to Tyre and Sidon, located along the Mediterranean Sea north of Galilee. His mission among the Gentiles was consistent with His ministry among the Jews in Galilee. Except for visiting synagogues to teach, He followed the same routines.

Jesus sought time to rest from the rigors of His ministry, hoping to find some peace and quiet, but in this Gentile region, people sought Him just as they did when He was in Galilee. His presence could not be kept secret.

Why did Jesus journey to Tyre and Sidon? Was it to broaden the scope of His ministry? Did He intend for the Gentiles to share in His message of repentance, or did He enter this region simply to get away from the huge, growing crowd that allowed Him no rest? Did He seek to get away from the ongoing accusations of the scribes and Pharisees?

In addition to seeking solitude, perhaps Jesus' reason for this sojourn into Gentile territory was to demonstrate in a graphic and practical way that there was nothing unclean except for man's heart. A Jew could travel among non-Jews and not be defiled. The disciples would learn valuable lessons from their life experiences with Jesus, and this lesson would confirm the validity of Jesus' earlier debate with His accusers.

7:25 *A woman whose little daughter had an evil spirit heard about Jesus. She went to him and bowed down.*

Obviously, Jesus' reputation as a healer had spread well beyond the borders of Galilee. He was also well known in the Gentile regions of Tyre and Sidon. In similar fashion, whenever people discovered Jesus' location, they came to Him, seeking help and relief from their earthly miseries. Likewise, this woman, though a Gentile, fell at the feet of this Jewish teacher. She acknowledged by her action that Jesus was of notable importance, and she bowed before Him in her grief, begging that her daughter be released from the possession of a demon.

7:26 *The woman happened to be Greek, born in Phoenicia in Syria. She asked him to force the demon out of her daughter.*

The text clarifies that this woman was a Greek born in the region of Syro-Phoencia and that she was, therefore, not a Jew. According to Jewish tradition, it was unlawful for Jews to interact with non-Jews. They viewed the Gentiles as unclean and beneath them on the social and spiritual ladder.

The woman wanted Jesus to heal her daughter of demon possession. Some translations reveal that she was persistent. Surely, the Lord would not ignore repeated pleas.

7:27 *Jesus said to her, "First, let the children eat all they want. It's not right to take the children's food and throw it to the dogs."*

If Jesus were to follow the edicts of the Jewish oral traditions as commanded by the Jewish scribes, He would have never even acknowledged this woman. As the disciples watched, perhaps with some degree of righteous horror, Jesus responded to her.

Jesus indicated that there existed an order to the message of God. While not denying her request, He told her that He was not yet finished teaching His own people. They were, after all, the children of the covenant. Those existing outside of this covenant relationship should not presume their significant role in God's plan. Therefore, Jesus told her that it was not right to take the food out of the children's mouths and offer it as scraps to the dogs.

7:28 *She answered him, "Lord, even the dogs under the table eat some of the children's scraps."*

This woman was very astute. Though not a Jew, she understood well what Jesus was saying, which starkly contrasted most of Jesus' discussions among His own people. This woman perceived that Jesus was not referring to food, children, or dogs but to the relationship that had existed for centuries between the Jews and all other nations. While acknowledging the truth of Jesus' words, she reminded Him of a common denominator that existed among all people. Though not the primary recipient of the food, even the dogs benefited from what the children neglected. Likewise, a receptive Gentile should not be ignored for the sake of a people that would not fully benefit from the "food" prepared for them.

7:29 *Jesus said to her, "Because you have said this, go! The demon has left your daughter."*

Jesus must have rejoiced at this woman's answer. In this Gentile region, He had found a Greek woman who understood what He was saying and still dared to ask for just a small crumb from His vast table. And that small crumb was more than enough. Jesus granted her request, and her daughter was released from the demon's control.

Imagine the amazement of the disciples as they watched this scene unfold before them. They would not speak to this woman because she was a Gentile. She was unclean. However, Jesus had spoken to her and granted her request. Jesus sent His own disciples a clear message of the meaning of "unclean," and the most important aspect of this message remained that cleanliness had absolutely nothing to do with outward characteristics whether material or physical. This woman demonstrated a faith that was indeed rare.

7:30 *The woman went home and found the little child lying on her bed, and the demon was gone.*

This remarkable woman returned home to find her daughter lying calmly on her bed. She no longer exhibited those characteristics that had consumed her while she was under the control of the demon. Jesus had granted the woman's earnest petition, and her daughter was now free.

Jesus did not even go to the house or issue a direct command to the demon. He never spoke to the daughter. This is the only case in Mark's gospel in which Jesus issued no spoken command and did not directly meet the afflicted person. His power and authority existed far beyond the limitations of human boundaries.

Notes/Applications

Jesus was previously involved in a heated discussion with the scribes and Pharisees from Jerusalem about the realities of the heart, the source of uncleanness. Jesus proclaimed that external rituals are meaningless when the motivation behind them is corrupt. Jesus then left that confrontation and took His disciples directly into "unclean" Gentile territory, where He issued a living lesson to the Twelve. He could not emphasize strongly enough how the Jewish tradition had perverted the living Word of God.

When the Syro-Phoenician woman approached Jesus, she crossed the societal boundaries that separated Gentiles from the Jews. Thus, we empathize with how desperate she must have been to reach the Savior because she willingly risked being scorned and perhaps even punished to gain deliverance for her daughter.

Jesus, moved by the woman's faith and persistence, granted her request. God is pleased by the kind of faith that believes outside of human parameters. Jesus told the disciples in Matthew, "I can guarantee this truth: If your faith is the size of a mustard seed, you can say to this mountain, 'Move from here to there,' and it will move. Nothing will be impossible for you" (*Matthew 17:20*). He is equally moved by a heart so sincere as to be honest enough to cry out, "I believe! Help my lack of faith."

Only on the altar of the sacrificed Son of God can our hearts be broken. Only then do we truly see ourselves. Only then does the reality of our sinful hearts overwhelm us, and only then can the Creator claim His rightful place in our hearts as the center of our worship and praise.

Mark 7:31–37

7:31 *Jesus then left the neighborhood of Tyre. He went through Sidon and the territory of the Ten Cities to the Sea of Galilee.*

Jesus and His disciples returned again to the Sea of Galilee. He did not go directly to the Jewish region of Capernaum but journeyed through the region east of the Sea of Galilee to the Ten Cities. These Ten Cities, also known as the Decapolis, in the Gentile region east of the Jordan River, were all centers of Gentile trade.

7:32 *Some people brought to him a man who was deaf and who also had a speech defect. They begged Jesus to lay his hand on him.*

We know that the demoniac who was previously released from the control of many demons called Legion, went throughout the region of Decapolis declaring what God had done for him as Jesus had instructed him to do: "[19]'Go home to your family, and tell them how much the Lord has done for you and how merciful he has been to you.' [20]So the man left. He began to tell how much Jesus had done for him in the Ten Cities. Everyone was amazed" (*Mark 5:19–20*). Therefore, we can conclude that many people in the region knew about Jesus and what He had done for this man, so it is no wonder that these Gentile people brought their sick to Jesus. The people brought a deaf man to Jesus and pled with Him to heal the man of his hearing loss and speech impediment.

7:33 *Jesus took him away from the crowd to be alone with him. He put his fingers into the man's ears, and after spitting, he touched the man's tongue.*

This miracle appears only in Mark's gospel. Jesus took this man aside from the crowd. Some of the disciples likely accompanied Jesus, but this miracle did not take place in front of a large audience. Jesus placed His fingers in the man's ears, spat, and then touched the man's tongue. We are not told the significance of these gestures, but it is obvious from earlier passages that Jesus did not have to be present to employ His healing power *(Mark 7:24–30)*. Perhaps these gestures had significance for the man who was deaf.

7:34 *Then he looked up to heaven, sighed, and said to the man, "Ephphatha!" which means, "Be opened!"*

Jesus looked upward to heaven and appealed to God the Father with a sigh. Many commentators assign much significance to the purpose of the Lord's sigh. A literal translation from the Greek text of the word *sigh* is "groan."[5] Such a specific inclusion in the text surely is intended to express an emotional response from the Lord, although to suggest that Jesus was grieving over the man's (or even humankind's) spiritual condition is mere speculation.

7:35 *At once the man could hear and talk normally.*

Jesus immediately released the man from the physical bondage of his impediment. This man could now hear and speak clearly. Although the content of this conversation is not disclosed, we are struck again with the power and authority of Jesus, even among these Gentile people.

7:36 *Jesus ordered the people not to tell anyone. But the more he ordered them, the more they spread the news.*

A familiar scene repeats itself. Jesus commanded the nearby people to remain silent about what they had witnessed. While they might not have observed the miracle that Jesus had just performed, they certainly could see and hear the results. What cause for joy and celebration! True to earlier experience and truer still to the obstinacy of human nature, the more Jesus urged them to be silent, the more they told everybody about this healer—how a deaf man with a speech impediment could now hear and speak clearly.

7:37 *Jesus completely amazed the people. They said, "He has done everything well. He makes the deaf hear and the mute talk."*

This narrative of Jesus' journey into Gentile territory concludes with a general statement that the people were amazed. The Greek word ὑπερπερισσῶσ (hyperperisose) describes the intensity of their astonishment, and this verse marks its only use in the New Testament. Certainly, Mark searched for unique words to properly describe how Jesus' life and miracles were so astounding that people everywhere were overwhelmed with the results.

Notes/Applications
Jesus' healing of a deaf man with a speech impediment illustrated a spiritual truth. Only Jesus the Messiah can open our plugged hearts so that we can truly "hear" and receive His Word. *"5And the ears of the deaf will be unplugged. 6Then those who are lame will leap like deer, and those who cannot speak will shout for joy. Water will gush out into the desert, and streams will gush out into the wilderness"* (Isaiah 35:5–6). ·

Can we hear Him speaking to us? Jesus' words resound in truth as they pierce our human perceptions, but He also whispers this message directly to our hearts through His Word as He sends out a call upon our lives. Fanny Crosby, beloved hymnist who fervently wrote for her Savior despite her blindness, had a keen ear for listening to the Lord. She penned the hymn entitled "Hark! There Comes a Whisper," which proclaims Jesus' standing invitation:

> *Hark! There comes a whisper*
> *Stealing on thine ear:*
> *Tis the Savior calling,*
> *Soft, soft and clear.*
> *'Give thy heart to Me,*
> *Once I died for thee';*
> *Hark! Hark! thy Savior calls;*
> *Come, sinner, Come!*[6]

Jesus alone heals our spiritual depravity, for without Him, our condition, called the sin nature, is terminal. He alone can open our hearts to redemption and, thereby, resurrect our spirits from the dead. Yes, Jesus physically heals, but even more, He restores spiritual life to human marrow. May we respond to His call and be able to pray as the psalmist did so long ago: "⁶You have dug out two ears for me. You did not ask for burnt offerings or sacrifices for sin. ⁷Then I said, 'I have come! (It is written about me in the scroll of the book.) ⁸I am happy to do your will, O my God.' Your teachings are deep within me" *(Psalm 40:6–8)*.

Jesus' Journeys to the Gentiles: Chapter Seven

1. Jesus started on the western shore of the Sea of Galilee.
2. Jesus traveled to region of Tyre and Sidon.
3. Jesus returned through the Ten Cities to the eastern shore of the Sea of Galilee.

Mark 8:1–7

8:1 *About that time there was once again a large crowd with nothing to eat. Jesus called his disciples and said to them,*

While Jesus remained in Gentile territory east of the Sea of Galilee, a huge crowd gathered, and He recognized that they had not eaten. Jesus called His disciples to bring this to their attention, and He prepared to address the needs of this crowd.

In chapter six when Jesus fed the five thousand, the disciples had noted the need for food. In this case, Jesus reminded His disciples of this physical requirement, demonstrating His awareness of the material world.

This was not the same crowd that Jesus previously fed. That multitude consisted primarily of Jewish people who had assembled during Jesus' travels. In this passage, while there were many Jews present, there was also a large segment of Gentile followers. The long journey to Tyre and Sidon and the eventual return through Decapolis would have eliminated a great majority of the initial crowd while at the same time gathering different people from the Gentile areas through which He traveled. Jesus, Son of Man, born of a Jewish virgin and reared in the Jewish tradition, broke the yoke of the cultural barrier by preaching to the Gentile territories around Galilee.

8:2 *"I feel sorry for the people. They have been with me three days now and have nothing to eat.*

In a remarkable statement, Jesus declared His compassion for this large gathering. If only the scribes and Pharisees could have seen Him now, they would have surely complained. They had previously criticized Jesus because He ate with publicans and sinners, but at least they were Jewish publicans and sinners. This was a continuing lesson by Jesus that "cleanness" or "uncleanness" was not a matter of physical location or other external conditions. Jesus had left His home in the region of Galilee, took His disciples into Gentile territory, and released a Greek woman's daughter from a demon. Now, upon returning to the Sea of Galilee, Jesus expressed compassion for the well-being of this largely Gentile crowd.

Perhaps this was the very reason that Jesus made His disciples aware of the crowd's need for food. The disciples must have been very nervous throughout their travels in Gentile regions. Jews may have traveled into pagan territories for the purpose of trade and business, but they never associated with non-Jews socially. Now, Jesus put their Jewish faith to a test. Who was correct in these matters? Was it the oral tradition of the scribes, or was it the new, radical teaching of this leader, Who had taught them that cleanliness before God is a matter of the heart? Certainly, a Jew would never show compassion on a Gentile. Jesus placed His disciples squarely in the middle of this theological dilemma. They would have to make some decisions.

8:3 *If I send them home before they've eaten, they will become exhausted on the road. Some of them have come a long distance."*

Jesus' concern was very practical. In three days, they had walked thirty to forty miles. Some of the crowd might have received small portions of food along the way, but for the most part, the crowd had not eaten. Jesus was concerned that they would faint when they journeyed back to their homes. Some had come a long way and would have to travel the same distance to return to their homes.

8:4 *His disciples asked him, "Where could anyone get enough bread to feed these people in this place where no one lives?"*

As already demonstrated, the twelve disciples really had a difficult time understanding the one Whom they were following. They had very short memories. Earlier, Mark told us how Jesus fed a crowd of greater than five thousand *(Mark 6:35–44)*. These circumstances were virtually the same. The entire entourage was located in a remote area in which there were no ready sources for food. Again, the disciples questioned Jesus and reminded Him of their physical surroundings. Despite their previous experience, the disciples could not conceive of any way to feed this large group of people in this remote area.

8:5 *Jesus asked them, "How many loaves of bread do you have?" They answered, "Seven."*

As before, Jesus asked His disciples to avoid looking at what they did not have. Rather, He called them to take account of what they did have. Jesus showed them again that there would always be plenty when He was with them. Their inventory showed that they had seven loaves of bread. Earlier, Jesus had fed five thousand with only five loaves and two fish.

8:6–7 *⁶He ordered the crowd to sit down on the ground. He took the seven loaves and gave thanks to God. Then he broke the bread and gave it to his disciples to serve to the people. ⁷They also had a few small fish. He blessed them and said that the fish should also be served to the people.*

With the meager supply of seven loaves of bread, Jesus clearly demonstrated His authority over the entire matter. After everyone was seated, Jesus acted decisively. He intended to feed this huge crowd. In the Greek, each action, *took*, *gave thanks*, and *broke*, is imbued with clear authority. Then, the verb tense changes. Just as in Mark chapter six, Jesus kept supplying the disciples with bread so that they, in turn, could distribute the food to the crowd.

Jesus repeated the entire procedure with a small number of fish, which was also distributed among the crowd.

Notes/Applications

Amazingly, the disciples still seemed incapable of perceiving Jesus' ability to create plenty out of little by feeding a crowd of thousands with only a few loaves and fish. They viewed the predicament through the lens of their own fallibility, wherein human reasoning is always shamed by God's infinite wisdom and power.

Lest we be too hard on these twelve men chosen by Jesus, we must also look in the mirror of our own vanity and acknowledge our lack of wisdom in matters concerning the kingdom of God. Again and again, we read God's promises in Scripture confirmed through the life of His Son, yet we still doubt. Can Jesus really meet all our needs? Can He really heal? Does He really forgive sin?

Such questions are natural but elementary. They may visit us, but we must not let them set up camp in the ridges of our minds.

> *⁵If any of you needs wisdom to know what you should do, you should ask God, and he will give it to you. God is generous to everyone and doesn't find fault with them. ⁶When you ask for something, don't have any doubts. A person who has doubts is like a wave that is*

blown by the wind and tossed by the sea. ⁷*A person who has doubts shouldn't expect to receive anything from the Lord.* ⁸*A person who has doubts is thinking about two different things at the same time and can't make up his mind about anything.* (James 1:5–8)

We all go through stages of spiritual maturity where God's Word becomes our creed backed by our obedience. However, if we do not progress beyond our doubts, we remain infants in the faith, unable to fulfill the leadership roles for which God has designed us.

Scripture records the disciples' journey of faith as they accompanied the master from miracle to miracle. Although they did not always understand Jesus' directives and continually questioned His methods, we must conclude by their actions that they sincerely desired spiritual growth. Otherwise, they would not have stayed in His ranks.

We, too, embark on a spiritual journey. No one can believe for us. That responsibility falls squarely on our shoulders. Situations will constantly arise that challenge our faith, but let us not be tossed about by the winds of circumstance. May we believe the promises of the one Who can do more than we can ever hope or imagine (Ephesians 3:20).

Mark 8:8–13

8:8 *The people ate as much as they wanted. The disciples picked up the leftover pieces and filled seven large baskets.*

The quantities of food Jesus gave His disciples to distribute were again large enough to yield leftovers. The people ate until they were full, and yet the remaining food filled seven large baskets. The Greek word used in this verse for "basket" is different from the basket that was used in Mark chapter six. This was a large rope basket, sometimes strong enough to carry a full-grown man.[1] Therefore, these seven baskets probably contained more food than the twelve reed baskets of Mark six. Jesus provided abundant quantities of food for the nourishment of the people.

8:9–10 *⁹About four thousand people were there. Then he sent the people on their way. ¹⁰After that, Jesus and his disciples got into a boat and went into the region of Dalmanutha.*

According to Mark, the number of people in the crowd amounted to about four thousand. He does not indicate that there were four thousand men, but Matthew's account of the same incident reports "four thousand men, besides women and children" (*Matthew 15:38*). The total group, therefore, likely exceeded this cited number, and all were served by seven loaves of bread and a few fish that had been blessed by Jesus. After feeding this multitude, Jesus sent them away.

From a practical perspective, Jesus might have taken this journey to avoid the large crowds assembled in the region of Galilee. Most of the Jews in the crowd would not follow Him into pagan territories, but the same thing happened in the pagan territories that happened in Galilee. People came to see and hear this remarkable person and to beg for healing and release, so the crowd continued to grow, and Jesus could find little rest. At the beginning of the passage, Jesus' intention had been for the people to return to their homes, but He demonstrated His compassion by feeding the crowd before He dismissed them.

Immediately, Jesus got into the boat with His disciples and crossed the Sea of Galilee to the region of Dalmanutha, also called Magadan (*Matthew 15:39*). This voyage across the middle of the sea, where they had had so much trouble on earlier voyages, passed without crisis.

8:11 *The Pharisees went to Jesus and began to argue with him. They tested him by demanding that he perform a miraculous sign from heaven.*

The minute Jesus disembarked, the Pharisees came with the intention of testing Him. Jesus had left Galilee after a confrontation with these self-righteous hypocrites (*Mark 7:1–16*). The moment Jesus returned to Jewish territory, He again faced their closed hearts and minds. These religious leaders thought nothing of debating with Jesus, though they had sufficient evidence of His authority.

The Pharisees had already charged Jesus with blasphemy by saying, "Beelzebul is in him," and, "He forces demons out of people with the help of the ruler of demons" (*Mark 3:22*). In this earlier debate, Jesus had shown them the folly of their logic: "²³How can Satan force out Satan? ²⁴If a kingdom is divided against itself, that kingdom cannot last. ²⁵And if a household is divided against itself, that household will not last. ²⁶So if Satan rebels against himself and is divided, he cannot last. That will be the end of him" (*Mark 3:23b–26*). Still, they refused to believe.

Although they had seen the spectacular miracles, they understood Jesus from their pharisaical perspective. Now, ironically, they asked Jesus for a sign. They knew He had healed people. What sign did they seek? They wanted Him to prove that God was the source of His authority and power.[2] They sought a sign to persuade their closed minds that Jesus was one of the prophets like the prophets of ancient times.

8:12 *With a deep sigh he asked, "Why do these people demand a sign? I can guarantee this truth: If these people are given a sign, it will be far different than what they want!"*

This verse portrays a very personal side to Jesus, Who showed the depth of His grief and anguish over these leaders with a measure of annoyance. Jesus' answer challenged these self-righteous Pharisees. Why did they want a sign? After all the evidence that had been given, nothing more could be done to open their blinded eyes. He told them emphatically that any sign He might give them would not be the sign they hoped for. Jesus knew that nothing would be enough to persuade them, and so He did not perform a sign for them.

In the context of this narrative, "these people" refers to a type of people (the Pharisees as representing the Jews) and not to all people of that time.[3] Apparently, Jesus' patience with them neared an end. They had rejected God's revelation, and He would do nothing further to validate His ministry.

8:13 *Then he left them there. He got into a boat again and crossed to the other side of the Sea of Galilee.*

Jesus did not remain to be further provoked by these religious leaders. He got into the boat and returned to the eastern shore of the Sea of Galilee, the territory of the pagans, where He would find more acceptance than He had found with the scribes and Pharisees from Jerusalem. As John stated, "He went to his own people, and his own people didn't accept him" *(John 1:11).*

Notes/Applications

The quickened pace of this passage foreshadows the approaching final weeks of Jesus' earthly life. He pressed to instill His message into His disciples' hearts because He knew His time was drawing near, and His disciples needed to be equipped to assume His ministry.

In contrast, the meandering pace of our lives can lull us into believing we have all the time in the world. *"God says,*

'At the right time I heard you. On the day of salvation I helped you'" (2 Corinthians 6:2). God warns that we never know when time will run out for us, and we will be called into eternity. We cannot afford the luxury of putting God off until later when we are not so busy or when we have exhausted our list of goals and appointments.

Now is the day of salvation, but now is also the day to live out our salvation. Today is the perfect opportunity to reach beyond ourselves and meet others' needs. Today is the day to surrender schedules that are consumed by worldly preoccupations and to spend quality time at the master's feet as we become proficient followers. Let us heed the urgency of the moment and live wisely, redeeming every moment to further God's kingdom.

Mark 8:14–21

8:14 *The disciples had forgotten to take any bread along and had only one loaf with them in the boat.*

As this small band of men rowed across the lake, they only had one loaf of bread with them. They had previously fed four thousand and had taken up seven baskets of leftover fragments. When they did have food at their disposal, they forgot it. Now, they rowed back across the Sea of Galilee with insufficient provisions.

8:15 *Jesus warned them, "Be careful! Watch out for the yeast of the Pharisees and the yeast of Herod!"*

Jesus warned the disciples about the yeast of the Pharisees and Herod. Yeast makes bread rise. During the Passover, the Hebrew people were to celebrate using unleavened bread (bread to which no yeast has been added). Jesus used a familiar illustration to symbolize the corrupting influence of Pharisees among the Jewish people. The connotation was that a small amount of yeast pervaded the whole loaf. Referring to the incident that had just occurred, Jesus grieved over the Pharisees' unbelief, and He cautioned His followers to reject their influence. Jesus warned them not to build their religious faith on external practices that left the heart unclean.

8:16 *They had been discussing with one another that they didn't have any bread.*

The disciples misunderstood Jesus' warning to avoid the influence of the religious leaders and assumed that He was referring to the one loaf of bread on board. It must have been very difficult and frustrating for Jesus to communicate God's ways to a creation so badly fouled by the yeast of sin.

8:17 *Jesus knew what they were saying and asked them, "Why are you discussing the fact that you don't have any bread? Don't you understand yet? Don't you catch on? Are your minds closed?*

Jesus knew that his disciples thought He was discussing a bread shortage. He confronted them with a battery of questions that must have hurt their pride since His questions challenged them and revealed their lack of spiritual comprehension. A bread shortage was of no consequence in light of the eternal matters He conveyed to them. Did they not yet understand what they had witnessed and experienced? These men, chosen by Jesus, must have been bewildered as Jesus' words rang true. Jesus had told them earlier, "[11]The mystery about the kingdom of God has been given directly to you. To those on the outside, it is given in stories: "[12]They see clearly but don't perceive. They hear clearly but don't understand. They never return to me and are never forgiven" *(Mark 4:11–12).*

8:18 *Are you blind and deaf? Don't you remember?*

Jesus further pressed the disciples by reiterating the same metaphor that He had used when speaking to the crowds. He emphasized the importance of paying attention to His teachings and allowing His truth to become firmly rooted in their hearts and minds.

8:19 *When I broke the five loaves for the five thousand, how many baskets did you fill with leftover pieces?" They told him, "Twelve."*

Jesus was grieved by the disciples' failure to comprehend what He was saying, and He had likely grown impatient with their spiritual stupor. Time was limited, and He needed the Twelve to apply themselves and to focus, so He referred back to the previous few weeks. How many baskets of fragments were collected after He fed the five thousand? The disciples responded to His question accordingly.

8:20 *"When I broke the seven loaves for the four thousand, how many large baskets did you fill with leftover pieces?" They answered him, "Seven."*

How many rope baskets full of fragments had the disciples collected after Jesus fed the crowd? The disciples again responded with the correct answer.

Somehow, in this simple test of their memory, Jesus longed to have these twelve spiritually immature men move beyond the mere physical manifestation. He wanted them to see Him for Who He was.

8:21 *He asked them, "Don't you catch on yet?"*

If the disciples remembered how much food was left over from these two events, how could they not remember the quantity of food with which Jesus began? Jesus, Son of God and Son of Man, marveled at the utter blindness of the disciples' minds, which seemed to have shutters pulled tightly closed against the realities of the world outside. However, the shutters on the disciples' minds prevented them from seeing what transpired on the inside. They could not understand the truth! They were indeed blind like the rest of the world. For all of the special times with the master, they might as well have been asleep. Their hearts were skeptical, and their spiritual eyes were not yet opened to the things of God.

Notes/Applications

After two years of teaching, preaching, and working miracles for all to see, Jesus had good reason to be frustrated with His disciples. When Jesus referred to the yeast of the Pharisees, He spoke figuratively. As yeast can overtake a batch of dough, unbelief penetrates people's hearts with hostility. Jesus warned His disciples to guard against such corruption that demanded continuous outward displays to confirm His identity and power. However, when Jesus referred to yeast, the disciples assumed He spoke of their bread shortage. When would they ever perceive Him as the embodiment of the spiritual reality that the signs and wonders merely confirmed?

Jesus provided ample evidence confirming His identity as the Son of God, but the Pharisees and the disciples demonstrated that signs went only so far in piercing man's spirit. Miracles should not be the foundation of our faith lest that faith crumble when challenged. Miracles should merely substantiate the living faith embedded in our hearts.

How would we answer if the Lord asked us directly, "Don't you understand yet? Don't you catch on? Are your minds closed?" The disciples were so absorbed by their present material concern that they missed the invaluable spiritual lesson before them. We, too, often miss the forest for the trees. We focus so much on our circumstances that we miss the purpose behind them and fail to understand that Jesus reigns supremely over them. Instead of scrambling to squelch life's fires, perhaps we should channel that spiritual energy into focusing on Jesus, the miracle of all miracles.

Mark 8:22–26

8:22 *As they came to Bethsaida, some people brought a blind man to Jesus. They begged Jesus to touch him.*

Jesus and His disciples finally arrived in Bethsaida on the northeast shore of the Sea of Galilee. As so often was the case, people brought to Jesus those who were in need, and mentioned here was a particular blind man. This and another similar event (*Mark 7:32–37*) are recorded only in Mark's gospel.

8:23 *Jesus took the blind man's hand and led him out of the village. He spit into the man's eyes and placed his hands on him. Jesus asked him, "Can you see anything?"*

Generally, Jesus' miracles were public events, but in this case, Jesus took the blind man by the hand and led him out of town. More and more, Jesus pulled away from the crowds to spend time alone with those He had called so that His disciples could better understand Him.

Jesus then spat on the man's eyes and touched Him. Jesus asked the man if he could see anything. Prior to this account, results of Jesus' healing acts have been immediate. Why would Jesus reach out to heal this man and then ask if he saw anything?

8:24 *The man looked up and said, "I see people. They look like trees walking around."*

The man looked up and dimly saw the disciples milling around. He saw them as walking trees, but he could not see clearly enough to identify them. Was Jesus' healing incomplete or insufficient to restore the man's eyesight completely the first time? We can hardly believe that such could ever be the case. Rather, it seems that Jesus was revealing a spiritual insight about the inability of men to have their blindness fully restored while still encumbered by their human inadequacy. *"Now we see a blurred image in a mirror. Then we will see very clearly"* (1 Corinthians 13:12a).

8:25 *Then Jesus placed his hands on the man's eyes a second time, and the man saw clearly. His sight was normal again. He could see everything clearly even at a distance.*

Jesus placed His hands on the man's eyes again and instructed him to look up. The healing was complete. The man then saw everyone clearly and could identify their distinguishing characteristics. He saw Jesus, Peter, James, John, and the rest of the disciples. Just as in the other cases, Jesus had answered the appeal of this man's friends by restoring his sight.

8:26 *Jesus told him when he sent him home, "Don't go into the village."*

Apparently, this man did not live in Bethsaida. Although that is where his friends brought him, Jesus told this man to go home and not to return to the town. He was not to tell anyone in the town about Jesus or what He had done for him. Apparently, this man complied with Jesus' request since no statement is made otherwise. However, when he returned to his home, his family would know without a doubt that this man who was once blind could now see. How could he not tell them about Jesus?

Notes/Applications

Some people see Jesus as a type of magician able to perform fantastic miracles. Others see Him as just a means to an end—a heavenly "Santa Claus" capable of filling their wish lists. Still others are like the scribes and Pharisees, who witnessed the power of God but split hairs over rules and regulations. Perhaps, like the blind man, we acknowledge Jesus Christ but only see people "like trees, walking" and still do not recognize that we have encountered the Son of God.

Is the realization too great? Are we simply overwhelmed by His presence? This is the miracle for which the spiritual forefathers longed. Abraham yearned for the day when God would bring about a new covenant that would supersede the old. When God told Abraham he would be the father of a great nation numbering as many as the stars in the sky, He was talking about all who call Him "Father" through Jesus Christ. Because of Jesus' death on the cross, man's severed relationship with God could finally be restored.

How do we perceive Jesus, the Son of Man and Son of God? Do we seek Him for what He can do for us, or for Who He is? Our prayer must be that our eyes be completely opened to the reality of Jesus as our Lord, Savior, and King.

Mark 8:27–30

8:27 *Then Jesus and his disciples went to the villages around Caesarea Philippi. On the way he asked his disciples, "Who do people say I am?"*

Jesus and His disciples left the region near Bethsaida and traveled to the region around Caesarea Philippi, about twenty-five miles north. As they walked along, Jesus asked the central question that surrounded His ministry and His teaching. These twelve men, personally chosen to be His followers, had been privileged to observe His actions and to receive His personal instruction. Jesus engaged them in conversation with a broad question, asking them what people said about His identity: "Who do people say I am?"

8:28 *They answered him, "Some say you are John the Baptizer, others Elijah, still others one of the prophets."*

Interestingly, they responded with the same answers recorded in Mark six. Herod had heard of Jesus and questioned his court about this man's identity.

> [14]*King Herod heard about Jesus, because Jesus' name had become well-known. Some people were saying, "John the Baptizer has come back to life. That's why he has the power to perform these miracles."* [15]*Others said, "He is Elijah." Still others said, "He is a prophet like one of the other prophets."* [16]*But when Herod heard about it, he said, "I had John's head cut off, and he has come back to life!"* (Mark 6:14–16)

Obviously, Herod, convinced that Jesus was John the Baptizer, was burdened with guilt for executing an innocent man. The disciples' answer indicated that public sentiment agreed with Herod—that the predominant opinion was that Jesus was John the Baptizer returned to life. Others contended that Jesus was one of the prophets.

8:29 *He asked them, "But who do you say I am?" Peter answered him, "You are the Messiah!"*

Now, Jesus redirected His question. It no longer concerned others but became personal. When Jesus asked, "Who do you say I am?" Peter, the outspoken leader of the Twelve, answered, "You are the Messiah."

With this answer, a great barrier crumbled. For the first time, the disciples realized that Jesus was the Christ. Peter was finally aware that he stood in the presence of the one promised by the prophets of old. Jesus was the fulfillment of Old Testament prophecies. No longer was He simply Jesus, the carpenter turned rabbi, but he was Jesus the Christ, God's Anointed.

Just as the populace concluded that Jesus was John the Baptist, Elijah, or another prophet, the disciples' revelation of Jesus as the Christ did not unveil full understanding of His role. This was yet to come.

Peter's confession offered hope that mankind might perceive the reality of Jesus and His unique position in the history of God's creation.

8:30 *He ordered them not to tell anyone about him.*

Jesus acknowledged that Peter was correct. Matthew's gospel gives us more detail on this dialogue. *"¹⁶Simon Peter answered, 'You are the Messiah, the Son of the living God!' ¹⁷Jesus replied, 'Simon, son of Jonah, you are blessed! No human revealed this to you, but my Father in heaven revealed it to you' "* (Matthew 16:16–17).

The disciples' perception of Jesus was no longer shrouded in a spiritual fog. Surely, in the time between that heated dialogue in the boat and this walk to Caesarea Philippi, the disciples must have had occasion to discuss recent events among themselves and to recall everything they had experienced along this faith journey.

However, now that His disciples more fully understood their teacher's true identity, Jesus reiterated that they were to tell no one about Him. He sternly commanded them to be quiet about this revelation that He was the Christ.

Notes/Applications

At last, the disciples began to perceive that Jesus really was the Christ. However, even Peter's bold, remarkable statement could not be credited to his own understanding. *"Simon, son of Jonah, you are blessed! No human revealed this to you, but my Father in heaven revealed it to you" (Matthew 16:17)*. The time had finally come for God to drop the scales from the disciples' eyes that they might see the Lord.

Once Peter proclaimed the truth about Jesus' identity, things started to change for this ragtag band of twelve men. Suddenly, they looked at their leader with new eyes. The events of the past two years now seemed to fall into place and to make sense to their finite minds. They had literally been in the presence of God!

A cloud of rebellion continues to block the truth that knowledge comes only through Jesus Christ. Down through the centuries of time, we hear Jesus calling, "Are you blind and deaf? Don't you remember?" *(Mark 8:18)*.

We ourselves remain a strangely dense and uncomprehending people. We argue for hours on end, debating the identity of Jesus with the Bible in our laps. We love to debate what other people say about His identity, but, God forbid, we should emphatically proclaim that we believe the truth of the Bible. For those who fail to accept Jesus as Lord and Savior, their eternal fate is written on the pages of God's Word and declared from the lips of the living Word. Have we come to the same conclusion as Peter that we can exclaim, "You are the Christ"?

Mark 8:31–38

8:31 *Then he began to teach them that the Son of Man would have to suffer a lot. He taught them that he would be rejected by the leaders, the chief priests, and the scribes. He would be killed, but after three days he would come back to life.*

Now the blinders were off. His closest followers, the Twelve, understood that He was the Christ, the promised Messiah, and with that meager beginning, Jesus began intense instruction regarding His mission. Jesus again identified Himself as the Son of Man. Although He had just acknowledged the truth about His identity, He kept this in the background. In the Jewish culture, the word *Messiah* carried a host of meanings that involved a king and a kingdom. There were battles to be fought. The Messiah was expected to break the yoke of political bondage.

While Jesus' message concerned the kingdom of God, it was not the type of kingdom the Jews expected. Jesus told His disciples that He, the Son of Man, must suffer many things, be killed, and rise again after three days. Jesus' disciples had come so far. They now acknowledged that He was the Christ, but they still perceived this in an earthly, historical sense. What Jesus now told them was impossible for them to comprehend.

All of these things had to happen. They were necessary to complete God's plan of redemption. The Greek word δει (day) means "necessary, as binding."[4] The entire purpose of Jesus' life was directed by the divine necessity that was placed on Him for the sins of man. This was a "necessity established by the counsel and decree of God, especially by that purpose of his which relates to the salvation of men by the intervention of Christ and which is disclosed in the Old Testament prophecies."[5]

As noted many times, Jesus faced the open opposition of the religious leaders of His day. As the Son of Man, He would succumb to an angry religious establishment. He would be rejected by the scribes and Pharisees. The Sanhedrin, the religious and civil "supreme court" comprised of the scribes, Pharisees, and Sadducees, would stand in judgment of the Son of Man. Jesus knew these people from the first day He met them. He knew their motive, and He knew what fate awaited Him at their hands.

8:32 *He told them very clearly what he meant. Peter took him aside and objected to this.*

Jesus spoke plainly to His disciples about these very disturbing developments. This was no time for allegory and parable. Only the straightforward facts were necessary. Peter took Jesus aside and rebuked Him for His negative attitude. We can just imagine Peter, probably physically bigger and stronger than Jesus, putting his arm around His leader and walking with Him to a place away from the others and earnestly admonishing Jesus for His dire predictions.

8:33 *Jesus turned, looked at his disciples, and objected to what Peter said. Jesus said, "Get out of my way, Satan! You aren't thinking the way God thinks but the way humans think."*

Jesus did not accept Peter's rebuke but turned around and brought the other disciples into the conversation. He confronted Peter, scolding him for failing to understand that little phrase "would have to" of which He spoke. Jesus knew that these events needed to occur.

Jesus' words must have pierced Peter to the core. Peter had just declared that Jesus was the Christ. However, Jesus now strongly reprimanded Peter by identifying Satan as the source behind the question.[6] Even at the poignancy of this moment when Peter recognized Jesus' true identity, Satan would do anything to obstruct once again the disciples' perception of Jesus and ultimately to destroy God's plan to redeem the lost. Even though Peter meant well, he forgot that he was addressing the Son of Man. Peter still peered through the eyes of his physical existence and could, therefore, not conceive of these things ever happening to the one Who had demonstrated so much control over His circumstances.

8:34 *Then Jesus called the crowd to himself along with his disciples. He said to them, "Those who want to follow me must say no to the things they want, pick up their crosses, and follow me.*

Jesus now gathered His disciples along with the rest of the people who had traveled with Him to Caesarea Philippi. He clearly challenged all who wished to follow Him by redefining the cost of discipleship. No longer would it suffice to simply follow Jesus around, listening to His teachings and marveling at His works. From this point forward, Jesus required an ardent, passionate commitment, which would yield heavy consequences. Selfish indulgences were to be sacrificed for the sole purpose of pursuing the will of God. The concept of taking up one's cross would not be fully appreciated until the fulfillment of His words recorded in verse thirty-one.

8:35 *Those who want to save their lives will lose them. But those who lose their lives for me and for the Good News will save them.*

While Jesus no longer spoke in parables, there was a strong paradoxical element in His discourse on discipleship. The losing and saving of one's life seemed unclear according to natural human understanding, but it is clear that Jesus meant every word that He said.

Most of us desire ways to make our lives easier and more enjoyable. We seek a better paying job to buy a bigger house and a newer car, but to Jesus, the end of such a self-centered existence is a life that is lost. Jesus urged His disciples to forget about making their human existence as smooth as possible. To follow Jesus is to "lose" oneself in Him. The road of life may be rough, often with staggering blows and grievous experiences, but in the end, abandoning our own will and desires for those of Christ and His gospel brings complete joy and fulfillment.

⁸It's far more than that! I consider everything else worthless because I'm much better off knowing Christ Jesus my Lord. It's because of him that I think of everything as worthless. I threw it all away in order to gain Christ ⁹and to have a relationship with him. This means that I didn't receive God's approval by obeying his laws. The opposite is true! I have God's approval through faith in Christ. This is the approval that comes from God and is based on faith. (Philippians 3:8–9)

8:36 *What good does it do for people to win the whole world yet lose their lives?*

The stakes in this game of life are high. Jesus taught the disciples the consequences of self-centered living. The constant pursuit of personal gain indicates a person's will to control the circumstances of his life, but it is foolish for man to believe that he is in control of anything. One stroke of unexpected misfortune can remove an entire life's work from man's control and result in an impoverished spirit, bereft of joy, happiness, and salvation. The ending of every person's life renders useless all of man's frantic efforts to control his life and to avoid the eternal God. Life in such an existence is futile, self-defeating, and eternally condemned. Consider Jesus' parable of the rich man.

¹⁶A rich man had land that produced good crops. ¹⁷He thought, "What should I do? I don't have enough room to store my crops." ¹⁸He said, "I know what I'll do. I'll tear down my barns and build bigger ones so that I can store all my grain and goods in them. ¹⁹Then I'll say to myself, 'You've stored up a lot of good things for years to come. Take life easy, eat, drink, and enjoy yourself.' ²⁰But God said to him, "You fool! I will demand your life from you tonight! Now who will get what you've accumulated?" ²¹That's how it is when a person has material riches but is not rich in his relationship with God. (Luke 12:16–21)

The implications of Jesus' statement are clear. Those who adopt such an arrogant perspective do so at the peril of their souls. There is no comparison on the balance sheet of life—one's soul is far more valuable than all the wealth in the world.

8:37 *Or what should a person give in exchange for life?*

Jesus concluded with a very simple question to emphasize His point. What could a man give in exchange for his soul? What price could be placed on someone's immortality? This rhetorical question in light of Jesus' previous statements was already answered. The eternal value of a man's soul far outweighed the wealth and power that this world system could offer.

8:38 *If people are ashamed of me and what I say in this unfaithful and sinful generation, the Son of Man will be ashamed of those people when he comes with the holy angels in his Father's glory."*

Jesus explained the personal nature of real life choices. Choosing the world and all it offered would be to deny the salvation offered by Jesus, God's Anointed One: "You unfaithful people! Don't you know that love for this evil world is hatred toward God? Whoever wants to be a friend of this world is an enemy of God" (*James 4:4*). Jesus would ultimately deny those who denied Him. What a terrifying statement! Jesus opened His discourse by stating the cost of discipleship and ended it by explaining the holy judgment for those who do not follow Him.

Note the end-times tone of this statement. Jesus would enter the court of judgment with God the Father and His holy angels. He revealed that the term *Son of Man* did, in fact, contain elements of a political kingdom: "In my visions during the night, I saw among the clouds in heaven someone like the Son of Man. He came to the Ancient One, who has lived for endless years, and was presented to him" (*Daniel 7:13*).

What a change from the suffering Son of Man seen in Mark 8:31.

Notes/Applications

With the declaration of His true identity, Jesus told the disciples about the approaching fearsome events, and He then zeroed in on the crux of His message: "Those who want to save their lives will lose them. But those who lose their lives for me and for the Good News will save them" (*Mark 8:35*).

Strange words indeed. So much of what Christ said was a paradox. To gain your life, you must lose it. To be rich in this life, you must store up treasure in heaven. To truly live, you must die to self. Blessed are those who mourn. Give, and it will be given to you.

While studying this passage, we can easily imagine ourselves among that first-century crowd or among the disciples. We have stumbled along blindly with them, ignorant of God's purposes even when Jesus spelled them out for us. Now that we have traveled with these people over the hills and through the valleys of Galilee, we come to the realization that Jesus is the Christ.

However, with that revelation fresh in our minds, we are confronted with the cost of such knowledge. Discipleship, following Jesus, comes at a cost. The challenge Jesus lays on the human heart seems overwhelming. We despair at the thought of trying to measure up to such standards. Although Jesus declares that the value of one person's soul is worth more than the world's riches, the cost of following Him seems too high a price to pay.

How can we possibly be His disciples? We journey through this life attempting to reconcile the sacred and the profane into a peaceful coexistence. We want Jesus, but we also want the things this world offers. We want to follow Jesus, but we also want to follow our own reasoning so that we can have the respect and praise of men. We may secretly cringe at the thought of being labeled a fanatic, one too conspicuous in Christian discipleship because we do not want to stand out from the crowd so starkly. Then, we hear the Spirit pricking our hearts with the eternal words of Christ: "If people are ashamed of me and what I say in this unfaithful and sinful generation, the Son of Man will be ashamed of those people when he comes with the holy angels in his Father's glory."

So, let us ask ourselves: What will it profit us if we gain the entire world yet lose our souls? And let us challenge ourselves: Will we die to ourselves in order to truly live?

Jesus' Journeys: Chapter Eight

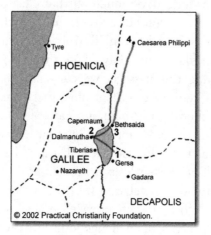

© 2002 Practical Christianity Foundation.

1. Jesus started on the eastern shore of the Sea of Galilee.
2. Jesus traveled by boat to the western shore and Dalmanutha.
3. Jesus traveled by boat to the eastern side and Bethsaida.
4. Jesus walked with His disciples to the region of Caesarea Philippi.

Mark 9:1–7

9:1 *He said to them, "I can guarantee this truth: Some people who are standing here will not die until they see the kingdom of God arrive with power."*

This verse better serves as a conclusion to the discourse in chapter eight than as an introduction to the following verses. After clarifying that the Son of Man would come "with the holy angels in his Father's glory" *(Mark 8:38)*, Jesus concluded His discourse with this statement, which has been a source of controversy for centuries. Interpretations vary widely regarding the event that would mark fulfillment of these prophetic words and range from Christ's resurrection to the destruction of Jerusalem and from the outpouring of the Holy Spirit at Pentecost to Christ's glorious return at His second coming.[1]

Mark records this discourse as a part of the more intimate instruction given to the Twelve and a few others. Within the confines of this small group, Jesus declared that some of them would see "the kingdom of God arrive with power." Six days after this discourse, Jesus was transfigured in the presence of Peter, James, and John. Understanding this verse requires an overview of Mark's record of the transfiguration. These three men were privileged to see Jesus arrayed in His divine glory. The veil of the flesh was stripped away, revealing to the disciples the splendor of the Son of God. Peter, James, and John truly witnessed the circumstance described in this verse.[2]

Without doubt, this declaration described some future event. However, the fulfillment of the prophecy only six days later does not make the prophecy less valid or false. It is unnecessary, therefore, to place any further apocalyptic emphasis on this verse. We must understand that this statement by Jesus was not a profound mystery to Mark or to his mentor, Peter the apostle, but merely serves as a transition to the event recorded in the following verses.[3]

9:2 *After six days Jesus took only Peter, James, and John and led them up a high mountain where they could be alone. Jesus' appearance changed in front of them.*

Six days passed. Jesus and His disciples remained in the area of Caesarea Philippi about twenty-five miles north of Bethsaida. Jesus took His inner circle of disciples, Peter, James, and John, and left the rest of His followers behind. He chose these three men to witness the glory of Jesus the Christ. They traveled several miles and climbed a high mountain where Jesus' appearance changed; He was transfigured before their eyes.

Much debate surrounds the location of this event since the text does not specify an exact location. Traditionally, Mount Tabor has been considered the place of Jesus' transfiguration.[4] However, Mount Tabor is situated among the hills in the southern regions of Galilee overlooking the Jezreel valley, and its peak stands approximately nineteen hundred feet above sea level. The problem in accepting this location is that Mark carefully describes the travels of Jesus and His disciples. In this gospel, the discourse concerning Jesus' identity (*Mark* 8:27) took place near Caesarea Philippi, which was some distance from Mount Tabor. It is more likely, therefore, that Jesus, along with Peter, James, and John, traveled a short distance (about twelve miles) north of Caesarea Philippi toward the mountainous area near Mount Hermon, which rises approximately 9,200 feet above sea level.[5]

Whatever the specific geographical location, the event itself overshadows any peripheral speculation. High on the slope of the mountain, Jesus was transfigured before these three men. Even in English, the word *transfigured* is confined to the Christian domain, specifically representing this scene that unfolded. The Greek word μετεμορφώθη (metemorphothay) is the direct root of the English word *metamorphosis*, which is the word used to describe a caterpillar's total change in form when it enters its cocoon and later emerges as a butterfly. Jesus was visually transformed from the familiar appearance of His earthly body into a supernatural radiance revealing His deity.

9:3 *His clothes became dazzling white, whiter than anyone on earth could bleach them.*

The proof of Jesus' total transformation rested in the appearance of His clothes, which became so bright that they probably hurt the eyes of the amazed disciples. That no one on earth could match the brightness emphasizes the divine nature of what they saw. It appeared that Jesus' body was illuminated. Nothing on earth that these men had ever seen could have adequately described this transformation.

9:4 *Then Elijah and Moses appeared to them and were talking with Jesus.*

In addition to witnessing the brightness of Jesus' transformed appearance, these men saw Elijah and Moses talking with Jesus. Imagine their shock and total bewilderment. Moses had lived approximately fifteen hundred years earlier, and Elijah had prophesized around 874 to 852 B.C. during the reign of King Ahab. These two men were extremely important figures in Old Testament history, Moses as the Lawgiver and Elijah as a great prophet. Moses' death was attended by God: "⁵As the Lord had predicted, the Lord's servant Moses died in Moab. ⁶He was buried in a valley in Moab, near Beth Peor. Even today no one knows where his grave is" (*Deuteronomy 34:5–6*). Elijah never saw death but was taken by a whirlwind to heaven: "As they continued walking and talking, a fiery chariot with fiery horses separated the two of them, and Elijah went to heaven in a windstorm" (*2 Kings 2:11*).

These two Old Testament saints were alive and well as they stood in the presence of Jesus and conversed with Him. They represented the Law and the Prophets of which Jesus was the fulfillment: "Don't ever think that I came to set aside Moses' Teachings or the Prophets. I didn't come to set them aside but to make them come true" (*Matthew 5:17*).

Arrayed in His glory, Jesus discussed His imminent death in Jerusalem. "*³⁰Suddenly, both Moses and Elijah were talking with him. ³¹They appeared in heavenly glory and were discussing Jesus' approaching death and what he was about to fulfill in Jerusalem*" (*Luke 9:30–31*). Jesus did not resist His destiny but embraced it.

DIG DEEPER: *Meeting On The Mountain*

During their respective lifetimes, Moses and Elijah individually met with the Lord God on mountaintops, and the glory of Jehovah was revealed to them. Moses met the Lord on Mount Sinai ("the Mountain of God") where he received the Law on tablets of stone (*Exodus 24:12–18*). Elijah, when pursued by Jezebel's military because he had destroyed the prophets of Baal, retreated to a cave on Mount Horeb, and there He met the God Whom he served (*1 Kings 19:8–13*). Centuries later, Peter, James, and John accompanied Jesus to a mountaintop near Caesarea Philippi where they witnessed God's Messiah meeting face to face with these two great prophets of the Lord.

9:5 *Peter said to Jesus, "Rabbi, it's good that we're here. Let's put up three tents—one for you, one for Moses, and one for Elijah."*

Peter, seeing Jesus, Moses, and Elijah talking, interrupted the conversation with a suggestion. This spectacular event eclipsed all other moments in their human experience. What could possibly be better than erecting three tabernacles on the very spot—one for Jesus, one for Moses, and one for Elijah? Apparently, Peter believed that such an event as this should have been commemorated by some kind of edifice identifying the spot where this phenomenal event occurred.

9:6 *(Peter didn't know how to respond. He and the others were terrified.)*

Peter experienced a loss of words at the frightening scene that unfolded before these ordinary men. No one in all of history had seen such piercing glory. This extended beyond the scope of man's expectations, but Peter, an impulsive fisherman, felt compelled to say something to hide his fear.

9:7 *Then a cloud overshadowed them. A voice came out of the cloud and said, "This is my Son, whom I love. Listen to him!"*

On the side of a high mountain, a cloud could be expected to envelop the peak. However, this was no ordinary circumstance, and this was no ordinary cloud. It overshadowed them by covering them in the presence of the Creator, the God of Abraham, Isaac, and Jacob. This was Yahweh, Who called Moses in the burning bush *(Exodus 3:2–3)* and guided the children of Israel from bondage in Egypt to the promised land in a cloud by day and a pillar of fire by night *(Exodus 13:21)*. This was the God Who met Elijah on Mount Horeb and came to him in "a quiet, whispering voice" *(1 Kings 19:12)*. This was the Father of Jesus, Who had called the three to discipleship and with Whom they had traveled the sea and walked the hills of Galilee. This was the Father Who would give His Son for the redemption of mankind.

They heard His voice coming out of the cloud saying, "This is my Son, whom I love. Listen to him!" Again, just as He had at Jesus' baptism, the Father identified Jesus as His Son and declared Himself to be Jesus' Father. These three disciples experienced a glimpse of a realm far beyond their human and physical understanding. No wonder they were frightened. No wonder they did not know what to say.

The Father forcefully commanded, "Listen to him!" The context of the narrative and the imperative form of the verb show that the Father was reprimanding Peter for his impulsive desire to build three tents in this location to commemorate the event. From his human perspective, Peter had again tried to do the right thing but had not waited for God's leading.

Notes/Applications

Once Peter stated that Jesus was the Christ, the fulfillment of messianic Old Testament prophecy, Jesus took pains to educate His disciples about the road He must travel. That road was not a pleasant one because an agonizing death lay ahead. However, now that they understood Who He was, they needed to know why He had come. Peter, James, and John were singled out for the most important revelation about the Son of God prior to His death and resurrection. They beheld in wonder and amazement the glory of God's Son and heard it endorsed by the Father Himself.

We can relate to Peter in his awkward attempt to honor God by building tabernacles on the Mount of Transfiguration. His effort to do "the right thing" earned him another rebuke of sorts—this time from Almighty God. In his bewilderment, he tried to respond to the glory of God by a feeble human act. Are we any different? How much better it would be to wait for God's command and then do His work. When we, like Peter, attempt to maneuver situations ahead of God's will, we get ourselves into all sorts of tangles, many of which have unnecessary and serious consequences.

The children of Israel circled Mount Sinai for forty years until the grumbling generation died off in the wilderness, and a new generation sprang up. God is not in a hurry. He has all the time in the world to mold us into the men and women He created us to be, but we hinder our own spiritual growth when we try to second-guess His intentions. Like a patient teacher, He waits until we come to the end of ourselves and collapse exasperated and surrendered at His feet.

Mark 9:8–13

9:8 *Suddenly, as they looked around, they saw no one with them but Jesus.*

When confronted by the Lord God on Mount Horeb, Elijah covered his face in his cloak because God's glory was too great to behold *(1 Kings 19:13)*. Peter, James, and John may also have hidden their faces from the dazzling presence of the Almighty. Then, when they looked up, they found that they were once again alone with Jesus. No longer were they in the presence of Jesus, the glorified Son of God. They were again in the familiar presence of Jesus as they knew Him before the Transfiguration.

9:9 *On their way down the mountain, Jesus ordered them not to tell anyone what they had seen. They were to wait until the Son of Man had come back to life.*

Just as He had on previous occasions, Jesus ordered these three disciples to keep this experience private. When the demons acknowledged Jesus as the Son of God, He commanded them to be silent. Usually, when He healed a person privately, He ordered him or her not to tell anyone. Although many of His miracles were performed in the presence of a crowd, it seems as though their perception of Jesus' identity was not based on recognition of His authority as Son of God. Though He had often referred to Himself as "Son of Man," the closer people drew to the true perception of His identity as the "Son of God," the more He commanded silence. Peter, James, and John had now seen Jesus in His heavenly glory. Peter's identification of Jesus as God's Messiah was confirmed in a personal experience that Peter would never forget. The three needed no further evidence to substantiate that Jesus was the Son of the Most High God.

The command of secrecy that Jesus placed on Peter, James, and John was temporary. After the Son of Man arose from the dead, they were to proclaim this spectacular experience. Further, after

Pentecost, the Holy Spirit would command them to incorporate the event of the Lord's transfiguration in the witness that they would give to the world. When speaking of their risen Lord, they would testify of every experience that they had shared with their master as evidence of Jesus' true identity, confirming His divine origins along with His sacrifice.

> [16]When we apostles told you about the powerful coming of our Lord Jesus Christ, we didn't base our message on clever myths that we made up. Rather, we witnessed his majesty with our own eyes. [17]For example, we were eyewitnesses when he received honor and glory from God the Father and when the voice of our majestic God spoke these words to him: "This is my Son, whom I love and in whom I delight." [18]We heard that voice speak to him from heaven when we were with him on the holy mountain. (2 Peter 1:16–18)

> The Word became human and lived among us. We saw his glory. It was the glory that the Father shares with his only Son, a glory full of kindness and truth. (John 1:14)

9:10 *They kept in mind what he said but argued among themselves what he meant by "come back to life."*

The three disciples obeyed Jesus by keeping silent about what might have been the most astounding experience that any human had ever witnessed. While they vividly remembered the experience, they probably had difficulty in comprehending its truest meaning until after the resurrection. They debated among themselves what Jesus meant when He spoke of the Son of Man rising from the dead.

Within the scope of Jewish thinking, there was life after death. However, this life existed in the murky shadows of some netherworld that was never clearly defined. The Jewish teaching held that there was a general resurrection during the last days but that it was not a personal resurrection. The Old Testament speaks of the place of the dead when it uses the Hebrew word *sheol*. In the New Testament and the Septuagint, the Greek word used is *hades*, which is sometimes translated as "grave" or "pit," indicating the location of the soul after physical death without distinguishing between the righteous or the wicked. It was simply the realm of the dead. All souls ended up there. Therefore, Peter, James, and John could not conceive what Jesus meant by "coming back to life." As far as their Jewish backgrounds were concerned, there was no return from this place. It was the permanent abode of departed souls. As a result, the main topic of conversation on their return to Caesarea Philippi did not center on the remarkable event that they witnessed but on what Jesus meant by stating that the Son of Man must rise from the dead.

9:11 *So they asked him, "Don't the scribes say that Elijah must come first?"*

The three disciples did not ask Jesus to expound on the concept of physical resurrection but on why Elijah would precede the Messiah. For some reason, they avoided the most pressing question that could have potentially changed their entire perspective on life and death. Perhaps the concept was too weighty for them to grasp despite the fact that they had just seen Moses and Elijah talking with Jesus.

In their study of the Scriptures, the scribes had determined that Elijah would precede the "day of the Lord": "I'm going to send you the prophet Elijah before that very terrifying day of the Lord comes" (*Malachi 4:5*). The disciples knew of this prophecy but did not understand its meaning. Perhaps they wondered if they had just experienced the fulfillment of this prophecy. It was much safer to engage Jesus in a theological discussion on the coming of Elijah than to probe the perplexing question concerning resurrection from the dead.

9:12 *Jesus said to them, "Elijah is coming first and will put everything in order again. But in what sense was it written that the Son of Man must suffer a lot and be treated shamefully?*

Jesus' answer confirmed the validity of the scribes' teaching about Elijah preceding the coming of the Son of Man. Jesus then brought them back to the issue of the treatment of the Son of Man, the subject that most occupied His mind at this time. Jesus essentially questioned them, "If you know what is written of Elijah, do you not also know what is written of the Son of Man?" Jesus stated clearly that the Scriptures testify that the Son of Man "must suffer a lot and be treated shamefully."

How could the scribes, as well as the disciples, know about Elijah but not about the Son of Man? Generally, the scribes taught that the Son of Man, God's Messiah, was a politically powerful figure who would destroy Israel's enemies and restore the kingdom of David. While this teaching was ultimately true, they had ignored references in their Scriptures to the Son of Man as a suffering servant *(Psalm 22; Isaiah 53)*. Nevertheless, Jesus reminded the three disciples that those passages served as a precursor to the Messiah and that those Scriptures must also be fulfilled.

9:13 *Indeed, I can guarantee that Elijah has come. Yet, people treated him as they pleased, as Scripture says about him."*

Jesus made a cryptic statement. He had said that Elijah must come first, confirming their understanding of the scribes' teaching, and then He declared that Elijah had already come. Clearly, this reference referred to John the Baptizer: "If you are willing to accept their message, John is the Elijah who was to come" *(Matthew 11:14)*. While John the Baptizer was not Elijah come back to earth, he was God's prophet who bore his witness much like Elijah had. They were similar in their appearance, in their styles of speaking, and in their steadfast focus on God's message. In the first chapter of Mark, John the Baptizer baptized people in the Jordan River and called them to repentance for their sins, but he also clarified that he was not the Messiah but the Messiah's predecessor. When Jesus came to John for baptism, he immediately recognized Jesus as the one Who came after him.

Notes/Applications

When Jesus spoke of the Son of Man rising from the dead, Peter, James, and John asked about Elijah. The idea that their long-awaited Messiah might die could not be broached. He was going to overthrow the Roman rule and restore a Davidic kingdom to the Jews, or so they thought. The disciples did not yet realize that the kingdom of God that Jesus described would not be a physical kingdom on this earth. They did not grasp that suffering and death were a part of God's plan for His beloved Son much less for themselves.

Who of us likes to think of suffering and hardship? It is an unpleasant topic, something we pray God will hold off from our lives. Oftentimes, though, God allows suffering in the lives of His saints to mature them spiritually. The apostle Paul knew all about suffering because he had been shipwrecked, beaten, imprisoned, homeless, hungry, and without adequate clothing. Everywhere he went, people hurled insults at him and sometimes plotted to kill him, yet he remained convinced that what he had to say for the sake of the gospel was eternally worthwhile: "I consider our present sufferings insignificant compared to the glory that will soon be revealed to us" (Romans 8:18).

At what times has our relationship with Jesus been the most trying yet also the most precious and dynamic? Has it not been during times of intense adversity?

> [16]*That is why we are not discouraged. Though outwardly we are wearing out, inwardly we are renewed day by day.* [17]*Our suffering is light and temporary and is producing for us an eternal glory that is greater than anything we can imagine.* [18]*We don't look for things that can be seen but for things that can't be seen. Things that can be seen are only temporary. But things that can't be seen last forever.* (2 Corinthians 4:16–18)

When we ponder the coming glory and Christ's abundant life already bestowed in immeasurable portions, our trials suddenly appear as merely a bridge to an eternity with Him:

O wondrous sight! O vision fair
A type of those bright rays on high
Of glory that the church shall share,
Which Christ upon the mountain shows,
Where brighter than the sun He glows!

With shining face and bright array,
Christ deigns to manifest that day
What glory shall be theirs above
Who joy in God with perfect love.

And faithful hearts are raised on high
By this great vision's mystery;
For which in joyful strains we raise
The voice of prayer, the hymn of praise.

O Father, with the eternal Son,
And Holy Spirit, ever One,
Vouchsafe to bring us by Thy grace
To see Thy glory face to face.[6]

Mark 9:14–18

9:14 *When they came to the other disciples, they saw a large crowd around them. Some scribes were arguing with them.*

When Jesus, Peter, James, and John returned to the area of Caesarea Philippi and joined the other disciples, a large gathering surrounded the other nine disciples. In the middle of the crowd, the scribes argued with His disciples. Jesus, of course, knew their hearts and preferred to debate with these teachers of the law Himself. Perhaps, in Jesus' absence, the disciples felt capable, maybe even duty-bound, to carry on the debate with the scribes. We can imagine Jesus wading into the crowd toward these chosen friends, anxious to weigh in on the debate and to address the scribe's questions directly.

9:15 *All the people were very surprised to see Jesus and ran to welcome him.*

When the people saw Jesus, they were thrilled to see the teacher again. They ran toward Him and greeted Him with great gladness. When Jesus was present, He was the focus of attention, drawing both friend and foe to Him. None were happier to see Him than the disciples.

9:16 *Jesus asked the scribes, "What are you arguing about with them?"*

When Jesus arrived, He directly questioned the scribes concerning their debate with His disciples. He wanted the scribes to bring their arguments to Him. Jesus was the one they despised. He was the one Who had repeatedly made them look foolish in the "wisdom" of their Judaic heritage. Therefore, He wanted that continuing debate brought to Him and not to His disciples, who were ill equipped to handle the sly traps the scribes would lay for them.

9:17 *A man in the crowd answered, "Teacher, I brought you my son. He is possessed by a spirit that won't let him talk.*

Before the scribes could answer Jesus, another person interrupted the discussion. He had brought to Jesus his son, who had a spirit preventing him from speaking. Was this the topic of discussion among the disciples and the scribes? It might have been that this man, accompanied by his mute son, had become the subject of the disciples' interaction with the scribes.

9:18 *Whenever the spirit brings on a seizure, it throws him to the ground. Then he foams at the mouth, grinds his teeth, and becomes exhausted. I asked your disciples to force the spirit out, but they didn't have the power to do it."*

The man further described his son's condition. The spirit seized the boy's body with excessive violence and threw him down, at which time the boy would foam at the mouth, grind his teeth, and become exhausted. It must have been heartbreaking for a father to watch helplessly while his son thrashed on the ground.

While Jesus and the three disciples were away, the remaining disciples apparently attempted to carry on the ministry. In the past, they had cast out demons and healed all sorts of illnesses. They tried to answer the plea of this father, but in this case, they failed. The father told Jesus that he had sought help from the disciples, but they could not cast out the demon.

Notes/Applications

Fresh from their mountaintop experience with the transfigured Christ, Peter, James, and John were plunged back into the river of human misery. When a man brought his demon-possessed son to be exorcised, the other disciples could not cast out the spirit.

Jesus fought the crowds to get to the center of the controversy with the scribes and found this desperate man and the disappointed disciples. It is easy to imagine the sheepish look on their faces as they admitted their failure.

None of us will have a perfect track record as we grow in our spiritual lives. Though Jesus chided the disciples for their faithless response (*verse 19*), it was no doubt part of their spiritual schooling, and God used this failure to remind them of the source of their power, their dependence on Him, and the reason for the miracles—to glorify the master.

Later, after Jesus had ascended to heaven, these same apostles were known for their powerful ministry, such as the time Peter and John went to the temple and saw a lame man begging: "Peter said to him, 'I don't have any money, but I'll give you what I do have. Through the power of Jesus Christ from Nazareth, walk!' " (*Acts 3:6*). Peter took him by the hand, and the man stood to his feet "walking, jumping, and praising God" (*Acts 3:8*).

God has much in store for us as we grow in the likeness of His Son. Though spiritual setbacks will come, we know that He leads us by His right hand: "My soul clings to you. Your right hand supports me" (*Psalm 63:8*).

Mark 9:19–27

9:19 *Jesus said to them, "You unbelieving generation! How long must I be with you? How long must I put up with you? Bring him to me!"*

Jesus' response to this man and to the futile efforts of His disciples was understandable frustration. When thrust back into the crowds that attended His every move, Jesus was again confronted with their blindness and inadequacy. The disciples themselves were at a loss to respond to this man's plight.

We know from Luke's gospel that Moses, Elijah, and Jesus had been discussing the road that the Son of Man must take *(Luke 9:30, 31)*. Jesus knew this road led to His condemnation in Jerusalem as a blasphemer and ultimately to the cross. As a result, Jesus cried out in grief at the human condition and questioned how long He must endure such a faithless generation. This generation was blessed beyond all others because they personally participated in the life of the Son of Man. They heard the words flow from His lips and saw great miracles, yet they failed miserably to understand the person they followed and were blind to His divinity. Jesus expressed the burden of being surrounded by people with an overwhelming lack of perception and faith by saying, "How long must I put up with you?"

Finally, Jesus asked for the son to be brought to him. He would personally respond to this need. The phrase "bring him to me" could be translated "carry him to me." Apparently, the boy possessed by the evil spirit had to be forcibly brought to Jesus. He could not or would not come voluntarily.

9:20 *They brought the boy to him. As soon as the spirit saw Jesus, it threw the boy into convulsions. He fell on the ground, rolled around, and foamed at the mouth.*

The man and possibly the disciples brought the boy to Jesus. As in previous instances of demon possession, the demonic spirit was terribly frightened when brought face-to-face with Jesus, Son of Man and Son of God. As a result, the spirit showed his fear with a violent demonstration, devastating the body of the young boy. The boy literally convulsed and foamed at the mouth as this demon contended with the master of the universe.

9:21 *Jesus asked his father, "How long has he been like this?" The father replied, "He has been this way since he was a child.*

Jesus was not at all fazed by the demon's violent demonstration. Despite the weakness in His disciples, there was no reason for concern on Jesus' part. The adversary had never been able to withstand the Lord's command. Jesus calmly asked the father how long the boy had endured this condition. The father answered that this condition had plagued his son since he was a young child.

9:22 *The demon has often thrown him into fire or into water to destroy him. If it's possible for you, put yourself in our place, and help us!"*

The father further informed Jesus of the intensity of the demon's activity in his son. There were times when the boy had been thrown into fire and into water, apparently in an attempt by the demon to destroy him. The son's condition was extreme.

The father had already been disappointed by the disciples' failure to restore his son, so in an effort to lessen any further disappointment, he carefully petitioned Jesus in desperation to see if there might be something—anything—that Jesus could do. Perhaps the man did not doubt Jesus' compassion toward the needy but doubted His ability to free the boy from the demon's clutches.

9:23 *Jesus said to him, "As far as possibilities go, everything is possible for the person who believes."*

Jesus responded with a clear statement that probed the depth of the man's faith. The man had expressed a conditional doubt about Jesus' ability to answer his plea. Jesus refocused the issue on the man's faith. The man obviously believed that Jesus might heal his son, but Jesus now challenged the father to believe that his son's ravaged body would be restored to health.

9:24 *The child's father cried out at once, "I believe! Help my lack of faith."*

The depth of this man's anguish was expressed in one of the most honest prayers in Scripture. It was a prayer of faith that acknowledged a struggle with doubt. This prayer reflects the condition of every believer who has walked the face of the earth. No matter where we are on our journey of faith, whether we are a new Christian recently rescued from the burden of sin or an older saint who has won and lost many battles of faith, we can all relate to this man's prayer: "I believe! Help my lack of faith." With tears streaming down his face, he looked at the face of Jesus and confessed that he was doubtful even as he dared to ask for his son to be healed and restored to wholeness.

9:25 *When Jesus saw that a crowd was running to the scene, he gave an order to the evil spirit. He said, "You spirit that won't let him talk, I command you to come out of him and never enter him again."*

It is interesting to observe how Jesus proceeded with the healing. He noticed the crowd running toward Him, eager to see His miracles. Those close enough to overhear the dialogue between Jesus and the distraught man anticipated the result, but Jesus, always interested in limiting the exaggeration of His reputation, seemed eager to help the boy before the crowd increased.

Jesus ordered the evil spirit to come out of the boy. This is the same term that Mark used previously when Jesus rebuked a demon in the man at the synagogue (*Mark 1:25*), when Jesus rebuked the wind (*Mark 4:39*), and when Jesus strongly admonished the evil spir-

its to keep silent about His identity as the Son of God *(Mark 3:12).*
Jesus' command to the evil spirit was direct and final. The spirit was
to leave the boy and never enter him again. Jesus procured a complete healing for the boy and his anguished father. The boy would
never again be plagued by this demon.

9:26 *The evil spirit screamed, shook the child violently, and*
came out. The boy looked as if he were dead, and everyone said,
"He's dead!"

The spirit, unable to survive Jesus' command, gave one desperate
demonstration of his limited power. The boy's body endured a final
major convulsion. He lay so still that those close to him thought he
was dead. In the process of Jesus' healing the young boy, it appeared,
perhaps, that the demon had won this confrontation with the powerful Son of God.

9:27 *Jesus took his hand and helped him to stand up.*

Jesus disregarded the conclusions of those around Him. He simply
took the boy by the hand and restored life and strength to his ravaged body. The boy rose with the life that had been preserved by his
Savior. Never again would he fear the destruction of a demon. Never
again would he be thrown in fire or water by an evil spirit. The boy
rose with gratitude to the one Who had delivered him from such
terrible bondage. He rose a whole person.

Notes/Applications
Jesus once again discussed the faith issue. Frustrated with the
"faithless generation," He, nonetheless, addressed the father of
the demon-possessed boy with compassion by saying, "As far as
possibilities go, everything is possible for the person who believes"
(verse 23).

What wonderful words! And how we long to believe them in the
depth of our souls. We can relate to the man's response—desperate

to believe yet afraid he did not "have it in him." The truth is, this man did not have it in him. In this passage, two miracles actually occurred in that Jesus transformed both father and son. He set the boy free from the demon's possession, and He released the father from overwhelming doubt by equipping him with the faith to believe. *"Because of the kindness that God has shown me, I ask you not to think of yourselves more highly than you should. Instead, your thoughts should lead you to use good judgment based on what God has given each of you as believers"* (Romans 12:3).

As Christians, we acknowledge Jesus to be our Savior and Lord. We confess the reality of the forgiveness we received at salvation, but that does not remove our vulnerability in falling prey to doubt. It does not completely unveil the mysterious, startling glory of the God we worship. With Paul, we, too, must admit that we "see through a glass darkly" (1 Corinthians 13:12, KJV). While we are "new creations" (2 Corinthians 5:17), we continually work out our salvation "with fear and trembling" (Philippians 2:12). Thankfully, God does not require us to conjure up an optimal level of faith before responding to our needs, but He wants us to exercise the faith that He has endowed to us. Faith is not our tool to operate but God's gift operating within us.

In what area of our lives do we need Jesus' touch? No matter where we find ourselves in our journey of faith, the Lord can untangle the web of conflicting emotions that strangle our spirits as we commit our longings to Him and cry out, "I believe! Help my lack of faith."

Mark 9:28-32

9:28 *When Jesus went into a house, his disciples asked him privately, "Why couldn't we force the spirit out of the boy?"*

Jesus and His disciples withdrew from the crowds in Caesarea Philippi and entered a house to face the disconcerting reality of their failure to cast the demon out of the boy. They had restored health to many when Jesus sent them out two by two *(Mark 6:7–12)*. Had their power left them? Had their faith failed?

In Mark six, Jesus had commissioned the disciples to perform a specific ministry. Not only did Jesus describe the ministry that He expected them to perform, but He "gave them authority over evil spirits" *(Mark 6:7)*. Jesus gave His disciples a task with the means to accomplish it. Was this power now withdrawn?

9:29 *He told them, "This kind of spirit can be forced out only by prayer."*

Jesus did not imply that the disciples' ministry had ceased. Rather, this violent demon required an additional measure of spiritual preparation accompanied by prayer and fasting. A special time of focused prayer was required to achieve the necessary spiritual strength to combat the adversary. It was clear that this demon possessed unusual power. The disciples' failure did not mean that they would be unable to perform such special healings in the future.

This experience provided Jesus an opportunity to respond to the anguished pleas of this father on behalf of his beleaguered son. It would further establish the validity of Jesus' power before the scribes and Pharisees. While the disciples had performed many miracles, it was necessary to confirm that Jesus was the source of their ability. They needed frequent reminding that "you can't produce anything without me" *(John 15:5)*.

9:30 *They left that place and were passing through Galilee. Jesus did not want anyone to know where he was*

Jesus and His small group of disciples left the area of Caesarea Philippi and traveled southwest to Capernaum. They traveled as inconspicuously as possible because Jesus evidently did not want to be hampered by the crowds. More and more, Jesus withdrew from the crowd to devote time to teaching His disciples. Difficult times lay ahead, and they needed to know the Father's plan for sending His Son into the world.

9:31 *because he was teaching his disciples. He taught them, "The Son of Man will be betrayed and handed over to people. They will kill him, but on the third day he will come back to life."*

Jesus spoke for the second time of His grim future and for the third time of His resurrection. In Mark 8:29, Peter declared that Jesus was the Messiah, and then Jesus predicted His death and resurrection. Then, after the Transfiguration, Jesus warned Peter, James, and John to keep silent about what they had just witnessed until the Son of Man was risen from the dead. Now, Jesus once again confirmed the reality of His impending death and resurrection.

9:32 *The disciples didn't understand what he meant and were afraid to ask him.*

Jesus' disciples did not understand His words. Nevertheless, they were afraid to seek an explanation. After so much time with Jesus, the disciples had progressed only marginally in their ability to perceive through the fog that enclosed their minds and hearts. Although they could hear His words, they could not comprehend their meaning because His concept of "coming back to life" was foreign to them (*verse 10*).

When the disciples did not understand, why were they afraid to ask Him? It seemed that their relationship with their teacher involved a strong mixture of respect, awe, and even fear. Jesus lived beyond the scope of their human frailties and experience, and His words and deeds did not correlate with what they understood about life and death.

Notes/Applications

When Jesus said, "This kind of spirit can be forced out only by prayer," He informed His followers that a unique closeness to God was required to command the demon to exit the boy. However, we must be very careful not to assume too much after reading this passage.

Often, we search for formulas by which we can evaluate our spiritual success or predict how situations will transpire. We convince ourselves that if we live by the letter of the Word and follow its "formulas," God will then grant us our wishes. How earthbound are our motives! How foolish and simplistic is our view of a sovereign God, Whose thoughts and ways are beyond our own!

> [8]"*My thoughts are not your thoughts,*
>   *and my ways are not your ways," declares the Lord.*
> [9] "*Just as the heavens are higher than the earth,*
>   *so my ways are higher than your ways,*
>   *and my thoughts are higher than your thoughts."*
>   (*Isaiah 55:8–9*)

A saved loved one is diagnosed with a terminal disease. If we conducted a three-day fast and a ten-minute prayer session every hour for those three days, would we then be able to secure our beloved one's cure? The answer registers as both yes and no. Yes, if physical healing is God's will. But what if God chooses to heal by carrying His child through the portals of death to a place where there is no more sickness or sorrow? Would not our loved one be totally healed in the most glorious sense? "*He will wipe every tear from their eyes. There won't be any more death. There won't be any grief, crying, or pain, because the first things have disappeared*" (*Revelation 21:4*). To God, the answer is yes. To us, the answer is bittersweet. If there is one thing that Scripture teaches, it is the clear, perplexing fact that God does not operate according to our understanding. He is sovereign, and He does not answer to any human (*Job 36:22–26*).

The word for this passage is caution—caution that we do not permit ourselves to subscribe to any extremities. If the Holy Spirit draws us to pray and fast for a spiritual or physical breakthrough, we must obey Him, trusting that God desires this exercise of faith. However, we must not subscribe to the fallacy that God is required to meet our demands or our ideals because of our works, for we dare not presume to know the mind of God.

We do not really know why the disciples were unable to cast out this demon, but we do know that Jesus did, and, by that singular, powerful act, He once again proved His identity as the Son of God.

Mark 9:33–37

9:33 *Then they came to Capernaum. While Jesus was at home, he asked the disciples, "What were you arguing about on the road?"*

Jesus and His disciples finally arrived in Capernaum, the city that had been the center of Jesus' Galilean ministry. There was something on Jesus' mind. During the journey, He had reiterated that He was to die at the hands of the religious leaders. The disciples could not understand this message and were afraid to discuss this with Him. However, there was something they did discuss, and Jesus questioned them about the matter.

9:34 *They were silent. On the road they had argued about who was the greatest.*

The disciples did not answer Jesus because they had not been discussing His impending death. Jesus desired for the Twelve to understand the difficulty of the immediate future. Ironically, the disciples were more concerned about their status in the coming kingdom. Since they clearly knew Jesus to be the Messiah, they expected Him to fulfill the Old Testament prophecies and free Israel from Roman domination. He would ascend the throne of David. These twelve men kept silent because they did not want to acknowledge the dispute fueled by their self-serving ambitions.

The journey from Caesarea Philippi would have taken several days. It seems as though Jesus may have often walked ahead while the Twelve followed at some distance, enabling them to have a private discussion. However, just as Jesus knew the thoughts of the Pharisees when they sought to trap Him, He also knew the thoughts of His closest friends.

9:35 *He sat down and called the twelve apostles. He told them, "Whoever wants to be the most important person must take the last place and be a servant to everyone else."*

Responding to their deafening silence, Jesus sat down and called the Twelve to Him. He would respond to their dispute, rebuking their concern about which of them would be the greatest in the new messianic kingdom. This was not the messianic kingdom that the disciples had imagined but the kingdom of God founded upon the theme "Repent and believe the Good News." In paradoxical fashion, Jesus established the criteria for greatness in His kingdom—the greatest would be the least. In other words, the one who was "servant to everyone else" on earth would hold the most esteemed position in the kingdom.

The word for "servant" as used in this verse is διακονος (diakonos), conveying the concept of one who voluntarily ministers to others, one who wants to serve.[7] This person has a heart attitude that is always looking to meet others' needs. This definition contrasts the word δουλος (doulos), which indicates a position of service rather than an attitude of service.[8] This is not a voluntary position, though even in such a position one can still serve with a willing attitude.

In essence, Jesus taught that the one who wants to be first must have a heart attitude that chooses to serve those around him and does not consider his own status. Position and status should not matter when one considers the needs and cries of humanity.

9:36–37 [36]*Then he took a little child and had him stand among them. He put his arms around the child and said to them,* [37]*"Whoever welcomes a child like this in my name welcomes me. Whoever welcomes me welcomes not me but the one who sent me."*

Jesus provided a vivid object lesson by giving them a visual example of His point. He took a small child and placed him in the middle of the group. Holding the child in His arms, He addressed them.

One must be willing to warmly receive a small child. We cannot assume that Jesus meant that we can achieve greatness in His kingdom simply by taking a young child in our arms. In light of the context of His teaching, we should conclude that we must be able to relate to the least important person, no matter how important we view ourselves. Again, the significance in the act of service was not in the performance but in the mind-set. Those who humbled themselves to serve another exemplified the meek attitude that Christ desired from His followers.

Notes/Applications

The disciples' childish dispute concerning who would be the greatest in the kingdom of heaven sounds so much like us. Jesus took the opportunity to give them a visual aid when He picked up a small child and proceeded to teach His bickering followers. Surely it was embarrassing to have a child placed in their midst as an example before them. Jesus did not display this child as a sinless model, for all who enter the world are born with an inherent sin nature. We know that even a child clamors for what he does not have. If Jesus' action was not a comment on youthful innocence, what was His point *(Matthew 18:1–5)?*

We are no different. Like the twelve disciples, we strive for promotion. We scratch, claw, and fight to establish ourselves in the world. We may even step on others if they pose obstacles in our way. Sometimes, we even use these worldly tactics to secure positions of rank within the church, but a spirit of humility is one of the true benchmarks of a Christ-follower. *"²⁴A servant of the Lord must not quarrel. Instead, he must be kind to everyone. He must be a good teacher. He must be willing to suffer wrong. ²⁵He must be gentle in correcting those who oppose the Good News. Maybe God will allow them to change the way they think and act and lead them to know the truth"* (2 Timothy 2:24–25). True believers, according to Proverbs, seek a path apart from pride, for the Lord abhors arrogance, evil behavior, and twisted speech *(Proverbs 8:13).*

As children depend on their parents for preservation, provision, teaching, and guidance, we are to be like children before the heavenly Father. Surely, this was the dynamic that Jesus emphasized in describing the kingdom of God. His kingdom code required humility—surrendering self and becoming a servant to all. In serving others, we ultimately serve the King.

Such behavior goes against our natural grain, and for this reason, many will never be vassals in His royal court. Nevertheless, let us pray that we may be counted as His loyal subjects. *"Be humbled by God's power so that when the right time comes he will honor you"* *(1 Peter 5:6)*. Let us, as a trusting child, serve our King with glad hearts, seeking the welfare of others before our own.

Mark 9:38–42

9:38 *John said to Jesus, "Teacher, we saw someone forcing demons out of a person by using the power and authority of your name. We tried to stop him because he was not one of us."*

The disciples did not respond directly to Jesus' admonition. Like children caught in the act, they changed the subject, hoping to divert the attention from their selfish search for status in the coming kingdom. Rather, John mentioned someone who was successfully casting out demons in Jesus' name even though the man was not one of the Twelve.

John and the other disciples judged this person for exorcising evil spirits without being a follower of Christ as they were. Evidently, the disciples were determined to fight for some recognition of their special place next to the master. They surmised that because this person did not belong to their group, he must not be a true follower. John no longer merely sought a special position for himself in the kingdom but was actually arguing for the exclusivity of the disciples.

9:39–40 *³⁹Jesus said, "Don't stop him! No one who works a miracle in my name can turn around and speak evil of me. ⁴⁰Whoever isn't against us is for us.*

Jesus responded candidly. Although this person was not counted among the Twelve, he could not perform a miracle in Jesus' name and simultaneously oppose Him. This person did not speak against God's Messiah. In fact, he apparently endorsed Jesus' ministry by casting out demons in His name.

Jesus' response should not be misconstrued to suggest that He counted among His faithful followers any and all who did not openly oppose Him. He was not necessarily endorsing this man's miracle-working ministry so much as urging the Twelve not to doubt or condemn the ministry of another simply because he was not among their group. Further, Jesus apparently cautioned them not to concern themselves with those who did works in His name while plenty of people openly opposed their efforts. The disciples wasted more time worrying about their friends than their enemies. Jesus alone had the authority and right to judge the true motives of those who claimed to be His. *"²²Many will say to me on that day, 'Lord, Lord, didn't we prophesy in your name? Didn't we force out demons and do many miracles by the power and authority of your name?' ²³Then I will tell them publicly, 'I've never known you. Get away from me, you evil people'"* (Matthew 7:22–23).

9:41 *I can guarantee this truth: Whoever gives you a cup of water to drink because you belong to Christ will certainly not lose his reward."*

Jesus endorsed acts of ministry that reflected a serving heart. A person who performed a simple act of kindness toward one of Christ's followers, even one as simple as giving a drink of water, would be rewarded. The text does not imply that the reward would be a spiritual one, such as an eternal reward. The benefactor might or might not belong to Christ. Nevertheless, those who stretched forth their hands in a simple gesture of giving would be rewarded for serving those who served the Lord.

9:42 *"These little ones believe in me. It would be best for the person who causes one of them to lose faith to be thrown into the sea with a large stone hung around his neck.*

Jesus emphasized the severe consequences of misleading young followers. The faith of the least significant person who had placed his hand in the grasp of the master's love must be nurtured into a mature confidence. Jesus very jealously guarded the faith of those who had been given to Him by His Father. Anyone who caused such newborn faith to falter would meet with swift and sure punishment worse than if he were weighted with a heavy stone and tossed into the sea to drown.

Notes/Applications

As John did, when the Christian message hits close to home, we attempt to shift the focus from ourselves to others by saying, "What about them?" Jesus did not allow such antics to divert Him from kingdom issues. He painted a world of black and white in this passage when He proclaimed, "Whoever isn't against us is for us."

Scripture continually warns about guarding against the evil influence of false doctrine within the body of Christ. False teachers will be greatly judged for perverting the truth. However, in this passage, we see how Jesus differentiated between false prophets and those who ministered in His name but were not of the intimate Twelve. He advised them to examine the power behind the teaching and not to rebuke those ministries that did not fit their blueprint.

> *²This is how you can recognize God's Spirit: Every person who declares that Jesus Christ has come as a human has the Spirit that is from God. ³But every person who doesn't declare that Jesus Christ has come as a human has a spirit that isn't from God. This is the spirit of the antichrist that you have heard is coming. That spirit is already in the world. (1 John 4:2–3)*

Do we set up spiritual smokescreens to draw attention away from kingdom issues and the condition of our hearts? Many times, we rashly judge other believers for differences in how they look, worship, or evangelize. We focus on our different methodologies instead of on our master. May we experience the heavenly fellowship found in partnering with other believers as we carry out the Lord's Great Commission. *"See how good and pleasant it is when brothers and sisters live together in harmony"* (Psalm 133:1)!

Mark 9:43–50

9:43 *"So if your hand causes you to lose your faith, cut it off! It is better for you to enter life disabled than to have two hands and go to hell, to the fire that cannot be put out.*

Jesus expounded on the requirements of discipleship. He had just placed a young child in their midst as an example of the humility and simplicity with which the disciples were to approach their ministry. Jesus now described the intense commitment required in following Him. He explained His point with an illustration about hands. He described how the human hand possessed the capability of bringing both delicate tenderness and terrible harm. Whatever deeds the hands performed depended upon the direction of the heart and mind controlling them. If the hand committed atrocities, Jesus urged that it would be better to maim oneself than to risk losing one's life because of such an encumbrance.

Jesus was speaking figuratively, admonishing His disciples to be committed completely to their ministry as His representatives in this world. Anything holding them back from such commitment was to be cast aside as completely as if one were to cut off an offending hand.

The intensity of such single-minded commitment was measured against horrible consequences. Christ's followers must endeavor by God's grace and with the intercession of the Holy Spirit to live with unfettered resolve. Failure to accept Jesus and His selfless sacrifice result in eternal condemnation in the fires of hell.

> **DIG DEEPER:** *Gehenna*
> The Greek word γέεννα ("Gehenna," translated "hell") is trans-literated from two Hebrew words meaning "Valley of Hinnom," a place south of Jerusalem where children were once sacrificed to the pagan god Molech (2 *Chronicles* 28:3, 33:6; *Jeremiah* 7:31, 19:5–6, 32:35). Later, during the reforms of Josiah (2 *Kings* 23:10), the site became Jerusalem's refuse dump where fires continually burned to consume regular deposits of worm-infested garbage. In Jewish thought, the imagery of fire and worms vividly portrayed the place of future eternal punishment for the wicked (compare the apocryphal *Judith* 16:17 and *Ecclesiasticus* 7:17). Jesus used the word *Gehenna* in eleven of its twelve New Testament occurrences; the one exception is in James 3:6.

9:44–46 *"In hell worms that eat the body never die, and the fire is never put out."*

Jesus described the horror of such an existence by quoting from the Book of Isaiah, in which the Lord God dealt the consequences of the people's disobedience.

> *Then they will go out*
> *and look at the corpses of those who have rebelled against me.*
> ‘　　*The worms that eat them will not die.*
> *The fire that burns them will not go out.*
> *All humanity will be disgusted by them. (Isaiah 66:24)*

God coveted a personal relationship with the Hebrew people, but they ran from His covenant and followed the patterns of the heathen nations that surrounded them. God had offered them life, but they preferred the path leading to death.

"Worms that eat the body never die" has often been interpreted to refer to the eternal conscience that will forever gnaw at and accuse those in hell.[9] The intention is to convey an unimaginable torment that will never end. In similar fashion, the fire that tortured them would not be extinguished but would endure forever.

9:45 *If your foot causes you to lose your faith, cut it off! It is better for you to enter life lame than to have two feet and be thrown into hell.*

Jesus reemphasized His statement about the offending hand, this time referring to the foot. A passage from the Book of Proverbs clearly demonstrates how the foot hastens toward evil.

> ¹⁰My son,
>> if sinners lure you, do not go along.
>
> ¹¹If they say,
>> "Come with us.
>>> Let's set an ambush to kill someone.
>>> Let's hide to ambush innocent people for fun.
>>> ¹²We'll swallow them alive like the grave,
>>>> like those in good health who go into the pit.
>>> ¹³We'll find all kinds of valuable possessions.
>>> We'll fill our homes with stolen goods.
>>
>> ¹⁴Join us.
>>> We'll split the loot equally.
>
> ¹⁵My son,
>> do not follow them in their way.
>> Do not even set foot on their path,
>>> ¹⁶because they rush to do evil
>>> and hurry to shed blood. (Proverbs 1:10–16)

Instead of traveling an evil path, the foot should flee wickedness as quickly as possible. In other words, Christ's followers must clearly avoid the path of evil and steer straight ahead toward the ministry that He has ordained for them. Again, all diversions must be avoided, cut off, and cast away, for the cause of Christ is of utmost importance.

9:47 *If your eye causes you to lose your faith, tear it out! It is better for you to enter the kingdom of God with one eye than to have two eyes and be thrown into hell.*

For a third time, Jesus restated the commitment that discipleship requires, this time using the eye as an example. The eye is the most precious sensory faculty. Where would we be if we could not see the world around us, especially the dangers lurking along our path? Jesus warned again that it would be better to lose physical sight and enter the kingdom of God than to allow the eye to encourage the heart toward wickedness.

> *15Don't love the world and what it offers. Those who love the world don't have the Father's love in them. 16Not everything that the world offers—physical gratification, greed, and extravagant lifestyles—comes from the Father. It comes from the world, and 17the world and its evil desires are passing away. But the person who does what God wants lives forever. (1 John 2:15–17)*

9:48 *In hell worms that eat the body never die, and the fire is never put out.*

Jesus again quoted Isaiah, confirming a third time the terrible consequence of rejecting the Lord God and His beloved Son. Using repetition, Jesus clearly stated the choices confronting humankind: accept and follow, or reject and die. Accept Him and enjoy eternal fellowship with the Creator, or reject Him and suffer eternal torment.

9:49 *Everyone will be salted with fire.*

Jesus alluded to scriptural imagery to describe the process by which one proved to be His disciple. All people are tested by fire, that is, by the adversity of life. Life itself is a test, refining who we are and increasing our degree of spiritual understanding and commitment. When faced with reversals of fortune, health, and prosperity, will the test grind us into dust or propel us toward a more profound, unwavering faith that will not refrain from praising the Lord God and the Creator?

Ultimately, Jesus promised that those who sacrificed themselves by denying the pleasures of this life would be "salt with fire." Those who followed Jesus would be tried, but these trials would enrich their ministry, condition their lives, and clarify their understanding of Him as God, Savior, Priest, and King. *"¹²Dear friends, don't be surprised by the fiery troubles that are coming in order to test you. Don't feel as though something strange is happening to you, ¹³but be happy as you share Christ's sufferings. Then you will also be full of joy when he appears again in his glory"* (1 Peter 4:12–13).

9:50 *Salt is good. But if salt loses its taste, how will you restore its flavor? Have salt within you, and live in peace with one another."*

Jesus often related to His audience in metaphors that could be clearly understood. Salt maintained a vital role in their everyday life since it enabled them to preserve meat. However, if the salt lost its flavor, it became worthless. Likewise, if the life of the disciple did not reflect holy characteristics in both word and deed, the disciple proved ineffective to Christ's cause.

Jesus' final admonition to His disciples exhorted them to possess this salt within themselves. They were encouraged to dig deep within their own souls and find those resources that enabled them to honor the Lord in everything. What was that single defining characteristic? It was the way in which Jesus had selflessly given Himself to the masses that pursued Him from that first day in Capernaum. While He sought solitude to commune with His Father, He did so in the middle of the night while the disciples and the crowd slept.

Jesus ended His discourse by admonishing the disciples to seek peace with one another. In so doing, He reminded them of the issues that initially prompted this discussion. He summarized His response to such self-centered thinking that led to debates over which of them would be greatest in His kingdom. Jesus essentially reproved the disciples to forget such selfish, worldly nonsense and to strive to serve one another and, thereby, live at peace with one another.

Notes/Applications

Jesus contended that each person would be "salted with fire." Those are not exactly comforting words, but we must heed everything the master said. Similarly, He warned that if we lose our "saltiness"—the flavor of the Holy Spirit within us that draws others to Him—we will become ineffective for the kingdom of God. He stated all of this against the backdrop of the disciples' petty argument about position and rank.

If there is one word in Scripture that characterizes what a disciple of Jesus should strive to become, it is *servant*, but one cannot be a servant of Christ without sacrifice—cutting loose anything that encumbers this commitment. The impact of our witness hinges on such focused action because it demonstrates to the world around us that we are His people.

The term *servant* carries a negative connotation in society because it brings to mind images of manual labor exerted for the sole benefit of others. Our world vigorously spins its wheels to get ahead and lead a life of luxury, but Jesus taught that serving Him by ministering to others should be our lifelong pursuit. Once we find the courage to live this radical lifestyle, we will discover the flipside to His wonderful, paradoxical kingdom: "Give, and you will receive. A large quantity, pressed together, shaken down, and running over will be put into your pocket. The standards you use for others will be applied to you" *(Luke 6:38)*.

Jesus' Journey: Chapter Nine

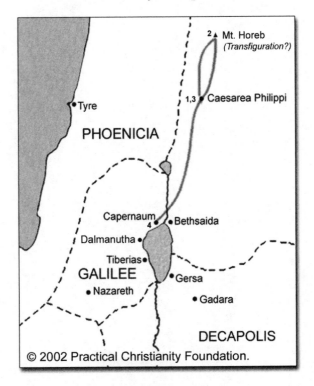

1. Jesus started at Caesarea Philippi.
2. Jesus, Peter, James, and John traveled to a mountain region where the Transfiguration occurred (Mount Horeb?).
3. Jesus and the three disciples returned to Caesarea Philippi and were joined by the other disciples.
4. Jesus and disciples journeyed to Capernaum.

MARK 10

Mark 10:1–6

10:1 *Jesus left there and went into the territory of Judea along the other side of the Jordan River. Crowds gathered around him again, and he taught them as he usually did.*

Following the events recounted in chapter nine, Jesus left Capernaum and headed to Jerusalem for what would be His last Passover feast. The small group of disciples traveled southward with their rabbi along the east side of the Jordan River. They left the province of Galilee and entered Judea via the regions of the Ten Cities and Perea. Along the way, the crowds swelled to great numbers. As in the past, Jesus took the time to teach them.

10:2 *Some Pharisees came to test him. They asked, "Can a husband divorce his wife?"*

This group of pious men placed a question before Jesus: "Can a husband divorce his wife?" Evidently, they did not truly seek guidance for their lives. Rather, they sought to trap Jesus into making a mistake so that they would have a reason to accuse Him.

If Jesus answered their question affirmatively, He contradicted His earlier teachings when He had taught that divorce was out of the question except in cases of sexual unfaithfulness: "But I can guarantee that any man who divorces his wife for any reason other than unfaithfulness makes her look as though she has committed adultery. Whoever marries a woman divorced in this way makes himself look as though he has committed adultery" *(Matthew 5:32)*. If Jesus answered negatively, He would be denying Mosaic Law, which generally permitted divorce: "This is what you must do if a husband writes out a certificate of divorce, gives it to his wife, and makes her leave his house. (He divorced her because he found out something indecent about her and she no longer pleased him)" *(Deuteronomy 24:1)*. The Pharisees surrounded Jesus and attempted to trick Him into either denying the authority of Mosaic Law or exposing Himself as an inconsistent teacher.

10:3 *Jesus answered them, "What command did Moses give you?"*

Knowing their intentions, Jesus surprised them with a question: "What command did Moses give you?" He asked them to clarify their understanding of the Law. Jesus turned the question back to these teachers of the Law and placed the burden of proof on them.

10:4 *They said, "Moses allowed a man to give his wife a written notice to divorce her."*

Jewish rabbinical tradition at this time contended that divorce was permissible, although not praiseworthy. If, according to Mosaic Law, a woman did not find favor in the eyes of her husband, he could give her a "certificate of divorce" and banish her from his house.

During Jesus' time, there was an ongoing debate between the rabbinical schools of Hillell and Shammai. Hillell allowed divorce for any cause, but Shammai, the more conservative school, allowed divorce only in the event of sexual unfaithfulness.[1]

10:5 *Jesus said to them, "He wrote this command for you because you're heartless.*

Jesus responded to these rabbis, who had quoted the Scriptures and invoked the name of their greatest patriarch, Moses. The religious leaders sat smugly secure in their knowledge of the Scriptures and in their interpretation of them.

In a straightforward and precise manner, Jesus blasted their traditional interpretation. True, Mosaic Law permitted divorce, but divorce was only granted to avoid more disastrous actions that a man might take against a woman who had lost favor in her husband's eyes. In the cultures surrounding the ancient Hebrew tribes, the woman was merely another possession of the man, much like his camel, donkey, or sheep. If the man decided that his "possession" did not please him, he could deem her a slave while he sought pleasure in another woman. If the wife-turned-slave became bitter and harassed the man, he might have her killed.[2] This was not to be the way among God's chosen people. Moses clearly taught the Hebrews to avoid the behaviors of the heathen nations around them. The Lord God of Israel expected a distinct behavior from His covenant people.

10:6 *But God made them male and female in the beginning, at creation.*

Jesus then reminded the Pharisees of God's original design for His creation. There was no question that from the beginning God intended the union of a man and a woman to be special. Only the hardness of man's heart invoked Moses' special provision. The heart of man was so degenerate that, if left to his own devices, he would rather strike out to wound or kill the woman than put up with her.

Notes/Applications

In this particular debate, Jesus clearly taught about the sanctity of the sacred marriage relationship between a man and woman as designed by the Creator at the beginning of time *(Genesis 2:18–25)*. Marriage is intended to be an ideal union in which each partner puts the other's needs first. *"¹⁸Let your own fountain be blessed, and enjoy the girl you married when you were young, ¹⁹a loving doe and a graceful deer. Always let her breasts satisfy you. Always be intoxicated with her love"* *(Proverbs 5:18–19)*. There is, perhaps, no sadder commentary on the church than the fact that divorce ravishes believers' homes in numbers equal to those outside of the faith. If the church of Jesus Christ was founded on principles of faith, hope, and love, should not our homes be as well?

This answer comes from the pages of God's holy Word, both the Old and New Testaments. Too many have chosen the path that the Pharisees endorsed by permitting divorce rather than heeding Jesus, the groom. *"So they are no longer two but one. Therefore, don't let anyone separate what God has joined together"* *(Mattthew 19:6)*. Believers are not exempt from the temptations of the flesh in whatever manner these sensual desires manifest themselves, but we must flee such evil trappings. Furthermore, there is no such thing as a victimless divorce. In fact, the lives of children, adults, churches, and communities are impaired, if not devastated, by divorce's far-reaching ramifications.

God remains the same throughout all generations. He has not changed His intentions for the marriage relationship, and neither should we. By cherishing Jesus' words and constant fellowship with the Holy Spirit, believers could provide the single most powerful testimony possible in this day and also enjoy the splendor of the second most fulfilling relationship this side of heaven. *"Wear me as a signet ring on your heart, as a ring on your hand. Love is as overpowering as death"* *(Song of Songs 8:6)*. This world seeks peace and stability, quiet and security. If we would show these qualities in our homes, how could the world deny the power of the living God?

Mark 10:7-12

10:7-8 *⁷That's why a man will leave his father and mother and will remain united with his wife, ⁸and the two will be one. So they are no longer two but one.*

Jesus reminded the Pharisees of God's divine intention for marriage. The Pharisees had chosen their scriptural text to support their position. In quoting from Mosaic Law, Jesus took them back to the creation of man and woman: "That is why a man will leave his father and mother and will be united with his wife, and they will become one flesh" *(Genesis 2:24)*. The Son of Man knew the Scriptures better than the Pharisees because He "wrote the Book." He threw the words of Moses back at the Pharisees and challenged them to refute the very rabbinical teachings from which they had quoted.

Jesus interpreted God's original intention for the union, whereas the Pharisees referred to Moses' provision for breaking the union. As was so often the case with the Pharisees, they elevated portions of Mosaic Law or rabbinical tradition that suited their own purposes—in this case, the writ of divorce—to be equal to or greater than the foundational laws of God. Marriage should take precedence over all other relationships, including that of a man to his father and mother. All other relationships should be forsaken to preserve this most important union. When a man and a woman leave father and mother to marry, they become one flesh. This is often interpreted only in the physical sense. However, this uniting merges two souls, two persons. They become complementary partners in the marriage personality. What a wonderful experience to find not only marriage partners who share physical pleasures but also soul mates who share the timeless pleasures of serving the Lord in the labor of their hands and the warmth of their married lives!

10:9 *Therefore, don't let anyone separate what God has joined together."*

The tremendous force of these words has been lost in recent years. This mandate imposed such an inviolable sanction on the marriage relationship that, should it be broken, one must fear the wrath of God. The Lord sanctioned the joining of a man and woman into one. Therefore, separation of the union offends God.

Therefore, no one, including the parties of the union, should dare think of breaking the marriage covenant. The rights of the individual parties were given up in a pledge, thus the obligation to preserve the marriage should remain paramount. The man must not allow himself to consider separation, just as the woman must maintain the sanctity of her vow. No parent, pastor, teacher, counselor, judge, lawyer, government, legislator, or any other human entity should challenge the union of the man and the woman.

10:10 *When they were in a house, the disciples asked him about this.*

Later, when the disciples were alone with Jesus, they questioned Him about divorce. Jesus had quoted the Mosaic Law, which the Jews believed to be ordained by the Lord God Himself. The teaching seemed clear and forthright, but the disciples were dissatisfied and sought further explanation.

10:11 *He answered them, "Whoever divorces his wife and marries another woman is committing adultery.*

Jesus did not repeat Himself. The disciples surely understood what He had just told the Pharisees. Rather, Jesus explained the negative consequences of separation. Everyone within earshot of Jesus should have conceded that divorce was not an option and that God deemed marriage as the most important relationship in the human experience. It is sacred and holy. It is God instituted, God blessed, and God endorsed.

However, human failure pervades human experience. As surely as marriages are made, marriages are also broken, regardless of the original intentions of the Creator. Jesus clarified why divorce is sinful. If a man chose to divorce his wife and then marry another, he committed adultery. In the minds of most people, the failure of a marriage is a terrible event. One can see the scars on the souls of the man and the woman written in the lines of their faces. Whether they have been enticed away from the marriage by another person or for any other reason, the stain of guilt and failure can trouble them for the remainder of their lives, and the sin of the marriage partners can be visited upon the children of the marriage in ways too profound to describe yet so visible.

10:12 *If a wife divorces her husband and marries another man, she is committing adultery."*

Jesus repeated the thought using the woman as the operative. If the woman chose to end the marriage, the judgment was the same, in that she, too, was guilty of adultery.

Jewish law permitted a man to divorce his wife but did not provide for a woman to leave her husband. There is little evidence that this was the practice in Jesus' time. Some indications from Josephus, a Jewish historian of Jesus' day, imply that it did occasionally occur, but it certainly was not the general rule.[3]

Perhaps Jesus used the woman as the operative to emphasize that both parties shared the guilt when a marriage failed. It speaks most clearly to our generation in which the man or woman can initiate divorce with equal impact under current law, and many do so with little consideration of the vows they made.

We must conclude, however, that the laws of men did not influence Jesus then or now. He reminded the Pharisees that God's intentions for His creation prevailed over anything that man could produce. In the purest sense of scriptural tradition, divorce is not an option in the mind of our Lord but a permission provided in the laws of men. We must acknowledge that these laws are the schemes devised by our fallen race to circumvent the will of our Creator.

Notes/Applications

Many of us know someone whose life has been impacted by divorce. Divorce is traumatic in the best of circumstances and devastating in the worst. Feelings of failure, which often get vented by angry, accusing words that further fuel the fire, overwhelm each person involved. Where have we gone so wrong?

Many people falsely believe that they can pledge themselves in marriage and yet still maintain their individual freedom and identity. Is this not the philosophy of today? Marry but do not give up a job, goals, or dreams for the sake of the marriage partner. Therefore, rather than the merging of two souls as one before the Lord, we have the joining of two people in a contractual relationship that firmly draws a line to maintain separation. The bodies may merge, seeking sexual gratification, but the souls live apart. As Christians, this should never be. *"I am my beloved's, and my beloved is mine"* (*Song of Songs 6:3*). A vain, self-centered philosophy of marriage dooms the partnership from the beginning. We cannot approach marriage seeking to maintain independence. We must approach it seeking interdependence. Is this not the message of Jesus' response to the Pharisees?

Truly, marriage challenges us on many spiritual levels because it exposes our prideful tendencies. Nevertheless, we must love, serve, and accept one another unreservedly as Christ loves us: "Love each other as I have loved you. This is what I'm commanding you to do" (*John 15:12*).

Jesus clearly said, "The two will be one," which denotes more than the merging of bodies in the physical act of love. The rule of behavior for all relationships that Jesus laid before His followers is that we must serve, support, and value one another. How much more should this become the rule in our homes? Christ described a union that put aside individualism for the betterment of a lifelong partner. When a husband and wife practice selfless love, they experience great fulfillment as they paint a beautiful illustration of Christian discipleship. *"Rather, serve each other through love"* (*Galatians 5:13*).

Mark 10:13-16

10:13 *Some people brought little children to Jesus to have him hold them. But the disciples told the people not to do that.*

As Jesus walked the shores along the Sea of Galilee and the hills of Judea, His charisma was abundantly evident. His demeanor drew people with great force, and they experienced His power and love. He did not reject the people. As the multitudes brought their sick, lame, and demon possessed, He spoke and relieved their misery.

Jesus' attraction was so strong that people brought their children to Him just so He could touch them. In His touch, they sought a special blessing from a special person. Amazingly, Jesus' disciples did not welcome these young ones. As the friends and followers of Jesus, they looked out for His welfare. They tried to protect Him from the overly zealous and to provide some space as He walked among the crowds that pressed Him from all sides. The disciples, probably with a note of irritation in their voices, rebuked these people.

10:14 *When Jesus saw this, he became irritated. He told them, "Don't stop the children from coming to me. Children like these are part of the kingdom of God.*

Jesus' response showed the marked contrast between His attitude and the disciples'. The disciples wanted to turn the children away, but Jesus wanted them brought to Him. The disciples sought to give Jesus some space among the crowd, but Jesus wanted that space filled with little children. He clearly stated that they should not only be allowed to come to Him but that they should be brought to Him. In these little upturned faces and in their simple trust, Jesus saw the best of the human race, the best example of what His followers should be. The kingdom of God would be comprised of those who, like children dependent on their parents, had placed their trust in Christ rather than in the things of the world. Would Jesus deny those who were an integral part of His kingdom?

10:15 *I can guarantee this truth: Whoever doesn't receive the kingdom of God as a little child receives it will never enter it."*

Jesus further explained why He likened the kingdom of God to little children. He firmly told His disciples that it would be impossible to enter His kingdom except as a little child. One must receive the kingdom with the awestruck wonder of a child, with the enthusiasm and energy of a child, and with the simple trust of a child. We are to believe even when we do not understand every nuance of that belief.

10:16 *Jesus put his arms around the children and blessed them by placing his hands on them.*

Jesus permitted the parents to bring their children so that He could touch them. He took the children in His arms as He embraced and blessed them. When Jesus took these little ones in His arms, He revealed a poignant picture of God's love. Surely, if these children were at the core of God's kingdom, let us strive to be as little children before the king.

Notes/Applications

Jesus had previously used a young child as a visual illustration. Now, in this heartwarming scene, the Son of God reached out His arms to gather up the little ones. In simple metaphoric language, He demonstrated another kingdom truth—the simple trust of a child is a highly valued characteristic in God's eyes.

Sometimes, we make things too complicated. In our "sophisticated" adult minds, we strive to prove the validity of the Scriptures with the precision of scientific research. We try to validate the Word by its psychological and emotional impact on the lives of those who believe it. While we desire to intellectualize the gospel, all that is needed is the simple trust that a child has in a parent. We must simply believe even when we do not understand all of the facets of that belief. We can only sing with the heart of a child that "Jesus loves me, this I know, for the Bible tells me so!"

Jesus showed us snapshots of the attitudes we should cultivate. All the money, positions, and futile struggles of mankind can never attain them. The world and its myriad voices clang so loudly in our ears that it is difficult for us to hear our Lord's still, small voice saying to our hearts: "Come home to me, for I will give you rest from your labors. Trust me, and I will give you significance and joy. I will pick you up in My arms and embrace you."

Mark 10:17-22

10:17 *As Jesus was coming out to the road, a man came running to him and knelt in front of him. He asked Jesus, "Good Teacher, what should I do to inherit eternal life?"*

Jesus and His disciples continued moving toward Jerusalem. As they walked along, with great crowds following them, a young man came running to Jesus. He knelt before Jesus, not necessarily in worship but to honor a great teacher.

He asked Jesus a question that most people ask one time or another. It was simple yet profound: "Good Teacher, what should I do to inherit eternal life?" Rather than rest his hopes on some vague concept of a future life, the young man straightforwardly asked Jesus what he could do to gain eternal life.

10:18 *Jesus said to him, "Why do you call me good? No one is good except God alone.*

Jesus responded to the young man's question with a light rebuke. Jesus redirected the man's thinking to the truth that God the Father, the Lord God of Israel, was the only one truly good. Humankind is not good, not as a species nor as individuals within the species. Although individuals sometimes do good deeds, in terms of the essential core of man's being, Jesus stated that no one was good.

> *²The Lord looks down from heaven on Adam's descendants*
> *to see if there is anyone who acts wisely,*
> *if there is anyone who seeks help from God.*
> *³Everyone has turned away.*
> *Together they have become rotten to the core.*
> *No one, not even one person, does good things.*
> *(Psalm 14:2–3)*

Only God is truly good in the very nature of His being. This statement affirms the central argument of all Scripture that humankind is lost. It confirms that man in his most lofty aspirations remains deeply and inevitably stained by sin. A person may find some degree of meaning by giving himself to a cause, but even in these worthy endeavors, man refuses to acknowledge the unique goodness of a loving God as revealed in His Son, Jesus Christ.

10:19 *You know the commandments: Never murder. Never commit adultery. Never steal. Never give false testimony. Never cheat. Honor your father and mother."*

Jesus reminded this earnest young man of the Ten Commandments. He did not cite every commandment but only those that spoke of personal conduct toward others. When Moses brought the commandments down from Mount Sinai, they were inscribed on two tablets of stone. The first four commandments were those concerning man's relationship to God. In this verse, Jesus spoke of the last six commandments, which addressed man's relations with other people *(Exodus 20:2–17)*.

Jesus affirmed the young man's knowledge of the Scriptures. As a Jew, He had known these precepts since childhood. His entire childhood environment was permeated with these rules of conduct that the Lord God had given His people.

10:20 *The man replied, "Teacher, I've obeyed all these commandments since I was a boy."*

The young man must have been thrilled by Jesus' response, for he was truly an obedient son of the law. He might have been a Pharisee since he believed in the resurrection, as indicated by his question concerning eternal life. When Jesus reminded the young man of the commandments, he proudly exclaimed that he had done all of these things from the time he was a boy.

Whether he was a Pharisee or not, it would have been pleasing to any Jewish man to know that his obedience to the law was commended. Indeed, this concept was at the core of the Pharisees' teaching. They were keepers of the law. Therefore, they would surely merit God's pleasure and be granted eternal life. To them, the law was supreme. Even the slightest detail of the law had to be followed. Even though Jesus had exposed flaws in their accumulated tradition and interpretation of the law, the zeal of the Pharisees had to be admired.

If obedience to the laws given by the Lord God could secure eternal life, this young man must have qualified, for he was truly a "good" man with a high regard for God and His law.

10:21 *Jesus looked at him and loved him. He told him, "You're still missing one thing. Sell everything you have. Give the money to the poor, and you will have treasure in heaven. Then follow me!"*

Jesus looked with godly love at this young man and heard the excitement in his voice, but Jesus now had to show him the importance of the first four commandments, which required total devotion to God. He could not simply keep those commands that pertained to his fellow man. He must also keep those pertaining to true worship of the Lord. Jesus, seeing the man's lack of complete devotion to God, instructed him to sell all that he had and to distribute the proceeds among the poor. This expression of placing his trust in Almighty God above his worldly possessions was what kept the young man from receiving eternal treasure in heaven. *"No one can serve two masters. He will hate the first master and love the second, or he will be devoted to the first and despise the second. You cannot serve God and wealth"* (Matthew 6:24).

Having said this, Jesus further instructed the man to follow Him. In essence, Jesus showed this young man the necessity of taking up the cross of discipleship by cleansing himself of his materialism. *"Whoever doesn't take up his cross and follow me doesn't deserve to be my disciple"* (Matthew 10:38).

10:22 *When the man heard that, he looked unhappy and went away sad, because he owned a lot of property.*

The young man's enthusiasm crumbled in a moment. His excitement about Jesus' first comment gave way to great sadness. He turned his back on the Lord and walked away because he refused to part with his wealth, take up the cross of discipleship, and follow Jesus. Full of sorrow, he went his own way, wealthy in earthly possessions but impoverished in the kingdom of God.

Jesus, by this incident, illustrated the true meaning of the first commandments.

> *³Never have any other god. ⁴Never make your own carved idols or statues that represent any creature in the sky, on the earth, or in the water. ⁵Never worship them or serve them, because I, the Lord your God, am a God who does not tolerate rivals. I punish children for their parents' sins to the third and fourth generation of those who hate me. (Exodus 20:3–5)*

The primary place that the Lord must hold in the life of His people is so vitally important that absolutely no person or possession can share His rightful place. God demands supreme worship from His people. Carving an image and worshiping an idol proved to be the downfall of the Hebrews in the days of Moses. This young man certainly had outwardly obeyed even this command, but God did not hold supreme authority in his young life or receive his greatest worship. Wealth and his position of prominence among his neighbors became the gods he served with his heart. Sadly, he would not give them up.

This man probably saw himself as a good person, kind and benevolent to those who were less fortunate than he was. Nevertheless, he did all of these things from the lofty perch of his wealth and his position in the community. Jesus was profoundly aware from the beginning of the conversation that this man's commitment ran shallow. Jesus knew that his "goodness" would be the stumbling block that would prevent him from gaining eternal life, the hope of his heart.

Notes/Applications

Mark relates the incident that occurred as Jesus and His disciples made their way toward Jerusalem. It is one of the most sobering events recorded in this gospel. Jesus loved the young man, who seemed to be an earnest seeker, but the cost of discipleship discouraged him. When Jesus pinpointed the one thing possessing the young man's heart, his wealth, it proved to be too great a sacrifice. The young man turned his back and walked away, refusing to surrender. He sought eternal life only on his terms, not on God's terms.

What a stark contrast to the reactions of the disciples when Jesus called them. Jesus simply entered their lives and said, "Come, follow me!" They set aside the nets they were mending or the taxes they were collecting to walk with the Savior. All of them except for Judas Iscariot went on to proclaim the gospel for the rest of their lives.

The cost of discipleship is a serious and telling matter, and Christ entreated us not to put our hand to the plow lightly:

> ²⁶*If people come to me and are not ready to abandon their fathers, mothers, wives, children, brothers, and sisters, as well as their own lives, they cannot be my disciples.* ²⁷*So those who do not carry their crosses and follow me cannot be my disciples.*
> ²⁸*Suppose you want to build a tower. You would first sit down and figure out what it costs. Then you would see if you have enough money to finish it.* ²⁹*Otherwise, if you lay a foundation and can't finish the building, everyone who watches will make fun of you.* ³⁰*They'll say, "This person started to build but couldn't finish the job."* (Luke 14:26–30)

Jesus' words sound harsh to our ears in these modern days. Abandon father, mother, wife, husband, children, and friends? In essence, if anything in our life occupies God's rightful place in our hearts, we cannot be His disciples. True followers of Christ must be willing to forsake everything they are and aspire to become in order to be conformed in Christ's image.

Have we counted the cost of following Jesus? Have we taken the commitment too lightly? If we are completely honest, even those of us who claim the name of Jesus would have to admit that we sometimes follow Him reluctantly. We have not turned our back and walked away, but we often drag our feet through the dirt on the way. We must resolve in our hearts and minds to take up the cross and follow the Savior, but may we first reaffirm within ourselves that we have truly put our hand to His plow.

> *[21]Not everyone who says to me, "Lord, Lord!" will enter the kingdom of heaven, but only the person who does what my Father in heaven wants. [22]Many will say to me on that day, "Lord, Lord, didn't we prophesy in your name? Didn't we force out demons and do many miracles by the power and authority of your name?" [23]Then I will tell them publicly, "I've never known you. Get away from me, you evil people." (Matthew 7:21–23)*

Mark 10:23-31

10:23 *Jesus looked around and said to his disciples, "How hard it will be for rich people to enter the kingdom of God!"*

Jesus continued to teach His disciples using the rich young man as an example. Little time remained until He would be taken from them, and they needed to be prepared for their apostolic ministry. They needed to learn the great lessons of life and discipleship. We can imagine Jesus watching the young man as he walked away. Jesus probably paused in great sadness as He bore the young man's rejection even though He loved him. Then, turning and looking intently at His disciples, He exclaimed how terribly difficult it was for the wealthy to enter the kingdom of God.

It is not the wealth that keeps the rich from following Jesus. It is simply the fact that those who have great wealth often come to rely on the provisions that their wealth affords them on earth rather than concern themselves with what lies beyond this life. Indeed, the very wealth that has given position and power has become their "god," their source of trust and security. In truth, it does provide for human essentials, but it only lasts for a season.

Jesus exhorted His disciples to look closely at this young man and realize that he could not enter the kingdom of God except by following Jesus.

10:24 *The disciples were stunned by his words. But Jesus said to them again, "Children, how hard it is to enter the kingdom of God!*

Earlier, when Peter rebuked Jesus for His negative attitude about the things He would suffer at the hands of the religious establishment, Jesus had reprimanded Peter in front of all the disciples, plainly telling him that he did not reason with the will of God but with the will of men *(Mark 8:33)*.

Now, once again, the disciples missed the point Jesus was trying to make: The rich young man could not participate in God's kingdom because he would not submit to the Lord as his king. He served only the god of his wealth, even though he was discontent. Even the disciples did not comprehend the character of the kingdom, so Jesus addressed them as "children." These grown men raised in the Jewish faith had the comprehension of little children. Jesus restated the lesson with kind and fatherly patience: Trusting in wealth would lead one away from the truth of Christ. In this case, wealth separated the young man from service in God's kingdom. He believed that his wealth had given him freedom to do as he chose.

We need to understand Jesus' view of this sad event. When we finally do comprehend the tragic truth of this example, we must plead for the mercy of our God and for the removal of all barriers that separate us from Him.

10:25 *It is easier for a camel to go through the eye of a needle than for a rich person to enter the kingdom of God."*

Jesus employed a typical Jewish proverb to explain the extremes presented in this experience. This phrase was common in Jesus' day and was used to express the utter infeasibility of a given situation.[4] Jesus metaphorically expressed the hopelessness of the situation by comparing it to a camel, the largest animal native to the region, squeezing through the eye of a sewing needle. The statement humorously described the implausibility of entering God's kingdom by trusting in earthly riches. Essentially, Jesus proclaimed that it was impossible to enter God's kingdom unless the Lord held absolute first place in an individual's life.

10:26 *This amazed his disciples more than ever. They asked each other, "Who, then, can be saved?"*

Again, the disciples were astounded. They simply could not comprehend what Jesus said. To the Jewish mind, wealth signified God's blessing, so this man was esteemed by others. In the disciples' minds, wealth should have been viewed as an asset to God's kingdom instead of a barrier.

The disciples did not question Jesus directly. Rather, they disputed among themselves about the difficulty of being saved. If Jesus' statement was true, their former perception of blessing was skewed. Jesus, in essence, undermined their understanding of what it meant to serve God. He had also utterly destroyed the measuring sticks by which they determined the blessings of God. If this was true, who was saved? Could anyone be saved? The disciples must have felt that everything they had believed to be true had just been torn away from them. Accordingly, they were "greatly astonished" and shocked to the point of disbelief.

10:27 *Jesus looked at them and said, "It's impossible for people to save themselves, but it's not impossible for God to save them. Everything is possible for God."*

When Jesus looked at His disciples, He must have seen the expressions on their faces—disbelief, doubt, even fear. Jesus had just stripped them of the most fundamental precepts of their Jewish faith that had been sown into the fabric of their being since childhood. They were His followers, but they were not ready for this.

Jesus knew the disciples were at a breaking point. They did not currently understand, but the time would come after He rose from the dead when they would remember and understand. Jesus gently told them that His Father, the Lord of all creation, could do all things. A man could be saved, but not by the merits of his behavior or his wealth but by the merits of God's grace. Rich and poor alike would be drawn by the Spirit and redeemed by the blood of God's sacrifice, Jesus Christ.

10:28 *Then Peter spoke up, "We've given up everything to follow you."*

Peter, so often the spokesman for the Twelve, captured an opportunity to elevate their own status. If Jesus claimed that one must leave all and follow Him to have eternal life, the Twelve were certainly qualified recipients. Only Matthew had accumulated any wealth, mainly from the fraudulent collection of taxes; most of them were just poor laborers. If the rich young man could not inherit eternal life because he refused to give up his possessions, there was a good chance for those who had left everything to follow Him.

Nevertheless, their ambitions for attaining the kingdom of God were neither selfless nor entirely accurate. Jesus had been transfigured before the amazed eyes of Peter, James, and John. Then, after traveling through Caesarea Philippi and returning to Capernaum, Jesus questioned them on the nature of a discussion they had while walking along the road: "³³'What were you arguing about on the road?' ³⁴They were silent. On the road they had argued about who was the greatest" *(Mark 9:33–34)*. These events showed that the disciples glimpsed the reality of their teacher as the Messiah and began to see the possibility of a new kingdom. Along with the excitement of this prospect, they began to discuss the positions that they might fill in this newly established kingdom. Jesus patiently taught them that being a servant would characterize the people of God's kingdom, but again, Peter expressed concern for the disciples' status, essentially saying to Jesus, "This rich young man turned his back on You and walked away, but we have left everything and followed You."

10:29–30 *²⁹Jesus said, "I can guarantee this truth: Anyone who gave up his home, brothers, sisters, mother, father, children, or fields because of me and the Good News ³⁰will certainly receive a hundred times as much here in this life. They will certainly receive homes, brothers, sisters, mothers, children and fields, along with persecutions. But in the world to come they will receive eternal life.*

Jesus responded to Peter with a heartwarming declaration of the bond holding the people of His kingdom together. Those who gave

up everything for Jesus would have a great reward. Those who sacrificed everything that they held dear for the sake of Jesus Christ
would be given a joy beyond measure. They would receive a hundred
times the amount that they sacrificed—that is "homes, brothers,
sisters, mothers, children and fields." These blessings should not be
understood in terms of earthly wealth and possessions. Those born
into the family of God share the birthright with those who counted
the cost of discipleship as nothing in view of the Savior's cross.[5]
In God's family, there is warmth, understanding, acceptance, and
forgiveness that the world cannot conceive. Even earthly flesh-and-
blood relatives may forsake us, but God's family is far greater than
anything we can imagine. Therefore, those who follow Christ receive
far more than we can ever give. Whether or not such blessings are
manifested in this life, they most assuredly will be in the next. God
will determine if, when, and what forms such earthly blessings will be
manifested in the lives of those who have sacrificially followed Him
(*Hebrews 11:32–38*).

"Along with persecutions" is a phrase that only appears in Mark's
gospel. It reminds us that discipleship will indeed result in hardships.
Sometimes, those tribulations cost believers their lives, yet they
immediately usher them into the Lord's presence. However, even
this cost pales when compared with the utter devastation of the soul
that refuses to bow to the king, the Lord and Savior Jesus Christ.
We do not bear these hardships alone. Within the arms of our loving
Father, the family of God provides strength and intercession. Just as
the bond with the heavenly Father cannot be broken, so the bond
of joy and pain that binds the family of believers together cannot be
broken.

The phrase "in this life" can be understood as "during their
lifetime." God's family will continue, day by day, week by week,
year by year, and even century by century until Jesus comes again
to establish the throne of David and take His rightful place as the
King of kings and Lord of lords. One day, this family will celebrate
together the glory of our God and His Christ. Then, all human bar-

riers that limit the faithful in their true worship of the Creator will be removed. All obstacles dividing Christians and tainting the "family" relationships in God's one true church will be erased. When all earthly fetters fall and we receive our resurrected bodies, we will see Jesus face-to-face. We will fall on our faces and praise the one and only God, Who redeemed us from the pit of destruction and brought us home to be with Him.

> *¹Consider this: The Father has given us his love. He loves us so much that we are actually called God's dear children. And that's what we are. For this reason the world doesn't recognize us, and it didn't recognize him either. ²Dear friends, now we are God's children. What we will be isn't completely clear yet. We do know that when Christ appears we will be like him because we will see him as he is. ³So all people who have this confidence in Christ keep themselves pure, as Christ is pure. (1 John 3:1–3)*

10:31 *But many who are first will be last, and the last will be first."*

The conjunction *but* joins this sentence to Jesus' earlier declaration of the joys and possessions that His followers will have in this life. In the midst of all the wonderful promises of our life as Jesus' disciples, we must remember the basic lesson of the series of events beginning in chapter nine. The ways of this world order are not His ways.

What man considers most important, God considers least. We are not to be concerned about our status now or in the future. Rather, we must desire that God's values pervade our hearts and, therefore, view our family of faith, even the "least important" with loving consideration. *"Live in harmony with each other. Don't be arrogant, but be friendly to humble people. Don't think that you are smarter than you really are"* (Romans 12:16).

Notes/Applications

Perceiving reality through a servant's eyes requires a new way of thinking—a new way of looking at the world. To do so, we must see this world in the context of the eternal. When Jesus confronted His disciples' limited, human perceptions, they had to come to grips with the profound contrast between the Lord and themselves. Of course, the realization probably left them shaking.

Jesus stripped away the disciples' preconceived notions of righteousness. These men were Jews, and as such, they counted themselves to be among God's chosen people. They believed they had a special covenant relationship with God, but Jesus quashed their complacent religiosity and destroyed their belief system. Consequently, the standards by which they judged the world were destroyed.

Throughout Mark's gospel, we see this basic concept drawn out for us in parables, in casual encounters between Jesus and the people, in disputes between Jesus and the Pharisees, and in question-answer sessions between Jesus and His disciples. Just as the Son of Man pushed, prodded, and forced His followers to confront the new order of God's kingdom, the Holy Spirit guides us step by tentative step into the same kingdom. Every step we take is progress. *"*[23]*A person's steps are directed by the Lord, and the Lord delights in his way.* [24]*When he falls, he will not be thrown down headfirst because the Lord holds on to his hand"* (Psalm 37:23–24).

Jesus offered kind words in response to Peter's declaration, "We've given up everything to follow you," by gently reminding His faithful followers that their sacrifice would not go unrewarded in this life or in the next. We may not always appreciate the "reward" for our faith along this earthly journey, but we can be sure it is there in the form of countless brothers and sisters in Christ, some of whom may have been brought to faith through our direct or indirect influence.

Mark 10:32-34

10:32 *Jesus and his disciples were on their way to Jerusalem. Jesus was walking ahead of them. His disciples were shocked that he was going to Jerusalem. The others who followed were afraid. Once again he took the twelve apostles aside. He began to tell them what was going to happen to him.*

Following the startling experience with the rich young man, the Twelve headed toward Jerusalem, following Jesus at a short distance. The disciples were shocked that Jesus would want to return to Jerusalem. Jesus had previously told them about future events concerning the Son of Man. Perhaps they remembered His remarks about the Son of Man and His death at the hands of the religious establishment in Jerusalem. With their discussion centered on the future of their teacher, we can understand why they were afraid. Who would want to go to Jerusalem, the center of the religious establishment? Who would want to walk directly into the enemies' camp? Would it not be smarter to go the other direction and stay in the hills of Galilee until Jesus could establish a force strong enough to defend Himself?

Nevertheless, Jesus led the way and walked straight toward Jerusalem, the center of Jewish worship and religious power (*Luke 9:51*). Jesus, Son of Man and Son of God, would not be dissuaded from the events that were yet to come. Such events would fulfill the purpose for which He came to earth.

As if to confirm their worst fears, Jesus again called the disciples together and told them of the things that would soon happen. He had first done this after Peter's declaration that He was the Christ. Once the disciples understood this, He could reveal more of the purposes of His life and His ministry (*Mark 8:31*). He repeated this startling future to them on the road from Caesarea Philippi to Capernaum (*Mark 9:31*). Now, Jesus drew these fearful men together as they traveled toward Jerusalem to tell them again of His future.

10:33 *"We're going to Jerusalem. There the Son of Man will be betrayed to the chief priests and the scribes. They will condemn him to death and hand him over to foreigners.*

Jesus very frankly told the Twelve why they were going to Jerusalem. He virtually repeated His previous statements. The chief priests and the scribes—those pillars of the Jewish faith, those righteous and upright men—would gain control over the Son of Man by an act of betrayal. They would falsely accuse Him of an offense worthy of the death sentence. Then, Jesus added a new piece of information, telling them that the Son of Man would be delivered into the hands of foreigners, the Gentiles.

Humanly speaking, something was dramatically wrong with this picture. How could it be so difficult for the religious establishment to endorse the ministry of one so obviously immersed in the Spirit of the living God? Nevertheless, they had been His major detractors from the earliest days of His ministry. But then to turn Him over to the Gentiles? The scenario continued to deteriorate. There were times in the past when the Jewish leaders condemned their own to death for offenses such as adultery, murder, and blasphemy. However, the Jewish people themselves carried out the sentence. Such would not be the case for Jesus.

The end of life for the Son of Man would be in the same fashion as His life and teaching. Only with eyes opened by the Spirit of God can we see the credible evidence of Jesus' life and death. As Christians, we understand the irony of Jesus' death at the hands of the most upright members of society whom He exposed as hypocrites.

10:34 *They will make fun of him, spit on him, whip him, and kill him. But after three days he will come back to life."*

Jesus revealed further details about the suffering that He would endure at the hands of the Gentiles. They would mock and ridicule Him. They intended to bring Jesus down to their level so that they would have no need to fear Him. They would, in effect, attempt to make His entire ministry meaningless. This Jesus, Who had done nothing but help and heal the miserable conditions of those who sought Him, would be brought low by their scorn.

> ⁶*Yet, I am a worm and not a man.*
> *I am scorned by humanity and despised by people.*
> ⁷*All who see me make fun of me.*
> > *Insults pour from their mouths.*
> > *They shake their heads and say,*
> > ⁸*"Put yourself in the Lord's hands*
> > *Let the Lord save him!*
> > *Let God rescue him since he is pleased with him!"*
> > (Psalm 22:6–8)

The Gentiles would scourge Jesus, that is, flog the Son of Man, Who had done nothing more than lift up the fallen and restore the broken. They would spray Jesus with spit from their mocking tongues and shame Him with this ultimate expression of disdain and rejection. Finally, they would kill Him. They would rid the world of this public nuisance Who challenged the authority of the Jewish religious establishment. He had become a threat to the tranquility of the state and required effective and permanent silencing.

Isaiah predicted all of the brutality and murder that would be inflicted upon Jesus centuries before the Messiah's birth. This vivid prophecy had been strangely ignored by the scribes and Pharisees then and by Jewish leaders of all generations since (Isaiah 52:13–53:12). However, all of man's efforts were futile because Jesus would rise again on the third day. Each time He told His disciples of His impending death, He promised them that He would rise again on the third day. God, the eternal Father, had planned a different outcome that would forever thwart the efforts of man to silence Him.

Jesus was constantly aware of what awaited Him in Jerusalem, but it was for this very purpose that He had come to share in the life of His creation. The Son of God in His human incarnation never deviated from His ultimate objective. Jesus, Son of Man and Son of God, would become the sacrifice for those who had rebelled against Him.

Notes/Applications

As Jesus and His disciples approached the holy city of Jerusalem, Jesus warned them about what lay ahead. Did the disciples suppose He used figurative language when He talked of His physical death? We have to wonder. Why else would they have seemed so stunned as the events became reality soon after this conversation? Jesus was not speaking metaphorically, however. He gave them graphic details of His rejection by the scribes and Pharisees that would end in humiliation at the hands of the Gentiles. He described the scourging, spitting, and impending death. But He also prophesied His resurrection from the dead.

Perhaps we know the story of Christ so well that we see what is coming, but if we put ourselves in the disciples' shoes, things stretch out of proportion. This was not supposed to happen. How could their long-awaited Messiah die? His descriptions were uttered in a straightforward manner, and He did not mince words when He told them what lay ahead in Jerusalem. Scripture does not disclose how the disciples responded to these devastating remarks. Perhaps they were shocked into silence. What had He done to deserve such treatment? How could someone with so much compassion for those who called on His name be construed as a common criminal? Why should He be mocked, scourged, spat upon, and killed?

The truth is that we, too, have participated in the humiliation of the Son of Man. We have mocked Jesus. We have made fun of Him. We have ridiculed Him. Every time we give credence to this world's wisdom, we denigrate the wisdom of God. In effect, we tell Him that we are capable of judging the events and circumstances around us. Every time we tell Him to leave us alone, we scourge the love He has shown us. We show our greatest disdain by raising our fist in His face and telling Him to give us our space. We spit on His interference in our lives. We do not want His opinions or His will for our lives.

The outcome of all our rebellion and rejection has been trampled and crushed by the relentless pursuit of God's Spirit, which convicts us of our sin and raises us to new life in Him. Just as Jesus turned His face toward Jerusalem and the cross, so, too, His Spirit turned His face toward us. He has chosen us to be His eternal possession, and through His blood, we are given entry to His kingdom, forever to share in the glory of His presence and the joy of His fellowship.

Just as Jesus would rise again on the third day, as He reminded the disciples, He has risen in the hearts of believers and wiped away all rebellion and rejection. His Spirit has opened our eyes so that we can behold His glory, and we can embrace Him with tears of shame and tears of joy.

Mark 10:35–45

10:35 *James and John, sons of Zebedee, went to Jesus. They said to him, "Teacher, we want you to do us a favor."*

Along the way to Jerusalem, two of the three prominent disciples approached Jesus. James and John, Zebedee's sons, whom Jesus called the "Thunderbolts" (*Mark 3:17*), boldly came to Jesus with a request. Evidently, Jesus had named them with clear insight into their persona. They asked Him to grant their request without revealing the content. Like little children bargaining with their parents for some wish, they shrewdly masked their actual question.

10:36 *"What do you want me to do for you?" he asked them.*

Although Jesus had previously demonstrated insight into the disciples' personalities and must have known the intentions of their hearts, He simply indulged James and John. Maybe, guided by the impression of Jesus' giving spirit, these two disciples thought that their request would be granted. By answering their request with a question, He put the ball in their court.

10:37 *They said to him, "Let one of us sit at your right and the other at your left in your glory."*

James and John then boldly exposed their desire to occupy the most honored positions next to Jesus at the throne of His glory. They were not necessarily speaking of some future heavenly event as would be revealed by Jesus' response. They expected Jesus the Messiah to reclaim the throne of David and to establish an earthly kingdom resplendent in glory, power, and wealth. Matthew's gospel states that their mother made the request for her sons to be given these positions of honor in Jesus' kingdom: "'What do you want?' he asked her. She said to him, 'Promise that one of my sons will sit at your right and the other at your left in your kingdom'" (*Matthew 20:21*). There is no reason these accounts cannot be harmonized since both depict the intent of these ambitious brothers regardless of the person who posed the request.[6]

Ironically, these two "inner circle" members campaigned for the two most esteemed seats in Jesus' kingdom just after He finished telling them of His future betrayal and death. They did so still believing that Jesus would soon establish His kingdom, and they desired positions of authority next to their Lord.

Such a pursuit for status had emerged on previous occasions, yet Jesus consistently responded that the disciples were to only strive to serve. That lesson remains hard to learn for the great majority of the human race. While we chastise the selfishness of James and John, we know from our own hearts that nothing has really changed. It seems as though each lesson that Jesus tried to teach these twelve men needed repeating several times under differing circumstances.

10:38 *Jesus said, "You don't realize what you're asking. Can you drink the cup that I'm going to drink? Can you be baptized with the baptism that I'm going to receive?"*

This time, Jesus did not immediately respond with a lesson on the godly virtue of service to others. The very nature of their question revealed their continued ignorance concerning His messianic role. Jesus candidly asked if they were able to "drink the cup" from which He would drink and if they were able to endure the suffering that He would have to withstand. Were they able to partake of the same things appointed for the Son of Man to endure?

Jesus asked a second question using a different metaphor: "Can you be baptized with the baptism that I'm going to receive?" Again, Jesus was not referring to baptism by water as experienced by the followers of John the Baptizer in the Jordan River. This was a much more powerful baptism. This was the baptism that the eternal God conferred upon His beloved Son, a baptism of suffering and death. This was a baptism that laid the sins of the world upon the man born to be the only acceptable sacrifice.

⁵Have the same attitude that Christ Jesus had.
⁶Although he was in the form of God and equal with God,
  he did not take advantage of this equality.
⁷Instead, he emptied himself by taking on the form of a servant,
  by becoming like other humans,
  by having a human appearance.
⁸He humbled himself by becoming obedient to the point of death,
  death on a cross. (Philippians 2:5–8)

10:39 "We can," they told him. Jesus told them, "You will drink the cup that I'm going to drink. You will be baptized with the baptism that I'm going to receive.

James and John quickly replied without knowing what they were saying. They confirmed with childish understanding and adult arrogance that they were, indeed, able to drink from the same cup and be baptized with the same baptism.

Then, Jesus confirmed their future participation in His cup and baptism. He affirmed that James and John would follow in their master's footsteps, but, surely, they had no idea what He really meant. He confirmed that they, too, would suffer pain, torture, and death at the hands of sinful men. They, too, would lose their lives and, in so doing, find eternal life. The cup would be similar in the form of their physical suffering for the sake of Jesus Christ, but it would not be identical to the cup that Jesus Himself would bear, nor would they have the same baptism from the eternal Father. That cup, baptism, and cross were reserved for Jesus, the Anointed One. He was the one appointed before creation to redeem and reconcile humanity to the eternal Creator.

10:40 But I don't have the authority to grant you a seat at my right or left. Those positions have already been prepared for certain people."

Jesus then informed James and John that these positions had already been assigned. It appears that time and eternity overlap in the plans that the Lord has revealed concerning man's redemption. We know that Jesus was with God as the agent of creation. *"¹In the beginning the Word already existed. The Word was with God, and the Word was God. ²He was already with God in the beginning. ³Everything came into existence through him. Not one thing that exists was made without him"* (John 1:1–3). The switch to the past perfect tense should not surprise us since it relates to an assignment that had already been prepared by God before the beginning of time.

10:41 *When the other ten apostles heard about it, they were irritated with James and John.*

Obviously, it was impossible to keep the matter quiet in such a small group. The ten other disciples were indignant, and rightly so. After all, had they not discussed all of this before *(Mark 9:33–34)*? Had they not been embarrassed when Jesus admonished them *(Mark 9:35)*? And, to be honest, were they not also guilty of harboring some of these same desires in their hearts? Yet, they resented James and John's selfish request for privileged status.

10:42 *Jesus called the apostles and said, "You know that the acknowledged rulers of nations have absolute power over people and their officials have absolute authority over people.*

Again, Jesus gathered the Twelve to define the character of the kingdom servant. They had to understand the way of His kingdom as compared with the kingdoms of this world.

This time, Jesus approached the subject by pointing them to the world. The dreaded Roman domination of their "promised land" daily reminded the Jews how the Gentiles held arbitrary and ruthless power over their subjects. They dominated them and crushed them for the slightest offenses. The Twelve were very familiar with this imagery.

With their Messiah in their midst, these disciples could barely contain their enthusiasm. When Jesus established His kingdom, it would be their turn to wield the authority. It would be their opportunity to repay the hated Romans for the injustices that the Jewish people had endured under the scourge of Roman rule.

10:43 *But that's not the way it's going to be among you. Whoever wants to become great among you will be your servant.*

The way of the Lord was not yet understood. The disciples could easily understand a newly restored kingdom in which the iron yoke of Roman bondage would be broken. They could envision positions of prominence for themselves, but Jesus reminded them that these were the ways of the world and not the way of the Lord.

Then, Jesus rephrased His earlier words: "Whoever wants to become great among you will be your servant." The Lord expected His disciples to assume the mantle of service. What kind of a kingdom was this? How could the disciples possibly establish authority and rule when they had to serve rather than dominate? This battle raged not between the Jews and the Romans. It was not for control of land or for world prominence. This battle erupted between man's sinful nature and the nature of the redeemed person. When this battle was ultimately won, Jesus would reign supremely, and man would be freed from the bondage of external influences and internal sin. Thus, the disciples were to attain greatness by deeds of kindness, love, and humble service instead of by shrewd maneuvers for prominence.

10:44 *Whoever wants to be most important among you will be a slave for everyone.*

Jesus proceeded by planting the seed of greatness in their human minds and hearts. Whichever one of His disciples yearned to be a prince in His new kingdom had to be a "slave for everyone." How did one become the "slave for everyone," and why would one seek such a humiliating position? What did Jesus mean by "slave"?

The disciples needed to understand what had happened in their lives. Jesus chose them to be His followers. As such, they were to learn everything necessary to understand the purpose of the one Who had called them from their daily occupations into a conse-crated service. Therefore, they were to understand that they should seek to serve the needs of others willingly. The disciples fell under obligation to the master Who had chosen them. The charge to serve was imposed on them by their teacher, the one they now knew to be the Christ. Therefore, they were to assume the character of a servant and a slave both by the claim of their Lord and by the voluntary will of their changed hearts and minds.

10:45 *It's the same way with the Son of Man. He didn't come so that others could serve him. He came to serve and to give his life as a ransom for many people."*

Jesus concluded this lesson with a graphic illustration of the servant-directed life. He cited His own life as the example for His followers at that time and for all of the centuries since.

How did Jesus do this? First, He told them that He did not come to be served by others. As the Christ, Jesus deserved their worship, yet He did not seek to be the object of worship but rather to be the servant responding to the needs of the great multitudes that followed Him. Therefore, by example, Jesus showed them a life lived in total disregard for personal health and safety. This life was sent by God into the world, a drama filled with deceit, treachery, and betrayal. Jesus was thrust into a sin-infested human race. They sought a mes-siah, not a Savior. They sought a king, not a servant. They sought victory over Roman domination but not victory over sin's domina-tion. Nevertheless, Jesus came to give them a Savior and victory over sin.

Jesus Christ opened a window into the very heart of God. In the past, He had spoken to the disciples about His future betrayal and death at the hands of the Jewish leaders and Gentile rulers. He now began to explain why all of this had to occur. The Son of Man would give His life as a "ransom for many people." The Father had placed the burden of this service wholly upon Jesus.

Notes/Applications

Sometime after Jesus' shocking words about His imminent death, James and John approached Him with a bold request. They desired to sit on either side of Jesus in His glory. What audacity! How could this request follow such a sobering account of Jesus' future! It simply smacks of arrogance, yet Jesus did not seem surprised at James and John's words. Instead, He calmly explained that they did not comprehend the ramifications of their request. Were they able to drink the cup that was appointed for Jesus to drink? He knew well that they would remain faithful to the end despite the suffering they, too, would experience. But how could such a question not pierce the human heart and jolt it to reality? Obviously, we are unable to drink the cup that Jesus drank, but are we willing to suffer and even die for His sake?

> [36]*As Scripture says:*
> *"We are being killed all day long because of you.*
> *We are thought of as sheep to be slaughtered."*
> [37]*The one who loves us gives us an overwhelming victory in all these difficulties.* [38]*I am convinced that nothing can ever separate us from God's love which Christ Jesus our Lord shows us. We can't be separated by death or life, by angels or rulers, by anything in the present or anything in the future, by forces* [39]*or powers in the world above or in the world below, or by anything else in creation.*
> (Romans 8:36–39)

As we observe the unfolding revelation of God's plan, we can rejoice with the angels, who watched this remarkable chain of events that resulted not in defeat but in Christ's victory over sin, death, and hell. The last few weeks of Jesus' life were dramatic and poignant. Christ possessed a selfless determination and love that propelled Him steadily toward Jerusalem. Surrounded by the doubt and fearful reluctance of His disciples, Jesus stood rooted in the baptism of His life by God the Father—a baptism of torture, death, and sacrifice—as He bore the world's sin simply because He loved us.

Mark 10:46–52

10:46 *Then they came to Jericho. As Jesus, his disciples, and many people were leaving Jericho, a blind beggar named Bartimaeus, son of Timaeus, was sitting by the road.*

While Jesus was truly master and worthy of sacrificial service, He was also the minister of healing and restoration. The indisputable evidence of these miracles demonstrated that Jesus was truly the Son of God. He met people's physical needs while earnestly desiring to expose their spiritual needs.

Continuing to Jerusalem, Jesus and His disciples, along with a great crowd, came to the city of Jericho. They did not remain in Jericho but continued on. As they left the city, they met a blind beggar who sat by the side of the road. His name was Bartimaeus, the son of Timaeus. In most cultures, a person with physical disabilities was generally reduced to begging. It was expected that those more fortunate would give money to the beggar so that he would be able to provide for his essential needs.

10:47 *When he heard that Jesus from Nazareth was passing by, he began to shout, "Jesus, Son of David, have mercy on me!"*

Although blind, Bartimaeus was certainly aware that this was no ordinary day and no ordinary crowd. As he listened, he discovered that this crowd followed Jesus of Nazareth. He apparently knew about Jesus because above the noise of the crowd he shouted, "Jesus, Son of David, have mercy on me!"

Interestingly, when Bartimaeus called out to Jesus, he referred to His lineage as the Son of David. Because Bartimaeus used this terminology, we might conclude that he knew that Jesus was the Messiah, for there would be no other reason for him to declare that Jesus was the Son of David.

10:48 *The people told him to be quiet. But he shouted even louder, "Son of David, have mercy on me!"*

Bartimaeus created quite a disturbance with his repeated cries. Those nearby probably were somewhat embarrassed and tried to silence him. That, however, only further encouraged this poor beggar to raise the volume of his cries for help. He knew of Jesus' reputation and did not want this opportune moment to pass. What did he have to lose? If Jesus just continued on His way, Bartimaeus would simply remain a blind beggar. But if Jesus heard him and stopped, what then? What could his future become if Jesus touched him and healed his blindness?

10:49 *Jesus stopped and said, "Call him!" They called the blind man and told him, "Cheer up! Get up! He's calling you."*

In the middle of the raucous crowd, Jesus heard this voice shouting to Him and asking Him for mercy. Hearing this desperate cry for help, Jesus stopped and commanded that Bartimaeus be brought to Him. The word was then passed along through the crowd. Now, the bystanders changed their tone. They told Bartimaeus to be happy because Jesus had summoned him. Imagine the heightened level of expectancy!

10:50 *The blind man threw off his coat, jumped up, and went to Jesus.*

Bartimaeus was overjoyed as he threw aside his coat. This garment had probably been spread before him to receive the coins tossed his way, but Bartimaeus quickly forgot this detail. With Jesus calling him, the coat became insignificant. He rose, and guided by the hands of those around him, he approached Jesus.

10:51 *Jesus asked him, "What do you want me to do for you?" The blind man said, "Teacher, I want to see again."*

Although his condition was obvious, Jesus posed the question: "What do you want me to do for you?" He asked Bartimaeus to state his request as an expression of his faith. Bartimaeus did not waver in his response nor in his confidence that Jesus could grant him the dearest desire of his heart. In the original language, he addressed Jesus as *Rabboni*, the emphatic form of the more common *Rabbi*. Excited, Bartimaeus declared his complete confidence in Jesus by addressing Him as "Teacher." The request for sight was articulated by the powerful faith exhibited in this man's confession of Jesus as his rabbi and master.

10:52 *Jesus told him, "Go, your faith has made you well." At once he could see again, and he followed Jesus on the road.*

Jesus responded by healing Bartimaeus and restoring his sight. He did so not with a touch but with a word.

As in so many other incidences, Bartimaeus' sight was immediately restored. No further action was needed because a word from the master sufficed. Bartimaeus could see instantly. He beheld the face of the one Who healed him, and with no hesitation, Bartimaeus followed Jesus along His journey to Jerusalem.

Notes/Applications

This powerful chapter leaves us with a remarkable image—that of a blind beggar crying out at the top of his lungs, "Jesus, Son of David, have mercy on me!" We are encouraged by the image of a blind beggar who refused to relinquish his one golden opportunity to be healed. Filled with mercy, Jesus stopped to minister to Bartimaeus despite the reprimands of those who hissed that the beggar should behave more respectfully. Jesus then did a peculiar thing. He asked, "What do you want me to do for you?" This strikes us as an odd question. Was it not obvious to Jesus that Bartimaeus wanted to receive his sight?

This miracle, the last one recorded in Mark, demonstrates a physical lesson that has profoundly deep meaning. Following Jesus' lesson on servanthood in God's kingdom, it is especially significant in showing us that discipleship is dependent on the ability of the heart to see through the fog of sin and selfishness. Jesus gives us this sight. To be His disciples, it is necessary to "see" Him, to know Who He is, and to accept what He has done.

Jesus meant what He said. Not all who come to Him really want to be "see again." Perhaps they move forward because the rest of the crowd does so. Maybe they are simply caught in the emotion of the moment. When Jesus asks this pointed question of us, how will we respond? Do we truly want His salvation and all that comes with being His disciple, or are we simply seeking fire insurance for the afterlife?

When standing in the presence of Jesus, Bartimaeus referred to him as "Teacher." With a word, Jesus gave him his sight. Like blind Bartimaeus, we must not relinquish the opportunity to be restored to health and wholeness. *"¹⁶Turn to me, and have pity on me. I am lonely and oppressed. ¹⁷Relieve my troubled heart, and bring me out of my distress"* (Psalm 25:16–17). We, too, need to have our eyes opened to the reality of the one we follow. We, too, must cry out at the top of our lungs, "Jesus, Son of David, have mercy on me!" *"⁵But I trust your mercy. My heart finds joy in your salvation. ⁶I will sing to the Lord because he has been good to me"* (Psalm 13:5–6).

Jesus' Journeys: Chapter Ten

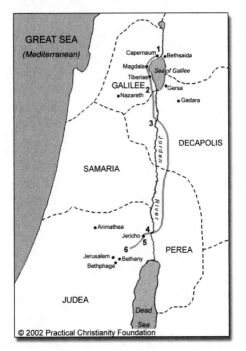

1. Jesus started at Capernaum.
2. Jesus, His disciples, and a crowd of pilgrims headed south toward Jerusalem for the Passover.
3. Jesus crossed the Jordan River, traveling through the Ten Cities and Perea.
4. Jesus crossed the Jordan River again and entered Judea.
5. Jesus healed blind Bartimaeus just south of Jericho.
6. Jesus continued on toward Jerusalem.

MARK 11

Mark 11:1–6

11:1 *When they came near Jerusalem, to Bethphage and Bethany, at the Mount of Olives, Jesus sent two of his disciples ahead of him.*

Jesus and His disciples had left Jericho and continued with the crowd of pilgrims toward Jerusalem, a journey of about twenty-one miles. He did not enter the city of Jerusalem but stopped at the Mount of Olives, a mountainous ridge separating Jerusalem from the two small villages of Bethphage and Bethany. On the slope of the mountain, overlooking the city in which His execution would soon be demanded, Jesus chose two of His disciples for a special task. Mark's account does not reveal their names.

11:2 *He said to them, "Go into the village ahead of you. As you enter it, you will find a young donkey tied there. No one has ever sat on it. Untie it, and bring it.*

Jesus gave explicit instructions to these two men to go into the village. There they would find a tethered colt that had never been sat upon. The directions were not complicated, and the disciples would not have to search through the streets since they would find the colt as soon as they entered the village. The colt would be tied so that it could not wander away, and Jesus instructed them to untie it and bring it to Him.

The point that the colt had never been worked resonates with Old Testament references regarding the selection of unblemished animals that were to be used in the service of God (*Numbers 19:2; Deuteronomy 21:3; 1 Samuel 6:7*). However, it is more important to note the significance in the type of animal chosen by Jesus. The Lord was not tired and in need of riding the colt the remainder of the short journey. Rather, the act would fulfill prophecy. The animal would reflect the servant attitude with which the Messiah would come to His people instead of the conqueror they anticipated[1], as Zechariah had prophesied: "Rejoice with all your heart, people of Zion! Shout in triumph, people of Jerusalem! Look! Your King is coming to you: He is righteous and victorious. He is humble and rides on a donkey, on a colt, a young pack animal" (*Zechariah 9:9*). Throughout His ministry, Jesus emphasized that humility and a servant attitude characterized those who would occupy the kingdom of God.

11:3 *If anyone asks you what you are doing, say that the Lord needs it. That person will send it here at once."*

Surely, this would be considered an act of thievery worthy of swift retribution, but Jesus instructed the disciples on how to reply if questioned about taking the colt. They should simply say, "The Lord needs it." With that explanation alone, any doubts would be satisfied.

The tone of this passage is perplexing. Certainly, the event had not yet occurred, yet Jesus spoke as though arrangements had already been made. However, we know that this was not the case since, otherwise, the owner of the colt would have welcomed the two disciples and sent the colt with them. As Jesus instructed His disciples to retrieve the colt, we sense that He was able to reach out beyond the limitations of His humanity. Surely, He was fully cognizant of even the smallest of details that would be woven together and result in His death.

For the most part, Jesus had said little about His identity. He questioned others regarding their perception of Who He was not because He valued their opinions but because He wanted to gauge their degree of understanding. This was the first occasion in which He referred to Himself as Lord.

11:4 *The disciples found the young donkey in the street. It was tied to the door of a house. As they were untying it,*

The disciples left without hesitation to obey their master's directive, and Jesus' awareness of future events proved true. The disciples followed His instructions and found everything exactly as He had described it. Just inside the village, they found a colt on the street tied outside a door, presumably that of its owner's house. The owner did not know that his colt would be taken by two strangers. Nevertheless, the two disciples untied the colt and prepared to lead it back to Jesus.

11:5 *some men standing there asked them, "Why are you untying that donkey?"*

Apparently, several witnesses observed the actions of the disciples. Luke's account implies that this colt belonged to more than one person: "While they were untying the young donkey, its owners asked them, 'Why are you untying the donkey?'" *(Luke 19:33)*. The disciples were unable to simply untie the colt and walk away with it. Several observers, including owners, saw what was happening and challenged the two strangers. Despite Jesus' specific forewarning that this would happen, the disciples surely hoped to avoid such an awkward encounter.

11:6 *The disciples answered them as Jesus had told them. So the men let them go.*

The disciples repeated the words that Jesus gave them for this situation, simply stating, "The Lord needs it." Satisfied with this explanation, the witnesses let the colt go in the hands of these two Galilean strangers. The challenge was resolved. The concern of the onlookers was put to rest.

It is likely that the owner(s) of the colt had heard about Jesus, Who had surely gained a reputation throughout the area as a great healer and teacher, especially in a village so close to Jerusalem. While Jesus' favorable reputation might account in part for the owner(s)' allowing the disciples to take the colt, it does not contradict Jesus' foreknowledge in the matter.

Notes/Applications

From the beginning of this gospel, compelling evidence has continued to mount and challenges us to consider one particular spiritual reality. We are prevented from drawing any other conclusion than the fact that Jesus is undoubtedly the Son of God. We are petitioned to look into the face of this man from Galilee, peering beyond His humanity to behold the face of God.

To the disciples' credit, they promptly obeyed when Jesus commanded them to find a specific colt. Obviously, Jesus had full cognizance of the colt's location and the nature of the conversation that would transpire when His disciples obtained the animal. Once they returned with the colt, Jesus would resolutely set about the task before Him by entering Jerusalem and facing His destiny. *"Through God's kindness he died on behalf of everyone" (Hebrews 2:9)*. How can we deny His omniscient awareness of details concerning future events?

As we study the progression of events beginning in this passage, we note that nothing overtly miraculous occurs, but something very profound becomes apparent. Jesus did not just foreknow the overall outcome of God's plan; He knew the specifics, and He executed every detail according to the Father's design. *"Then I said, 'I have come! (It is written about me in the scroll of the book.) I have come to do what you want, my God.'"* (Hebrews 10:7). He played an intimate, active, yet humble role in fulfilling the destiny set before Him.

By riding into Jerusalem on a colt, Jesus revealed that He did not come as a king to be served but as the Son of Man to serve humankind.

> *⁵Have the same attitude that Christ Jesus had.*
> *⁶Although he was in the form of God and equal with God,*
>   *he did not take advantage of this equality.*
> *⁷Instead, he emptied himself by taking on the form of a servant,*
>   *by becoming like other humans,*
>   *by having a human appearance.*
> *⁸He humbled himself by becoming obedient to the point of death, death on a cross. (Philippians 2:5–8)*

Through His miracles and teachings, the calming of the seas and the careful explanations, preparations, and instructions, we must conclude that Jesus was more than a man.

Mark 11:7–11

11:7 *They brought the donkey to Jesus, put their coats on it, and he sat on it.*

The disciples returned with the colt from a nearby village to the Mount of Olives, where Jesus and the others awaited their arrival. Though the colt had never been ridden, it stood quietly as some of those in Jesus' company threw their coats on its back. Then, for the first time, this donkey bore the weight of a rider, the Son of Man. Jesus, the servant Messiah, prepared to enter Jerusalem riding on the back of this humble beast of burden.

11:8 *Many spread their coats on the road. Others cut leafy branches in the fields and spread them on the road.*

Jesus and His disciples had traveled to Jerusalem from Capernaum (*Mark 9:33*) to attend the Feast of the Passover. Now, as they made their final descent down the slopes of the Mount of Olives, the crowds thronged around Him, and anticipating His triumphal entrance into the city, they spread coats and tree fronds on the road before the slow-moving donkey and its celebrated rider. The crowd fervently hoped that this prophet would be the salvation of Israel. Consequently, they behaved as though Jesus was their king. Jerusalem was already overflowing with Jewish pilgrims who had traveled by foot from great distances. They came to celebrate their history, specifically God's redemption of His people from slavery in Egypt. The people of the city exhibited a cheerful mood, and Jesus' celebrated arrival fanned the festive atmosphere.

11:9–10 *⁹Those who went ahead and those who followed him were shouting, "Hosanna! Blessed is the one who comes in the name of the Lord! ¹⁰Blessed is our ancestor David's kingdom that is coming! Hosanna in the highest heaven!"*

The fervor and the passion of the crowd escalated as they hailed their king. Apparently, the crowd that followed Jesus from Jericho merged with a crowd of people who came out from Jerusalem to greet Him.

As Jesus rode toward Jerusalem, the crowd lifted shouts of praise from the great Hallel *(Psalms 114–118)*, a familiar part of the Feast of Tabernacles celebration[2]: "Blessed is the one who comes in the name of the Lord" *(Psalm 118:26)*. The word *hosanna* comes from a Hebrew root word meaning "save, we pray."[3] In reciting this psalm as Jesus entered the city, the crowd acknowledged Him as its long-awaited Messiah and Redeemer. But did they realize the significance of this particular Passover? Did they truly recognize the one Who came to them riding on a colt? Did they understand the many cross currents that converged at this moment? Did they realize that this Passover would become a crucial point in history where Old Testament prophecies reached their fulfillment in the person of Jesus?

The crowd further acknowledged God's blessing on the kingdom of David—a kingdom that would be established by God's representative "in the name of the Lord." Psalm 118 was based on a promise that God gave David through the prophet Nathan: "He will build a house for my name, and I will establish the throne of his kingdom forever" *(2 Samuel 7:13)*. Later, a psalmist would repeat God's promise: "[3]I have made a promise to my chosen one. I swore this oath to my servant David: [4]I will make your dynasty continue forever. I built your throne to last throughout every generation'" *(Psalm 89:3–4)*.

In the same psalm, the promise is confirmed:

> [34]*I will not dishonor my promise*
> *or alter my own agreement.*
> [35]*On my holiness I have taken an oath once and for all:*
> *I will not lie to David.*
> [36]*His dynasty will last forever.*
> *His throne will be in my presence like the sun.*

37Like the moon his throne will stand firm forever.
It will be like a faithful witness in heaven. (Psalm 89:34–37)

The prophets of the Lord continually reminded the people of this covenant that God had established. We find references to it in the prophecies of Isaiah, Jeremiah, Ezekiel, Daniel, Hosea, Amos, and Zechariah. This promise to David became a significant turning point in Israel's history. It became a focal point for the manner in which Jewish people perceived themselves. This was the seal of God on the covenant that He had made with Abraham many generations earlier. Jesus now became the center of this Jewish hope. So, they sang in loud voices, "Blessed is our ancestor David's kingdom that is coming!"

They concluded their song with the repetition of the first line: "Hosanna in the highest heaven," a plea for salvation reaching to heaven: "Save us, O God Most High," or "Save us, O God, Who lives on High."

11:11 *Jesus came into Jerusalem and went into the temple courtyard, where he looked around at everything. Since it was already late, he went out with the twelve apostles to Bethany.*

This 11:seems almost anticlimactic. We would expect that the exultation of the crowds would have ended with a soaring acclamation praising God and, perhaps, pushing Jesus to establish the throne of David. But that was not God's plan. Rather, Jesus entered Jerusalem and went into the temple. There, He watched closely as people transacted the "business" of the temple. After observing the activity for a while, Jesus quietly left because it was already late in the day. He took the Twelve and departed for Bethany.

Notes/Applications
The images that come to mind while reviewing this passage replay with a familiar nostalgia. During the church year, most believers

anticipate the celebration of Palm Sunday, and some enter the sanctuary carrying palm branches in honor of the day.

The biblical text portrays a festive mood during this Passover celebration as the cheering crowd welcomed Jesus when He entered Jerusalem. However, was this truly a "triumphal" entry, as some refer to it? Throughout Mark's gospel, we have seen too many occasions in which people did things without realizing the full impact of their actions. The disciples walked closely alongside their teacher and still failed to understand His teaching or comprehend the miracles He performed before their eyes. Evidently, this crowd was no different. One week later, these people would crucify the king of glory and hurl insults at Him, mocking Him as the "king of the Jews."

If we could have walked with Jesus at this point in time, we most certainly would have noticed the shadow of sadness that must have lined His face: "When he came closer and saw the city, he began to cry" (Luke 19:41). This ride was not one of triumph. It was a ride to betrayal and death. Those who cheered Him now would crucify Him before seven days passed. Nevertheless, through the multitudes' cheering and through the anguish piercing the Savior's heart, centuries of Jewish prophecy and spiritual warfare would culminate as God's plan of salvation moved unwaveringly toward the cross. Nearer and nearer, no crowd of people could stop Him. No individual could stop Him. Not even the powers of hell could stop Him. As expressed in the following excerpt from the classic hymn entitled "Through This Holy Week of Our Salvation," God's character demanded righteousness for redemption, which could only be purchased by the blood of His Son, Jesus:

> Lord, through this holy week of our salvation,
> Which Thou hast won for us who went astray,
> In all the conflict of Thy sore temptation,
> We would continue with Thee day by day . . .
>
> Along that sacred way where Thou art leading,
> Which Thou didst take to save our souls from loss,

Let us go also, till we see Thee pleading
In all prevailing prayer upon Thy cross.

Until Thou see Thy bitter travail's ending,
The world redeemed, the will of God complete,
And, to Thy Father's hands Thy soul commending,
Thou lay the work He gave Thee at His feet.[4]

Mark 11:12–19

11:12–13 *¹²The next day, when they left Bethany, Jesus became hungry. ¹³In the distance he saw a fig tree with leaves. He went to see if he could find any figs on it. When he came to it, he found nothing but leaves because it wasn't the season for figs.*

The next morning, Jesus and His disciples returned to Jerusalem from Bethany. As He made His way toward the city, we are told that He was hungry. At a distance, Jesus saw a flourishing fig tree. He went to the tree hoping to find something to eat. Though full of leaves, the tree yielded nothing in the way of food because figs were not in season at that time.

11:14 *Then he said to the tree, "No one will ever eat fruit from you again!" His disciples heard this.*

When Jesus saw the condition of the fig tree, He spoke to it as if it could hear Him, and His disciples were close enough to overhear His words. Was this a fit of rage? Would Jesus destroy this fig tree just because He could not get anything to eat from it? It was not the season for figs, so it should not have been expected to have ripened fruit ready to be picked from its branches. Was this the tree's fault? If not, was Jesus unjust in expecting something more than what was natural for a fig tree?

This was not the case at all. Rather, Jesus was continuing to teach His disciples using the same methods He had employed in the past. He gave His disciples an illustration with far-reaching implications, though the lesson would not come on this same day. Consequently, He verbally cursed the fig tree not in a fit of rage but as a visual object lesson that His disciples would soon learn and never forget.

11:15 *When they came to Jerusalem, Jesus went into the temple courtyard and began to throw out those who were buying and selling there. He overturned the moneychangers' tables and the chairs of those who sold pigeons.*

Upon His arrival in Jerusalem, Jesus proceeded directly to the temple, as He had on the previous day when he stood quietly observing the activity of those who occupied the temple grounds. He likely had stood in the outer courts where the markets were set up. He had said nothing at that time, but this occasion was dramatically different. Although His actions might suggest He was angry, Mark makes no comment that Jesus was in a mindless rage. Rather, He was acting on His authority as the Messiah and chastising the Jewish people for desecrating the temple with their commerce. Jesus could no longer tolerate the abuses of God's people in the house of God.

Commerce had become an integral part of the temple activity, but it had nothing to do with the worship of God. The ruling priests had established a lucrative sideline business whereby they could enhance their earnings. For a hefty price, they permitted vendors to sell items that were acceptable for sacrifice to those who could not, for whatever reasons, supply their own. Though it may have outwardly appeared that these merchants were providing a service of convenience to the less fortunate, their true motivation was to turn profits. As such, Jesus brought an end to these godless activities that were being done in the name of the Lord.

Jesus drove out the sellers, the buyers, and the moneychangers, who exchanged Roman and provincial currencies for Jewish coinage, the only currency accepted for the temple transactions.[5] Special mention is also made of "those who sold pigeons" since pigeons were such a plentiful and common sacrifice for those of little means.[6]

11:16 *He would not let anyone carry anything across the temple courtyard.*

Furthermore, Jesus forbade anyone to use the outer courts as a passage to other parts of the city. Apparently, rather than travel around the circumference of the temple, many people passed through the courtyard as though it were a city street. While traveling through the portico, they transported the wares of their commerce. These people were now forced to go around the temple, adding a significant distance to their daily travels.

The temple of the living God was consecrated for worship. It was not to be used for the greed and deceit of men.

11:17 *Then he taught them by saying, "Scripture says, 'My house will be called a house of prayer for all nations,' but you have turned it into a gathering place for thieves."*

Contrary to the Lord's design, His people did not maintain the purpose He had intended for the temple. Rather, they had made it a "gathering place for thieves." They had gone far beyond the scope of business within the walls of God's house. The system of commerce was rife with extortion and bribery. Jesus made it clear that He would uphold His Father's original plans for the temple. He would restore the temple to its primary purpose—the worship of the eternal God.

Jesus did not simply disrupt the temple commerce and then walk away. He chastised those whose tables were overthrown by appealing to the authority of the Scriptures, as was His custom: "Then I will bring them to my holy mountain and make them happy in my house of prayer. Their burnt offerings and their sacrifices will be acceptable on my altar, because my house will be called a house of prayer for all nations" (*Isaiah 56:7*). Jesus' own authority was confirmed by His interpretation of the Scriptures. He reminded His listeners of the basic, God-given principles that the people had chosen to distort for their own benefit. They ignored the will of the Lord Who had brought them out of the land of Egypt.

Only in Mark's gospel do we read the phrase "for all nations." We have come to understand that Mark broadened the message of his gospel account to include people who were not of Jewish heritage. He wanted his Roman readers to understand that the temple was designed to include Gentiles in God's plan. It is comforting to realize that the Lord has always intended for all nations to share in the act of worship. Although the Christian faith is deeply rooted in the history of the Jewish people, all nations of the earth will participate in the Lord's kingdom.

11:18 *When the chief priests and scribes heard him, they looked for a way to kill him. They were afraid of him because he amazed all the crowds with his teaching.*

The scribes and chief priests were quickly informed of Jesus' actions. They must have been outraged that He had dismantled their temple commerce and halted their abilities to gain profit through those resources. Their aspirations to destroy Jesus intensified as He undercut their finances and undermined their authority.

Mark opens a small window of understanding into the motives of the scribes and the chief priests. It was not for some lofty theological disagreement that they wanted Jesus silenced. It was not for the protection of the political, social, or financial structure of the temple organization. It was because they feared Him. They were deeply troubled by His popularity. The crowds continued to be amazed by His teaching, His authority, and His grasp of the Scriptures. The scribes and chief priests feared that Jesus' continued popularity could result in the overthrow of their control over the political and social structure of Jewish life.

11:19 *(Every evening Jesus and his disciples would leave the city.)*

At the end of a long day, a day of turmoil, conflict, and teaching, Jesus and His twelve disciples left Jerusalem. Presumably, they returned to Bethany, where they had spent the previous night.

Notes/Applications
When Jesus arrived at His Father's house, the great temple in Jerusalem, He found not a house of worship but a "gathering place for thieves." Extortionists and pigeon merchants had set up shop in the temple to capitalize on Jewish trade, so Jesus toppled the tables

of the moneychangers in an act of judgment. Jesus announced to all those within the sound of His voice that He would uphold His Father's original plans for the temple. He would restore the temple usage to its primary purpose—the worship of the eternal God.

It is easy to see the parallel this holds for churches today. The central purpose for believers to assemble together must always be to honor and magnify the Lord through worship and praise. *"Indeed, the time is coming, and it is now here, when the true worshipers will worship the Father in spirit and truth. The Father is looking for people like that to worship him"* (John 4:23). In many cases, however, we have allowed our churches to become nothing more than social clubs or charitable organizations. We must make sure that the church-sponsored activities that so often overflow our calendars do not overshadow or undermine the primary intent of the church—to gather together fellow believers in wholehearted worship to God.

Fellowship among the local body must be fostered, and committee meetings serve a vital purpose in church administration. However, let us follow the example from the early church and not neglect worshipping together through prayer, Bible study, and the breaking of bread: *"*[46]*The believers had a single purpose and went to the temple every day. They were joyful and humble as they ate at each other's homes and shared their food.* [47]*At the same time, they praised God and had the good will of all the people. Every day the Lord saved people, and they were added to the group"* (Acts 2:46–47).

When we enter the house of God, He must remain preeminent in our thoughts and actions. Let us not go to His house only seeking what we might gain but giving a sacrifice of praise to Him. *"*[1]*I will give thanks to you with all my heart. I will make music to praise you in front of the false gods.* [2]*I will bow toward your holy temple. I will give thanks to your name because of your mercy and truth. You have made your name and your promise greater than everything"* (Psalm 138:1–2).

Mark 11:20–26

11:20–21 *²⁰While Jesus and his disciples were walking early in the morning, they saw that the fig tree had dried up. ²¹Peter remembered what Jesus had said, so he said to Jesus, "Rabbi, look! The fig tree you cursed has dried up."*

The next morning, Jesus and His disciples returned to Jerusalem along the path they had previously traveled. They passed the same fig tree that was in full leaf the day before and observed that it "had dried up." Twenty-four hours after they had first passed the fruitless tree that Jesus had cursed, they found the tree completely withered. Peter remembered Jesus' curse on the fig tree and, stating the obvious, voiced the wonder of all the disciples that the tree was now dead.

Many commentators link Jesus' curse of the fig tree with His judgment on the hypocrisy of the religious establishment in that the pronunciation of doom on the fig tree reflected the Lord God's pronunciation of judgment against the house of Israel.[7] In some Old Testament references, a fig tree represented the nation of Israel (*Micah 7:1; Hosea 9:10; Jeremiah 8:13*). There can be little doubt that Jesus was fully aware of this prophetic background. However, if there were any justification in drawing a parallel between the barren fig tree and the spiritual condition of Israel, it should be properly viewed as a supplemental illustration applied by commentators with the benefit of New Testament insight. It should not be supposed that Jesus expected His disciples to understand this comparison because such was clearly not the lesson He conveyed to His followers. Rather, the fate of the fig tree served as an illustration on faith in a discourse that begins in the following verses.

11:22 *Jesus said to them, "Have faith in God!*

Jesus responded to the disciples with a simple encouragement: "Have faith in God." He began His lesson by exhorting His disciples to rely solely on the Lord. Only a deep, abiding faith would sustain them as they were taken through the world-changing events just on the horizon, and there should be only one focal point of their faith—God Himself. All else would be swept away in a rising tide of animosity and betrayal that surrounded Jesus. During those times, they would need faith to understand that the transpiring events were not necessarily what they seemed. Despite how things appeared, the events they witnessed would not validate the success of man's plan to destroy Jesus but rather would validate Jesus' plan to redeem man. *"Faith convinces us that God created the world through his word. This means what can be seen was made by something that could not be seen"* (Hebrews 11:3).

It is also important to note before the various elements of this discourse unfold that Jesus was not suggesting that the fig tree He cursed died as a result of faith. As the Son of God, Jesus had sovereign control over all His creation and had no need to accomplish this or any other miraculous feat through a demonstration of faith. The fig tree withered simply because Jesus commanded it to die, and nothing else was required to seal its fate. The cursing of the fig tree, therefore, serves as an illustration not of how Jesus accomplished the feat but of the astounding nature of the act itself.

11:23 *I can guarantee this truth: This is what will be done for someone who doesn't doubt but believes what he says will happen: He can say to this mountain, 'Be uprooted and thrown into the sea,' and it will be done for him.*

Jesus then addressed His disciples with solemn assurance. Faith would be the core of their existence, the foundation of their future hope. Faith was the root, the center of their relationship with their God, their Creator, and their Savior. *"Faith assures us of things we expect and convinces us of the existence of things we cannot see"* (Hebrews 11:1).

Jesus followed these words with a comment on faith that was, and is, virtually impossible to comprehend. Jesus and His disciples were standing on or near the Mount of Olives. To the west lay Jerusalem and to the southeast the Dead Sea. He used tangible geographical features to illustrate the quality of true faith. If their faith were properly founded upon the almighty Creator, even the inconceivable act of uprooting the Mount of Olives and throwing it into the Dead Sea would be a simple feat. However, there were conditions placed on such an act of faith. Primarily, there could be no doubt on the part of the person making the request but only a complete, abiding faith that what was asked would be accomplished.

11:24 *That's why I tell you to have faith that you have already received whatever you pray for, and it will be yours.*

Jesus seemed to give His disciples carte blanche, an open wish book. It seems as though the disciples could request anything their hearts desired and God would grant their request.

Was that all there was to it? The disciples only needed to ask and believe that it would be given to them? Then all their requests would be granted? Do we really comprehend what Jesus said to His disciples as they stood there looking intently at the withered fig tree?

Many Christians, even many Bible teachers, point to this verse as characterizing the attitude with which we must approach God if we expect Him to answer our prayers. However, we must not presume that God would obligate Himself to answer our prayers in proportion to the amount of certainty that we can muster. We dare not suppose that the more we can convince ourselves that our prayers will be answered, the more we increase the likelihood that they will be. Such conclusions breed dangerous motivations wherein the expectation of answered prayers lies in human fervor more than in the will of God. As such, these conditions do not characterize the attitude with which we must approach God but instead characterize the attributes of one who already possesses such a faith—a faith that is only possible within the will of God. This verse should not be viewed as a recipe for a successful prayer life. It is not an "if we believe hard enough, then God will surely answer our prayers" formula. Rather, it

is a matter of a faith founded in God that will develop these characteristics in our prayer lives.

Accordingly, the cursing of the fig tree should serve as an illustration not of what miraculous things we could accomplish if only
we possessed enough faith, but of what miraculous things the power
of God could accomplish through us if we were able to express such
unobstructed faith. These verses should not be viewed as a step-by-
step formula whereby we can receive anything we ask for, but as a
list of common hindrances that keep us from expressing our faith in
God and permitting Him to work through us. God will not ask us
to do the impossible, though it may appear so if we lack faith. *"Jesus
said, 'The things that are impossible for people to do are possible for God to
do'" (Luke 18:27).* Only when we tear down the obstacles to our faith
are we able to receive all that we ask for in accordance with His will.
*"When you pray for things, you don't get them because you want them for
the wrong reason—for your own pleasure" (James 4:3). "We are confident
that God listens to us if we ask for anything that has his approval" (1 John
5:14).*

11:25 *Whenever you pray, forgive anything you have against
anyone. Then your Father in heaven will forgive your failures."*

Jesus introduced another aspect of prayer and faith. One who peti-
tions God with any expectation that God will hear the prayer must
be in such an emotional and spiritual condition that there is no
offense among his acquaintances. A person whose faith is centered
on the living God can exemplify faith only if he is at total peace with
everyone else.

This forgiveness of others can be understood in two ways. First,
if someone has offended us, we are to forgive that person through
the process of prayer. Second, there is an attitude associated with
the offense, and Jesus exhorts us to release our anger through the
process of prayer.

By the tone of the verse, we learn that the offenses that exist
among the people of the world are simple. The disputes in our

earthly relationships are relatively minor in comparison with our offenses against our Creator. Jesus tells us that our heavenly Father is willing and able to forgive us our greater transgressions against Him. Our indebtedness for the forgiveness we have received from a holy God should give us perspective on our quarrels with one another. Nevertheless, we have difficulty forgiving each other for disputes both real and imagined.

Jesus introduced a startling new principle about the importance of relationships in regard to faith. Our behavior toward others directly reflects our relationship with the Lord. These two elements are inseparable. The assurance of God's forgiveness is predicated by our willingness to forgive each other *(Matthew 18:21–22; Luke 17:3–4).*

11:26 *"But if you don't forgive, your Father in heaven will not forgive your failures."*

This verse places even stronger emphasis on the importance of our human relationships. If we refuse to forgive or if we are so angry that we cannot forgive, God will not forgive us our sins. If we are to understand the forgiveness offered to us by our heavenly Father, how can we not understand the need to extend forgiveness to one another? Even more, if we have experienced the forgiveness of our Lord God through the blood of Jesus Christ, how can we possibly fail to forgive those relatively minor offenses dividing us?

Notes/Applications

Jesus made a connection between three aspects of a disciple's life that have a vital role in his walk—faith, prayer, and forgiveness. Although these could be looked at separately, somehow, the Lord wove them together by drawing an object lesson from a fig tree.

When the disciples could not believe that the tree Jesus cursed had withered, Jesus reminded them of the incomprehensible power of God. The truth is that although we have never moved mountains, we also have never acted on many other adventures in faith. We have never dared to ask for many other things, thereby putting Jesus' statement to the test. Often, when life seems to swamp us with humanly insurmountable obstacles, we avoid calling out to God for help because the task seems too great. And so we go on, afraid to ask God for anything. We prefer to live in the strength of our human existence rather than seek the help of a God Who is able and willing to do all things if only we will demonstrate a properly motivated faith. Consequently, we often feel as though we are struggling along in a deep valley between faith and doubt. We want to see the hand of God, but we are blinded by our own lack of faith.

The heart of this difficult passage is forgiveness—our forgiveness of others because God first forgave us and the realization that our sins will not be forgiven by God if we do not forgive others. *"²⁶Be angry without sinning. Don't go to bed angry. ²⁷Don't give the devil any opportunity to work" (Ephesians 4:26–27)*. We cling to our petty grudges. We harbor our schemes of revenge. We thrive on a diet of "Do unto others before they do unto you." What a shameful contrast to Christ's example on the cross.

When we look at this passage, we must admit that we do not always know how to interpret the words of Jesus. We only know that this kind of faith, immersed in prayer and forgiveness, is intended to be part of our daily experience. Our relationship with Jesus offers the only glimpse of faith possible within the parameters of our human comprehension. Jesus provides this object lesson on faith, prayer, and forgiveness to move His followers into a more dynamic and powerful communion with Him.

Mark 11:27-33

11:27 *Jesus and his disciples returned to Jerusalem. As he was walking in the temple courtyard, the chief priests, the scribes, and the leaders came to him.*

As the morning continued, Jesus and His disciples returned to Jerusalem and the scene of the previous day's events. Whether or not the temple commerce had reconvened after Jesus' scathing judgment is unknown.

Immediately the chief priests, scribes, and elders approached Him. This group comprised the Sanhedrin, the highest judicial and religious body in the Jewish community. From previous encounters, we know that they bitterly opposed this revolutionary prophet from Galilee. And now, Jesus and His disciples returned to the scene where only one day earlier He had openly challenged and physically overthrown the temple commerce system.

11:28 *They asked him, "What gives you the right to do these things? Who told you that you could do this?"*

These religious leaders, the final authority over all legal and religious matters concerning Jewish life and conduct, confronted Jesus with two blunt questions. First, they demanded that He explain by what authority His actions could be justified. Second, they wanted to know who had sanctioned His authority. If someone in authority had encouraged Jesus to clean out the temple, they wanted to deal with that person as well. The Sanhedrin was sure of only one thing: they had not instructed Jesus to dismantle the temple marketplace. If Jesus' authority did not come from them, where did it come from? They apparently believed that this was just another example of Jesus' unorthodox behavior. If Jesus had not been commissioned by an authoritative body that they acknowledged, He had signed His own death warrant. He had crossed the line. He had disregarded the recognized authority of the Jewish faith, and this kind of open rebellion could not—would not—be tolerated.

11:29 *Jesus said to them, "I'll ask you a question. Answer me, and then I'll tell you why I have the right to do these things.*

We can almost picture this scene unfolding. Jesus certainly appeared quiet and calm. He did not appear agitated. In typical style of rabbinical debate, Jesus responded to their questions with a question of His own. Such an appeal did not seem unreasonable. He desired only one answer from them. If they answered His question, He would answer their questions and reveal the source of His authority.

11:30 *Did John's right to baptize come from heaven or from humans? Answer me!"*

Calmly, Jesus asked His question. From where had John the Baptizer received his authority for ministry? Had John entered his ministry because some earthly authority commissioned him, or had he become a prophet by the authority of heaven?

11:31–32 *³¹They discussed this among themselves. They said, "If we say, 'from heaven,' he will ask, 'Then why didn't you believe him?' ³²But if we say, 'from humans,' then what will happen?" They were afraid of the people. All the people thought of John as a true prophet.*

These learned men were suddenly stumped. They were the highest authority on the Law and the Prophets. They were smart enough to recognize that they had walked into a trap. This carpenter from Galilee, this rabbi without formal education or rabbinical training had outwitted them. Every time the scribes confronted Jesus, He made them look foolish.

If they responded that John the Baptist was called into his ministry from heaven, they had a big problem since they had not endorsed his ministry. If they acknowledged that John was commissioned by heaven, they would then be questioned for not accepting his message. They had not gone out to the Jordan River to adopt John's message, and they had not been baptized. Therefore, they could not respond that John the Baptizer was sent from heaven. The alternative answer was equally unacceptable. If they voiced their opinion that John's ministry was authorized by humans, they would evoke the anger of the people who were convinced that John the Baptist was a prophet of the living God. They needed the ongoing support of the Jewish people in order to maintain the temple worship system and to sustain their positions as the leaders of Jewish life and practice.

11:33 *So they answered Jesus, "We don't know." Jesus told them, "Then I won't tell you why I have the right to do these things."*

These religious leaders were humiliated. When the chief priests, scribes, and elders arrived on the scene, others probably gathered with the twelve disciples to witness the encounter between these now-familiar opponents. In front of this group, however large or small, the best-educated men in all Judea were forced to admit that they did not have an answer. Once again, Jesus had managed to bring these proud men to their knees.

Jesus then responded very simply, "Then I won't tell you why I have the right to do these things." The real problem was much deeper than the question concerning the legitimacy of John's ministry. If these men could not produce a clear answer regarding John's ministry, there was no reason to pursue further debate. Forcing the issue would require the ruling priests to similarly consider Jesus' authority. In their pride, self-righteousness, and blind religious confidence, they could not and would not endorse the ministry and the mission of the carpenter from Galilee. To do so would require not only that they accept His teaching and healing ministry but also that they acknowledge Him as their long-awaited Messiah. Such validation would devastate the established religious structure as well as destroy the ruling council's political and social status and financial earnings.

Notes/Applications

When Jesus entered the temple and overturned the commercial system endorsed by the Jewish religious leaders, He displayed the great scope of His authority. This one highly charged act demonstrated that Jesus' authority defied the authority of the Sanhedrin. Jesus proved beyond doubt that His position before God the Father gave Him the authority to destroy this man-made debacle of the temple. The very fact that no one dared to challenge Him confirmed that His authority was not to be questioned. Only on the following day, and probably after much heated debate, did the chief priests, scribes, and elders dare to confront Jesus about His behavior. He had not just overturned their physical accessories of commerce, He had confronted their rabbinical religious system. In response, the religious leaders plotted to destroy Jesus, as described in Isaac Watts' hymn, "Why Did the Jews Proclaim Their Rage?"

> Why did the Jews proclaim their rage?
> The Romans, why their swords employ?
> Against the Lord their powers engage,
> His dear Anointed to destroy?
>
> "Come, let us break His bands," they say;
> "This Man shall never give us laws":
> And thus they cast His yoke away,
> And nail'd the Monarch to the cross.
>
> But God, Who high in glory reigns,
> Laughs at their pride, their rage controls;
> He'll vex their hearts with inward pains
> And speak in thunder to their souls.
>
> But nations that resist His grace
> Shall fall beneath His iron stroke;

His rod shall crush His foes with ease,
As potters' earthen work is broke.

Now, ye that sit on earthly thrones,
Be wise, and serve the Lord, the Lamb;
Now at His feet submit your crowns,
Rejoice and tremble at His Name. . . . [8]

In the most basic sense, Jesus confronts our personal authority as He did the scribes' and Pharisees'. We may consider ourselves intellectually, educationally, and even religiously superior to those who lived in Jesus' day. We fall into the trap of self-adulation and the resulting self-confidence, making it hard to face Jesus' penetrating analysis of our sinful nature. We do not appreciate being challenged and then beaten by the overriding clarity of Jesus' authoritative word, for we prefer not to see ourselves as God sees us. When Jesus overturns the wrong motives of our hearts, how do we respond? When He exposes our sin, do we seek His forgiveness? Truly, when Jesus enters the realm of our awareness and exposes our motives, we may be deeply offended, but if we are wise, we will heed the gentle voice of the Spirit and repent.

Jesus drew a line in the sands of time. Dare we cross this line? If we take that step, we must do so on our knees with tears in our eyes as we individually confess: "Jesus, I am guilty as charged. Save me!"

MARK 12

Mark 12:1–6

12:1 *Then, using this illustration, Jesus spoke to them. He said, "A man planted a vineyard. He put a wall around it, made a vat for the winepress, and built a watchtower. Then he leased it to vineyard workers and went on a trip.*

Jesus had just refused to tell the chief priests, scribes, and elders by Whose authority He conducted His ministry. Jesus, His disciples, the religious leaders, and a crowd of curious onlookers were still standing in the temple. Now, Jesus began to shed light on the controversy they had just witnessed by further exposing the dilemma facing the religious leaders. Unwilling to implicate themselves on the question concerning John's baptism, they stood near Jesus as He told them a parable.

A man planted a vineyard and set a wall around it to provide security for his workers and his crop. He constructed a vat to press the grapes into wine and built a watchtower for protection. The man then leased the property to vinedressers, left his investment in their hands, and departed to a foreign land.

12:2 *"At the right time he sent a servant to the workers to collect from them a share of the grapes from the vineyard.*

It was expected under the terms of the agreement that the owner would collect a percentage of the profits.[1] The caretakers would bring the harvest to the wine vat, crush the grapes, and produce wine, and the owner would collect his percentage from the caretakers. Since the owner was out of the country, he sent one of his servants to collect his share of the profits.

12:3 *The workers took the servant, beat him, and sent him back with nothing.*

When the owner's servant arrived, the vinedressers beat him and sent him away without the profits. The vinedressers took matters into their own hands and disregarded the very person who had established their livelihood. The battered servant returned to the owner of the vineyard empty-handed.

12:4 *So the man sent another servant to them. They hit the servant on the head and treated him shamefully.*

In another attempt to collect his expected profits, the owner sent a second servant to his property. The caretakers intensified their adversarial behavior; they struck him in the head and sent him away just as they did the first servant.

12:5 *The man sent another, and they killed that servant. Then he sent many other servants. Some of these they beat, and others they killed.*

In a third attempt, the owner sent another servant. This time, the caretakers showed their total disdain for the owner by killing the servant. The owner had constructed the vineyard and invested much time and money to make it safe and profitable, but the hired vinedressers ignored the owner's investment and care for them. The vinedressers likewise accosted each and every subsequent person the owner sent. Some were wounded and returned to the owner to tell him of their mistreatment, and some received fatal injuries. How could the field-workers treat the owner and his representatives with such contempt?

12:6 *"He had one more person to send. That person was his son, whom he loved. Finally, he sent his son to them. He thought, 'They will respect my son.'*

In one last attempt to collect the profits due him, the man sent his own son, whom he dearly loved. The owner expected that the caretakers would respect the fact that he sent his son to collect the profits.

Notes/Applications
It was not unusual in the early first century for rich landowners to contract with tenant farmers to care for their investment. While much of the income from these investments was needed to pay the tenant farmers, the owner retained all rights to the profits.

If the parable went no further, our sense of justice would demand that these ungrateful tenants be driven off the property and punished for their mistreatment of the owner's representatives. Without further detail, we might conclude that Jesus spoke about the fair treatment of God's people. Once again, though, He was referring to something of spiritual depth that had ominous overtones for the listeners. Specifically He was describing how the Jews had treated God's messengers (the prophets) and His Son.

God's faithfulness is incomparable. Day by day, year by year, and even generation by generation, the richness of His grace has surrounded our lives and given us genuine peace in the midst of this chaotic world. Even though we are the recipients of His constant care, we repeatedly take for granted His goodness toward us. Even though He has demonstrated innumerable times in countless ways that He cares for us, we are dissatisfied working in His service. We ignore the message of His holy Scriptures. We avoid the hearing and sharing of His Word. Our prayers are only the dull repetition of well-worn phrases. Our passion and warmth wane as we disregard the close relationship that our Lord yearns for us to enjoy.

If we are quick to pronounce judgment on these ungrateful care-takers, are we not also quick to evoke judgment on ourselves? *"¹Stop judging so that you will not be judged. ²Otherwise, you will be judged by the same standard you use to judge others. The standards you use for others will be applied to you"* (Matthew 7:1–2). When Jesus addressed the crowd at large and the Sanhedrin in particular, a strong element of truth was unveiled for us as well. Have we treated God's beloved messenger with derision? Even as recipients of His boundless grace, have we treated our owner carelessly? Let us not allow the fire of our first love to cool to a faint ember by brushing aside His direction, conviction, encouragement, and love. May ours not be a cold and inexpressive faith.

Mark 12:7-12

12:7 *"But those workers said to one another, 'This is the heir. Let's kill him, and the inheritance will be ours.'*

As the caretakers watched the owner's son coming, they discussed their strategy. Having beaten and killed previous representatives, what would they do now that the owner's son was approaching?

Their answer was clear and strong. They reasoned that if they killed the son and no one else lay claim to the property, the land would become theirs by default. They would no longer be caretakers; they would be the owners.

It was a matter of law that "ownerless property" was available to anyone who laid first claim to the land.[2] Perhaps they believed that if they killed the only heir to the property that the owner, who feared for his life, would dare not return to reclaim the property, whereupon the caretakers would inherit the land they worked. However, the method by which these thieves, liars, and murderers schemed was irrational. They would break the law by committing murder and then exercise the provisions of the law in order to claim the property.

12:8 *So they took him, killed him, and threw him out of the vineyard.*

When the son arrived, the vinedressers carried out their evil scheme. They killed the owner's son and threw his body out of the vineyard. The murder took place within the confines of the owner's property, where the caretakers had been given the opportunity to earn a living by the gracious owner they now abhorred.

12:9 *"What will the owner of the vineyard do? He will come and destroy the workers and give the vineyard to others.*

We can assume that the crowd responded to Jesus' parable in the same manner that we do when we hear the story. Who would not argue that these ungrateful, murderous men should be destroyed?

Surely, the crowd sympathized with the owner's right to execute the unworthy caretakers.

After the vinedressers were destroyed, the owner would then place the property under the care of others. New caretakers would be given the owner's trust in his investment. He would care for them as he cared for those who had disregarded his rights of ownership.

12:10–11 *¹⁰Have you never read the Scripture passage: 'The stone that the builders rejected has become the cornerstone. ¹¹The Lord has done this, and it is amazing for us to see'?"*

With perfect timing and understanding, Jesus concluded His parable with a quotation from the Holy Scriptures. He interpreted His illustration not with a personalized explanation but with the authority of Scripture, quoting from the psalms *(Psalm 118:22–23)*.

By citing this Scripture, Jesus identified the roles of the parable with its real-life counterparts. Jesus was the cornerstone rejected by the builders and the Son rejected by the vinedressers; the religious leaders were the hateful, brutal vinedressers and the builders. Most unbelievable, this rejection was the work of the Lord. God Almighty would establish His Son as the cornerstone of a new structure. Consequently, the new structure would be built by God's hands on the foundation of the Son. It would be God's work and God's alone, and the result would be marvelous to behold.

12:12 *They wanted to arrest him but were afraid of the crowd. They knew that he had directed this illustration at them. So they left him alone and went away.*

Imagine the scribes, elders, and chief priests biting their tongues with fury! Not only had Jesus made them look foolish, He had added fuel to the fire. Not only had Jesus embarrassed them in front of their constituents, but He now illustrated a scenario that clearly pointed an accusing finger at them. These "righteous" men knew the

Scripture that Jesus quoted, and they knew that Jesus was speaking about them.

How dare He accuse them of being the murderous caretakers of the Lord's vineyard? How dare He accuse them—the religious elite of their society—of killing the representatives of God? How dare He suggest that the owner would come and destroy them? They were God's representatives. They were charged with caring for the social, political, and moral welfare of the Jewish people. They alone were the proper interpreters of the Holy Scriptures. If not them, who would be entrusted as the new caretakers of the vineyard? And this uneducated carpenter from Galilee dared to bring judgment upon them?

The religious leaders probably believed that Jesus had carefully constructed the story to win the favor of the crowd, which was incensed by the injustice of the caretakers. Therefore, they avoided rushing Jesus as an attempt to stop His insulting words. They were left with very few options, so they turned quietly and walked away.

Notes/Applications
Although Jesus' audiences rarely understood the full thrust of His messages, the religious leaders recognized very well the meaning of this parable. So well, in fact, that they wanted to seize Jesus. They realized that He had judged them and that His judgment bore a heavy verdict—their destruction. With divine wisdom, Jesus pronounced a death sentence on His accusers just a few days before they would crucify Him on a cross.

Jesus identified Himself as the stone that the builders rejected, which would become the cornerstone. Generally, a cornerstone was the first stone from which the first two walls were laid to form a new building. It was the foundational stone by which all other stones were aligned and constructed. Certainly, Christ was and is the cornerstone of His church. He instituted the church, establishing cohesion and unity and consummating the bond among the family of

God: "You are built on the foundation of the apostles and prophets. Christ Jesus himself is the cornerstone" (*Ephesians 2:20*).

The scribes and Pharisees were so self-righteous that they were able to recognize neither their sin nor the Son of God, Who stood before them. It was not that they would not see but that they could not see. They had built their religion on their drive for position and on their misinterpretations of the Law—a sinful and weak foundation. They rejected the precious jewel that would have given their faith purpose and stability.

> *This is what the Almighty Lord says:*
> *I am going to lay a rock in Zion,*
> *a rock that has been tested,*
> *a precious cornerstone,*
> *a solid foundation.*
> *Whoever believes in him will not worry. (Isaiah 28:16)*

It is Jesus, the cornerstone, that believers have been admonished to build the temple of their lives upon. Only when we see ourselves in the light of God's righteousness can we begin to see the enormity of God's free gift to us, salvation through His Son, Jesus Christ.

> ⁴*You are coming to Christ, the living stone who was rejected by humans but was chosen as precious by God.* ⁵*You come to him as living stones, a spiritual house that is being built into a holy priesthood. So offer spiritual sacrifices that God accepts through Jesus Christ. . . .*
>
> ⁹*You are chosen people, a royal priesthood, a holy nation, people who belong to God. You were chosen to tell about the excellent qualities of God, who called you out of darkness into his marvelous light.* ¹⁰*Once you were not God's people, but now you are. Once you were not shown mercy, but now you have been shown mercy.* (1 Peter 2:4–5, 9–10)

Mark 12:13-17

12:13 *The leaders sent some of the Pharisees and some of Herod's followers to Jesus. They wanted to trap him into saying the wrong thing.*

Although the group of angry and frustrated religious leaders had withdrawn, they were determined to trap Jesus. Their hearts were hardened, and their egos would not allow them to back down without a fight. We can imagine the whole group moving to some other location within the temple complex and plotting their next move. Consequently, they sent a representative group back out to the temple courts to further challenge Jesus.

This group consisted of Pharisees and Herodians. The Pharisees were generally separatists who believed in the supremacy of the Jewish mind and faith over their Gentile rulers. They believed in a coming Messiah who would be God's anointed king and would break the yoke of Roman oppression and restore the glory of Israel as in the days of King David. The Herodians usually opposed the Pharisees. They accepted Roman rule and even profited from it. They were called Herodians because they endorsed Herod Antipas, the Jewish king placed in authority by the Roman Caesar.

In Jesus, the Pharisees and Herodians had a common enemy, so together they came out to challenge Jesus and to ensnare Him in some error for which they could arrest Him. Both groups hated Jesus—the Herodians for political reasons and the Pharisees for religious reasons. By their evil scheming, they merged their efforts to prevent Jesus from further interfering in their religious and political routines. Their past experience should have discouraged them from attempts to entrap Him, especially considering that day's earlier humiliation.

12:14 *When they came to him, they said, "Teacher, we know that you tell the truth. You don't favor individuals because of who they are. Rather, you teach the way of God truthfully. Is it right to pay taxes to the emperor or not? Should we pay taxes or not?"*

These men again approached Jesus but this time with flattering words. They called Him "Teacher" but avoided using the title "Rabbi", which would have implied that they acknowledged Him as a legitimate teacher. Then they said, "We know that you tell the truth," though they did not believe that Jesus was the embodiment of truth. When they said that Jesus did not favor individuals because of who they were, they were not suggesting that Jesus was uncaring but that He would speak the truth impartially without regard for the way His words might impact public opinion toward Him. Finally, as if to demonstrate their sincerity, they added, "You teach the way of God truthfully." What sheer hypocrisy flowed from their deceitful lips! How ironic that they could even articulate these words!

Jesus was all of these things and certainly did speak the way of God in truth, but coming from the lips of these religious and pious hypocrites, these words were not compliments. They did not believe one word of what they had just said to Jesus. If they did, would they have proceeded with the trap they had set for Him? Would they not have repented of their hypocrisy and embraced Him? Would they not have looked to Him for release from the bondage of their sin?

Without pause for response, the Pharisees and Herodians flowed right into one more question, and with that, the trap had been set. They inquired about whether it was lawful to pay taxes to Caesar. If Jesus answered, "Yes," then He would be in big trouble with the crowd, who hated the Romans and the tax that reminded them that they were a people under subjection. Even the Pharisees would have preferred not to pay such a tax. However, if Jesus answered, "No," then He would anger the Herodians, who endorsed the tax. More importantly, He would seem to endorse a defiance of governmental authority, which would then be notified of this dangerous political rebel. Either way, Jesus appeared certain to lose!

12:15 *Jesus recognized their hypocrisy, so he asked them, "Why do you test me? Bring me a coin so that I can look at it."*

By posing the question to Him in a short, direct fashion, the Pharisees and Herodians had hoped to evoke a simple yes-or-no answer. Immediately, though, Jesus knew the intent of their minds and hearts. Perceiving that they sought to trap Him, Jesus asked to see a denarius, the Roman coin with Caesar's image on one side and a tribute to Caesar's glory on the other side.[3]

12:16 *They brought a coin. He said to them, "Whose face and name is this?" They told him, "The emperor's."*

Someone nearby handed a coin to Jesus, Who then entered the debate by asking whose image was represented on the face of the coin. Some might have snickered at this question, wondering how Jesus could not know something that was so patently obvious. Nevertheless, they replied, "The emperor's."

12:17 *Jesus said to them, "Give the emperor what belongs to the emperor, and give God what belongs to God." They were surprised at his reply.*

Not knowing what to expect, the Herodians and Pharisees showed Jesus the image of the emperor, Caesar. Jesus looked at the coin and then at His adversaries and told them to give to Caesar what belonged to Caesar and to give to God what belonged to God. How could Jesus have eluded their cleverly devised trap? What kind of an answer was this?

If Jesus taught the way of God in truth, this was the only answer that was needed. Jesus thereby acknowledged that Rome, the governmental authority, was in power by the hand of the sovereign God. Therefore, Caesar had a right to his governmental tax. It was not a question of liking the tax or not. Their duty as a subject nation required that the tax be given to their Roman rulers. Jesus also acknowledged that God is supreme and had a right to the tribute due Him. The Jews should pay their earthly authorities the financial dues owed to them in the same manner that they should pay their heavenly authority the worship and devotion owed to Him. *"Every person should obey the government in power. No government would exist if it hadn't been established by God. The governments which exist have been put in place by God" (Romans 13:1).*

Notes/Applications

Once again, the religious leaders tried to trap Jesus by His own words, but their ploy backfired. This time, they brought up the issue of money in relation to paying taxes to the Roman emperor, who harshly ruled over the Jews in their own God-given land. Jesus' calm reply turned the tables on the religious leaders and brought the issue of giving God what was owed Him to the foreground.

The answers to many of life's questions lie hidden in the confused applications that sinful man has adopted throughout the years. Confident in human knowledge and opinion, people blunder through life on the basis of trial and error rather than on absolute truth. Without this divine anchor, they grow more arrogant and hostile toward God and wallow in the mire of their own human thinking. Like the Sanhedrin, they believe they sit far above the misguided lives of other people. *"The Teachings were given through Moses, but kindness and truth came into existence through Jesus Christ" (John 1:17). "Jesus answered him, 'I am the way, the truth, and the life. No one goes to the Father except through me'" (John 14:6).*

So, what do we owe God? Everything. Our allegiance, praise, worship, time, attention, money, hearts, and lives. The Bible reminds us that every breath we breathe is a gift from God. If we are talented in a certain area, it is because He has gifted us for that particular work. Only through the Holy Spirit can we see our need, our depravity, and then realize that we must accept the Savior:

[20]But that is not what you learned from Christ's teachings. [21]You have certainly heard his message and have been taught his ways. The truth is in Jesus. [22]You were taught to change the way you were living. The person you used to be will ruin you through desires that deceive you. [23]However, you were taught to have a new attitude. [24]You were also taught to become a new person created to be like God, truly righteous and holy. (Ephesians 4:20–24)

May God give us eyes to see, ears to hear, and hearts to understand that we are stewards of His physical and spiritual provisions.

Mark 12:18–27

12:18 *Some Sadducees, who say that people will never come back to life, came to Jesus. They asked him,*

Many members of the Sanhedrin were Sadducees, who were the most liberal of the religious leaders. Contrary to the common Jewish traditions, the Sadducees did not believe in the resurrection. To them, such a concept was beyond the realm of possibility. They also did not believe in angels or spirits.[4] These beliefs influenced their line of reasoning. When reports came back to the Sanhedrin that Jesus had cast out demons and had brought a young girl back from the dead, the Sadducees must surely have regarded it as an exaggeration of misguided observers. Seeing themselves as rationalists, they must have held Jesus in intellectual contempt.

After the failure of the Pharisees and Herodians to trap Jesus in His words, the Sadducees took their turn in trying to undermine Jesus' authority. They were confident they would be able to silence this troublemaker or at least embarrass Him in the presence of the crowd.

12:19 *"Teacher, Moses wrote for us, 'If a man dies and leaves a wife but no child, his brother should marry his widow and have children for his brother.'*

The Sadducees, who accepted only the Pentateuch (the first five books of the Bible, written by Moses) as authoritative, put forth a hypothetical circumstance expecting that Jesus would be unable to provide a satisfactory answer to the quandary. They first set the background for their question by reciting the portion of Mosaic Law that dealt with the situation in which a man died without an heir:

> [5]*When brothers live together and one of them dies without having a son, his widow must not marry outside the family. Her husband's brother must marry her and sleep with her. He must do*

his duty as her brother-in-law. ⁶Then the first son she has will carry the dead brother's name so that his name won't die out in Israel.

⁷But if the man doesn't want to marry his brother's widow, she must go to the leaders of the city at the city gate. She must say, "My brother-in-law refuses to let his brother's name continue in Israel. He doesn't want to do his duty as my brother-in-law." ⁸Then the leaders of the city must summon him and talk to him. If he persists in saying that he doesn't want to marry her, ⁹his brother's widow must go up to him in the presence of the leaders. She must take off one of his sandals and spit in his face. She must make this formal statement: "This is what happens to a man who refuses to continue his brother's family line." ¹⁰Then in Israel his family will be called the Family of the Man Without a Sandal. (Deuteronomy 25:5–10)

12:20–22 *²⁰There were seven brothers. The first got married and died without having children. ²¹The second married her and died without having children. So did the third. ²²None of the seven brothers had any children. Last of all, the woman died.*

Once they set the stage, the Sadducees exaggerated the circumstance by posing an unlikely scenario in which this situation occurred multiple times to the same woman. A man died leaving his wife childless, and as prescribed by the Law, the man's brother married the woman. Similarly, that brother died, and the situation repeated itself until each of seven brothers had died, leaving the woman childless. It must be assumed from the story that each man had tried to comply with his obligatory duty. Nevertheless, they all died without producing an heir to honor their brother's name. Eventually, the woman also died.

12:23 *When the dead come back to life, whose wife will she be? The seven brothers had married her."*

The Sadducees finally concluded their implausible story by posing the question that they believed would stump Jesus and discredit Him before a crowd of witnesses. When the resurrection occurred, of the seven brothers whose wife would she be? It is ironic that these men would ask this question since they did not even believe in the resurrection. The question not only was an attempt to confound Jesus, but it also mocked the very concept of the resurrection.

12:24 *Jesus said to them, "Aren't you mistaken because you don't know the Scriptures or God's power?*

Jesus' response showed His contempt for these self-righteous "representatives of God." He asked them a question in such a way as to express that He expected a positive answer. "You are mistaken, aren't you?" Of course, the Sadducees could not agree with Jesus because they would be admitting that they were wrong if they did.

Jesus was not asking the Sadducees so much as telling them that they did not know the Scriptures or the power of God. Jesus publicly exposed their ignorance. He defied their intelligence, the very core of their vanity. These men could only demonstrate the outward expression of a religious perspective that was empty and vain.

12:25 *When the dead come back to life, they don't marry. Rather, they are like the angels in heaven.*

Contradicting everything the Sadducees believed, Jesus confirmed the validity of a resurrection from the dead. However, at the resurrection, the need for human propagation would no longer exist. Rather, when resurrected, humankind would be more like the "angels in heaven." There would be no purpose for marriage, so the Sadducees' carefully drawn scenario was irrelevant.

12:26 *Haven't you read in the book of Moses that the dead come back to life? It's in the passage about the bush, where God said, 'I am the God of Abraham, Isaac, and Jacob.'*

Jesus then challenged their erroneous belief that there was no resurrection. He continued His argument, basing His responses on the Scriptures, even on the ones the Sadducees accepted. He reminded them of Moses, the only person that these men revéred. He recalled that moment when Moses encountered God by the burning bush.

> ⁴*God called to him from the bush, "Moses, Moses!"*
> *Moses answered, "Here I am!"*
> ⁵*God said, "Don't come any closer! Take off your sandals because this place where you are standing is holy ground.* ⁶*I am the God of your ancestors, the God of Abraham, Isaac, and Jacob." Moses hid his face because he was afraid to look at God.*
> *(Exodus 3:4–6)*

Jesus, using logical methods of argument similar to the Sadducees', reminded them that God had told Moses, "I Am." Within that continuing sense of the verb, God stated that He is the God of Abraham, Isaac, and Jacob. If these men were dead, God would have used the past tense of the verb, saying, "I was the God of your father, Abraham, Isaac, and Jacob." This would confirm that the time of Moses' ancestors was past. However, that was not the case. These men were no longer alive in the flesh, but they were certainly alive within the scope of Jehovah's eternity.

Jesus had responded to the Sadducees' challenge by redirecting their attention to the Scriptures that they had ignored concerning the resurrection. He pointed out that the very same Scriptures on which they based their opposition also declared that God's power would be revealed in the resurrection of the dead.

12:27 He's not the God of the dead but of the living. You're badly mistaken!"

Jesus' conclusion was clear. The Sadducees were terribly wrong because they had not sought the truth from the totality of the Scriptures. If God said that He *is* the God of those who were assumed to be dead, the only conclusion was that they were not dead. "He's not the God of the dead but of the living." The God of Moses, Abraham, Isaac, and Jacob, and the God of the chosen people of Israel is a living God, and those He numbers among the redeemed are the blessed recipients of a living inheritance. There will indeed be a resurrection of the dead.

Notes/Applications

In this passage, Jesus pinpointed another truth that the religious leaders would have preferred to avoid. They again sought to trap Him by bringing up a question that they thought would be unanswerable, but He drove to the heart of the matter. Jesus confirmed that there is life after death, and He continues to affirm this truth to His faithful followers throughout all generations.

Jesus' response to the religious leaders has far-reaching implications. We may forget the question that the Sadducees put to the Son of God in the futile effort to discredit Him, but we will never forget His answer. Essentially, Jesus promised that all who believe in Him would live again through the power of the living God. Death and the grave will not hold them. For the believer, to be physically dead is to be present with the Lord.

Soon after this exchange, Jesus provided the greatest empirical evidence to support His claim when He died and three days later arose, becoming the firstfruit of many.

> [20]*But now Christ has come back from the dead. He is the very first person of those who have died to come back to life.* [21]*Since a man brought death, a man also brought life back from death.* [22]*As everyone dies because of Adam, so also everyone will be made alive because of Christ.* [23]*This will happen to each person in his own turn. Christ is the first, then at his coming, those who belong to him will be made alive. (1 Corinthians 15:20–23)*

After Jesus' resurrection, the disciples walked, ate, and fished with Him. They did all of these things after they saw Him die on the cross. They did all of these things after they saw Him laid in a tomb.

We can praise God and His risen Son for the assurance of eternal life, a gift purchased by Jesus' death and resurrection.

⁵¹I'm telling you a mystery. Not all of us will die, but we will all be changed. ⁵²It will happen in an instant, in a split second at the sound of the last trumpet. Indeed, that trumpet will sound, and then the dead will come back to life. They will be changed so that they can live forever. ⁵³This body that decays must be changed into a body that cannot decay. This mortal body must be changed into a body that will live forever. ⁵⁴When this body that decays is changed into a body that cannot decay, and this mortal body is changed into a body that will live forever, then the teaching of Scripture will come true:

"Death is turned into victory!
⁵⁵Death, where is your victory?
Death, where is your sting?"

⁵⁶Sin gives death its sting, and God's standards give sin its power. ⁵⁷Thank God that he gives us the victory through our Lord Jesus Christ. (1 Corinthians 15:51–57)

Mark 12:28–34

12:28 *One of the scribes went to Jesus during the argument with the Sadducees. He saw how well Jesus answered them, so he asked him, "Which commandment is the most important of them all?"*

One of the scribes had heard the unfolding debate with the Pharisees, the Herodians, and the Sadducees and was impressed with Jesus' response to these hypocritical religious leaders. Jesus was able to answer their most difficult questions with a knowledge and authority that the best of them never possessed. Apparently, this man approached Jesus on his own without the counsel of other members of the Sanhedrin.

This scribe, most likely a Pharisee, wanted to get past all of their oral tradition and get to the heart of the matter, so he simply asked Jesus, "Which commandment is the most important of them all?"

12:29–30 *²⁹Jesus answered, "The most important is, 'Listen, Israel, the Lord our God is the only Lord. ³⁰So love the Lord your God with all your heart, with all your soul, with all your mind, and with all your strength.'*

Jesus answered with the basic creed of the Old Testament, one that every Jew recited twice daily—once in the morning and once in the evening. From the cradle to the grave, it was the one overriding doctrine that governed Jewish religious devotion. It was called the *Shema*, referring to the first Hebrew word of the phrase, and Jesus quoted it verbatim[5]: *"⁴Listen, Israel: The Lord is our God. The Lord is the only God. ⁵Love the Lord your God with all your heart, with all your soul, and with all your strength"* (Deuteronomy 6:4–5). This phrase would warm the heart of every person within earshot of Jesus' voice. While the Pharisees and the Sadducees reveled in the intricacy of verbal debate, trying to show their great intellect and understanding of the Scriptures, Jesus went directly to the passionate core of the Jewish faith. While the Pharisees loved to debate the value of the oral traditions that required strict adherence to a legalistic code of conduct, Jesus went straight to the intimacy of a relationship with God that focused the mind and heart on praise and devotion.

12:31 *The second most important commandment is this: 'Love your neighbor as you love yourself.' No other commandment is greater than these."*

Jesus had answered the scribe's question with the most revered phrase in all of Judaism, but He went on to remind him that acceptance of the first commandment required a similar commitment to the second greatest commandment: "Never get revenge. Never hold a grudge against any of your people. Instead, love your neighbor as you love yourself. I am the Lord" *(Leviticus 19:18)*.

Jesus then stated that nothing could compare with these two commands, which encompassed all of the Mosaic Law. All other rules and regulations were enacted only to ensure that these primary commandments were obeyed.

12:32–33 *³²The scribe said to Jesus, "Teacher, that was well said! You've told the truth that there is only one God and no other besides him! ³³To love him with all your heart, with all your understanding, with all your strength, and to love your neighbor as you love yourself is more important than all the burnt offerings and sacrifices."*

The scribe responded to Jesus with hearty approval. He paraphrased Jesus' quotations of the Old Testament Scriptures and acknowledged God's uniqueness. In His position as supreme Creator and Redeemer of Israel, God alone is worthy of the wholehearted devotion of His people.

Encouraged by Jesus' accurate teaching, the scribe added his own summary to these two great commandments by fervently agreeing that they were greater than all of the rituals of the Jewish faith, which centered on burnt offerings and sacrifices. This conversation occurred within the confines of the temple and in the presence of the other ruling leaders who relentlessly sought to maintain a temple worship system centered on burnt offerings and sacrifices. These debates were the result of Jesus' bold actions of the previous day when He had overturned all of the booths where business was being conducted in God's temple. This was a significant statement considering that it was made by one of the members of the Sanhedrin.

12:34 *When Jesus heard how wisely the man answered, he told the man, "You're not too far from the kingdom of God." After that, no one dared to ask him another question.*

Jesus saw into the man's heart and acknowledged his sincerity. He saw him as a man in search of resolution to centuries of rabbinical debate. Jesus did not see him as a scribe. He did not see him as an adversary. He saw him only as someone genuinely seeking peace in the midst of this heated controversy. Jesus told the man that he was "not too far from the kingdom of God," referring, it seems, to the sincerity of the man's heart. Still, apart from the scribe's acceptance of Jesus as his Messiah, all of his sincerity and devotion was in vain.

After this statement, no one dared to question Jesus anymore. The debates were over. Finally, the religious leaders—the Pharisees, Sadducees, Herodians, scribes, and elders—had come to a startling revelation. They were unable to debate with this man. On every occasion throughout the time of His public ministry, these men had lost every challenge that they placed before Him.

Notes/Applications

If in the earlier passage Jesus rekindled our assurance of the reality of the resurrection, this passage gives us the principles by which we should live before God. Jesus commended a man's faith and knowledge of the Scriptures. By proclaiming the two greatest commandments, He established that nothing testifies to a disciple's devotion to Him more than one's love of God first and love of neighbor second—and, in that, to love one's neighbor as oneself. The fact that no one dared question Him demonstrated the authority with which Jesus spoke these commandments.

Some people would argue that they do not truly love themselves, and by their actions, we might be tempted to believe them. Nevertheless, most of us take extensive pains to feed, clothe, and comfort our bodies of flesh and bone. More often than not, we seek personal betterment before another's contentment. Our finances show this to be true. Our time schedules prove it as well. Truly, our attitudes reveal in what esteem we hold others. Indeed, we do love ourselves.

If we are the recipients of God's eternal grace, how then should we conduct ourselves among those who walk this road with us? *"¹²Love each other as I have loved you. This is what I'm commanding you to do. ¹³The greatest love you can show is to give your life for your friends"* (John 15:12–13).

How do we actually love others as ourselves?

⁹Love sincerely. Hate evil. Hold on to what is good. ¹⁰Be devoted to each other like a loving family. Excel in showing respect for each other. ¹¹Don't be lazy in showing your devotion. Use your energy to serve the Lord. ¹²Be happy in your confidence, be patient in trouble, and pray continually. ¹³Share what you have with God's people who are in need. Be hospitable.

¹⁴Bless those who persecute you. Bless them, and don't curse them. ¹⁵Be happy with those who are happy. Be sad with those who are sad. (Romans 12:9–15)

What higher calling is there than to live in unity and harmony before the God Who created us and calls us His sons and daughters? Despite the century or culture to which these words were originally issued, Jesus' words remain as absolute and relevant and as challenging to us today: Love the Lord your God with all your heart, soul, and mind, and love your neighbors as yourself.

Mark 12:35–40

12:35 *While Jesus was teaching in the temple courtyard, he asked, "How can the scribes say that the Messiah is David's son?*

While no one dared to ask Jesus any more questions, Jesus continued teaching in the temple and revealing His true identity to those willing to listen. To those remaining scribes, Pharisees, Sadducees, and the general audience who had witnessed the ongoing debate, Jesus posed a question about a foundational belief of the entire Jewish culture. There was no debate that the Christ, the Anointed One, was to be the descendent of David.

We can imagine the growing excitement of the crowd as Jesus spoke these words. Many in the group followed Jesus because they believed that His miracles proved He was the Anointed One. Nevertheless, they believed that the Messiah would be one Who would ascend the throne of David. They believed the Messiah would be a political figure who would break the bondage of Roman rule and return Israel to her days of greatest glory and power under David. Was Jesus now going to discuss His political objectives? Would He now declare His kingship?

12:36 *David, guided by the Holy Spirit, said, 'The Lord said to my Lord: "Take the highest position in heaven until I put your enemies under your control." '*

Jesus did not claim any earthly throne but sought to prove the divine authority of His ministry and the emptiness of the established religious structure. First, He declared that David wrote this psalm under the control of the Holy Spirit. He affirmed that the Scriptures were revealed to God's chosen nation under the inspiration and authority of the Holy Spirit. Next, Jesus quoted a messianic psalm, which David had written nearly one thousand years earlier[6]: "The Lord said to my Lord, 'Sit in the highest position in heaven until I make your enemies your footstool' " *(Psalm 110:1).* Jesus quoted this passage to challenge the interpretive process used by the scribes. Interestingly, the New Testament has more references to Psalm 110 than to any other Old Testament passage *(Acts 2:29–35; Hebrews 1:5–13; 5:6; 7:17, 21).*

12:37 *David calls him Lord. So how can he be his son?" The large crowd enjoyed listening to him.*

Jesus then posed a question that really confounded the people. David had addressed the Messiah as his Lord. How could the Messiah simultaneously be David's Lord and also David's son? This dilemma could not be answered through any deductive or inductive reasoning. Jesus posed this dilemma to the learned men of Judea to demonstrate that human logic failed to decipher the divine wisdom of God. Everything that the members of the Sanhedrin held dear was undermined when Jesus placed this question before them. Their pride, their position, and their ability to debate were rendered use-less when Jesus accurately and appropriately interpreted the words of Scripture. Without doubt, He crushed any vestiges of human pride in these men, though they dared not come apart under humiliation by Jesus. In fact, this exchange fueled their hatred and animos-ity. Their pride and spiritual blindness kept them from seeing the Messiah Who stood in their midst. The paradox and irony of God's wisdom was all around them, yet they had no clue that they would be the instruments of God's eternal design for the redemption of the world.

In contrast to the religious elite, "the large crowd enjoyed listen-ing to him." They probably enjoyed seeing these self-important men rattled at the hands of Jesus. They surely enjoyed seeing Jesus stand up to these learned men, who were silenced by the teachings of the one that many hoped would be their Messiah. However, even those pleased with the outcome of the debate did not comprehend the scope of the eternal battle being waged before their eyes.

12:38–39 *³⁸As he taught, he said, "Watch out for the scribes! They like to walk around in long robes, to be greeted in the marketplaces, ³⁹and to have the front seats in synagogues and the places of honor at dinners.*

Whether or not the ruling priests were still present is uncertain. Regardless, Jesus focused his attention on the "common people," and in unveiled discourse, He directly warned them to be mindful of the true nature of the scribes. While the scribes considered themselves the epitome of God's design for His people, they were empty shells. Jesus began by citing some outward characteristics that reflected the inward attitude for which they were to be faulted.

First, they loved to "walk around in long robes." Jesus was not criticizing them for wearing the robes but for their motivations behind adorning themselves in this ceremonial dress, which was to flaunt their important positions as teachers of the law. They also loved to exchange greetings in the marketplaces. Again, the problem was not that they liked meeting others in the marketplaces but that they loved to be seen by others for the purpose of parading their position before the people. They also yearned to occupy the best seats in the synagogue and at the dinners (feasts). The seats at the front of the synagogue facing the congregation were reserved for officials and other persons of distinction. The scribes sought to be seen in these positions in order to be revered by the common people. They also loved to claim the place of highest honor and respect at various feasts. Their efforts seemed to be directed at exalting themselves before the people.

12:40 *They rob widows by taking their houses and then say long prayers to make themselves look good. The scribes will receive the most severe punishment."*

The previous phrases reflected the scribes' continual efforts of flaunting their position before the public. However, Jesus also referred to their handling of legal matters. Not only did their pride affect their outward behavior, but their greed influenced their practices behind closed doors. The despicable level of their greed drew an analogy that Jesus illustrated as "robbing widows of their houses." This likely referred to underhanded practices by which the scribes duped widows out of most, if not all, of their material possessions. Such perverted and self-serving justice hardly reflected the Lord's intentions for taking care of the less fortunate members of Jewish society.

Finally, they loved to demonstrate their superior piety in public places by saying long prayers. Their prayers were not heartfelt. Though eloquent, they were empty words spoken to inflate their egos before one another and others. In essence, their prayers were spoken for the sake of people and not God.

Jesus concluded with a scathing summary of the scribes' ultimate destiny. The statement assumed a clear comprehension of His earlier debate with the Sadducees. There would surely be a resurrection of the dead, and there would surely be a judgment. Furthermore, these self-serving men would receive a harsher judgment for abusing their position of authority to rob and defraud the common people. Their vacant piety was more than arrogant. It was a cover used to enhance their selfish aims. God certainly did not condone such behavior in His people, let alone their leaders.

Notes/Applications

Contrasted with the earlier passage in which Jesus outlined the principles of a praise-filled life, the Messiah now revealed the meaningless consequence of a vain, self-serving, and hypocritical lifestyle. We can imagine that the people felt vindicated when Jesus exposed how false and empty the scribes really were. Everything these religious elitists did was self-motivated. They loved to worship man and money and used the cloak of religious piety to gain an inside position in society.

Sadly, life has not changed much since the Messiah walked the earth. Hypocrisy, pride, and rebellion against the truth are still prevalent. Seemingly, the wicked prosper while the righteous suffer. However, let us not be dismayed, for the power of God moves steadily toward that great day when the Messiah will come again, restoring justice and peace to those who remain faithful to His call.

> ⁷*Surrender yourself to the Lord, and wait patiently for him.*
> *Do not be preoccupied with an evildoer who succeeds in his way*
>   *when he carries out his schemes.*
> ⁸*Let go of anger, and leave rage behind.*
> *Do not be preoccupied.*
> *It only leads to evil.*
> ⁹*Evildoers will be cut off from their inheritance,*
>   *but those who wait with hope for the Lord will inherit*
>   *the land. (Psalm 37:7–9)*

Eternity with Almighty God: Cast against the backdrop of modern-day evil and hypocrisy, this promise continues to be worth the wait.

Mark 12:41–44

12:41 *As Jesus sat facing the temple offering box, he watched how much money people put into it. Many rich people put in large amounts.*

Having concluded His teaching in the outer court of the temple, Jesus entered the inner court, where no Gentile was permitted to enter. Thirteen receptacles lined the walls of this courtyard, and each receptacle was designated for a specific type of offering.[7] The treasury of the temple housed these containers where people brought their financial gifts.

Jesus sat in an area where He could watch the people put their offerings in the receptacles. Many of these people were wealthy and gave much money.

12:42 *A poor widow dropped in two small coins, worth less than a cent.*

Jesus observed a poor widow who threw in two small coins. These are often referred to as *mites*, the smallest unit of Jewish currency, worth a fraction of a penny. This woman had nothing and was poverty-stricken.

12:43 *He called his disciples and said to them, "I can guarantee this truth: This poor widow has given more than all the others.*

The disciples may have been milling about marveling at the glory of the temple structure *(Mark 13:1)* or, like Jesus, simply observing the people. Jesus called His disciples together for a brief lesson. He pointed to the widow, the picture of poverty, then told them what she had contributed to the temple. In human terms, her gift was insignificant, but in spiritual terms, it exceeded the gifts of all the others He had observed. Jesus, while observing all who contributed to the treasury, was also able to discern the motivations with which those offerings were given.

12:44 *All of them have given what they could spare. But she, in her poverty, has given everything she had to live on."*

Jesus contrasted the widow's meager contribution with the offerings of those who provided substantial sums of money to the temple. Many who gave did so from a much greater level of prosperity. Compared with the widow, however, they gave proportionately very little. The widow contributed an amount that equaled everything she had. Nothing was left even to buy the next day's bread. She gave money that was desperately needed for her daily provisions. The next day, she would have to rely on God's provision for her needs. Her gift is forever remembered as "the widow's mite."

Notes/Applications

The story of the widow's mite offers a moving glimpse into the heart of God and a stark contrast to the hypocrisy of the scribes. This woman was poor in material things but rich in eternal resources. As Jesus said, the rich gave out of their abundance, but she gave out of her poverty. Therefore, the little she gave amounted to much, according to God's accounting. The lesson here contrasts the faithful attitude with which this widow committed her all and the greed with which the more fortunate members in the synagogue withheld their devotion.

Whether or not we ever experience such dire material circumstances, imagine being down to the last dollar and giving that to God. What does God do with faith like that? He rewards it through supernatural provision. We see His provision in a parallel account of the widow of Zeraphath, who fed the prophet Elijah her last bit of food, even though she knew that she and her son might soon die of starvation: *"¹³Then Elijah told her, 'Don't be afraid. Go home, and do as you've said. But first make a small loaf and bring it to me. Then prepare something for yourself and your son.* *¹⁴This is what the Lord God of Israel says: Until the Lord sends rain on the land, the jar of flour will never be empty and the jug will always contain oil"* *(1 Kings 17:13–14).*

What resources have we withheld from the Lord? God, Who owns the "cattle on a thousand hills" *(Psalm 50:10)*, does not need our money to achieve His purposes. However, He desires that our love of Him and our trust in His provision be expressed through willing surrender. *"²⁵So I tell you to stop worrying about what you will eat, drink, or wear. Isn't life more than food and the body more than clothes? ²⁶Look at the birds. They don't plant, harvest, or gather the harvest into barns. Yet, your heavenly Father feeds them. Aren't you worth more than they?"* *(Matthew 6:25–26).*

Of infinite value to God is the condition of our hearts. We need the change in heart that comes from trusting Him to provide for our every need even in the face of frightening circumstances, the kind of heart that rejoices in obeying Him and in expressing our gratitude by returning to Him a portion of what He first gave us:

> *⁶Remember this: The farmer who plants a few seeds will have a very small harvest. But the farmer who plants because he has received God's blessings will receive a harvest of God's blessings in return. ⁷Each of you should give whatever you have decided. You shouldn't be sorry that you gave or feel forced to give, since God loves a cheerful giver. ⁸Besides, God will give you his constantly overflowing kindness. Then, when you always have everything you need, you can do more and more good things. ¹⁵I thank God for his gift that words cannot describe (2 Corinthians 9:6–8, 15).*

MARK 13

Chapter thirteen and its parallel passages in the synoptic Gospels *(Matthew 24 and Luke 21)* are commonly referred to as the "Olivet Discourse" and are considered among the most difficult passages in the New Testament to interpret. Jesus' words were undoubtedly prophetic as He responded to the disciples' question, "Tell us, when will this happen?" *(Mark 13:4)*. However, interpretations regarding the fulfillment of this prophecy vary widely, and as a result, these passages remain controversial.

The account begins with the disciples' awed admiration of the temple's magnificence and enormity *(verse 1)*, at which time Jesus advised them of its inevitable doom with His bleak words, "Not one of these stones will be left on top of another. Each one will be torn down" *(verse 2)*. Unable to fathom such an implausible fate for the colossal structure, the disciples seemingly equated its devastation with the end of the world. Parallel passages more vividly convey these thoughts with the disciples' further inquiries to know when the world would end *(Matthew 24:3)*. Though it may have seemed unlikely at the time, most of these events would come to pass with the destruction of the temple in A.D. 70 at the hands of the notorious Roman emperor, Titus.

Whereas the historical facts surrounding the destruction of Jerusalem serve as the initial fulfillment of this prophecy, many elements within Jesus' discourse cannot be reconciled with that event. Therefore, we must conclude that this discourse, as with many biblical prophecies, requires a progressive, or "telescopic," treatment; that is, the fulfillment of such prophecies had both initial (or partial) fulfillment in events relevant to the age in which the prophecy was given and also an ultimate fulfillment by a future event, specifically "the Son of Man coming in clouds" *(verse 26)*. In a sense, Jesus answered both questions posed by the disciples regarding the destruction of the temple and the coming of the Son of Man, even though they themselves were unable to understand that these events would not happen concurrently. Through the benefit of historical record, as well as through a more comprehensive understanding of the New Testament, today's readers can more easily appreciate Jesus' prophecy as having been initially fulfilled in A.D. 70 and having yet to be ultimately fulfilled. Accordingly, we must exercise caution lest we conclude that this prophecy has been or will be entirely fulfilled at only one time or the other.

We approach the commentary to this chapter with such a mindset. Whereas many passages of the Olivet Discourse have been treated to address simultaneously the relevance within both time frames, for the purposes of simplicity, we opt to pursue the handling of the chapter in reference to the events of A.D. 70 insomuch as the historical facts will allow. Only when such prophetic elements can no longer be reconciled by the fall of Jerusalem in the late first century will verses be treated as pertaining to a future, glorious day when the Son of Man will come again, as described in other scriptural accounts. This is not done to place more validity or emphasis on one particular interpretation but merely to harmonize the events described herein as clearly and as accurately as possible within the confines of a historical and scriptural balance.

Mark 13:1–7

13:1 *As Jesus was going out of the temple courtyard, one of his disciples said to him, "Teacher, look at these huge stones and these beautiful buildings!"*

After a grueling debate with the Jewish leaders, Jesus and His disciples left the temple, and one of the disciples remarked about its amazing grandeur. This was not the temple that Solomon built around 967 B.C. That temple, one of the most magnificent structures in the ancient world, was destroyed in 586 B.C. when Nebuchadnezzar, king of Babylon, captured Jerusalem and demolished the temple. The temple in Jesus' day was originally constructed by Nehemiah when Cyrus permitted the Jews to return to Jerusalem to rebuild the temple. Due to a lack of funds and commitment on the part of God's people, the structure was far inferior to Solomon's glorious temple. The temple complex was architecturally adorned under Herod, the Roman tetrarch of Galilee. While it still lacked the richness of Solomon's temple, it was the most prominent structure in Jerusalem. According to Josephus, some of the stones of the structure measured thirty-seven feet long by eighteen feet deep by twelve feet high and were polished until they gleamed in their whiteness.[1] The porches, courtyards, and colonnades were reminiscent of the glorious status Israel had possessed as God's chosen nation. Surely, this sight must have inspired awe and wonder in even the most casual observer.

13:2 *Jesus said to him, "Do you see these large buildings? Not one of these stones will be left on top of another. Each one will be torn down."*

The innocent exclamation of wonder from one of the disciples deeply moved Jesus. While acknowledging the grandeur of the temple structure, He was also profoundly aware of the hypocrisy within its walls. The day before, He had turned the entire court of the Gentiles upside down, forbidding the fraudulent transactions that characterized temple business. Even earlier on this same day, He had met the blistering hostility of the Sanhedrin, and although He had defended Himself from their accusations, Jesus knew that His days were numbered and that He would soon be crucified.

He looked at the grandeur of the temple and exclaimed to His disciples that those great buildings, even those tremendous stones, would be leveled. Stones weighing several tons would be moved from their foundations and the glory of Herod's temple would crumble to dust. Everything would be demolished so that no one would recognize that this was once the center of Jewish devotion and worship.

13:3–4 *³As Jesus was sitting on the Mount of Olives facing the temple buildings, Peter, James, John, and Andrew asked him privately, ⁴"Tell us, when will this happen? What will be the sign when all this will come to an end?"*

Jesus and His small band of devoted followers continued to walk out of the temple area and leave Jerusalem behind. They crossed the Kidron Valley to the east and ascended the Mount of Olives, whose ridge was slightly higher than the east wall of Jerusalem. Sitting there, they could see the holy city and the temple itself. Pondering the ramifications of Jesus' prophecy during the short walk and looking back at the magnificence of the temple, we can imagine the deep uneasiness that swelled in the hearts of these men. This was all that they knew. What would happen to God's chosen people when this devastating event occurred? Were they to suffer a second defeat like the one they experienced when Nebuchadnezzar destroyed Solomon's temple? How much were the Hebrew children expected to bear? This was unthinkable!

Yet, we do not read that they argued with Jesus. They did not protest this horrible prophecy. In fact, since Jesus Himself spoke the words of prophecy, its fulfillment was certain. The only question concerned timing. Would they live to see this prophecy come true? Would they be forced to bear witness to the devastation of God's holy city? Four of Jesus' closest disciples approached the Lord and inquired about when this event would occur and what events would precede it to show them that the time of fulfillment was near.

The men had great difficulty understanding that the destruction of the temple and the end of the world would not be the same thing: "Tell us, when will this happen? What will be the sign that you are coming again, and when will the world come to an end?" (*Matthew 24:3*). To them, the temple's destruction would signify at the very least the end of the Jewish culture—the end of the social, political, and religious structure that had guided God's chosen people throughout centuries of upheaval. In its greatest extreme, however, they perceived the destruction of the temple as signaling the end of the world or resulting from it.

13:5 *Jesus answered them, "Be careful not to let anyone deceive you.*

The first words from Jesus' mouth consisted of both warning and caution for He was concerned that His disciples would be deceived. This warning occurs four more times in this discourse. The Greek implies an emphatic "Watch out!"[2] The disciples were to be continually aware of their social, political, and religious environment. Things were going to happen that would be a source of perplexity and concern to them. Firmly grounded in Jesus' teaching, they had to depend on all of their God-given resources to avoid falling prey to wrong interpretations of coming events.

13:6 *Many will come using my name. They will say, 'I am he,' and they will deceive many people.*

Jesus gave the reason for His words of caution. As the four sat with Him and viewed the glory of the temple, He informed them of the course of future events. He warned that many would come using His holy, sacred name, wrongfully claiming to be the messiah. These would be imposters, since Jesus' identity, position in history, and God-given role as Redeemer were unique and exclusive.

This was a terrible affront to the divine author of salvation for the sins of mankind. Nevertheless, Jesus was not concerned about what people thought they could do to Him. His major concern was that His followers would be deceived by these imposters. Jesus had gladly taken on His shoulders the mantle of Redeemer. He would never be misled by the chaos and confusion generated among the ranks of the human race, but that certainty did not inhabit the minds of men. With skills damaged by sin, their perception of the truth remained clouded. Jesus was concerned to think of the terrible consequences that would occur among His followers because of these imposters. These godless pretenders would deceive a great number of people.

13:7 *"When you hear of wars and rumors of wars, don't be alarmed! These things must happen, but they don't mean that the end has come.*

A warring mentality has always characterized every political and social environment. In the midst of all these national confrontations, Jesus urged His disciples to remain calm and not be afraid. Jesus' prophecy frightened the tough but simple men, but these events were not to unduly impact their lives, which were to be characterized by a calm and peaceful spirit.

Jesus told them that these things must happen and affirmed that such wars among the nations were not indications that the end was near. While the nations of the earth pursued their own interests, a divine imperative would direct the future events.

Notes/Applications

Jesus admonished His followers to be cautious, alert, and watchful. He told them that many false prophets would rise up claiming His name. We are subject, as were the disciples, to the philosophies and opinions of those around us. Today, man's view on how to live and interact in a global, pluralistic, and international climate bombards us. The handwriting seems to be on the wall: Senseless violence, rampant promiscuity, "wars and rumors of wars," natural disasters, false prophets emerging with regularity all seem to bear apocalyptic portent.

As Christians, our security is assured for all eternity. Therefore, we have every reason to remain calm and confident. We look through the eyes of Scripture and find that the world is a foreign place whose tenets sharply contrast the principles of the kingdom of God. We need to seek refuge in the Word of God, knowing that our hope and security are not based on the temporal events of today's news. Rather, our foundation is laid in the chief cornerstone of faith, the Lord Jesus Christ.

Mark 13:8–13

13:8 *Nation will fight against nation and kingdom against kingdom. There will be earthquakes and famines in various places. These are only the beginning pains of the end.*

Jesus continued His lesson on future events after urging His disciples to remain calm amid impending disasters. Catastrophes such as warring nations, earthquakes, famines, and other calamities are not unnatural. Such events had occurred prior to Jesus' statement and will continue to occur throughout all ages until the end. Therefore, such events should not be perceived as signaling the end of the world.[3] As terrible as they might appear to those living through them, they represent only the "beginning pains of the end." Especially considering the disciples' expectations that the devastation of the temple paralleled the end of the world, it should be no surprise that Jesus urged them to remain calm when the world appeared to be unraveling. Imagine how reassuring this statement must have been to them during events like the widespread droughts, famines, and devastating earthquakes that ravaged Middle Eastern and Mediterranean regions in the first century[4] (*see also* Acts 11:28). Likewise, neither should Christians of any era point to such calamities, no matter how violent or destructive, as signals that the end is at hand.

13:9 *"Be on your guard! People will hand you over to the Jewish courts and whip you in their synagogues. You will stand in front of governors and kings to testify to them because of me.*

Jesus urged His disciples to watch out for themselves because many of them would be brought to trial and be beaten. Although not guilty of any legal infractions, they would stand trial and be punished for their faith in Christ. This verse serves as a reminder that God's people, past and present, suffer ridicule and physical abuse at the hands of unbelievers.

The phrase "to testify to them because of me" can also be translated to mean that these trials would serve as testimony against those who brought the faithful to trial. All proclamations of Jesus' gospel are submitted as an exhortation to believe the message. For those who choose to walk away, like the rich young man *(Mark 10:22)*, it certainly becomes a testimony against them. No alternative to salvation exists other than the call of Jesus Christ to repent and believe. After Jesus' death and resurrection, Jesus' disciples would have many opportunities to stand before both religious and political rulers and proclaim the truth in Christ *(Acts 4; 5; 6:12–7:60; 13:6–7; 16:19–35; 21:33–26:32)*.

Peter's ministry after Pentecost serves as a perfect example of this twofold presentation of the gospel's testimony. He was brought before the high priest, Caiaphas, the same man before whom Jesus was tried and condemned to death. Peter's answer was clear.

> *⁹Today you are cross-examining us about the good we did for a crippled man. You want to know how he was made well. ¹⁰You and all the people of Israel must understand that this man stands in your presence with a healthy body because of the power of Jesus Christ from Nazareth. You crucified Jesus Christ, but God has brought him back to life. ¹¹He is the stone that the builders rejected, the stone that has become the cornerstone. ¹²No one else can save us. Indeed, we can be saved only by the power of the one named Jesus and not by any other person.* (Acts 4:9–12)

13:10 *But first, the Good News must be spread to all nations.*

This verse has often been applied strictly to the second coming of Christ, such that before this glorious event can occur every individual or kindred on earth must have an opportunity to hear and respond to the gospel message.[5] The difficulty with this interpretation is threefold. First, it implies that God's timing concerning the second coming is subject to humankind's success in missionary efforts, thereby denigrating a believer's evangelistic motivation from

God-serving obedience to self-serving anticipation. However, God's providence is not confined to man's accomplishments. Second, the interpretation assumes a task that seems implausible both in scope and measurability. Can it really be supposed (by people if not by God) that we must locate and proclaim the gospel to each and every person of every generation? And if so, could we ever know if and when that "goal" was achieved? Third, this interpretation disregards any application of this verse to the first-century destruction of Jerusalem.

This verse can be properly applied both to time frames (A.D. 70 and an unknown future time) and to fulfillments (the destruction of the temple and the second coming of Christ) more easily than an initial reading of the verse might suggest. Primarily, Jesus' reference to "nations" is clearly ἔθνη (ethnos), which commonly differentiates between Jew and non-Jew[6] (*Luke 7:5; John 11:48–52; Acts 10:22; 24:2,10,17*). In this sense, after the final rejection by the Jews of Jesus as their Messiah, salvation would also be extended to the Gentiles (*Romans 9–11*). While this is an indisputable truth to modern Christians, it was a concept as perplexing and incomprehensible to Jesus' disciples as was the destruction of the temple. Nevertheless, the gospel would be preached to Gentile nations even within the disciples' own lifetimes, and the Jews' understanding of God's chosen people would be changed forever (*Acts 10–11*). Moreover, in the context of the previous verse, it seems that the trials and persecutions the disciples suffered would be a means by which they would have opportunity to proclaim the gospel to other nations.

In regard to this verse's application to the second coming of Christ, we must not define God's timeline based on our ability to fulfill the task of reaching every nation within our own abilities, regardless of how one might define this verse. This passage should not be understood as a divine checklist that must be fully satisfied before Jesus will return. We must preach to all nations out of obedience to our Lord (*Matthew 28:19–20*) and not out of obligation to our perceived role in the fulfillment of this verse. When the time for Jesus' return is at hand—according to His time and His purposes—He will satisfy this requirement. *"⁶I saw another angel flying overhead with the everlasting Good News to spread to those who live on earth—to every nation, tribe, language, and people. ⁷The angel said in a loud voice, 'Fear God and give him glory, because the time has come for him to judge. Worship the one who made heaven and earth, the sea and springs'"* (Revelation 14:6–7).

Fortunately, the challenge to preach to all nations, per the Great Commission, is not equivalent to the necessity to reach all nations, a feat that perhaps only God can accomplish *(1 Timothy 2:6)*.

13:11 *When they take you away to hand you over to the authorities, don't worry ahead of time about what you will say. Instead, say whatever is given to you to say when the time comes. Indeed, you are not the one who will be speaking, but the Holy Spirit will.*

Again, Jesus admonished His disciples to remain calm though they would be arrested for His sake. When they were handed over to the authorities, their faces were to confirm their inner calm and confidence. Even under these stressful circumstances, they needed to forsake their natural inclinations of fear and rely instead on their faith in God. This statement marked the first occasion where Jesus promised to empower His followers with the Holy Spirit. The authority of their words would be from God through the Spirit, so they were not to be concerned with what they should say. It would not be them speaking but the Spirit speaking through them. Therefore, the court would hear what God wanted it to hear *(Acts 4:8, 7:55)*.

13:12 *"Brother will hand over brother to death; a father will hand over his child. Children will rebel against their parents and kill them.*

In this statement, Jesus emphasized the severity of persecution His disciples would face. Believers would be hated for His sake not only by authorities but even by their own kin. The hostility they were to expect was not simply a matter of political and religious opposition but also a matter that severed the intimate relationships of their own families. *"34Don't think that I came to bring peace to earth. I didn't come to bring peace but conflict. 35I came to turn a man against his father, a daughter against her mother, a daughter-in-law against her mother-in-law. 36A person's enemies will be the members of his own family"* (Matthew 10:34–36). Because of the fear produced by violent persecution, members of the same household would turn against each other, presumably in a futile effort to save their own lives. The outcome would succeed. Many of Jesus' followers would die because of these betrayals. The same principle applies even today. Worldly propensities to disassociate from Christians often result in the collapse of traditional family loyalties.

13:13 *Everyone will hate you because you are committed to me. But the person who endures to the end will be saved.*

All of the events Jesus warned His disciples about in the preceding verses culminate as a result of one fact. The disciples would be hated by everyone "because you are committed to me," yet they were expected to stand firm in the face of open hostility and outright hatred. Jesus, however, did not just convey dismal words of warning; He also provided a message of encouragement and hope. Those who endured to the end would "be saved." This phrase is difficult to interpret because we cannot be certain what Jesus meant by "the end." Surely, we are to persevere through the hardships we face in the sense of not giving up or giving in to the circumstances. However, we must be encouraged that, even if those hardships cost us our very lives, we have endured to the end and will receive our heavenly inheritance. *"Christ means everything to me in this life, and when I die I'll have even more"* (Philippians 1:21).

Notes/Applications

Surrounded by events that seem to fulfill this passage, Christian disciples who commit themselves to standing forth with the clear salvation message will likely be swamped with opposition. Amid reports of wars, famines, violence, death, and despair, we hear Jesus' words echo from the pages of Scripture: "Be careful! Watch! Be alert!" *(Mark 13:33, 37)*. Although, as Christians, we are often forced into postures that depict us as weak and defenseless, Jesus exhorts us to endure to the end.

The most precious words of this passage are found in verse eleven: "When they take you away to hand you over to the authorities, don't worry ahead of time about what you will say. Instead, say whatever is given to you to say when the time comes. Indeed, you are not the one who will be speaking, but the Holy Spirit will." The hour of decision may come when we are called to testify or face punishment and even death for our beliefs. In many parts of the world, Christian martyrdom is not something read about in dusty books or in ancient Scriptures; it is a very real and present danger. If a day comes when we are persecuted for our beliefs, we have Jesus' promise that the Holy Spirit will speak through us, answering when we are speechless.

Jesus bids us to look beyond the physical environment that surrounds us. He bids us to focus on Him and understand that we are only players on the stage of history, ordained by God to be His witnesses. He bids us to understand that reality exists not in the struggle we face here on earth but in the terrible struggle between the Lord of heaven and the principalities of this world *(Ephesians 6:12)*. He bids us to comprehend the wondrous fact that we are blessed to be the children of the most high God, for the blood of Jesus Christ saves us in this life and throughout eternity.

Even if we should face death for His sake, we need not be afraid. Do we not enter the gates of heaven where we shall meet our Redeemer face-to-face? Surely, at that moment, we will be standing in His glorious, eternal presence *(1 John 5:4–5; 2 Timothy 4:17–18)*.

Mark 13:14-23

13:14 *"When you see the disgusting thing that will cause destruction standing where it should not (let the reader take note), those of you in Judea should flee to the mountains.*

Jesus further accentuated His discourse by citing the words of Daniel the prophet. Some commentators suggest that Daniel 11:31 was Jesus' intended reference.[7] However, it is generally accepted by most biblical historians that Daniel chapter eleven points to the treacherous exploits of Antiochus Epiphanes nearly two hundred years before Jesus spoke these words, and therefore, this reference seems to be an unlikely option.[8] A more fitting explanation is to reconcile Jesus' reference with Daniel 9:26–27.[9]

> [26]*But after the sixty-two sets of seven time periods, the Anointed One will be cut off and have nothing. The city and the holy place will be destroyed with the prince who is to come. His end will come with a flood until the end of the destructive war that has been determined.* [27]*He will confirm his promise with many for one set of seven time periods. In the middle of the seven time periods, he will stop the sacrifices and food offerings. This will happen along with disgusting things that cause destruction until those time periods come to an end. It has been determined that this will happen to those who destroy the city.* (Daniel 9:26–27)

Nearly six hundred years before Jesus conveyed these words to His disciples, an angel of the Lord appeared to the prophet Daniel and foretold the same events that would come to pass in A.D. 70, when all sacrifices and offerings would be forced to an end by the destruction of the temple.[10]

The phrase "standing where it should not" has been widely interpreted but requires little explanation to be resolved satisfactorily. Basically, the abomination, whatever it represents, was identified as an abomination by the mere fact that it profaned the holy city and temple by its inappropriate presence. In this case, the Roman armies' occupation of Jerusalem in general and the temple in particular may adequately account for this phrase.[11]

Mark inserts a personal encouragement for his readers to understand both the prophecy in the Book of Daniel and Jesus' words regarding that prophecy.

Jesus confirmed that the location of this devastation would be in the region of Judea. The only reason to emphasize that this sacrilege would occur in Judea, and specifically in Jerusalem, appears to be to avoid spiritualized interpretations that would suggest that this prophecy pertains to global events. Jesus clarified that this would be a specific event happening in a specific location at a specific point in history.

When His disciples saw these events unfolding, they were told to "flee to the mountains." It seems unusual that after encouraging His disciples to stand firm in the face of opposition in earlier verses, Jesus would then urge them to flee as far from Judea as possible. Surely, this must emphasize the intensity of the sweeping atrocities that would be brought against the temple and the city of Jerusalem at that time. Whereas the disciples were expected to face harsh persecutions (brought against them even by their own family members) with confidence and boldness through the Holy Spirit, those events would pale in comparison to the unimaginable violence that lay ahead. This seems to be why it was so imperative for them to understand. When Jesus' followers recognized the events as moving beyond direct persecution to destruction, they were not only permitted but compelled to escape from the region. The urgency of the matter was reiterated in the verses that follow.

13:15–16 *15Those who are on the roof should not come down to get anything out of their houses. 16Those who are in the field should not turn back to get their coats.*

When this devastation was visited upon Jerusalem, it would be necessary to flee immediately, suggesting not only the extent but also the speed with which the atrocities would occur. Those working in their fields when these events began were not even to return to their homes to retrieve more clothes. This was not to be some orderly retreat in which one had the time or leisure to pack his belongings before moving to a safer location.

13:17 *"How horrible it will be for the women who are pregnant or who are nursing babies in those days.*

Jesus acknowledged that these events would come at a time when many were not prepared for the rigors of a hasty flight. He expressed His concern and compassion for pregnant and nursing mothers. Jesus still encouraged them to flee Judea, but He did not minimize the hardship that would befall new and expectant mothers.

13:18 *Pray that it will not be in winter.*

Jesus also recognized that wintertime would make it more difficult to flee. The weather would be an additional burden to face. The forces of nature would escalate the hardships and conditions under which those in Judea would have to evacuate their homeland.

13:19 *It will be a time of misery that has not happened from the beginning of God's creation until now, and will certainly never happen again.*

This would be a period of tremendous suffering. It would be a horrific experience unparalleled by any other moment in history. In his account of Jerusalem's destruction, first-century historian Josephus similarly depicted a period of unprecedented violence and carnage the Jewish people experienced.[12] However, Jesus' specific mention of this being a time worse than any that would ever be resonates with apocalyptic undertones. It should not be assumed that the horrors surrounding the first-century destruction of the temple would exceed those of the period traditionally referred to as the great tribulation, as described in the Book of Revelation. Accordingly, the next several verses of this passage seem to be most appropriately treated as transitional; that is, while referring to both time frames, the progression of events described in the remainder of this discourse rapidly fades as a reference to the events of A.D. 70 and expands in allusion to that still-future period of intense persecution directly preceding the second coming of the Lord Jesus Christ.

13:20 *If the Lord does not reduce that time, no one will be saved. But those days will be reduced because of those whom God has chosen.*

Jesus continued to reveal the arduous times of both the near and distant future. The Lord in His sovereignty promised to curb the length of this perilous time. Man and beast would be annihilated if the Lord would not mercifully spare His chosen ones by limiting the duration of the events that Jesus predicted.

The affirmation that the Lord would "reduce that time" does not mean that the days would have fewer than twenty-four hours but that God would restrict the period of terrible suffering. In fact, the tense of the verb "reduce" implies that the cataclysmic period had been predetermined. Although the events would be extremely frightening, Jesus' assurance of God's sovereignty over the calamitous events should serve as reassurance to His chosen ones.

13:21–22 *²¹"At that time don't believe anyone who tells you, 'Here is the Messiah!' or 'There he is!' ²²False messiahs and false prophets will appear. They will work miraculous signs and do wonderful things to deceive, if possible, those whom God has chosen.*

As Jesus indicated in verse six, there would be those who claimed to be messiahs. This manifestation of "false christs" would occur prior to and during this intense tribulation.

These pseudo christs would deceive great numbers of people by corroborating their claims with "miracles." *"²ᵇThe serpent gave its power, kingdom, and far-reaching authority to the beast. ³One of the beast's heads looked like it had a fatal wound, but its fatal wound was healed. All the people of the world were amazed and followed the beast"* (Revelation 13:2b–3). The general population would be astounded by these deceivers just as the crowds that had followed Jesus had been continually astonished by His acts of healing and restoration. The miracles performed by these imposters would be so convincing that, if it were possible, even those whom God had chosen would be deceived. It is extremely important to understand that those individuals chosen by the Lord to be His can never be taken away from Him either by force or by falsehood.

13:23 *Be on your guard! I have told you everything before it happens.*

Jesus warned His listeners to be alert. Whether or not this is a reference by which to gauge the march of history, He admonished His followers not to be alarmed. When these things came to pass, His followers could be encouraged by the fact that Jesus had foretold the events, thereby demonstrating His sovereignty over the adversities, no matter how terrifying they might be.

Notes/Applications

Jesus began His discourse by discussing a specific judgment that would befall Jerusalem and the Jewish temple. It quickly becomes evident, however, that elements of a future period of tribulation are interwoven within the context of Jesus' prophecy. During this future time, the intensity of the persecution and suffering will be much greater than that experienced in A.D. 70. Jesus counseled His followers to remain alert and watchful when these things happened.

Even now we do not like to ponder the afflictions that Jesus described to the disciples. Such a dismal picture riddled with frightening prospects can catapult us into an extreme state of panic or euphoria. Without minimizing the consuming judgment that He described, Christ issued a message of hope. He will permit such devastation to occur for a purpose and will limit its duration.

Why would God allow such a time of trial and then mandate His followers to remain alert, calm, and loyal to Him? How can believers truly rest at the door of such calamity? Scripture adamantly establishes that God does not tempt, but He does test (James 1:12–18). Through tumultuous circumstances, God will further conform His beloved ones into what He wants them to be. He will usher in His kingdom and glorify Himself.

> *⁵I am the Lord, and there is no other.*
> *There is no other God besides me.*
> *I will strengthen you, although you don't know me,*
> *⁶so that from the east to the west people will know*
> *that there is no God except me.*
> *I am the Lord, and there is no other.*
> *⁷I make light and create darkness.*
> *I make blessings and create disasters.*
> *I, the Lord, do all these things. (Isaiah 45:5–7)*

Although God has admonished believers to remain grounded in faith throughout frightening times, the miraculous truth holds firm that He has equipped believers with the power of the Holy Spirit to accomplish what they cannot do on their own.

Certainly, God has not required anything from us that He will not provide. His faithfulness to us makes it possible for us to be faithful to Him no matter what we face. His children will not be tested beyond what they can bear. His children will not be seduced by false prophets, and His children will not fail the ultimate test. They will remain faithful to His end for them. These dire warnings about perilous times should cause us to live continually in sober reverence, thankful that our lives are in God's hands. *"The Lord guards you from every evil. He guards your life"* (Psalm 121:7).

Mark 13:24–27

13:24–25 [24]*"Now, after the misery of those days, the sun will turn dark, the moon will not give light, [25]the stars will fall from the sky, and the powers of the universe will be shaken.*

The nature of Jesus' discourse by this time digressed from personal persecution to widespread suffering and appeared to be worsening to involve even the celestial realm. Some commentators spiritualize these verses as allegorical phrases still referring to the aftermath of Jerusalem's destruction.[13] However, this has not been the tone of the discourse to this point, and therefore, it seems difficult to prove that such is the case now. Rather, it appears that Jesus' words by this point in His exposition are markedly apocalyptic, especially in light of other scriptural passages about the cataclysmic events preceding the Lord's second coming.

> [30]*I will work miracles in the sky and on the earth:*
> *blood, fire, and clouds of smoke.*
> [31]*The sun will become dark,*
> *and the moon will become as red as blood*
> *before the terrifying day of the Lord comes. (Joel 2:30–31)*

> [12]*I watched as the lamb opened the sixth seal. A powerful earthquake struck. The sun turned as black as sackcloth made of hair. The full moon turned as red as blood. [13]The stars fell from the sky to the earth like figs dropping from a fig tree when it is shaken by a strong wind. [14]The sky vanished like a scroll being rolled up. Every mountain and island was moved from its place. (Revelation 6:12–14)*

We must, therefore, conclude that at some future time the whole universe will be embroiled in the cosmic battle between the Lord and Lucifer. It seems that the entire earth will be enveloped in physical darkness when the elements of the heavens that have produced light for the earth for thousands of years will be dimmed and, perhaps, extinguished. Life-giving light will no longer radiate from the sun and the moon. Even the secondary sources of light, the stars far beyond the realm of our galaxy, will also fade. All of the powers of the universe will be shaken. When this sign is given in the sky above, it will not be a joyous spectacle to behold. Rather, it will be a sign of impending doom and judgment for the people of the world.

13:26 *"Then people will see the Son of Man coming in clouds with great power and glory.*

Evidently, "people" refers to all people throughout the world: *"Look! He is coming in the clouds. Every eye will see him, even those who pierced him" (Revelation 1:7).* No longer the suffering Messiah Whose death would come at the hands of sinful men, the mighty King will triumphantly return in the clouds of the sky.

> *⁹After he had said this, he was taken to heaven. A cloud hid him so that they could no longer see him.*
> *¹⁰They were staring into the sky as he departed. Suddenly, two men in white clothes stood near them. ¹¹They asked, "Why are you men from Galilee standing here looking at the sky? Jesus, who was taken from you to heaven, will come back in the same way that you saw him go to heaven. (Acts 1:9–11)*

His power and glory will be profoundly evident.

> *¹³There was someone like the Son of Man among the lamp stands. He was wearing a robe that reached his feet. He wore a gold belt around his waist. ¹⁴His head and his hair were white like wool—like snow. His eyes were like flames of fire. ¹⁵His feet were like glowing bronze refined in a furnace. His voice was like the sound of raging waters. ¹⁶In his right hand he held seven stars, and out of his mouth came a sharp, two-edged sword. His face was like the sun when it shines in all its brightness. (Revelation 1:13–16)*

In His early discourses with His disciples, Jesus told them of His future and how He would be betrayed and would suffer and die.

Now, Jesus again identified Himself as the Son of Man Who would return to His creation as a powerful and conquering king.

Jesus had already warned His disciples of imposters who would come claiming to be the Messiah. While these false christs would perform many spectacular miracles, they would never be able to duplicate the power of this glorious event. Only the Lord Jesus Christ can shake the heavens to their very foundations. Only the Lord of all creation will appear in the clouds and ascend the throne reserved for God's Anointed.

13:27 *He will send out his angels, and from every direction under the sky, they will gather those whom God has chosen.*

Jesus informed His disciples that, on that day, the Son of Man will send His angels to gather all those who belong to Him wherever they may be spread around the globe (*Revelation 14:14–16*).

Notes/Applications
While candidly describing future events, Jesus exhorted His followers to "Be aware. Be assured." In the midst of devastating news, He reminded His loved ones that He remained in control, and He affirmed that He would return in power, glory, and might to gather His beloved home. *"²Dear friends, now we are God's children. What we will be isn't completely clear yet. We do know that when Christ appears we will be like him because we will see him as he is. ³So all people who have this confidence in Christ keep themselves pure, as Christ is pure"* (*1 John 3:2–3*).

We should not waste too much time worrying about time frames because it may keep us from a productive life for Christ here and now. At the same time, we must remain alert as Jesus cautioned, and rest in His promises as we look to the day when He will return in heavenly splendor.

Come, Thou long-expected Jesus,
Born to set Thy people free;

From our fears and sins release us,
Let us find our rest in thee:
Israel's Strength and Consolation,
Hope of all the saints Thou art;
Dear Desire of every nation,
Joy of every longing heart.

Born, Thy people to deliver;
Born a child, and yet a King!
Born to reign in us forever,
Now Thy precious kingdom bring:
By Thine own eternal Spirit,
Rule in all our hearts alone;
By Thine all-sufficient merit,
Raise us to Thy glorious throne.[14]

Mark 13:28–37

13:28 *"Learn from the story of the fig tree. When its branch becomes tender and it sprouts leaves, you know summer is near.*

As Jesus drew His discourse to an end, He illustrated a crucial point of His message with an ordinary fig tree. He encouraged His disciples to regard the progression of future events as similar to the foliage of the tree. During the winter, a tree loses its leaves and the branches become cold and brittle. When spring arrives, the branches become more pliant, leaves develop, and one can safely conclude that the harshness of winter is nearing its end and that the promise of summer will soon be realized.

13:29 *In the same way, when you see these things happen, you know that he is near, at the door.*

Just as one anticipates summer by the blooming of the trees, so, too, is the disciple to recognize that the day of the Lord is near when the described events begin to transpire. So near, in fact, were the events that would comprise the initial fulfillment of this prophecy that Jesus described it as "at the door" to indicate that the disciples were standing on the threshold and ready to pass through.

13:30 *"I can guarantee this truth: This generation will not disappear until all these things take place.*

Even within the interpretive difficulty of the Olivet Discourse, this verse poses unique challenges in its explanation. For instance, the modern-day Christian faces difficulty in trying to reconcile the statement that "all these things [would] take place" in regard to the A.D. 70 time frame when we advocate that the Son of Man has not yet returned "in clouds" *(verse 26)*. Likewise, any conclusion that treats this verse as having relevance only to the second coming without regard to Jesus' first-century audience does grave injustice to the entire passage.[15] Fortunately, the independent arguments relating this verse specifically to one time frame or the other are compelling enough to address both time frames sufficiently.

In a sense, the elements of Jesus' discourse would come to pass within the disciples' literal generation. They lived through times of terrible persecution and were time and again brought before rulers and magistrates in defense of their faith. They were often beaten for preaching the gospel. Tradition holds that each of the twelve disciples except Judas and John were ultimately martyred for the cause of Christ. Within this context, the "coming of the Son of Man" would eventually be manifested not in a physical sense but a spiritual one such that God's judgment would fall utterly upon Jerusalem and the temple in order to bring the continuing sacrilege of the old covenant sacrifices and offerings to a decisive end.[16]

Moreover, these events will realize their ultimate fulfillment during the tribulation period preceding the second coming of the Lord Jesus Christ. As verified by other Scriptures, these final days will be marked by a physical manifestation of the dreadful images depicted in verses twenty-four through twenty-seven. The use of the word *generation* in this interpretation denotes a reference not to a time frame but to a race, specifically the Jewish people, similar to its use elsewhere in the Bible[17] (*Deuteronomy 32:5, 20; Psalm 12:7; 78:8*).

13:31 *The earth and the heavens will disappear, but my words will never disappear.*

Jesus confirmed the reliability of these prophecies with this dramatic statement. In our human mind-set, the physical world is the only existence that we know. We rely on the stability of routine, expecting one day to follow the next. However, Jesus told His disciples that the world as they knew it would someday disappear. This material world, which embodies the tangible things in our physical existence, will certainly come to an end. Unlike our temporary physical world, however, Jesus' words are eternal. His entire ministry, from His first message in the synagogue, was rooted in authority. Many who heard Him commented on the authority with which He taught. Now, in this private moment with His disciples, Jesus confirmed that His authority is eternal and will last long after this world fades from its temporal existence. *"¹⁰The day of the Lord will come like a thief. On that day heaven will pass away with a roaring sound. Everything that makes up the universe will burn and be destroyed. The earth and everything that people have done on it will be exposed. ¹¹All these things will be destroyed in this way. So think of the kind of holy and godly lives you must live"* (2 Peter 3:10–11).

13:32 *"No one knows when that day or hour will come. Even the angels in heaven and the Son don't know. Only the Father knows.*

Jesus could not tell the disciples when these events would occur. In that precise, foreordained moment, the Father in heaven will commence His plan. No man on earth nor angel in heaven—not even the Son of Man, in His humanity—could know the time of this appointment when the world will cease. Only Almighty God knows.

13:33 *Be careful! Watch! You don't know the exact time.*

Again, Jesus emphasized His words with the warning that His disciples should be careful, or literally "be on their guard," because no one knew when that time would come. While there is absolute certainty about the events that Jesus described, their timing will remain unknown until that moment when they befall us. We are exhorted to watch carefully, as further illustrated in the following verses.

13:34 *It is like a man who went on a trip. As he left home, he put his servants in charge. He assigned work to each one and ordered the guard to be alert.*

Jesus accentuated the seriousness of His warning by using a simple parable. He explained the elements of His prophecy and His second coming by relating them to a man who left his home to embark on a journey to a distant place. The man assigned respective tasks to his servants and identified the chores that he expected them to accomplish while he was gone. He also charged a watchman to stand guard of his household and keep an eye on the operations. It might appear at first a close parallel to the parable that Jesus communicated in the temple earlier that day about the wicked vinedressers (*Mark 12:1–9*).

In this verse, however, the Lord was urging His disciples to stay focused on their assigned tasks in His absence. Even though the master would not always be in their presence, it did not mean that they would be orphaned or forsaken. Rather, they were still expected to diligently persevere in their commission under the comforting presence and convicting guidance of the Holy Spirit.

Like the man who went on a distant journey and left important tasks in the hands of his servants, so, too, the Lord would return to His Father soon after commissioning His disciples to carry on with their critical responsibilities. Jesus did not want them to become so concerned about the future events that they neglected their present duties, so He exhorted them to watch and work regardless of the surrounding hostilities and deteriorating circumstances.

13:35–36 *³⁵Therefore, be alert, because you don't know when the owner of the house will return. It could be in the evening or at midnight or at dawn or in the morning. ³⁶Make sure he doesn't come suddenly and find you asleep.*

Jesus continued to speak to the disciples in the context of the parable. In fact, He addressed them directly, as if they themselves were the servants entrusted with the care of the home front in the master's absence. Accordingly, Jesus exhorted them to heed His caution and remain watchful because they knew neither the day nor the hour when the master of the house would return.

Jesus called on them not only to be watchful but also to guard against the negative consequences of idleness. The servant needed to be vigilant and hard at work so that he would be found faithful

and obedient when the master returned unannounced. The caution to the servant to remain watchful was not so much a plea to be
looking for the arrival of the master but, rather, to be aggressively
about the master's business lest the servant be found negligent of his
assignment. Jesus was outlining the tangible benefits of being watchful and faithful.

13:37 *I'm telling everyone what I'm telling you: 'Be alert!' "*

Jesus concluded His discourse with a final and emphatic, "Be alert!"
Jesus' main concern seemed to be the reaction of His disciples to this
prophecy. Four times, Jesus had encouraged the Twelve to observe
the events around them and to conclude that the end was near when
they saw the escalation of hostilities. Now, three times in four verses,
Jesus warned them to be alert, to be on guard. Plainly, His concern
was that their fears and apprehensions about Jerusalem, the temple,
and their Jewish heritage would not control their lives and deter
them from doing His work.

Likewise, Christians throughout the ages must understand that
Jesus' exhortation is timeless and every bit as applicable today as it
was then. We must not allow any internal or external influences to
render us ineffective at accomplishing what the Lord has called us
to do. Surely, there will be persecution. All of nature may appear to
be in sheer turmoil. The political and social structures to which we
have grown accustomed may crumble. Nevertheless, His servants
are to be working.

Notes/Applications

In the midst of the controversies surrounding the "end times,"
nothing is clearer than Jesus' constant and repeated warnings to
watch and work. The church has spent tremendous amounts of
time in heated debate about the great tribulation and the rapture.
Entire ministries are devoted to the discussion of such future events.

Detailed analyses of current events show "signs of the times" that the end is near and Jesus will return at any moment.

Over the centuries since the life of Jesus, many have thought that their particular time period would usher in the return of Christ. Some have declared the date and the hour of His return. Some have gone so far as to sell all their possessions and wait throughout the night, certain that Jesus would return to earth the next day. In each case, the wait has been futile. Jesus has not yet returned! As a result, some have turned away and lost faith.

How could so many people be so terribly misled? Does this not also fulfill Jesus' prophecy in this chapter? Jesus contended that no one knows the time or date of this long-awaited event and that many would be deceived. He admonished us to watch and to remain on guard *(1 Corinthians 16:13)*.

In the midst of so much frenetic activity about the end times, we have not heard the words of Jesus. We have been fascinated and, perhaps, even hypnotized by wild conjectures on what the future will hold, but we have avoided Jesus' admonition to work. Thus, we fail our Lord in not obeying His command. We put the eternal lives of thousands at risk because we would rather talk about the apocalyptic future than about the saving grace of Jesus Christ.

Like the original disciples, we want to know about the future. We are drawn by our earthly curiosity to ask with them, "When will this happen?" May God forgive us for not heeding His call to work while we watch and wait. Let us embrace the labor of the kingdom as well as our future redemption when the Son of Man will return again to rule the world in justice and righteousness.

MARK 14

Mark 14:1-9

14:1 *It was two days before the Passover and the Festival of Unleavened Bread. The chief priests and the scribes were looking for some underhanded way to arrest Jesus and to kill him.*

Two days after Jesus' discourse on the Mount of Olives, a conspiracy was being contrived by the Jewish religious leaders as the Passover and Feast (Festival) of Unleavened Bread began. Jesus had made them look foolish during their attempts to discredit Him.

They could no longer hide their contempt. The Pharisees, Sadducees, and scribes comprised the Sanhedrin, and although bitter enemies in their differing philosophies, they united in their determination to get rid of Jesus. He had offended every faction of the Sanhedrin, and their hatred for the Son of Man consumed them.

14:2 *However, they said, "We shouldn't arrest him during the festival, or else there will be a riot among the people."*

These religious rulers agreed that it would be risky to mount an attack against Jesus during Passover. There were several reasons such actions could backfire on them. First, it would not look good for them to mar the festivities with an attack on Jesus, Whom many considered to be a great prophet. Second, if a sufficient number of Jesus' followers were among the crowds, an open rebellion might break out, and the Sanhedrin's power over the people would be tested on the streets of Jerusalem. Third, such a riot might jeopardize the favor of Pilate or Herod, the Roman governors whose support the Sanhedrin would need to be successful in putting Jesus to death. The Sanhedrin had tremendous judicial power over matters pertaining to Jewish law, but under Roman law they were not permitted to administer the death penalty.

Although Jerusalem's estimated population at that time was fifty thousand, Josephus recorded that the crowds of pilgrims attending Passover in the holy city could swell to more than three million.[1] Regardless of the accuracy of the estimated population, it can be safely assumed that the city was overcrowded during this most sacred of Jewish holy days. A riot, while undesirable at any time, would have considerably worse consequences when the potential accomplices grew to such great numbers.

14:3 *Jesus was in Bethany at the home of Simon, a man who had suffered from a skin disease. While Jesus was sitting there, a woman went to him. She had a bottle of very expensive perfume made from pure nard. She opened the bottle and poured the perfume on his head.*

Every evening, after spending the day in Jerusalem, Jesus and the Twelve returned to Bethany. On this particular night, they dined at the home of Simon, a leper whom Jesus had presumably healed.

A woman approached Jesus as the group reclined at the table, broke a flask, and poured fragrant oil over Jesus' head. The Gospel of John identifies this woman as Mary, the sister of Lazarus (John 12:1–8).

This was an expensive demonstration of adoration. The container was made of alabaster, a gypsum that is virtually pure white.[2] The flask most likely would have been gourd shaped with a narrow neck. When the flask was broken, the contents spilled forth from the opened neck. This particular flask contained spikenard, a rare oil made from the root of a plant native to the Himalayan region.[3] Mark describes it as "very expensive," and, indeed, its worth equaled more than three hundred denarii, which amounted to a year's wages.[4]

14:4 *Some who were there were irritated and said to one another, "Why was the perfume wasted like this?*

Some of those around the table perceived this demonstration to be a waste of money that could have been better spent elsewhere. One of the main points of Jesus' message about the kingdom clearly expressed a concern for the poor. Now, money was literally being poured away when many mouths could have been fed with the funds secured from the sale of such a valuable item.

14:5 *This perfume could have been sold for a high price, and the money could have been given to the poor." So they said some very unkind things to her.*

In keeping with Jesus' concern for the poor, it would have seemed more sensible to sell this valuable product and distribute the proceeds to the poor. Eventually, the complaints broke forth into a strong verbal attack against Mary.

14:6 *Jesus said, "Leave her alone! Why are you bothering her? She has done a beautiful thing for me.*

Jesus responded to the disciples' opposition with a strong reprimand to leave the woman alone. Jesus, contrary to their expectations, commended her act of devotion.

Imagine the astonishment of Jesus' disciples. Why did He always seem to be so critical of them? Why did He now commend this woman and reprimand them? Were they not correct in their interpretations of His teachings? Had they not been exhorted to give to the poor even at the expense of their personal interests? Not many could have disagreed with the validity of the disciples' contention, yet the disciples failed to recognize that Mary's act exemplified the attitude and motivation Jesus sought through all of His teachings—a heart of obedience, service, and most important, worship.

14:7 *You will always have the poor with you and can help them whenever you want. But you will not always have me with you.*

Jesus gave them the reason for His reprimand. His time with them was short. Jesus knew this and accepted the woman's amazing act of devotion. There would be many future opportunities for the disciples to help the poor. It almost appears that Mary understood better than the rest about Jesus' dire predictions concerning His impending death.[5] Whether or not this was the case, Jesus used her expression as an illustration to focus the disciples.

14:8 *She did what she could. She came to pour perfume on my body before it is placed in a tomb.*

Jesus again commended Mary for anointing Him with precious oil. He then informed His disciples that this act was done in preparation for His death. His statement must have shocked the disciples. Surely, the Twelve thought Jesus was too preoccupied with His death. All of the recent events should have convinced Jesus that His life was not endangered. With much fanfare, He had ridden into Jerusalem thronged by a huge crowd shouting, "Hosanna!" He had been in the temple and had a very successful campaign against the hypocrisy of temple commerce. In confronting the members of the Sanhedrin, He had gained the favor of the common people, who privately relished the humiliation of the self-righteous leaders.

14:9 *I can guarantee this truth: Wherever the Good News is spoken in the world, what she has done will also be told in memory of her."*

Jesus conferred His blessing on the woman's devotion. He had previously told them that the gospel must be preached to the whole world. Now, He told them that this woman's act of devotion and worship would be an integral part of this gospel message. Her story would be told time and again as a lasting memorial to her.

Notes/Applications

When Mary poured expensive perfumed oil on the Messiah's head, Jesus prophetically stated that she was preparing His body for burial. How did those gathered react to this strange comment?

In light of the disciples' response, we observe the single-minded attention to money and wealth pervading humanity's thoughts and perceptions, for who among us would not agree with the disciples? Why would it not have been best to distribute the proceeds from the sale of this valuable perfume to the poor? Indeed, we might conclude that we would have preferred to sell the product, acquire the proceeds, and invest the sum so that we could feed the poor in perpetuity. We would rather do that than worship our Lord as Mary did.

Certainly, there is a time to "waste" our substance on the Lord. There is a time for action, but there is also a time for worship. *"Let go of your concerns! Then you will know that I am God"* (Psalm 46:10a). Sometimes, it is far better to stop, rest, and remain quiet as we ponder the love of God that drove His only Son, Jesus the Christ, to give His life for our sins and to be "the Lamb of God who takes away the sin of the world" (John 1:29). As we take time to refrain from hectic schedules, the world may criticize us, but the Lord will commend us for worshipping at His feet.

Mark 14:10-21

14:10 *Judas Iscariot, one of the twelve apostles, went to the chief priests to betray Jesus.*

Previous passages in the book of Mark have already established that Jesus predicted His death *(Mark 8:31)* and by whose betrayal His death would come *(Mark 3:19)*. In the book of John we glean insight into Judas' character, even in relation to this specific account: "⁴One of his disciples, Judas Iscariot, who was going to betray him, asked, ⁵'Why wasn't this perfume sold for a high price and the money given to the poor?' ⁶(Judas didn't say this because he cared about the poor but because he was a thief. He was in charge of the moneybag and carried the contributions)" *(John 12:4–6)*.

Whether or not this particular event served as the catalyst that spurred Judas' decision to betray Jesus, ultimately, the sovereign God had preordained this treacherous act to accomplish His plan of redemption *(John 17:12; Psalm 41:9)*. The account of Judas' betrayal begins with this verse, as he arose from the table and left Jesus and the others to seek out the chief priests.

14:11 *They were pleased to hear what Judas had to say and promised to give him money. So he kept looking for a chance to betray Jesus.*

Obviously, the chief priests and scribes were pleased to hear from one of the Twelve, and we can certainly understand their satisfaction. Judas was counted among the chosen ones, Jesus' inner circle *(John 6:70–71)*. The chief priests would gain tremendous advantages by employing an "insider" because Judas could track Jesus' movements about Jerusalem. He might even be able to quietly get Him off the streets to a place where the Passover crowd could not offer any opposition. Though the religious rulers had decided to postpone attempts on Jesus' life until after the Passover *(verse 2)*, this proved to be an opportunity too good to pass up, so they changed their plans and now waited on Judas, who sought an opportune moment to betray Jesus.

14:12 *Killing the Passover lamb was customary on the first day of the Festival of Unleavened Bread. The disciples asked Jesus, "Where do you want us to prepare the Passover meal for you?"*

The Festival of Unleavened Bread was one of the several celebrations required under the Mosaic Law and was to be observed yearly to commemorate the Lord's deliverance of the Israelites from their Egyptian bondage *(Deuteronomy 16:1–17)*. According to Jewish custom, this Passover festival was to be celebrated in the home of every Jewish family. However, those who traveled to Jerusalem were expected to remain within the walls of the holy city for the entire night.[6] Therefore, Jesus would not celebrate this Passover at the home of Simon or anywhere else in Bethany but within the walls of Jerusalem. Accordingly, the disciples asked Jesus for specific instructions regarding where they should make arrangements to observe the festival.

14:13 *He sent two of his disciples and told them, "Go into the city. You will meet a man carrying a jug of water. Follow him.*

Jesus responded by taking aside two of His disciples and instructing them on preparations. According to another account, these two disciples were Peter and John *(Luke 22:8)*. Jesus instructed them to go into Jerusalem where they would find a man carrying a pitcher of water. Finding the right man among the crowd would not have been as difficult a task as it might seem, since women were generally responsible for carrying water.[7] When they found this man, they were to follow him. This account resembles a previous occasion when Jesus sent some disciples into Bethphage to retrieve a donkey, which later carried Him into Jerusalem *(Mark 11:1–4)*. Both events revealed Jesus' divine cognizance of even the smallest details.

14:14 *When he goes into a house, tell the owner that the teacher asks, 'Where is my room where I can eat the Passover meal with my disciples?'*

When the man entered a house, the disciples were to ask the master of the house where Jesus could eat the Passover with His disciples.

We do not know the location of the house or the identity of its master. However, we can assume that he must have been someone of moderate wealth since the house was large enough to accommodate thirteen men around a table without interfering with the rest of the household, which also would have been celebrating the Festival of Unleavened Bread.

14:15 *He will take you upstairs and show you a large room. The room will be completely furnished. Get everything ready for us there."*

Whoever the owner was, Jesus indicated that he would willingly and happily make it available to them. We know from this verse that the room was already furnished. Perhaps this simply implies that the accommodations were suitable for the feast and that all of the elements were arranged for use during this most important feast. Peter and John were then to make the final preparations.

DIG DEEPER: *Seder*

The meal prepared on the first day of Passover was called σεδερ (Seder). The primary elements of this feast were a roasted lamb, special wine, bitter herbs, and unleavened bread *(Exodus 12; Numbers 9)*. Also, a thick paste was prepared to remind the celebrants of the mud that their ancestors mixed to make bricks for Pharaoh's building projects. This paste, called *charoseth*, consisted of apples, nuts, and raisins mixed in wine and vinegar. The celebrants would dip the bitter herbs in this mixture as they remembered their bondage in Egypt.

14:16 *The disciples left. They went into the city and found every-thing as Jesus had told them. So they prepared the Passover.*

Once again, the disciples discovered that Jesus knew everything ahead of time because the instructions He had given them concerning the person and place appointed to serve this purpose were accurate. They found everything just as He had told them. They spent the rest of the day preparing for the Passover celebration they would share with Jesus and their fellow disciples. The disciples had again exercised faith in taking Jesus at His word and obeying Him, by now a matter of routine.

14:17 *When evening came, Jesus arrived with the twelve apostles.*

After the preparations were completed, Jesus arrived at the house where the Passover meal was set. He came with the remaining ten disciples, including Judas, who had returned to join the others after conspiring with the chief priests. Jesus did not preclude Judas from sharing in the occasion even though He knew where he had just come from and what his intentions were. Jesus desired to enter the city without fanfare because He wanted to celebrate the Passover alone with His disciples, without any of the commotion they usually experienced.

14:18 *While they were at the table eating, Jesus said, "I can guarantee this truth: One of you is going to betray me, one who is eating with me!"*

During the course of the meal, Jesus interjected a comment that brought all other conversations to an immediate halt. He had spoken earlier of His betrayal as He described the future of the Son of Man (Mark 8:31; 9:31). Jesus had forewarned them that the Son of Man would be killed, but the disciples never imagined that such treachery would come from within their own ranks. Would one of the chosen twelve really cause the death of their beloved friend and master? It was simply unthinkable!

Jesus clearly affirmed that He would be betrayed by one of the Twelve. It was a Jewish idiom to express betrayal as coming at the hands of one who had intimately shared bread with the master.[8]

14:19 *Feeling hurt, they asked him one by one, "You don't mean me, do you?"*

Obviously, any doubts or hopes of avoiding Jesus' predictions of His own death were now dashed to pieces. The Twelve no longer questioned the validity of their rabbi's words. He had proven His authority and accuracy in all of His teachings. The disciples were consumed with overwhelming sorrow. The greatest concern preoccupying each one was the fearful possibility that he might be the traitor about which Jesus spoke. Their questions were asked in the negative, as if to solicit a solemn assurance, "No, it is not you." Each disciple entreated Jesus to affirm his innocence while agonizing within himself, "You don't mean me, do you?"

14:20 *He said to them, "It's one of you twelve, someone dipping his hand into the bowl with me.*

Jesus reaffirmed that one of the Twelve would indeed betray Him. In fact, He offered a tangible clue identifying the traitor. His betrayer would share the Passover supper with Him from the same dish.

As noted in John 13:26, no sooner had Jesus spoken His words than Judas fulfilled them by dipping his bread concurrently with the Lord. This simple action, so innocuous and so common, now pointed an accusatory finger at Judas Iscariot.

By this point, Judas had already betrayed his master by conspiring with the chief priests. Now, Judas' fellow disciples, who had shared in the teachings and admonitions of Jesus for three years, saw Judas for what he was—a spy in their midst. He was the betrayer.

14:21 *The Son of Man is going to die as the Scriptures say he will. But how horrible it will be for that person who betrays the Son of Man! It would have been better for that person if he had never been born."*

The Son of Man was sent to earth precisely for the events that would result from this moment. All of the teachings, all of the miracles, and all of the debates were but a preface to His betrayal, death, and resurrection. The will of the sovereign God could not be altered, yet Jesus still lamented the tragic circumstances by which He would be betrayed.

Jesus depicted the calamity awaiting Judas, for it would have been far better if Judas had never been born than to be the agent of such insidious treason. True, Jesus had chosen Judas to be one of the Twelve, but Judas was chosen for a unique purpose distinct from the ministries to which the other eleven were called. Jesus did not exonerate Judas of his actions even though he fulfilled a specific role within God's redemptive plan.

> [19]*You may ask me, "Why does God still find fault with anyone? Who can resist whatever God wants to do?"*
> [20]*Who do you think you are to talk back to God like that? Can an object that was made say to its maker, "Why did you make me like this?"* [21]*A potter has the right to do whatever he wants with his clay. He can make something for a special occasion or something for everyday use from the same lump of clay.* (Romans 9:19–21)

Notes/Applications

When Jesus informed the disciples that one among them would betray Him, He already knew the guilty party within His group. After Satan entered him, Judas concocted a devious plan with the chief priests and captains *(Luke 22:3–4)*. Nothing would have thwarted the Son of God from fulfilling the Father's plan. Nevertheless, this did not exonerate the one who traded Jesus for thirty pieces of silver, for this man would heap condemnation on his own soul.

The disciples pleaded with Jesus, "You don't mean me, do you?" Perhaps we need to examine ourselves with such fear and trembling. How are we disloyal to the master? We may disguise our hearts behind words dripping with religious finery while infidelity resides in our hearts. *"²⁷You are like whitewashed graves that look beautiful on the outside but inside are full of dead people's bones and every kind of impurity. ²⁸So on the outside you look as though you have God's approval, but inside you are full of hypocrisy and lawlessness"* (Matthew 23:27b–28). We, too, may outwardly appear to be intimate with Jesus yet internally have only known Him as an acquaintance. How can we, like Judas, stand so close to the fire of the Messiah's being and still rebel against the transforming power available to us?

Only the Spirit of the living God can draw us to salvation. Only the Spirit of the living God can fire our souls with passion and devotion. Only the Spirit of the living God can infuse our lives with the joy of being counted as His disciples. However, we are still held accountable for how we respond to Lord Jesus Christ's sacrificial gift: "All of us will have to give an account of ourselves to God" *(Romans 14:12).*

Mark 14:22–26

14:22 *While they were eating, Jesus took bread and blessed it. He broke the bread, gave it to them, and said, "Take this. This is my body."*

At this precise time in history, Jesus and His disciples celebrated a unique and unprecedented Passover feast. While still commemorating Israel's deliverance from Egyptian bondage, this exceptional occasion marked the pivotal moment when the symbolism of the old covenant was replaced with the imagery of the new covenant. By concluding the old feast and inaugurating the new one at the same high occasion, Jesus signified the essential purpose of both celebrations.[9] He introduced new symbolism that embodied the true meaning of both the old and new observances.

Jesus Christ, the Son of God, the celebrant of this Passover meal, presided over the liturgy of the feast. He broke the solemn tradition of the Passover meal. It was at this point in the meal that the celebrant would break the unleavened bread and say, "Blessed be Thou, O Lord our God, King of the Universe, who bringest forth fruit out of the earth."[10] He would then distribute a piece of bread to each person around him, saying, "This is the Bread of Affliction which our fathers did eat in the land of Egypt."[11] However, Jesus amended the significance of this most sacred point of the celebration. No longer was the symbol of broken bread to remind them of the affliction their fathers endured in the cruel slavery of the Egyptian taskmasters. From this moment on, the bread was to remind them of the body of Jesus. The Messiah, God's only Son, would now fulfill His mission as announced by John the Baptizer: "John saw Jesus coming toward him the next day and said, 'Look! This is the Lamb of God who takes away the sin of the world'" (*John 1:29*). From this point on, the disciples would partake of the bread in remembrance of Christ's body broken for their sins.

> **DIG DEEPER:** *Old and New Covenants*
>
> The Passover meal was rich in symbolism for the Jew because it per-
> petuated the memory of Israel's deliverance from Egyptian bondage by
> the almighty arm of the Lord their God *(Exodus 12:21–28)*. This was
> why the children of Israel were commanded to observe the occasion
> every year. Likewise, the Lord's Supper is equally rich in symbolism
> for Christians, who are admonished to remember that the Lord God
> redeemed them from the bondage of sin through the broken body
> and shed blood of the new covenant. While the Passover feast of the
> old covenant pointed to the hope of redemption through Christ, the
> Lord's Supper confirms the fulfillment of salvation through the sacri-
> fice of the Passover lamb on Calvary *(1 Corinthians 5:7–8)*.

14:23–24 *²³Then he took a cup, spoke a prayer of thanksgiving, and gave the cup to them. They all drank from it. ²⁴He said
to them, "This is my blood, the blood of the promise. It is poured
out for many people.*

Following the distribution of the bread, Jesus took the cup and after
thanking God for it, offered it to His disciples. The text implies that
they all partook of the same cup by passing it around. Again, Jesus
broke with the sacred, ancient tradition of the seder. Instead of
continuing with the expected liturgy, Jesus proclaimed the eternal
significance of the cup in that it symbolized His blood that would
soon be shed for the remission of the sins of the world. The cup
would perpetually commemorate the shed blood of the Lamb of God
and signify the deliverance and victory of God's redemption over sin
and bondage.

His disciples must have been listening with amazed curiosity.
The bread now symbolized Jesus' broken body, and this cup of bless-
ing now represented Jesus' blood. Passover would never be the same
again. Jesus' followers were no longer to commemorate the bitter
Egyptian bondage as descendents of the ancient Hebrew people.
They would now celebrate Jesus the Christ, His broken body and

spilled blood, sacrificed for the sins of the world. No longer would they remember that a lamb was sacrificed and its blood brushed on the lintels of their ancestors' doorways so that death would pass over their households. They would now commemorate that Jesus, the Lamb of God, was sacrificed and that His blood would cover the sins of His people for all generations to come.

This new covenant is a unilateral promise on the part of God the Father. The Greek word διαθήκη (diathaykay) means an arrangement established by only one party. It is not a contract between two equal parties. This covenant was established by God with the blood of Jesus Christ, the perfect sacrificial Passover lamb. As the other party to the covenant, humankind can only accept or reject the terms of this arrangement. We can never change them, for they are written by God Himself in the blood of His Son.

14:25 *"I can guarantee this truth: I won't drink this wine again until that day when I drink new wine in the kingdom of God."*

Jesus declared that He would not "drink this wine again," implying that this was the last Passover meal He would celebrate with them. His death was imminent. However, consistent with His previous promise to His disciples, He affirmed that He would drink again at some future time. He had dramatically changed the seder liturgy and told them that the bread represented His body and the cup, His blood. Nevertheless, Jesus looked beyond the immediate circumstances that marked the end of His earthly life and declared that His death was not the end.

In saying this, Jesus also assured His disciples that they, too, would enjoy the fruit of the vine together in the kingdom of God. However, He first had to fulfill the requirements of the new covenant, which they had just celebrated by the feast.

14:26 *After they sang a hymn, they went to the Mount of Olives.*

Jesus and His disciples concluded the Passover feast by singing the traditional hymn, the Hallel, which consisted of the text recorded in Psalms 115 through 118.[12] These psalms ended the Feast of Unleavened Bread and praised the Lord God for His salvation. Jesus and His disciples left the room where they had celebrated the Passover feast and returned to the Mount of Olives. The night sky had fallen upon the region, but Jesus and His disciples proceeded to the mountain for a special time of seclusion. Quietly trekking up the hill, the disciples probably considered the many things that Jesus had taught them during the feast. For them, this observance would never be the same.

14:27 *Then Jesus said to them, "All of you will abandon me. Scripture says, 'I will strike the shepherd, and the sheep will be scattered.'*

As He and His disciples left Jerusalem for the Mount of Olives, Jesus forewarned them concerning their inevitable collapse under the pressure surrounding the events of His suffering that very night. The text implies that they would all fail to stand with Him in this moment of betrayal. Jesus reminded His disciples of their frailties in light of the extreme suffering that their master would endure.

> "Arise, sword, against my shepherd,
>   against the man who is my friend,"
>   declares the Lord of Armies.
> "Strike the shepherd, and the sheep will be scattered.
>   Then I will turn my hand against the little ones." (Zechariah 13:7)

These men began to recognize that their journey with Jesus was nearly over. They were grief stricken by the implications of His words predicting His death. Now, He told them that they would all forsake Him, and He would face His final hours alone. This was not a statement of disappointment by Jesus, for it had been prophesied centuries earlier.

> [5]He was wounded for our rebellious acts.
> He was crushed for our sins.
> > He was punished so that we could have peace,
> > > and we received healing from his wounds.
> > [6]We have all strayed like sheep.
> > Each one of us has turned to go his own way,
> > > and the Lord has laid all our sins on him.
> [7]He was abused and punished,
> > but he didn't open his mouth.
> He was led like a lamb to the slaughter.
> He was like a sheep that is silent
> > when its wool is cut off.
> > > He didn't open his mouth. (Isaiah 53:5–7)

While Jesus' abandonment exposed the infirmities of the disciples in the face of frightening circumstances, the truth of Christ's unique mission would, nonetheless, be publicly confirmed by the sufferings He bore alone for the sake of the lost.

14:28 *"But after I am brought back to life, I will go to Galilee ahead of you."*

Jesus put the devastating news of His sufferings and the disciples' scattering in perspective. He would suffer humiliation and death on the cross. However, He assured them that He would be raised from the dead and that He would return to Galilee. There, He would meet them and revitalize their relationship. This time, they would know that He was not simply another prophet or rabbi but that He was indeed the Son of God, the risen victor.

14:29 *Peter said to him, "Even if everyone else abandons you, I won't."*

Peter, in typical fashion, was unwilling to accept Jesus' words. He argued with Jesus, just as he had when Jesus first told them about His betrayal and death (Mark 8:32). Peter had lost that argument, but he had not learned his lesson. He again argued with Jesus and adamantly declared his loyalty to Him. While he did not doubt that the rest of his fellow disciples might fail the master, Peter insisted that he was above reproach. Not yet realizing the extent of his own weakness, Peter convinced himself of his steadfastness because he truly loved Jesus and believed in Him.

14:30 *Jesus said to Peter, "I can guarantee this truth: Tonight, before a rooster crows twice, you will say three times that you don't know me."*

Because Peter openly challenged Jesus' prediction, Jesus exposed the specifics of Peter's denial. Peter would not only deny his relationship with Jesus but would do so three times. Even more discouraging was that his denial would be corroborated with indisputable evidence. He would make these denials before the "rooster crows twice," or before the dawn of the next day. That meant that Peter would deny his teacher and friend three times within a few hours of his hearty declaration of allegiance. Jesus had predicted the sudden reversal of Peter's loyalties. In a sense, Peter's denial would be three times more evident than his words of devotion.

14:31 *But Peter said very strongly, "Even if I have to die with you, I will never say that I don't know you." All the other disciples said the same thing.*

Peter would not accept such disheartening predictions from Jesus. His volatile temper incited him to reaffirm his loyalty by stating that he was willing to die with Jesus rather than turn away from Him in His final hours. His indignation was contagious. The rest of the disciples echoed Peter's commitment to die for his master.

Peter could not conceive of any circumstance, even death, that would cause him to turn away from his master. He had seen this man do so many things for so many people. He had carefully listened to Jesus and was convinced that He was the Christ *(Mark 8:29)*. Even now, Peter was willing to fight for his Messiah. But Peter had not listened carefully enough. Jesus was, indeed, the Messiah Who came to establish His kingdom in the hearts of His followers. Peter was probably still thinking of Jesus as the deliverer Who had come to establish His kingdom and set God's people free. Consequently, he could not stand quietly, because a dead Messiah would be no Messiah at all. He would have died fighting for the Lord until Jesus established His kingdom. Peter obviously spoke as a truly temporal man who put much credence in the thoughts of his carnal mind.

Notes/Applications

This passage can be deeply disturbing to anyone who thinks carefully about its implications. What makes this passage so disturbing is the fact that the denials did not come from Jesus' enemies but from His closest friends.

By this time, Jesus had challenged every faction of the religious and political leadership of His day. Through His stringent words, He had earned avowed enemies, and these men looked for some way to silence Him. Judas Iscariot determined to join forces with these "respected" men and betray Jesus. We are not privy to the gradual unraveling of his loyalty. Still, we recognize that the son of perdition had to emerge on the scene to fulfill prophecy. But how did these eleven remaining men account for their betrayal?

We do understand them. Perhaps we understand them too well. Our personal experience shows us that we are fickle creatures, bold with our mouths yet weak with our wills. At times, our faith and commitment run shallow.

Just as the disciples failed to live up to their declarations of loyalty, we do the same—not once, but repeatedly. And why? Because we fear the mild ridicule of those around us. *"If people are ashamed of me and what I say in this unfaithful and sinful generation, the Son of Man will be ashamed of those people when he comes with the holy angels in his Father's glory"* (Mark 8:38). *"I'm not ashamed of the Good News. It is*

God's power to save everyone who believes, Jews first and Greeks as well" *(Romans 1:16).*

The cost of becoming a Christian and declaring one's loyalty to Jesus Christ is a test of faith that could end in trial and persecution. May God grant us His Holy Spirit to empower our witness to a world that likely may not want to hear about the Way, the Truth, and the Life.

Mark 14:32–42

14:32 *Then they came to a place called Gethsemane. He said to his disciples, "Stay here while I pray."*

Gethsemane was a small garden area at the foot of the Mount of Olives.[13] At this special location, Jesus stopped and asked His disciples to wait for Him while He prayed.

14:33 *He took Peter, James, and John with him and began to feel distressed and anguished.*

Jesus separated Peter, James, and John from the rest of the disciples. These three men had also been privileged to witness His glorious transfiguration on a mountaintop near Caesarea Philippi *(Mark 9:2–8)*. Now, they were separated again from the rest of the group to witness the agony of their beloved master. They would not see His glory but His humanity as he struggled with His imminent death.

Before praying, even as He walked a little farther into the garden, Jesus was deeply disturbed by the anticipation of His impending suffering. Profoundly aware of the mission that had been eternally appointed for Him, the reality of His looming agony and death overwhelmed Him as the moment approached.

14:34 *He said to them, "My anguish is so great that I feel as if I'm dying. Wait here, and stay awake."*

Jesus shared the depth of His grief with His closest friends. He was immersed in grief because He was to bear the sin of the world. *"God had Christ, who was sinless, take our sin so that we might receive God's approval through him"* (2 Corinthians 5:21). He asked Peter, James, and John to stay where they were and to stay awake. They were to stand by while He prayed.

14:35 *After walking a little farther, he fell to the ground and prayed that if it were possible he might not have to suffer what was ahead of him.*

No commentary can fully describe this scene. As He walked a short distance farther into the garden, Jesus collapsed on the ground, where He poured all of His agony, grief, and loneliness out to the Father. Undoubtedly, Jesus knew that His moment was at hand. He had walked from Galilee to Jerusalem with firm resolution, and His moment had at last arrived. Surely, just as He had known where to find the colt for His triumphal entry into Jerusalem *(Mark 11:2)* and where to find the man carrying water who would lead His disciples to the upper room *(Mark 14:13)*, Jesus foreknew each and every excruciating detail of what lay ahead. In His human condition, He wanted to avoid this final hour. He did not want to endure the brutal suffering awaiting Him.

14:36 *He said, "Abba! Father! You can do anything. Take this cup of suffering away from me. But let your will be done rather than mine."*

By quoting the very words of His prayer, this verse captures the sentiment at the core of Jesus' emotion. He addressed His Father as "Abba," an Aramaic word denoting a warm, intimate relationship. This was not some figurehead Father. This was a Father Who dearly loved His Son, and the Son addressed Him intimately—Daddy! The short prayer reveals great detail about the relationship of Jesus to His Father *(see also John 17)*.

The ache of betrayal. The anticipation of unbearable torture. The concern for those He would leave behind. The depth of the sin for which He would die. All of these emotions culminated into a single moment when Jesus in His humanity sought escape from the cup that had been prepared for Him to drink: "Take this cup of suffering away from me." Even at His greatest moment of misgiving and reluctance, Jesus yielded the sway of His human emotion to the divine purpose for which He had come into the world, and rather than surrender to His hesitations, He offered His utter submission to His Father's will even at the ultimate cost.

14:37 *He went back and found them asleep. He said to Peter, "Simon, are you sleeping? Couldn't you stay awake for one hour?*

After His profoundly human struggle, Jesus returned to the place where He left the three disciples and found them asleep. He chided Peter for his failure to watch. However, Jesus addressed him not by the name He had given him, Peter, but by Simon, His family name. At that moment, Simon was not Peter ("Rock"), and Jesus addressed him accordingly. Despite the vehemence of Peter's earlier declaration of loyalty *(verse 29)*, he was sleeping! He demonstrated the weakness of human resolve. Jesus asked nothing of these three except to stand watch during this difficult time. This was not the picture of individuals prepared to defend their master. One brief period of time, only one short hour. Nevertheless, exhausted from a day filled with conflicting emotions, the three disciples slept.

14:38 *Stay awake, and pray that you won't be tempted. You want to do what's right, but you're weak."*

Again, Jesus admonished them to be on their guard. Furthermore, they were to follow their master's example and pray. That was the only way to avoid crumbling in the face of the coming trial. Jesus clearly recognized the inner conflict of humans. Despite the best intentions and strong convictions of the spirit, human sinfulness so often prevails and smothers those things that God seeks to accomplish.

14:39 *He went away again and prayed the same prayer as before.*

Contrary to the behavior of His disciples, Jesus again moved a short distance away and repeated His earlier prayer. Once more, Jesus likely fell prostrate on the ground, driven to the earth by His overwhelming grief yet surrendered to the will of His Father.

14:40 *He found them asleep because they couldn't keep their eyes open. They didn't even know what they should say to him.*

When Jesus returned for the second time, He again found His three friends sleeping. They "couldn't keep their eyes open," being beleaguered by the revelations of that day, and they could not resist their longing to sleep. Jesus again awakened them, and when they discovered that they yet again failed their master, they were speechless. Despite their professions of loyalty even unto death, they could not deny their vulnerability.

14:41 *He came back a third time and said to them, "You might as well sleep now. It's all over. The time has come for the Son of Man to be handed over to sinners.*

Once again, Jesus walked away from the others to pray, and once again, when He returned, He found them sleeping. Somehow, Jesus expressed compassion for His friends in this moment: "You might as well sleep now." He had struggled against compelling human pressure to resist His destiny, and even though He had won the battle, He understood the persuasive influence of the flesh. His next words were ominous. The wait was over. The moment of His betrayal had now arrived. The Son of Man, by yielding His human uncertainty to the eternal will of His Father, had also subjected Himself to the will of His treacherous enemies.

14:42 *Get up! Let's go! The one who is betraying me is near."*

Jesus awakened the three sleeping men and informed them that it was time to depart. Judas, the betrayer, had entered the garden prepared to surrender his master into the hands of the Jewish and Roman authorities.

Notes/Applications

Alone, forsaken by His friends, Jesus faced the agony of His death. He asked Peter, James, and John to pray and stand guard for Him, but they slept instead. Even before the betrayal by Judas Iscariot, Jesus' disciples had emotionally abandoned Him, and in this passage, Jesus prayed alone.

> 'Tis midnight, and on olive's brow
> The star is dimmed that lately shone;
>
> 'Tis midnight in the garden now
> The suffering Savior prays alone.
> 'Tis midnight, and from all removed,
> Emmanuel wrestles lone with fears;
> E'en that disciple whom He loved
> Heeds not his Master's grief or tears.
>
> 'Tis midnight, and for others guilt
> The Man of Sorrows weeps in blood;
> Yet He Who hath in anguish knelt
> Is not forsaken by His God.[14]

Jesus accepted the lonely, burdensome, horrendous task of bearing others' sin upon Himself (*Luke 22:44-46*). He willingly separated from heaven's glory to provide others with the opportunity to be reconciled with the Father. He Who knew no sin renounced Himself for those who knew nothing but sin.

In our humanity, we can never grasp the horrors of that somber moment—the fear, the disappointment, and yet the resolve—when Jesus faced His death alone, redeeming those that would rather sleep than pray and those that would swear loyalty in one moment and then flee the next. However, as the Father escorted His Son through the dark tunnel of rejection leading to Calvary's cross, we can be assured that He never abandons us even if no human being stands with us. He remains faithful to His promises: "He won't abandon you or leave you. So don't be afraid or terrified" *(Deuteronomy 31:8).* "God has said, 'I will never abandon you or leave you'" *(Hebrews 13:5b).*

Mark 14:43–50

14:43 *Just then, while Jesus was still speaking, Judas, one of the twelve apostles, arrived. A crowd carrying swords and clubs was with him. They were from the chief priests, scribes, and leaders of the people.*

No sooner had Jesus announced that His betrayer was at hand than Judas appeared in the garden with a heavily armed group. What a shocking moment for the disciples! Their friend Judas led the attack and aided Jesus' most hostile enemies in the capture of their teacher. He was accompanied by a large number of armed men who were dispatched by the Sanhedrin. Although some Roman foot soldiers were likely present, this was not a contingent sent by Roman authorities.

14:44 *Now, the traitor had given them a signal. He said, "The one I kiss is the man you want. Arrest him, and guard him closely as you take him away."*

Judas had prearranged a signal to clearly identify Jesus among the rest of the group. Jesus was widely known throughout all of Galilee and much of Judea. He was certainly known by many members of the Sanhedrin, since they had debated with Jesus many times. However, it can be easily understood that many of the military personnel might not have recognized Jesus because He had not had any direct confrontations with Roman authorities.

Judas would betray his teacher with a kiss. This was not an unusual gesture in the Jewish or Middle Eastern culture. It was common for a student to greet his teacher with a kiss as a sign of respect. With this gesture, Judas demonstrated the dichotomy of the human spirit. Externally, there appeared to be devotion and respect, but in the heart lurked hatred and hypocrisy.

Judas had told the men to seize Jesus immediately and safely lead Him away. They needed to exercise extreme caution lest the disciples mount a defense for their master, or lest Jesus calmly walk away from the confrontation and disappear among the crowd as He had done before. Even now in the garden, Jesus could have walked away from this bitter experience, but He did not. Rather, He subjected Himself to humiliation and death at the hands of those He came to save, and He did so by His holy will.

14:45 *Then Judas quickly stepped up to Jesus and said, "Rabbi!" and kissed him.*

Judas wasted no time. He immediately approached Jesus, calling Him "Rabbi," then kissed Him. The treachery of Judas' soul was laid bare in the planning and execution of his deception and betrayal.

14:46 *Some men took hold of Jesus and arrested him.*

The band of soldiers noted Judas' signal and promptly took hold of Jesus, Who submitted to their control. Though He had escaped their grasp on several previous occasions, His time was now at hand, and the will of the eternal God was enacted. Unknown to them, their evil actions would result in the salvation of mankind.

14:47 *One of those standing there pulled out his sword and cut off the ear of the chief priest's servant.*

Though Jesus did not protest, one of His disciples did. Mark does not identify the assailant, though other accounts confirm that it was Peter *(John 18:10)*. In his haste, Peter drew a short sword and cut off the ear of the personal servant of Caiaphas, the high priest. Peter had planned for the moment *(Luke 22:38)*, and, seemingly, he acted without hesitation when the opportunity arose. This was the closest Peter came to keeping his word that he would not allow harm to come to Jesus.

14:48 *Jesus asked them, "Have you come out with swords and clubs to arrest me as if I were a criminal?*

The Gospel of Luke records that Jesus healed and restored the ear of Caiaphas' servant *(Luke 22:51)*, and Matthew quotes Jesus' amazing words: "⁵²Then Jesus said to him, 'Put your sword away! All who use a sword will be killed by a sword. ⁵³Don't you think that I could call on my Father to send more than twelve legions of angels to help me now? ⁵⁴How, then, are the Scriptures to be fulfilled that say this must happen?'" *(Matthew 26:52–54)*.

Mark only conveys Jesus' comments to His captors. He chided them that His "crime" did not merit such treatment. He had never picked up a sword. He had never encouraged rebellion or insurrection against Jewish or Roman authority, yet they were treating Him as though He were a felon.

14:49 *I used to teach in the temple courtyard every day. But you didn't arrest me then. But what the Scriptures say must come true.*"

Jesus reminded these men that He had been in the temple every day that week teaching them and showing them the character of God's kingdom. He had been a public figure and had not hidden from them. He had vigorously debated with their leaders, yet they had not had the courage to arrest Him during those encounters. Jesus' response exposed a stark contrast between His public ministry and the scheming of the Sanhedrin as they moved under the cover of darkness to arrest Him. The Sanhedrin, the highest legal and moral authority in Judea, would break most of their own laws in the trial and condemnation of Jesus. But for them, political expediency was far more important than legal or moral propriety. Nevertheless, it was not the cunning of the Sanhedrin that finally led to Jesus' capture, but the fulfillment of God's will as prophesied in Scripture *(Psalm 22:6; Isaiah 53:7)*.

14:50 *Then all the disciples abandoned him and ran away.*

These might be among the saddest words recorded in Scripture. When the disciples saw that no real defense was possible and that Jesus would not make an attempt to escape, they ran away as fast as they could. They did not want to share in their master's fate. Alone, Jesus faced the legal authorities of the Sanhedrin and Rome. He had no friend to help Him, no one to come to His defense. Though the disciples had denied that any such thing would ever happen, Jesus' words from earlier that night had come to pass: "All of you will abandon me. Scripture says, 'I will strike the shepherd, and the sheep will be scattered'" (*Mark 14:27*).

Notes/Applications
"Then all the disciples abandoned him and ran away." We read these sad words and remember the boldness of Peter, who asserted that he would not abandon the Lord even if all the others did. Nevertheless, in the hour of danger, fear seized him as it likely would have gripped us all.

As we will read, the Gospel of John records a touching passage not included in the other three gospels (*John 21:1–19*). Even the subtitle of this passage in some Bibles has a loving sound to it: "Jesus Restores Peter." The disciples had returned to their everyday fishing jobs in the wake of Jesus' death, but one night, they caught nothing. When morning came, a figure hailed them from the shore and told them to cast their nets on the right side of the boat. When they did, the net was so heavy with fish that they could not draw it into the boat. "It is the Lord!" Peter cried as he jumped into the water and swam to shore.

Jesus prepared a breakfast of fresh fish for them on the shore of the Sea of Galilee, and when they had eaten, He said, "Peter, do you love Me?" Peter replied affirmatively. "Then feed My lambs," Jesus said. Christ asked the question a second and third time, and each time, Peter responded, "Yes, Lord, you know I do." With each affirmation, Jesus said, "Feed My sheep." Three times to make up for the three times Peter denied Christ on the night He was arrested. Three times to show this dejected, humbled sinner that He loved him and had a wonderful destiny for him to fulfill. Best of all, Jesus restored Peter and validated his worth to the kingdom of God in the presence of the others.

Yes, Jesus knew the purpose of His betrayal in the garden of Gethsemane. While others slept, He assumed the weight of His God-given ordination. He would bear the sins of the world upon His immortal soul. Why give Himself up for such a faithless bunch? For one purpose only. To bring redemption to an otherwise condemned creation.

Mark 14:51–56

14:51–52 *⁵¹A certain young man was following Jesus. He had nothing on but a linen sheet.* *They tried to arrest him,* *⁵²but he left the linen sheet behind and ran away naked.*

Since the inclusion of this side story occurs only in the Gospel of Mark, many scholars believe that Mark was recounting his own personal experience of that frightening night.[15] Whoever this elusive guest was, it appears that he was lurking around observing the goings-on and was present, though hidden, when the other disciples fled. It almost seems that he had jumped out of bed in an attempt to find Jesus and warn Him about His pursuers. This would account for the fact that the bed linen was not securely tied around his waist with a belt. When the soldiers saw him, they attempted to seize him. However, since the linen was not secured to his body, he slipped away from the soldiers, leaving the linen cloth behind.

14:53 *The men took Jesus to the chief priest. All the chief priests, leaders, and scribes had gathered together.*

Jesus and His host of captors left the Mount of Olives and arrived at the home of the chief priest (Caiaphas) (*Matthew 26:57*). The full Sanhedrin had assembled with him and awaited the arrival of this "blasphemer."

Although these men were bound by Mosaic Law and their traditions to execute justice for the Jewish people, there was nothing just about this trial. Generally, the Sanhedrin met publicly in the temple's marketplace. However, they now assembled at nighttime in Caiaphas' home still hoping to avoid a riot (*verse 2*). Under the cover of darkness and out of sight of the people, they met in secret to determine the fate of this one Who had posed a threat to their status and political power.

14:54 *Peter followed him at a distance and went into the chief priest's courtyard. He sat with the guards and warmed himself facing the glow of a fire.*

Peter, who had at first fled the scene in Gethsemane, apparently followed the procession from a distance. He even dared to enter the courtyard of the high priest, but he did not enter the room where the Sanhedrin congregated, prepared to try Jesus for a yet unstated crime. He even joined others around an open fire and warmed himself, while trying desperately to regain his composure.

14:55 *The chief priests and the whole Jewish council were searching for some testimony against Jesus in order to execute him. But they couldn't find any.*

The members of the Sanhedrin had arrested Jesus and taken Him into custody intending to silence Him. However, they sought to do so without clear evidence against Him. Jesus now stood before them as the object of their scorn, and these legal scholars looked for concrete evidence that would give merit to the death sentence that they had imposed on the Son of Man. It seems that they had already condemned Jesus to die, and all they lacked was an indictment worthy of the verdict. However, this proved to be very difficult because they could not find anyone with incriminating testimony against Jesus.

14:56 *Many gave false testimony against him, but their statements did not agree.*

Many who fabricated evidence against Jesus were found to be frauds whose statements were contradictory. Although political expediency had thrown caution to the winds, they still felt constrained to condemn Jesus with evidence that met the criteria of the Law of Moses, even if that evidence had been falsely contrived. However, according to Mosaic Law, the evidence had to be confirmed by at least two witnesses (*Deuteronomy 19:15–19*).

The sacred Mosaic Law had been compromised. They sought the death penalty for Jesus, but false witnesses clearly could not agree on the evidence against Him. Ironically, their lies went unpunished despite a clear penalty for lying in court. In this court on this night, lying witnesses were encouraged as long as two of them could offer corroborating stories.

Notes/Applications

When Jesus stood trial before the Sanhedrin, the greatest war between God and Satan rapidly approached. At the cross of Jesus, Satan assumed he had won this battle because, he thought, the Son of God was silenced. However, Jesus had control over that event. When He arose from death on the third day, Satan's doom was sealed. In Revelation 1:17–18, a victorious Lamb of God proclaimed, "Don't be afraid! I am the first and the last, the living one. I was dead, but now I am alive forever. I have the keys of death and hell."

Narcissism runs through our veins as it did Peter's. Personal preservation and advancement guide our actions. We will do anything to protect ourselves from ridicule or harm. While Jesus stands on trial in the world's courtrooms, do we, like Peter, stand outside and warm our hands by the fire?

Nevertheless, the battle goes on. Satan will continue to use every means at his disposal to take as many with him to hell as possible. Therefore, we dare not stand by the fire warming our hands while Jesus goes to trial undefended. Like Peter, we must rise from the defeat of abandoning Jesus. We must again and again enter the battlefield equipped with the truth of our risen Lord and girded with the armor of our faith.

Mark 14:57–65

14:57–58 *⁵⁷Then some men stood up and gave false testimony against him. They said, ⁵⁸"We heard him say, 'I'll tear down this temple made by humans, and in three days I'll build another temple, one not made by human hands.'"*

As Jesus stood before the court, men rose up to give false testimony against Him. A certain frenzy pervaded the atmosphere in this unseemly trial. The testimony against Jesus referred to a comment not recorded in the synoptic Gospels, but presented in the Gospel of John. Jesus had entered the temple and, seeing the godless commerce within its walls, was moved with indignation against the vendors. He immediately demonstrated His displeasure as He overturned their tables and scattered their merchandise.

> *¹⁸The Jews reacted by asking Jesus, "What miracle can you show us to justify what you're doing?"*
>
> *¹⁹Jesus replied, "Tear down this temple, and I'll rebuild it in three days." ²⁰The Jews said, "It took forty-six years to build this temple. Do you really think you're going to rebuild it in three days?"*
>
> *²¹But the temple Jesus spoke about was his own body. ²²After he came back to life, his disciples remembered that he had said this. So they believed the Scripture and this statement that Jesus had made. (John 2:18–22)*

Though the witnesses clearly reiterated Jesus' words, they did not understand the context of their meaning.

14:59 *But their testimony did not agree even on this point.*

The witnesses against Jesus still could not corroborate their testimonies. Jesus' outrageous behavior against the temple vendors was not the focus of their accusation since the penalty for this action did not warrant death. They needed a serious offense, so they referred to Jesus' statement that He could destroy the temple and rebuild it in three days. However, their statement was inaccurate. Jesus never said that He would destroy the temple. In fact, He had used a play on words to veil the truth about His statement. John, of course, correctly interpreted Jesus' words as a reference about His own body being destroyed by death and then raised again in three days.

It is easy to understand why the average person would have found it difficult to comprehend the spiritual meaning of Jesus' statement. It would have been nearly impossible to believe that someone could die and then rise from the dead three days later. In any case, their testimony misrepresented Jesus' original statement, and discrepancies between their statements were apparent.

14:60 *So the chief priest stood up in the center and asked Jesus, "Don't you have any answer to what these men testify against you?"*

Up to this point, no consistent or accurate evidence against Jesus had been presented. Even the liars could not agree on exactly what Jesus had said. If the witnesses could at least agree that Jesus said He would destroy the temple, the Sanhedrin could then execute Him for His intention to destroy the sacred place. To level a place of worship was an offense punishable by death, so in the middle of such conflicting evidence, Caiaphas challenged Jesus to defend Himself. Certainly, Jesus was fully aware of the perjured evidence being presented. There would be no reason to say anything because there was insufficient evidence to keep Him in custody, let alone to have Him executed.

14:61 *But he was silent. The chief priest asked him again, "Are you the Messiah, the Son of the Blessed One?"*

Amid the chaos and shouting, Jesus remained silent. Untouched by their malicious accusations, He stood quietly. Finally, in exasperation, the high priest directly addressed Jesus and asked if He was the Christ, the Son of the Blessed One. The high priest, religiously cautious to the smallest detail, used the word *blessed* to avoid saying the name of the Lord.[16] As priests and scribes, students of the Holy Scriptures, they knew the prophecies about God's Anointed One. They knew that the Messiah would be the son of David and that He would be the Son of God.

14:62 *Jesus answered, "Yes, I am, and you will see the Son of Man in the highest position in heaven. He will be coming with the clouds of heaven."*

Jesus would not deny His true identity. For the first time, He publicly acknowledged His deity. Before, He had spoken only to His disciples about His holy commission. Now, before His ardent enemies, Jesus declared that He was indeed the Messiah.

Jesus could have stopped right there. He could have simply answered, "I am," and that would have been sufficient. That statement alone sealed His death warrant. Such "blasphemy" could not be endured. Jesus had now said that He was the Son of God. However, He did not stop with a simple "I am." He further declared His authority by saying that He would sit in the highest position in heaven. He also gave a veiled reference to a messianic prophecy found in the book of Daniel.

> [13]*In my visions during the night, I saw among the clouds in heaven someone like the Son of Man. He came to the Ancient One, who has lived for endless years, and was presented to him. [14]He was given power, honor, and a kingdom. People from every province, nation, and language were to serve him. His power is an eternal power that will not be taken away. His kingdom will never be destroyed. (Daniel 7:13–14)*

These religious leaders knew exactly what Jesus was saying, and there could be absolutely no doubt that He declared Himself to be the Messiah. Jesus had given the Sanhedrin the only evidence they needed to put Him to death. They had found no evidence to condemn Jesus apart from His own testimony. Certainly, the Son of

Man, even though now their prisoner, directed and controlled His own destiny.

14:63 *The chief priest tore his clothes in horror and said, "Why do we need any more witnesses?*

At this, the high priest ripped his clothes as a symbolic gesture of repugnance.[17] He had heard the "blasphemy" of Jesus with his own ears. Jesus had claimed authority that belonged only to God. Regardless of his excessive gestures, the high priest was surely relieved because he required no further proof against Jesus. Before the entire Sanhedrin, Jesus had declared Himself to be the Son of God.

14:64 *You've heard him dishonor God! What's your verdict?" All of them condemned him with the death sentence.*

Caiaphas called on the assembly for their verdict immediately after Jesus' statement. They could not deny what they had heard. Nothing could have been more blasphemous to their ears. The vote was cast. They unanimously condemned Him to die. Only Joseph of Arimathea did not give consent to this verdict: "[50]There was a good man who had God's approval. His name was Joseph. He was a member of the Jewish council, [51]but he had not agreed with what they had done. He was from the Jewish city of Arimathea, and he was waiting for the kingdom of God" *(Luke 23:50–51)*.

The penalty for blasphemy according to Jewish law was death by stoning. "[15]Also tell the Israelites: Those who treat their God with contempt will be punished for their sin. [16]But those who curse the Lord's name must be put to death. The whole congregation must stone them to death. It makes no difference whether they are Israelites or foreigners. Whoever curses the Lord's name must die" *(Leviticus 24:15–16)*. The death penalty had been decided, but the Sanhedrin faced another major problem. While Rome afforded wide latitude for the Sanhedrin to handle Jewish affairs, they were not permitted to execute anyone without Rome's permission.

14:65 *Some of them began to spit on him. They covered his face and hit him with their fists. They said to him, "Prophesy!" Even the guards took him and slapped him.*

Unsatisfied with their death penalty, some of the members of the Sanhedrin spat on Jesus as a gesture of their complete loathing and hatred. His blasphemy appalled them, and they wished to express their revulsion by spitting in His face.

They went even further. They blindfolded Jesus and then struck Him, demanding that He tell them who had delivered the blow. By doing so, they mocked Him as if to see whether He could determine what was happening around Him without the benefit of His sight.

Jesus did not answer them, though. Standing quietly before them, He simply received their abuse as prophesized in the Book of Isaiah nearly seven hundred years earlier.

> ⁶I will offer my back to those who whip me
>   and my cheeks to those who pluck hairs out of my beard.
> I will not turn my face away from those who humiliate me and spit
> on me.
>   ⁷The Almighty Lord helps me.
>   That is why I will not be ashamed.
>   I have set my face like a flint.
>   I know that I will not be put to shame."
>   (Isaiah 50:6–7)

Notes/Applications

Is Jesus the Son of God? He healed many. He cast out demons from tormented souls. He fed thousands by supernaturally multiplying food. He calmed stormy seas. Mark sets before us the evidence of eyewitness testimony, explaining in great detail the events that led to the death of this remarkable rabbi.

"Are you the Son of God?" The Sanhedrin put this question to Jesus, and they considered His reply—"I am"—as enough proof for Him to die. No one could blaspheme God in such a way and live. That is, no one but the real Messiah, the true Son of God. Jesus spoke the truth in their presence, but they would not, and could not, hear it.

How will we judge this bold claim by Jesus? Do we really believe He is the Son of God? Obviously, we have to evaluate Him differently than the Sanhedrin did. Although we have the record of the four Gospels and the weight of history, not everyone will come to the same conclusion. The godly evidence supplied in the Gospel of Mark must be confirmed in our hearts by the Spirit of the living God. He is the only one who can lead us into the absolute truth concerning the identity of Jesus of Nazareth. *"¹³When the Spirit of Truth comes, he will guide you into the full truth. He won't speak on his own. He will speak what he hears and will tell you about things to come. ¹⁴He will give me glory, because he will tell you what I say"* (John 16:13–14).

Mark 14:66–72

14:66–67 *⁶⁶Peter was in the courtyard. One of the chief priest's female servants ⁶⁷saw Peter warming himself. She looked at him and said, "You, too, were with Jesus from Nazareth!"*

While Jesus stood on trial inside, enduring the scorn of the most esteemed leaders of the Jewish nation, Peter remained outside warming himself by the fire in the courtyard *(verse 54)*. One of the girls who served at the high priest's bidding approached the same fire in the courtyard.

This girl looked at Peter and seemed to recognize him. Perhaps she had been a part of the crowds that had followed Jesus and recognized Peter as one of the rabbi's disciples. She might even have been in the multitude that hailed Jesus on the previous Sunday as He rode into Jerusalem. Nevertheless, we read that "she looked at him," examining him almost as if searching her memory for where she had seen him. Only after careful observation did she identify him as one of the Twelve, one of those closely associated with Jesus.

14:68 *But Peter denied it by saying, "I don't know him, and I don't understand what you're talking about." He went to the entrance. Then a rooster crowed.*

Peter denied the girl's allegation that he was one of Jesus' disciples. He declared that he was so far removed from Jesus that he was unaware of her implications. Not only was the girl wrong, but he did not even know what she was saying.

Peter departed a short distance to minimize the likelihood of being identified again. He went to the entryway that led to the street, and then a rooster crowed. However, Peter attached no significance to this signal of which Jesus had spoken. Peter only recognized how close he had come to being identified. His main concern probably stemmed from not wanting to be plunged into the same fate as his teacher, Whom he had declared to be the Messiah.

14:69 *The servant saw him. Once again she said to those who were standing around, "This man is one of them!"*

The servant girl probably continued to watch Peter closely as she went about her household duties, but this time, she did not address Peter directly. Rather, she addressed her comments to the people standing nearby. She no longer questioned but emphatically contended that Peter was "one of them," one of Jesus' followers.

14:70 *Peter again denied it. After a little while the men standing there said to Peter again, "It's obvious you're one of them. You're a Galilean!"*

Again, Peter denied any knowledge of Jesus. Peter apparently became the main topic of conversation around the small fire. Those gathered approached him a short time later and commented that he certainly must have been one of Jesus' disciples. They could identify Peter as a Galilean by his accent. They knew that Jesus came from Nazareth in Galilee, and, therefore, they surmised that Peter was an associate of Jesus.

14:71 *Then Peter began to curse and swear with an oath, "I don't know this man you're talking about!"*

Terrified by the possibility that he would suffer the same fate as Jesus, Peter lost control. When the bystanders continued to insist that he was one of Jesus' disciples, Peter cursed and violently swore as he renounced knowing Jesus.

14:72 *Just then a rooster crowed a second time. Peter remembered that Jesus said to him, "Before a rooster crows twice, you will say three times that you don't know me." Then Peter began to cry very hard.*

Standing at the doorway on the porch leading to the street, Peter heard the rooster crow again. This time the sound of the rooster triggered Peter's memory, and Jesus' words instantly came to mind. Peter had vehemently argued with Jesus about his loyalty and his willingness to die in the defense of his master. He loved Jesus. Still, as this day broke, the rooster crowed a second time, and Peter, remembering Jesus' words, broke down and wept. Despite his adamant vow of allegiance, cowardice prevailed, and he had failed his friend after all.

Notes/Applications
This passage models one of the most graphic descriptions of human failure in Scripture. We certainly understand the numerous failings of the Jewish people described in the Old Testament. We understand that they failed to live in a covenant relationship with their God, the one Who had brought them out of bondage in Egypt. However, to know Jesus, to walk with Him, to share intimate conversations with Him over a period of three years, to see Him transfigured on the mountain, to see Him speaking with Moses and Elijah, only to then turn away and deny any knowledge of Him is virtually incomprehensible.

On a personal level, we can relate to Peter only too well. We see in ourselves the numerous occasions of our own denials. We have never personally walked with Jesus. We have never heard His audible voice. We have never seen Him transfigured in a dazzling white light. Nevertheless, many of us have declared our loyalty to Him. We have walked with Him in faith, heard Him speak to us through the words of Scripture, and believed that He rose from the grave and ascended to heaven. Still, we may find ourselves ashamed to admit that we know Jesus. We do not fear a physical cross like Peter did. We fear only questioning looks from those who might wonder if we are religious fanatics. Yet even in our treachery, God remains faithful: "If we are unfaithful, he remains faithful because he cannot be untrue to himself" (2 Timothy 2:13). He will lovingly restore us. What a great testimony it would be to others if we could ultimately admit our failures and weep as Peter did before the king, the Messiah, Who remains constant and true in His merciful love for us.

MARK 15

Mark 15:1–5

15:1 *Early in the morning the chief priests immediately came to a decision with the leaders and the scribes. The whole Jewish council decided to tie Jesus up, lead him away, and hand him over to Pilate.*

The Sanhedrin wasted no time. In an early morning consultation, they declared Jesus guilty of blasphemy and sentenced Him to die. As mentioned in chapter fourteen, though they could pronounce a death sentence, they could not carry out the execution.

The subject of their deliberations was not revealed, though surely they were contriving a plan to present Jesus before Pilate in such a way that the Roman magistrate would have to uphold and confirm their death sentence. Having concluded their strategy session, they bound Jesus and took Him to Pilate. If Pilate could be persuaded, Jesus would be put to death. However, if Pilate determined that Jesus was either innocent or that His "crime" was not worthy of a death sentence, all of the Sanhedrin's scheming would have been in vain and Jesus might be set free.

15:2 *Pilate asked him, "Are you the king of the Jews?" "Yes, I am," Jesus answered him.*

In Pilate's question, we discover the Sanhedrin's strategy. According to Jewish law, blasphemy was an offense deserving of death, but they did not accuse Jesus of blasphemy because Roman law did not recognize it as a crime. Therefore, the Sanhedrin portrayed Jesus as a threat to the Roman Empire in that He claimed to be the king of the Jews. In essence, they accused Him of insurrection. Treason against Rome was a capital offense, so Pilate could not dismiss this accusation.

Interestingly, there is no record of Jesus ever claiming to be the king of the Jews. Nevertheless, the Sanhedrin had taken Jesus' declaration as the Son of God to be a messianic claim. Undoubtedly, the Jews anticipated that the Messiah would be their king, and as a result, they concluded that Jesus was claiming to be the king of the Jews.

Pilate was a Roman magistrate appointed by Caesar (A.D. 26–36) to govern over Judea even though he despised the Jews and everything for which they stood.[1] Nevertheless, because of his position, he had to give the Jews audience to hear and resolve their legal matters.

Pilate could have easily granted their wishes and ordered Jesus' execution. However, it seems that Pilate did not necessarily agree with Jesus' accusers. The governor decided to hear the case for himself, and he personally questioned Jesus. Though Jesus made no direct claim to be the king of the Jews, neither did He deny it.

15:3 *The chief priests were accusing him of many things.*

To add weight to their political accusation regarding Jesus' claim, the Sanhedrin continued to bring more accusations against Jesus. They wished to levy such a barrage of accusations that Pilate's only option would be to find Him guilty of crimes mandating the death penalty. Jesus, however, said nothing to defend Himself against these fabricated allegations. If the accused was not guilty of the charges, he would be expected to offer some evidence of his innocence or at least adamantly protest the accusations, especially when a guilty verdict would result in his death. It seems that the Sanhedrin was building its case on the principle that the accused was guilty until proven innocent.

15:4 *So Pilate asked him again, "Don't you have any answer? Look how many accusations they're bringing against you!"*

When Pilate heard all of the accusations against Jesus, he nearly begged Jesus to offer some kind of defense. Among the allegations wielded against Jesus was His claim that He would destroy the temple and rebuild it again in three days. This would further paint a picture of a violent man intent on overthrowing the establishment:

> [59]The chief priests and the whole council were searching for false testimony to use against Jesus in order to execute him. [60]But they did not find any, although many came forward with false testimony. At last two men came forward. [61]They stated, "This man said, 'I can tear down God's temple and rebuild it in three days.' " (Matthew 26:59–61)

Pilate heard these allegations and exclaimed that he could not merely ignore the charges being leveled against Jesus.

15:5 *But Jesus no longer answered anything, so Pilate was surprised.*

Jesus still offered no defense. Instead, He stood before Pilate and said nothing, which amazed the governor. Most men would have been begging for their lives. They would have been loudly proclaiming their innocence. Pilate simply could not believe that Jesus said nothing.

Notes/Applications

The hearing by the Sanhedrin was little more than a mock trial. They accused Jesus with false witnesses that could not even agree in their testimonials against Him. In the end, Jesus' own words brought the death penalty on His head, but after confirming His identity as the king of the Jews, Jesus remained silent throughout the remainder of the proceeding.

We may wonder why Jesus did not protest the derogatory accusations. He Who had silenced unclean spirits surely could have sealed the lips of His critics. Again, we see another piece in the puzzle of Jesus' life. From a heavenly perspective, He had no need to set the record straight, for He had been falsely condemned. He walked the path to Calvary absolutely innocent of any crime in order to bear the burden of man's sin under the Father's indictment.

When we sing songs of praise about the Lamb of God, do we realize the gravity of what He did for us? As time passes, it is easy to go through the motions and merely sing the words, read the stories, and live the life without reflecting on the greatness of the matter. We dare not continue in such a foggy spiritual state, which lulls us into indifference. Rather, may the Lord renew our understanding of what Jesus' sacrifice entailed.

Mark 15:6–15

15:6 *At every Passover festival, Pilate would free one prisoner whom the people asked for.*

As Pilate carefully weighed the evidence, he supposed that Jesus was not guilty of the crimes that the chief priests had leveled against Him. The governor's words and actions seem to indicate that he had concluded that Jesus was innocent of a crime against the Roman empire.

As a goodwill gesture toward its subject people, Rome would set one prisoner free each year at Passover. The people would choose the recipient of amnesty, and regardless of the severity of the crime, Rome would set that prisoner free. Pilate sought a loophole to avoid putting an innocent man to death, and this Passover tradition provided the perfect opportunity.

15:7 *There was a man named Barabbas in prison. He was with some rebels who had committed murder during a riot.*

Pilate brought out a man named Barabbas, which means "son of father."[2] Barabbas was an insurrectionist guilty of the very crime for which Jesus stood accused. Little is known about him except for what is recorded in the gospels. Along with his comrades, Barabbas had apparently mounted some sort of rebellion against Rome. Perhaps he envisioned himself as a patriot much like the celebrated Maccabees, the Jewish zealots who achieved some degree of success against the Seleucid king Antiochus Epiphanes around 160 B.C.[3] Even at this time, small groups of zealots still contended for their freedom from Gentile rule. Barabbas was one of these rebel leaders awaiting execution by the Roman authority.

In the course of his rebel activities, Barabbas had achieved notoriety by slaying some of the enemy, probably Roman foot soldiers. Pilate, therefore, had no love for this man. Rome had brought law and order to the entire known world, and men like Barabbas needed to be destroyed to guarantee the peace of this region.

15:8 *The crowd asked Pilate to do for them what he always did.*

A large crowd had gathered to watch the legal proceedings against Jesus. Perhaps many of the people in the crowd were Jewish zealots who hated the oppressive hand of Rome and supported the cause for which Barabbas had fought. These people began to raise their voices in an uproar to release a prisoner to them.

15:9–10 *⁹Pilate answered them, "Do you want me to free the king of the Jews for you?" ¹⁰Pilate knew that the chief priests had handed Jesus over to him because they were jealous.*

Pilate suggested to the crowd that Jesus was the better candidate for release. After all, Jesus was not a dangerous murderer like Barabbas. Pilate hoped that if the crowd compared the demeanor and history of these two men, they would rather have Jesus released than the true criminal, Barabbas.

Pilate was a shrewd politician. He could see right through these pious, hypocritical religious leaders. They had no just cause against Jesus of Nazareth. They simply considered Him to be a threat to the stability of the Jewish religious establishment. Pilate identified the truth about the motives underlying their accusations. Their case against Jesus was based solely on jealousy and fear of losing their own power and positions.

15:11 *The chief priests stirred up the crowd so that Pilate would free Barabbas for them instead.*

The chief priests were the victims of their own jealousy. They had determined for many months, possibly years, that Jesus had to die. It was the only way to silence this rabbi from Galilee. Out of their hatred for Jesus, they urged the crowd to ask for the release of

Barabbas, a known insurrectionist. They wanted Jesus eliminated. Pilate had perhaps underestimated the outright hatred that these men had for Jesus. They preferred the release of Barabbas, despite his criminal record, rather than Jesus, against Whom there was no real evidence.

15:12 *So Pilate again asked them, "Then what should I do with the king of the Jews?"*

Hearing the uproar of the crowd, Pilate realized that his attempt to free Jesus was not working. These fanatic Jews had called for the release of Barabbas instead. In one final, futile attempt to save Jesus, Pilate asked the people what they wanted him to do with Jesus, Whom they called the king of the Jews.

15:13 *"Crucify him!" they shouted back.*

The crowd roared back, "Crucify Him!" It did not matter that Jesus was not guilty of a crime or that He had never harmed anyone. It did not matter that He stood before them without a shred of convicting evidence. In one united cry, the crowd called for the death of this rabbi by means of crucifixion—the most cruel method of capital punishment ever devised by man.

15:14 *Pilate said to them, "Why? What has he done wrong?" But they shouted even louder, "Crucify him!"*

Pilate remained unconvinced. He asked again for them to define the crime that Jesus had committed. Why would they want Jesus—or any man—to be put to death if He had committed no crime?

The crowd did not answer Pilate's question. There was no answer that they could give that would convince Pilate of Jesus' threat to Rome. This was no longer a legal proceeding. It had become mob rule. The chief priests continued to incite the riot, and rather than raise a single voice to justify their accusations, they roared all the louder, "Crucify Him!"

15:15 *Pilate wanted to satisfy the people, so he freed Barabbas for them. But he had Jesus whipped and handed over to be crucified.*

Because he had raised the ire of the people in the past, Pilate sought to placate the will of the mob by releasing Barabbas to them. By granting these people their wish, he hoped to quiet the tumultuous rioters. After all, what was the value of the life of one more Jew?

Rome consented to crucify Jesus not because of His guilt but for political expediency. Barabbas, the true insurrectionist, was released, and Jesus, the innocent victim of hatred and jealousy, was delivered into the hands of the executioners.

Jesus was first scourged, which was part of the death-penalty process. Usually, the prisoner was stripped of his clothes, tied to a post, and then flogged by several soldiers.[4] The whips were designed to flay the back. Many of the whip's thongs contained pieces of bone and metal that would cut deeply into the prisoner's flesh.[5] Flogging itself sometimes was the only penalty for certain crimes.[6] In many cases, the prisoner would die from the flogging before the execution could be administered.

Notes/Applications

Jesus' trials serve as a remarkable example of the duplicity of the human spirit, for we see humankind at its worst. Jesus was innocent of crime, but in the end, reason did not prevail. The mob's contentions guided the hand of the law. Pilate buckled by submitting to the mob's will, although he "washed his hands" of Christ's innocent blood to clear his conscience *(Matthew 27:24)*. The Prince of Peace would be put to death to keep the peace in Jerusalem, but God remained in complete control of the situation.

In their hatred of the Son of Man, the members of the Sanhedrin unwittingly participated in God's plan to bring the hope of salvation to a lost humanity. Their depravity served God's purpose for bringing His Son to this point in history where time met eternity and sin would be eradicated by the blood of Jesus' sacrifice.

Many living in Jerusalem at that time probably thought that Jesus was just another common criminal being executed. Meanwhile, all the courts of heaven and hell watched as these eternal, momentous events unfolded, wherein salvation was being accomplished for sinful man.

> [10]The prophets carefully researched and investigated this salvation. Long ago they spoke about God's kindness that would come to you. [11]So they tried to find out what time or situation the Spirit of Christ kept referring to whenever he predicted Christ's sufferings and the glory that would follow. [12]God revealed to the prophets that the things they had spoken were not for their own benefit but for yours. What the prophets had spoken, the Holy Spirit, who was sent from heaven, has now made known to you by those who spread the Good News among you. These are things that even the angels want to look into. (1 Peter 1:10–12)

Thank You, Father, that You willingly gave Your Son to die at Calvary for us. Thank You, Jesus, for being obedient unto death so that we might, in You, have life.

Mark 15:16–20

15:16 *The soldiers led Jesus into the courtyard of the palace and called together the whole troop.*

After Pilate had Jesus flogged, he turned Him over to the soldiers, who led Jesus into the courtyard of the palace, which was the governor's residence.[7] When Jesus was escorted into the large courtyard of Pilate's palace, "the whole troop," or garrison, which generally signified a company of six hundred soldiers,[8] was called together. Apparently, Herod, the Rome-appointed ruler of Galilee, was in Jerusalem at the time. He most likely had come with additional military personnel to bolster the troops in the region. During Passover, the tremendous influx of pilgrims into Jerusalem made it necessary to increase the forces in order to maintain the peace.

15:17–18 *¹⁷They dressed him in purple, twisted some thorns into a crown, and placed it on his head. ¹⁸Then they began to greet him, "Long live the king of the Jews!"*

These rough, brutal soldiers had seen much bloodshed on the battlefields of Roman conquest, but at the moment, they were drawing easy duty, just standing by in case some disturbance erupted among the people. Jesus provided great diversion from their boredom of lingering around the palace.

In a mock gesture of regal deference, the soldiers adorned Jesus in improvised royal apparel. They placed a purple cloak around Jesus' body and fashioned a crown of thorns to place on His head. After all, He was the king of the Jews. Jesus, already physically battered, now became the object of their perverted humor with this mock coronation ceremony.

It seems Mark inserts an editorial statement in his choice of words to designate "crown." He did not use the word δίαδημα (diadema), which typically depicts a kingly crown. Instead, the Greek word used for "crown" in this verse is στέφανο (stefanos), which signifies "a victor's crown, a symbol of triumph."[9] The soldiers made this crown to ridicule Jesus, but Mark considered it a crown of victory. This bloodied and beaten man was, in truth, the victor Who conquered sin and death for the lost human race.

The entire troop of soldiers joined the fun as they saluted Jesus as king. They used the same phrase that they would have used if Caesar himself were in their presence—"Hail! Long live the king!" Even though these soldiers were doing everything possible to express disdain and loathing for this Jewish king, they unknowingly hailed the greatest majesty of all—the king Who loved His subjects enough to endure the humiliation of those He came to redeem.

15:19 *They kept hitting him on the head with a stick, spitting on him, and kneeling in front of him with false humility.*

This verse further describes the intensity of the beating that Jesus endured at the hands of the soldiers. The severity of His mistreatment cannot be measured. With a garrison of soldiers, only a few had to participate in this debacle to make it unbearable. Jesus' back was already profusely bleeding from the flogging He had received, and now, rivulets of blood streaked down His face and neck as the thorns of His crown were driven deeper into His scalp by the soldiers' repeated blows to His head. If they had been there, Jesus' own disciples probably would not have recognized their master. The soldiers, however, were not deterred by the bloody visage before them. What did they have to lose? There would be no loss in beating to death a man Who was sentenced to die anyway. As such, they continued their assault without reservation and expressed contempt for their prisoner by spitting on Him. To further demonstrate their ridicule, they bowed their knees to the bloody spectacle and "worshiped" Him. There simply were no limits to the extent that they would go to in order to physically and mentally wound Jesus.

15:20 *After the soldiers finished making fun of Jesus, they took off the purple cape and put his own clothes back on him. Then they led him out to crucify him.*

At last, their fun was over. The soldiers soon tired of their game, especially since Jesus would not respond to their actions, no matter how harsh. The time for execution had arrived, so they removed the "royal" cloak from Jesus and put His own clothes back on Him. Leaving the crown of thorns on His head, they led Him away to be crucified.

Notes/Applications
This horrifying scene was bathed in the people's mockery and disdain for One Who did not deserve such treatment. Something profoundly evil pervaded the atmosphere in Jerusalem on that day—an evil that would not be denied.

Surely, Satan thought his day had come. He ruled the hearts of these men—Jews and Romans alike. He laughed as he saw Jesus broken and spilled out. He laughed as he goaded the soldiers to commit crimes of blasphemy against the beaten, bloodied, and mutilated Son of God. Satan smelled victory in the foul Jerusalem air, and it smelled good to him.

Lucifer's pride has been his problem throughout his miserable existence. He thought he could match wits with Almighty God in heaven and in the garden of Eden. He lost on the Judean hillsides when Jesus rejected his most generous offerings (*Matthew 4:1–11; Luke 4:1–13*). He would lose again even though the Son of Man appeared broken in body with blood running freely down His back, through His hair, and into His eyes. His blood covered the multitude of sins of those who surrender to His calling upon their lives.

At this moment in time, Satan laughed, believing that Jesus' death would grant him victory. Meanwhile, God the Father grieved because He was offering His Son for the world's sins. Satan's demonic scorn would soon turn to awe and terror, for what Satan perceived as his victory would soon become his ultimate defeat.

> [8]*He humbled himself by becoming obedient to the point of death, death on a cross.*
> [9]*This is why God has given him an exceptional honor—*
> *the name honored above all other names—*
> [10]*so that at the name of Jesus everyone in heaven, on earth,*
> *and in the world below will kneel*
> [11]*and confess that Jesus Christ is Lord*
> *to the glory of God the Father.*
> *(Philippians 2:8–11)*

Mark 15:21–28

15:21 *A man named Simon from the city of Cyrene was coming into Jerusalem from his home in the country. He was the father of Alexander and Rufus. As he was about to pass by, the soldiers forced him to carry Jesus' cross.*

Mark does not mention why the Roman execution squad ordered Simon to bear the cross of Jesus, nor do any of the other gospels. Generally, a condemned man was expected to carry to his own execution the crossbeam from which he would be hung. The cross-beam could weigh about one hundred pounds.[10] Apparently, after the repeated beatings Jesus had endured throughout the night and into the morning, He was in no physical condition to transport the cumbersome load.

Simon was probably one of the thousands of pilgrims visiting the holy city for Passover. Cyrene was a Mediterranean coastal city in North Africa, so Simon had traveled a great distance to observe these holy days in Jerusalem.[11] Mark is the only evangelist to mention that Simon was the father of Alexander and Rufus. It is possible that Mark mentions the names of Simon's sons because they were known to Mark's Roman readers *(Romans 16:13)*. Nevertheless, as one of many spectators of these unusual events, Simon was forced into service to help Jesus bear the weight of His crossbeam.

15:22 *They took Jesus to Golgotha (which means "the place of the skull").*

The Roman execution squad led Jesus to a place called Golgotha. As the verse itself attests, *Golgotha* is an Aramaic word that means "the place of the skull."[12] It was likely so named because of the shape of the hill.[13] Calvary, the name by which this place is known to most English-speaking Christians, comes from the Latin Vulgate, which translates this verse using the word *Calvariæ*, meaning "a bare skull."[14]

15:23 *They tried to give him wine mixed with a drug called myrrh, but he wouldn't take it.*

According to some historians, this act was not a Roman custom but originated with the Jews.[15] In some final gesture of mercy to condemned criminals, the soldiers offered a potion of cheap wine into which they stirred myrrh, which had some anesthetic properties. It is believed that this mixture would lessen the pain of crucifixion.[16] Surprisingly, Jesus did not accept it but preferred instead to endure the excruciating pain of the cross without any relief. The sacrifice for which He died was too important to be faced with dulled senses.

15:24 *Next they crucified him. Then they divided his clothes among themselves by throwing dice to see what each one would get.*

Without further elaboration about Jesus' crucifixion, Mark recaps how the people dealt with Jesus' garments. At the time of His crucifixion, Jesus would have been stripped of His clothes and laid on His back, and stakes would have been driven through His wrists just above the hands into the crossbeam. The crossbeam would have then been raised and fastened to an upright beam.[17] Next, His feet would have been nailed to the beam to help keep the wrists from bearing His entire body weight.[18] Thus pilloried, He would endure excruciating hours, torn between the need to breathe and the incessant pain of extended weight on the nails. It was not uncommon for a condemned person to continue through this agonizing routine for as long as three days before succumbing to suffocation rather than blood loss.

The soldiers were unconcerned about Jesus' pain. Waiting for Him to die, they spent their time casting lots for possession of His garments. Even this detail provides evidence of God's foreordained plan of redemption: "They divide my clothes among themselves. They throw dice for my clothing" (Psalm 22:18). Even now, we can trace the hand of the sovereign Lord guiding history from generation to generation to this moment when the Son of Man hung on a cross and His executioners played games to determine who would keep His clothes.

15:25 *It was nine in the morning when they crucified him.*

This is the only gospel account that records the time at which Jesus' crucifixion occurred. According to the Jewish method of time computation by counting days from sunset of one day to sunset of the next day, "the third hour," as this time is referred to in some translations, would mean the third hour from sunrise—nine o'clock in the morning. To prevent a misunderstanding of the time, which seems to contradict the time given by the apostle John *(John 19:14)*, it is important to note that Mark documents this event by the Jewish method, whereas John used the Roman method of time computation.[19]

15:26 *There was a written notice of the accusation against him. It read, "The king of the Jews."*

Part of the routine of Roman execution included posting the crime of the condemned man. The prisoner usually wore this sign around his neck while he was led to his execution, and the soldiers then posted it above the prisoner while he hung on the cross.[20] Jesus' "crime" was publicized for all to see. The sign simply read, "The king of the Jews." No one else in history would ever be condemned for this reason. Certainly, we understand that crimes of murder or insurrection might have demanded the death penalty. But to be sentenced to death for being the king of the Jews? Pilate, having found no fault in Jesus and unwilling to agree with the despised Sanhedrin, refused to post Jesus' crime as "Insurrectionist." While Pilate yielded to the angry demands of the crowds and agreed to put Jesus to death, he would not change his verdict, as the chief priests demanded, declaring instead, "I have written what I've written" *(John 19:21–22)*. Though Jesus' accusers viewed the inscription with mockery and reproach, Jesus hung on the cross under the proclamation of His true title.

15:27 *They crucified two criminals with him, one on his right and the other on his left.*

Pilate further tried to minimize the impact of his submission to the Jewish outcry for the crucifixion of Jesus by executing two convicted criminals alongside Jesus. Robbery was generally not punishable by death, so these men were likely insurrectionists or rebels.[21] It almost seems that Pilate made a final attempt to demonstrate his contempt for the Jewish leaders by executing two men who were guilty of the same crime as Barabbas, the one he believed should be hanging on a cross in Jesus' place. This detail further exemplifies God's providence over the situation, as explained in the following verse.

15:28 *"And what the Scriptures said came true: 'He was counted with criminals.' "*

Jesus had never advocated the overthrow of Rome. He had never spoken against any civil authority. However, in the continued irony of God's plan, Jesus was executed side by side with two men who were guilty of the very crime for which the Son of Man was condemned.

Mark, in a rare departure from his normal style, calls on the authority of the Scriptures to confirm that this moment had been prophesied many centuries earlier: "So I will give him a share among the mighty, and he will divide the prize with the strong, because he poured out his life in death and he was counted with sinners. He carried the sins of many. He intercedes for those who are rebellious" *(Isaiah 53:12)*. During His life and now at His crucifixion, Jesus fulfilled each and every prophecy regarding the legacy of God's redeeming work among the lost human race.

Notes/Applications

Isaiah had prophesied that God's Messiah would be numbered among transgressors. In this passage of Mark's gospel, we see yet another messianic prophecy fulfilled in Jesus Christ. He hung on the cross with two criminals being executed on either side of Him. He was thrust into the moving tides of history as the righteous Son of God, into the tides of human misery and sin. Jesus lived His entire life walking among transgressors and then dying for them.

> ⁶*Although he was in the form of God and equal with God,*
> *he did not take advantage of this equality.*
> ⁷*Instead, he emptied himself by taking on the form of a servant,*
> *by becoming like other humans,*
> *by having a human appearance.*
> ⁸*He humbled himself by becoming obedient to the point of death,*
> *death on a cross.* (Philippians 2:6–8)

We stand among the transgressors of the human race. We deserve death as the penalty for our sin against the righteous, holy God. We are the insurrectionists who have rebelled against the God Who created us. We want nothing to do with Him. We desire to be free of Him because we despise the yoke of His righteous standard.

Nevertheless, Jesus came to us. He walked among us. He healed our diseases. He cast out our demons. He showed us the Father. Yet this innocent man was condemned to death in our place, bearing the penalty of our sin.

> ¹²*Sin came into the world through one person, and death came through sin. So death spread to everyone, because everyone sinned. . . .*
> ¹⁸*Everyone received God's life-giving approval through one verdict.*
> ¹⁹*Clearly, through one person's disobedience humanity became sinful, and through one person's obedience humanity will receive God's approval.* (Romans 5:12,18–19)

Have we taken up our cross to follow Him?

Mark 15:29–32

15:29–30 *²⁹Those who passed by insulted him. They shook their heads and said, "What a joke! You were going to tear down God's temple and build it again in three days. ³⁰Come down from the cross, and save yourself!"*

Those who passed by the scene of Jesus' execution mocked Him by repeating the words with which He was charged. They spoke to Him with loathing and without any compassion for His suffering on the cross.

These people felt no fear in ridiculing Jesus. They merely figured Him to be an imposter. He could not possibly have been their Messiah. This was the man Who had made such unbelievable claims of authority far beyond human comprehension.

The bystanders continued their mockery by daring Jesus to defy the cross and display His power once again. In their minds, if He was truly their Messiah, a Roman cross could not have held Him. Surely, the true Messiah would never have allowed Himself to be so easily captured and executed. Their Messiah would be strong and powerful, the heir to the throne of David. He would be their king! This poor, mutilated, breathing corpse could not possibly be their Messiah. If He were, He could have corrected their opinions by coming down from the cross, but they did not really expect Him to prove anything to them. Their words were the ravings of unbelief and were not worthy of divine credence.

15:31 *The chief priests and the scribes made fun of him among themselves in the same way. They said, "He saved others, but he can't save himself.*

Finally, their moment had arrived. As Jesus hung on the cross, the Jewish rulers reveled in what they surely considered their greatest victory. They had successfully and permanently silenced this radical rabbi and ensured their continued positions of wealth and power.

Hiding behind their sanctioned positions, the chief priests and scribes joined those who mocked Jesus and derided the suffering Messiah with scornful words. Their acknowledgment that "He saved others" undoubtedly referred to the far-reaching impact of Jesus' ministry. Whether or not the members of the Sanhedrin actually placed any credibility in those incidents, they unwittingly acknowledged that countless lives had been transformed by Jesus' miracles of healing and deliverance.

However, they misrepresented Jesus' commitment to the cross as evidence of His alleged blasphemy. Even though Jesus had been ridiculed and challenged to prove that He was the Messiah, it became obvious that He was not going to come down from that cross, which, in the minds of the Jewish religious rulers, only supported their opinion that Jesus was not Who He claimed to be. While others concluded that He *could* not save Himself, Jesus determined that He *would* not save Himself.

15:32 *Let the Messiah, the king of Israel, come down from the cross now so that we may see and believe." Even those who were crucified with him were insulting him.*

The chief priests and scribes rephrased the challenge with words that revealed their interpretation regarding the role the Messiah would assume when he came. He would be the king of Israel. He would not look like this man before them, with arms spread wide and nails in His hands, hanging on a cross and gasping for breath. He would be their king! Despite their declarations, the Sanhedrin's track record suggests that they most certainly would not have believed Jesus even if He did miraculously free Himself from the cross. Had they truly known the Scriptures as well as they professed, they would have recognized that this crucifixion embodied the very proof they sought for their Messiah.

Along with the people who passed by the cross and the self-righteous members of the Jewish council, even the two criminals being crucified beside Jesus mocked Him. They seemed to believe, too, that if Jesus were the true Messiah, He surely would save Himself from this cruel torture and, perhaps, spare them as well. The Gospel of Luke reveals greater insight into this exchange, as well as one ray of light beaming through this darkness.

> ³⁹One of the criminals hanging there insulted Jesus by saying, "So you're really the Messiah, are you? Well, save yourself and us!"
>
> ⁴⁰But the other criminal scolded him: "Don't you fear God at all? Can't you see that you're condemned in the same way that he is? ⁴¹Our punishment is fair. We're getting what we deserve. But this man hasn't done anything wrong."
>
> ⁴²Then he said, "Jesus, remember me when you enter your kingdom."
>
> ⁴³Jesus said to him, "I can guarantee this truth: Today you will be with me in paradise." (Luke 23:39–43)

Notes/Applications

As the crowd stood at the foot of Golgotha's hill and witnessed this horrible event, they continually hurled insults at their adversary. They taunted Jesus to save Himself without realizing that He could have summoned heaven's armies to His rescue: "⁵²Then Jesus said to him, 'Put your sword away! All who use a sword will be killed by a sword. ⁵³Don't you think that I could call on my Father to send more than twelve legions of angels to help me now? ⁵⁴How, then, are the Scriptures to be fulfilled that say this must happen?' " (Matthew 26:52–54). Jesus' torture was compounded between the blows of physical and verbal abuse. As a man, He felt the pain of His agonizing death, and yet as the Son of God, He would not be deterred from fulfilling His Father's perfect plan.

The religious leaders and the people over whom they presided did not want a "suffering Savior." They desired the grandiose—a Messiah cloaked in royalty and military power. They yearned for a king who would offer release from political bondage, but they thought little of the spiritual bondage eternally entangling them.

Even those of us who have believed Jesus, who have embraced redemption at the price of His blood, and who have pledged allegiance to the Savior seek to circumvent physical and verbal persecution. We dodge ridicule by not standing out from the crowd. We sacrifice only those resources that are in excess of what we need. Although we cling to the benefits associated with being Christ followers, we do not want to pay the price that such obedience requires. In actuality, the struggle resides internally between our flesh and the Holy Spirit dwelling within us. Our souls may soar with joy as we envision our Savior high and lifted up, but we remain sorely defeated by our self-preoccupation and the ways we shame the Lord Whom we claim to love.

How fickle our human frame! How unreliable our witness to His saving grace! Since Jesus remained faithful to the cross despite the arduous miles before Him, how can we not be moved to bear whatever is required by commitment to Him? How can we offer to Him something that costs us nothing? Surely, whatever we go through is miniscule compared with what Jesus endured for us. *"¹⁶The Spirit himself testifies with our spirit that we are God's children. ¹⁷If we are his children, we are also God's heirs. If we share in Christ's suffering in order to share his glory, we are heirs together with him. ¹⁸I consider our present sufferings insignificant compared to the glory that will soon be revealed to us"* (Romans 8:16–18).

May we resolve to allow the Holy Spirit to transform our lives into living testimonies of the grace, power, and sacrifice of our Lord.

Mark 15:33–39

15:33 *At noon darkness came over the whole land until three in the afternoon.*

It was now midday, and Jesus had been on the cross for three hours. For reasons that scholars cannot determine, the world was suddenly enveloped in utter darkness. Though some might argue that this was a coincidental eclipse, the season of its occurrence seems to preclude this explanation. Furthermore, a solar eclipse lasts only a short duration and cannot account for the three hours of darkness. Therefore, this darkness must have been a supernatural occurrence wherein all of creation experienced the impact of this cataclysmic moment in history. One of the early church fathers, Tertullian (A.D. 160–230), confirmed the historical evidence of this spectacle by reviewing Roman archives; and Suidas, another early historian, claimed that Dionysius the Areopagite observed the phenomenon in Egypt and commented, "Either the divine being suffers, or suffers with him that suffers, or the frame of the world is dissolving."[22]

Amazingly, many Jews believed that such a darkness always accompanied God's judgment. However, they could not conceive this darkness that settled over the earth as Jesus suffered on the cross.

> [9]On that day, declares the Almighty Lord,
>   I will make the sun go down at noon
>   and darken the earth in broad daylight.
> [10]I will turn your festivals into funerals
>   and all your songs into funeral songs.
>   I will put sackcloth around everyone's waist
>   and shave everyone's head.
>   I will make that day seem like a funeral for an only child,
>   and its end will be bitter. (Amos 8:9–10)

15:34 *At three o'clock Jesus cried out in a loud voice, "Eloi, Eloi, lema sabachthani?" which means, "My God, my God, why have you abandoned me?"*

After six hours on the cross, the Son of Man cried out above the noise of His detractors. Mark records Jesus' actual words and then translates them for His readers: "My God, my God, why have you abandoned me?" In His moment of greatest pain and deepest sorrow, Jesus uttered a line from the prophetic words that King David had chronicled nearly one thousand years earlier: "My God, my God, why have you abandoned me? Why are you so far away from helping me, so far away from the words of my groaning?" *(Psalm 22:1).*

Denied by the Jewish people and deserted by His own disciples, Jesus cried out in agony. When He had prayed in the garden of Gethsemane for "this cup" to pass from Him, it was this very anguish that Jesus, in His humanity, dreaded to suffer. The pain, the torture, the rebuke, and the derision of His adversaries created a formidable experience that anyone would hope to avoid, yet these were all part of the cup appointed for the Son of Man to bear for the sins of the world. *"Jesus said, 'You don't realize what you're asking. Can you drink the cup that I'm going to drink? Can you be baptized with the baptism that I'm going to receive?'" (Mark 10:38).* Forsaken by the Father, He endured all that needed to be accomplished for the atonement of man's sins. Even as He hung on the cross and cried out in His moment of utmost grief, He would receive no relief, no assistance, and no consolation from God the Father in heaven. Even so, this was the destiny of the Messiah. Jesus—sinless, perfect, and righteous—became the sin-bearer for man's transgressions against a holy God: "God had Christ, who was sinless, take our sin so that we might receive God's approval through him" *(2 Corinthians 5:21).*

This was the moment for which the Son of God was sent to earth. Though certainly the most appalling and tragic moment in human history, it also was the most awesome, most holy, most gracious, and most merciful moment of all time. This was the moment that all Old Testament sacrifices foreshadowed and so many Old Testament prophecies foretold. This was the moment when the Son of Man atoned for the sins of the world. This was the sacrifice of the Paschal Lamb of God. God the Father gave His Son, and the Son gave Himself. *"¹⁷The Father loves me because I give my life in order to take it back again. ¹⁸No one takes my life from me. I give my life of my own free will. I have the authority to give my life, and I have the authority to take my life back again. This is what my Father ordered me to do"* (John 10:17–18). Although inexplicable in human terms, Jesus the Christ not only felt the physical and spiritual suffering of the moment but also bore the weight of being forsaken by the heavenly Father when the sin of mankind was placed upon Him. *"We have all strayed like sheep. Each one of us has turned to go his own way, and the Lord has laid all our sins on him"* (Isaiah 53:6). Finally, this moment was also the glorification of the Son of God because, despite being distanced from Almighty God's intervention, He had faithfully completed the Father's sovereign plan of redemption. *"³This is eternal life: to know you, the only true God, and Jesus Christ, whom you sent. ⁴On earth I have given you glory by finishing the work you gave me to do. ⁵Now, Father, give me glory in your presence with the glory I had with you before the world existed"* (John 17:3–5).

The ultimate mystery of God's eternal providence is that He provided within Himself the divine means to satisfy the Law, to dispense His mercy by providing the means of salvation, and to accomplish His perfect will.

> *¹⁰Yet, it was the Lord's will to crush him with suffering.*
> *When the Lord has made his life a sacrifice for our wrongdoings,*
>   *he will see his descendants for many days.*
>   *The will of the Lord will succeed through him.*
> *¹¹He will see and be satisfied because of his suffering.*
> *My righteous servant will acquit many people*
>   *because of what he has learned through suffering.*
> *He will carry their sins as a burden.*

> [12]*So I will give him a share among the mighty,*
>   *and he will divide the prize with the strong,*
>   *because he poured out his life in death*
>   *and he was counted with sinners.*
>   *He carried the sins of many.*
>   *He intercedes for those who are rebellious. (Isaiah 53:10–12)*

15:35 **When some of the people standing there heard him say that, they said, "Listen! He's calling Elijah."**

Some standing nearby misunderstood Jesus' words and thought that He was calling for Elijah, one of the two prophets who appeared with Jesus during His transfiguration *(Mark 9:1–13)*. The anguish of the suffering Lamb of God was dismissed as a cry for help to a prophet of old. Some commentators suggest that onlookers ignorantly mistook Jesus' words based on tenets of the rabbinic tradition that declared that Elijah would come before the Messiah.[23] However, it seems that the Jews who overheard Jesus' cries would not have made such a mistake but instead were continuing in their heartless mockery of the Lord even in His darkest hour and deepest grief.[24]

15:36 **Someone ran and soaked a sponge in vinegar. Then he put it on a stick and offered Jesus a drink. The man said, "Let's see if Elijah comes to take him down."**

A person standing nearby filled a sponge with vinegar, fastened it to a reed, and offered it to Jesus, apparently in response to His statement, "I'm thirsty" *(John 19:28)*. This was likely an inexpensive concoction of vinegar wine diluted with water.[25] It is doubtful that the intent of this action was humanitarian since Jesus was already so near death. Rather, it seems they attempted to prolong His life so they could continue their abusive fun at His expense. While the person offered Jesus the vinegar, the people mockingly wondered whether Jesus' cry for help would be answered. He had already shown that He would not free Himself from the cross, and it seems no more probable that they expected Elijah to come and rescue the dying man. This was simply another way in which they could direct their animosity toward Jesus, the king of the Jews.

15:37 *Then Jesus cried out in a loud voice and died.*

Having wet His lips with the tart mixture, Jesus expressed His utmost anguish with a penetrating cry. *"After Jesus had taken the vinegar, he said, 'It is finished!' Then he bowed his head and died"* (*John 19:30*). In horrible agony—that of a body crucified and a soul forsaken—Jesus cried out loudly enough for all nearby to hear and then exhaled His final breath.

There is great significance in the fact that Jesus cried out loudly just before His final breath. In crucifixion, death followed an agonizing two- or three-day process of slow asphyxiation, dehydration, and torn muscles.[26] A condemned man's last few hours were usually spent in a state of semiconscious struggle until he eventually lapsed into a coma and then died. The fact that Jesus cried out "in a loud voice" just before He died indicates that He remained fully conscious to the end. He knew exactly where He was and why He was there.

15:38 *The curtain in the temple was split in two from top to bottom.*

At the moment that Jesus took His final breath, the veil of the temple was "split in two from top to bottom." The veil was a thick and massive woven curtain sixty feet in length that separated the holy place from the most holy place.[27] The curtain's size and construction made it virtually indestructible. The fact that it was torn from top to bottom rather than bottom to top certainly points to God's hands in its destruction and not man's doing.[28]

Finally, the profound significance that this event occurred at the precise moment of Jesus' death settles the matter as a supernatural happening, and one that forever changed the relationship between a righteous God and the human race. Until this moment, only the high priest entered the holy of holies, and even then only once a year. Jesus' death at the very hour of the evening sacrifice forever ended the need for the Jewish sacrificial system. Jesus was now the sacrificed Paschal Lamb that atoned for all the sins of the world. Never again would there be a physical or spiritual curtain separating God from His faithful.

15:39 *When the officer who stood facing Jesus saw how he gave up his spirit, he said, "Certainly, this man was the Son of God!"*

A Roman officer, or centurion, standing nearby had observed all that happened. He had seen many crucifixions, but this one was different. This man did not curse and swear and scream at the injustice done to Him. He bore the humiliation and the ridicule of His fellow countrymen. He even prayed for His enemies: "Then Jesus said, 'Father, forgive them. They don't know what they're doing.' Meanwhile, the soldiers divided his clothes among themselves by throwing dice" *(Luke 23:34)*. Fully conscious of all that was happening, He finally died after calling on His God: "Jesus cried out in a loud voice, 'Father, into your hands I entrust my spirit.' After he said this, he died" *(Luke 23:46)*. Overwhelmed with awe and astonishment, this rugged Roman soldier declared, "Certainly, this man was the Son of God!"

This soldier saw in Jesus a man like no one else he had ever known. He had experienced the ultimate testimony of Jesus' true identity as he came face-to-face with the reality of God's salvation. At the foot of the cross, this Roman officer openly acknowledged what the Jewish people failed to recognize—this man was surely the Messiah, the Son of God.

Notes/Applications

Throned upon the awful tree,
King of grief, I watch with Thee,

Darkness veils Thine anguished face;
None its lines of woe can trace;
None can tell what pangs unknown
Hold Thee silent and alone.

Silent through those three dread hours,
Wrestling with the evil powers,
Left alone with human sin,
Gloom around Thee and within,
Till th' appointed time is nigh,
Till the Lamb of God must die.

Hark, that cry that peals aloud
Upward through the whelming cloud!
Thou, the Father's only Son,
Thou, His own Anointed One,
Thou dost ask Him—can it be?
'Why hast Thou forsaken Me?'[29]

The moment had arrived. Jesus cried out to His Father and breathed His last breath. The sacrifice was complete. The price was paid. The temple veil covering the entrance to the holy of holies, the most sacred place of the temple, was torn from top to bottom. If accomplished by human hands, the veil would have most likely been split from bottom to top, but something supernatural had just occurred.

This symbolic act on the part of God demonstrated that the veil separating man from God had been rent. We are now free to approach Him as our Father through the blood of His Son. The writer of Hebrews penned these magnificent words so that we might hold fast to our confession.

> [19]*Brothers and sisters, because of the blood of Jesus we can now confidently go into the holy place.* [20]*Jesus has opened a new and living way for us to go through the curtain. (The curtain is his own body.)* [21]*We have a superior priest in charge of God's house.* [22]*We have been sprinkled with his blood to free us from a guilty*

conscience, and our bodies have been washed with clean water. So we must continue to come to him with a sincere heart and strong faith. (Hebrews 10:19–22)

Mark 15:40–47

15:40–41 *⁴⁰Some women were watching from a distance. Among them were Mary from Magdala, Mary (the mother of young James and Joseph), and Salome. ⁴¹They had followed him and supported him while he was in Galilee. Many other women who had come to Jerusalem with him were there too.*

At the scene of the cross stood a group of women watching the execution. These women may not have been close enough to hear everything, but they observed every detail of the proceedings.

Among these women were Mary from Magdala, commonly referred to as Mary Magdalene, and Mary the mother of Jesus (John 19:27), who was also the mother of young James and Joseph. These sons are named so that she can be distinguished from others with the same name and, perhaps, because James and Joseph were known in the early church. A third woman mentioned was Salome, the wife of Zebedee and the mother of Jesus' disciples James and John (Matthew 27:56).

These women were among a group of dedicated followers who had committed themselves to caring for Jesus as He traveled.³⁰ These women had assumed the task of providing food during His ministry. Apparently, other women also traveled with this core group as they made their way to Jerusalem for the Passover feast, and now, they had watched Jesus as the grueling hours of His crucifixion ground down to an inevitable conclusion.

15:42–43 *⁴²It was Friday evening, before the day of worship, ⁴³when Joseph arrived. He was from the city of Arimathea and was an important member of the Jewish council. He, too, was waiting for the kingdom of God. Joseph boldly went to Pilate's quarters to ask for the body of Jesus.*

Jesus died at the ninth hour, around three o'clock in the afternoon. The Sabbath would begin at six, so "evening" would indicate some time in those hours in between, perhaps as late as five o'clock. Mark again informs his Gentile readers about the requirements of the Jewish traditions. According to Jewish law, it would be necessary to bury the dead before the Sabbath.[31] If Jesus was to be buried on this day, it would have to happen quickly, or He would not be buried until Sunday.

Another element of Mosaic Law presented additional pressure for an immediate burial: "[22]When a convicted person is put to death, [23]never leave his dead body hung on a pole overnight. Be sure to bury him that same day, because anyone whose body is hung on a pole is cursed by God. The land that the Lord your God is giving you must never become unclean" (*Deuteronomy 21:22–23*). While we are acutely aware that Jesus was not guilty of any offense, the Jewish leadership would still do everything possible to conform to the Law.

Though the task awaited, there seemed few prospects to step forward and actually do what needed to be done. The women could not do it, and Jesus' disciples had fled in fear for their lives. Events had developed too quickly for anyone to be prepared to carry out this legal mandate.

The volunteer was a surprise. Joseph, who lived in a village called Arimathea about twenty miles northwest of Jerusalem, was a member of the Sanhedrin.[32] The Gospel of Luke tells us that Joseph dissented from the Sanhedrin's decision to condemn Jesus to death: "[50]There was a good man who had God's approval. His name was Joseph. He was a member of the Jewish council, [51]but he had not agreed with what they had done. He was from the Jewish city of Arimathea, and he was waiting for the kingdom of God" (*Luke 23:50–51*). Both Mark's and Luke's gospels note that he was "waiting for the kingdom of God." This could be said of any good Jew, which might be all we would think of Joseph were it not for the additional insight offered by the apostle John's account of this man: "Joseph was a disciple of Jesus but secretly because he was afraid of the Jews" (*John 19:38b*).

It is important to understand Joseph's position as he approached Pilate. He had already endangered his membership in the council when he objected to Jesus' sentence. Now, he took it a step further by proposing to handle a dead body, which was considered ceremonially unclean and would render him unfit to serve *(Numbers 19:11–13)*. In worldly terms, Joseph had more to lose than any of Jesus' disciples. Loss of position in the council would mean a loss of his status and possibly his wealth. Despite these risks, Joseph had the courage to come before Pilate and ask for Jesus' body. Joseph of Arimathea, wealthy council member, would no longer be a secret follower of Jesus.

15:44 *Pilate wondered if Jesus had already died. So he summoned the officer to ask him if Jesus was, in fact, dead.*

Pilate should not have been surprised by this news. He himself was responsible for the scourging that Jesus had initially received *(verse 15)*. After being escorted from Pilate's presence, Jesus had received another round of merciless cruelty at the hands of the Roman soldiers before He was led to the cross *(verses 17–19)*. Though innocent of any crime, Jesus had received a beating even more severe than was likely to be received by the most hardened of criminals, yet Pilate seemed surprised by the news that Jesus was dead after having been crucified only seven or eight hours earlier. Therefore, Pilate summoned the centurion to confirm this information before he agreed to release the body of Jesus to Joseph.

15:45 *When the officer had assured him that Jesus was dead, Pilate let Joseph have the corpse.*

The centurion eventually returned and confirmed the report that Jesus indeed dead. Pilate granted Joseph's request. We get the impression that Pilate wanted to get this episode behind him as quickly as possible. He apparently offered little protest that Joseph was not a family member of the deceased. Mark hereby confirms for his Roman readers the fact that Jesus' death was validated by Roman authorities.

15:46 *Joseph had purchased some linen cloth. He took the body down from the cross and wrapped it in the cloth. Then he laid the body in a tomb, which had been cut out of rock, and he rolled a stone against the door of the tomb.*

There was little time left before the Sabbath began. Being a wealthy man, Joseph probably had the help of several servants to perform the gruesome task. They took Jesus' body from the cross and, according to Jewish custom, wrapped it in the linen that Joseph had purchased. We find in John's gospel that Joseph also received help from Nicodemus, one of his colleagues in the Sanhedrin. *"³⁹Nicodemus, the one who had first come to Jesus at night, went with Joseph and brought 75 pounds of a myrrh and aloe mixture. ⁴⁰These two men took the body of Jesus and bound it with strips of linen. They laced the strips with spices. This was the Jewish custom for burial"* (John 19:39–40).

Together they laid the body of Jesus in a tomb located very near the place of His crucifixion: *"⁴¹A garden was located in the place where Jesus was crucified. In that garden was a new tomb in which no one had yet been placed. ⁴²Joseph and Nicodemus put Jesus in that tomb, since that day was the Jewish day of preparation and since the tomb was nearby"* (John 19:41–42). Such man-made caves were often used as burial chambers, and the chamber usually contained several stone beds upon which corpses could be laid.[33]

15:47 *Mary from Magdala and Mary (the mother of Joses) watched where Jesus was laid.*

Many had returned to their host families to prepare for the Sabbath, but apparently two of the women mentioned in verse forty were still present and watching all that was going on. They followed the actions of Joseph and Nicodemus as they removed Jesus' body from the cross and took Him to the tomb for burial. Nothing escaped their scrutiny as the two men handled the dead body of their beloved Jesus.

Notes/Applications

Sealed in a nearby tomb, Jesus lay dead. It was incomprehensible that this same exciting teacher, prophet, and healer took His place among the tombs of the dead.

We can barely imagine the gloom that settled over Jerusalem. The stain of Jesus' death had infused the disciples with despair and hopelessness. All of the plans, hope, and excitement of following Jesus dissipated. Only the great void of His absence remained. His disciples wandered through the city streets in shock. Eventually, they retreated to the upper room in tears.

> O come and mourn with me awhile;
> And tarry here the cross beside;
> O come, together let us mourn;
> Jesus, our Lord, is crucified!

> How fast His hands and feet are nailed;
> His blessed tongue with thirst is tied,
> His failing eyes are blind with blood:
> Jesus, our Lord, is crucified.

> Seven times He spoke, seven words of love;
> And all three hours His silence cried
> For mercy on the souls of men:
> Jesus, our Lord, is crucified.

> O break, O break, hard heart of mine!
> Thy weak self-love and guilty pride
> His Pilate and His Judas were:
> Jesus, our Lord, is crucified!

> A broken heart, a fount of tears,
> Ask, and they will not be denied;

A broken heart love's cradle is:
Jesus, our Lord, is crucified.

O love of God! O sin of man!
In this dread act your strength is tried;
And victory remains with love;
For Thou our Lord, art crucified![34]

Thousands of years before this event, a psalmist penned words inspired by the Holy Spirit: "Weeping may last for the night, but there is a song of joy in the morning" *(Psalm 30:5).* Those words were about to come true for the miserable little band huddled together in the upper room.

Mark 16:1–8

16:1 *When the day of worship was over, Mary from Magdala, Mary (the mother of James), and Salome bought spices to go and anoint Jesus.*

With the Sabbath past, three women brought spices to the tomb so that they could properly anoint Jesus' body according to Jewish customs. These same three women had stood some distance away from the scene of Jesus' crucifixion and had carefully observed all of the developments of that fateful afternoon (Mark 15:40–41). They had observed Joseph of Arimathea as he and Nicodemus removed Jesus' body from the cross and buried it in a nearby tomb (Mark 15:47). Their love for Jesus now brought them to the tomb at the earliest possible time to perform this final burial rite.

16:2 *On Sunday they were going to the tomb very early when the sun had just come up.*

Just after sunrise on Sunday morning, the first day after the Sabbath, these women came to Jesus' tomb. Their actions, though motivated by their love for Jesus, clearly demonstrated that they believed He was dead. Even though Jesus had told the Twelve on numerous occasions that He would rise on the third day, it is evident that they either did not comprehend His words or did not believe them. Despite the fact that these women had seen or at least heard that Jesus had brought Lazarus back from the dead *(John 11:32–44)*, they apparently did not expect the same to happen in this situation.

16:3 *They said to one another, "Who will roll away the stone for us from the entrance to the tomb?"*

As they walked along the road to Jesus' tomb, they thought of a major obstacle to the successful completion of their labor of love. They had seen a heavy stone rolled over the mouth of the tomb, and they feared it would be impossible for them to remove the stone so that they could enter the tomb and anoint Jesus' body. The Roman authorities had sealed the tomb, and a group of soldiers stood guard. This had been done at the request of the high priest so that the disciples could not steal the body and then declare that He had risen from the dead *(Matthew 27:62–66)*. The religious leaders remembered that Jesus had said He would rise again on the third day, but the disciples, Jesus' closest followers, were not thinking that far ahead. Fearful for their own lives, they were keeping out of sight. Ironically, Jesus' adversaries remembered the promise of His resurrection, but His faithful followers had forgotten.

As the women approached, their only problem, as far as they knew, would be the removal of the massive stone. If they had been aware of the deployment of Roman soldiers, they might never have made the journey. It was simply too dangerous to challenge the authority of Rome.

16:4 *When they looked up, they saw that the stone had been rolled away. It was a very large stone.*

As the women approached the tomb, they looked and saw that the stone had already been rolled away from the tomb's entrance. The stone was so large and so heavy that these faithful women could not have budged it themselves. Although they had anticipated the imposing obstacle to hinder their task, they were amazed and probably relieved to discover that their worrying was in vain. The tomb was open!

16:5 *As they went into the tomb, they saw a young man. He was dressed in a white robe and sat on the right side. They were panic-stricken.*

With this barrier removed, the three women entered the tomb expecting to anoint the body of Jesus. Suddenly, they came face-to-face with a young man dressed in white, who was an angel, according to this description and other gospel accounts *(Matthew 28:1–4)*. This angel was sitting to the right as they entered the tomb. When the women saw this young man, they were terribly frightened.

16:6 *The young man said to them, "Don't panic! You're looking for Jesus from Nazareth, who was crucified. He has been brought back to life. He's not here. Look at the place where they laid him.*

The holy messenger saw fear on the faces of the three women, and he encouraged them not to be afraid. He knew they had come to the tomb to anoint the body of Jesus. They were certainly not expecting to find anyone like this young man in the burial chamber, but the angel brought wonderful news of the greatest significance. Though He had been crucified and buried, Jesus was no longer in the tomb! He had risen again just as He said He would!

To verify the truth of his statement, the messenger invited the women to inspect the burial vault closely. The place where they had laid the dead body of Jesus was now empty! This rabbi, Jesus of Nazareth—the one Whom these women had known so well, the one to Whom they had ministered throughout His ministry, the one Whose death they had witnessed, and the one Whose body they had seen laid in the tomb—was alive!

16:7 *Go and tell his disciples and Peter that he's going ahead of them to Galilee. There they will see him, just as he told them."*

The angel instructed the women to go and tell the disciples what they had just seen and learned. He specifically mentioned Peter, as if to emphasize that the Lord still loved the disciple despite his denial. The particular mention of Peter is found only in the Gospel of Mark. However, as Peter's protégé, Mark would have been able to offer this particular detail that others may not have known.[1]

The messenger then instructed these faithful women to tell the disciples that Jesus would meet them in Galilee. There, they would experience for themselves the reality of Jesus' resurrection, which would fulfill a promise that Jesus had made to them before His crucifixion: "But after I am brought back to life, I will go to Galilee ahead of you" *(Mark 14:28)*.

16:8 *They went out of the tomb and ran away. Shock and trembling had overwhelmed them. They didn't say a thing to anyone, because they were afraid.*

The women turned and left the scene as quickly as their feet would carry them. They literally trembled with fear. The message was so unbelievable that they had no inclinations to tell anyone else about what they had just experienced. Would anyone believe them anyway? Shaking and frightened, they did not know what to do. Surely, the tomb was empty. They had seen it for themselves.

The women faced a terrible burden. Under Jewish law, only men were considered suitable witnesses.[2] Therefore, if they were to tell someone of their experience, their message could be disregarded. The validity of their testimony about Jesus' resurrection could have been jeopardized, and so they told no one.

Notes/Applications

The description of the women's encounter with an angel at the tomb dramatically portrays the final and most compelling evidence revealing Jesus' identity as the Son of God. Do we find it difficult to believe that Jesus did and said the things recorded in Mark? Can we possibly believe that there was such a person as Jesus—that He suffered a cruel and unjust condemnation, that He was forsaken by His Father for the purpose of redeeming the lost, and that He came back to life?

From the very first verse of this gospel, the author unequivocally states his conclusion that Jesus is the Son of God. With a fast-paced narrative pointing out the paradox of the human dilemma contrasted by the plan of God to save man from the hopelessness of his sin condition, Mark desired for others to know Jesus, to evaluate the evidence presented to them, and to arrive at the same conclusion.

God's plan was fulfilled not in Jesus' ministry, although the evidence of His life was remarkable. Rather, Jesus' death was the only acceptable atoning sacrifice for sin. The historical fact that Jesus rose from the dead proved that God's plan was fully carried out.

The Christian faith rests on Jesus' resurrection. Without the resurrection, we have no faith, no hope, and no reason to believe in eternal life, but with the evidence of Jesus' resurrection, we can look forward to the day when we will see Him in all His glory. Each of us will pass away from this life and will undergo a resurrection of our mortal bodies and stand before God at the great white throne of judgment. *"[11]I saw a large, white throne and the one who was sitting on it. The earth and the sky fled from his presence, but no place was found for them. [12]I saw the dead, both important and unimportant people, standing in front of the throne. Books were opened, including the Book of Life. The dead were judged on the basis of what they had done, as recorded in the books"* (Revelation 20:11–12).

How we have responded to the gospel message concerning the Son of God will determine if we will spend eternity with Him.

Mark 16:9–13

Some scholars believe that Mark's Gospel ends at verse eight since, among other reasons, the earliest Greek manuscripts do not contain verses nine through twenty.[3] Some manuscripts include just one additional verse, which is referred to as the "Shorter Ending."[4] However, verses nine through twenty, called the "Longer Ending," are found in a great majority of the early manuscripts.[5]

It is impossible to draw a dogmatic conclusion about these discrepancies. However, it may be best to summarize these disparities by maintaining that it really makes little difference to our understanding of Mark's Gospel or any other New Testament writing. Nothing in the remaining verses conflicts with the positions of other canonical writers.[6] The recognition of these verses as part of the New Testament is generally accepted, regardless of disputes concerning authorship. Since opinions for or against the authority of these verses can be neither proven nor rejected with any measure of certainty, it is essential to include them in any commentary on the book as a whole.

16:9 *After Jesus came back to life early on Sunday, he appeared first to Mary from Magdala, from whom he had forced out seven demons.*

Jesus had not yet been seen by anyone. The only testimony to His resurrection was an empty tomb and an angel's words. When He appeared, He did so first to Mary of Magdala, commonly known as Mary Magdalene. Apparently, Mary Magdalene, Mary the mother of Joses, and Salome had left the tomb frightened by what they had seen and heard. Shortly thereafter, Jesus appeared to Mary Magdalene.

Although Mark had mentioned Mary Magdalene on three previous occasions, this is the first reference to her life before she met Jesus. We are told that Jesus had rescued her from seven demons. This reference is verified in Luke's gospel: "Also, some women were with him. They had been cured from evil spirits and various illnesses.

. . . Mary, also called Magdalene, from whom seven demons had gone out" *(Luke 8:2)*.

16:10 *She went and told his friends, who were grieving and crying.*

Mary Magdalene went to the disciples and announced the good news of Jesus' resurrection. When she located them, they were mourning His death. Their grief was intense. They had lost their friend, the one Whom they thought was Israel's Messiah. Undoubtedly, their despair was compounded by their own failure to stand by Jesus' side. Each one of them had forsaken their master and fled.

16:11 *They didn't believe her when they heard that he was alive and that she had seen him.*

Mary Magdalene told the disciples that Jesus was alive and that she had seen Him, but they could not accept her eyewitness testimony of His resurrection. To them, these were the hysterical ramblings of a woman distraught in her grief. She could not be believed.

Why couldn't the disciples remember Jesus' words from only a few nights earlier at the celebration of the Passover feast? *"²⁷All of you will abandon me. Scripture says, 'I will strike the shepherd, and the sheep will be scattered.' ²⁸But after I am brought back to life, I will go to Galilee ahead of you"* (Mark 14:27–28). Is it possible that they understood their dismal failure but forgot Jesus' message of hope? Repeatedly, Jesus had told them that He would rise from the dead, but this statement was always met with doubt and misunderstanding because the concept was nearly impossible for the disciples to grasp. *"They kept in mind what he said but argued among themselves what he meant by 'come back to life'"* (Mark 9:10).

16:12 *Later Jesus appeared to two disciples as they were walking to their home in the country. He did not look as he usually did.*

Later, Jesus appeared to two of the disciples as they left Jerusalem. We can conclude that these two were likely present when Mary Magdalene said that she had seen Jesus.

According to a parallel account, these two disciples were returning to their home in Emmaus when they were joined by a stranger. A dialogue ensued in which the stranger revealed the Scriptures relating to Israel's Messiah, God's Anointed One. Finally, the stranger joined them for supper, and when He broke the bread and blessed it, their eyes were opened to the miraculous fact that this stranger was Jesus (*Luke 24:13–35*).

16:13 *They went back and told the others, who did not believe them either.*

These two disciples immediately returned to Jerusalem (*Luke 24:33*). There, they sought out the other disciples and related the remarkable events of their journey, that they had walked, talked, and broken bread with Jesus. Mary Magdalene had told the truth. Jesus was alive again!

Nevertheless, the remaining disciples could not accept the testimony of these two witnesses, either. It was inconceivable to hope that Jesus was alive again. Remarkably, they denied one of the basic tenets of Jewish law, which stated that the testimony of two witnesses validated the truthfulness of an account (*Deuteronomy 19:15*). Mary Magdalene's testimony could be discarded because she was a woman and because it was the testimony of only one person. However, they now had the testimony of two men who emphatically confirmed that they had seen Jesus. Why would they rush back to Jerusalem from Emmaus to tell the others if it were not true? Why would they expose themselves to the ridicule of others by promoting false reports about such implausible events?

Notes/Applications

In reading Mark's gospel we are drawn toward conclusions based on clear evidence—factual, historical evidence of the life, ministry, death, and resurrection of Jesus of Nazareth. Like the Roman centurion, we must stand at the foot of the cross and declare, "Certainly, this man was the Son of God!" Yet it is not cold hard facts that convince us but the excitement in our hearts *(Luke 24:32)*. The presence of the indwelling Spirit and the evidence of a changed life are the most powerful witnesses testifying that we are truly sons and daughters of the living God: "¹⁶The Spirit himself testifies with our spirit that we are God's children. ¹⁷If we are his children, we are also God's heirs. If we share in Christ's suffering in order to share his glory, we are heirs together with him" *(Romans 8:16–17)*.

Throughout this gospel account, we have walked the mountaintops and crossed the valleys. We have been taken to safety from the stormy seas. We have seen Jesus speaking to Moses and Elijah. We have seen Him prostrate on the ground in Gethsemane. We have heard the awful cry, "My God, My God! Why have You abandoned Me?" We have heard the testimonies of Mary Magdalene and the two disciples from Emmaus. The only acceptable conclusion to the matters presented to us is that Jesus is the Son of God. His words, His actions, His atoning death, and His resurrection rekindle in our hapless lives the spark of hope. By responding to His call to salvation, we become participants in the message of His kingdom, and we share the joys and responsibilities of those early disciples.

Mark 16:14-20

16:14 *Still later Jesus appeared to the eleven apostles while they were eating. He put them to shame for their unbelief and because they were too stubborn to believe those who had seen him alive.*

Jesus finally appeared to His grief-stricken followers while they were eating. He strongly rebuked them for failing to believe trustworthy eyewitnesses. Despite His special care and His many private discussions with them, these men continued to be exceedingly cynical in both heart and mind. They were still unable to comprehend the scope of the greatest message ever given to humankind. Jesus, therefore, reproached His chosen ones for their refusal to believe.

16:15 *Then Jesus said to them, "So wherever you go in the world, tell everyone the Good News.*

The risen Lord now provided His final earthly instructions to His followers. Only Mark and Matthew record these instructions (*Matthew 28:19*). They both begin with the same wording. Those who follow Jesus are instructed to go everywhere and preach the Good News to everyone. Whatever our occupation, wherever the journey of life takes us, we are to carry the gospel (the Good News) with us. This Good News is the same message Jesus had proclaimed since beginning of His public ministry. It is the message of the kingdom of God brought to earth by the Son of Man. On the foundation of Jesus' sacrifice for the sins of the world and proven by the indisputable evidence of His resurrection, we experience forgiveness for our sin and reconciliation to God the Father.

16:16 *Whoever believes and is baptized will be saved, but whoever does not believe will be condemned.*

As noted in chapter fourteen, the new covenant is not an agreement of two parties who stand on equal terms (*Mark 14:24*). This new covenant is a unilateral offer established by God through the blood of Jesus Christ, the perfect sacrificial Passover lamb. We can only accept or reject this arrangement. We can never alter the terms of this God-ordained covenant. Having sent into the world His only Son, Almighty God can offer nothing more to humankind. He has given us His best. He has purchased our redemption through the blood sacrifice of His Son.

Accordingly, Jesus now plainly communicated the two alternatives that lay before each individual. A person's response to this decision has eternal implications. We can either believe the testimony of many eyewitnesses or avoid the evidence that is presented to us. Belief results in eternal life in heaven; rejection results in eternal condemnation in hell. The Greek word translated in this verse as "saved" is the future tense of $\sigma o \zeta \omega$ (sowdso).[7] The full impact of that word means that we have been healed, we have been made whole.[8] We are complete, but only after we have accepted the evidence of God's gift of His Son. Only when we accept God's forgiving grace by the convicting power of the Holy Spirit can we come home to the one Who has made us and redeemed us.

It is critical to establish that this verse does not affirm that baptism is essential for salvation.[9] As preached by both John the Baptizer and Jesus Christ Himself, baptism is an outward, symbolic gesture of an inward commitment to the Lord. Repentance, not baptism, is the key to salvation (Mark 1:15; Mark 6:12; Luke 13:3–5). Any assertion that baptism is fundamental to salvation contradicts other scriptural accounts (John 10:9; Acts 2:21; Acts 16:31; Romans 5:10; 10:9,13; Ephesians 2:8; Titus 3:5). Rather, Jesus mentioned baptism because it is a natural response after salvation (Acts 2:41; 8:12; 18:8). Humankind is not condemned because of its refusal to be baptized but because of its refusal to believe in the Lord Jesus Christ as the once-and-for-all atonement for the sins of the world[10] (Hebrews 10:10).

16:17–18 [17]*"These are the miraculous signs that will accompany believers: They will use the power and authority of my name to force demons out of people. They will speak new languages.* [18]*They will pick up snakes, and if they drink any deadly poison, it will not hurt them. They will place their hands on the sick and cure them."*

Jesus then spoke of evidences that would confirm the message of the evangelists. In the name of Jesus, they would cast out demons. The Twelve had already done this under Jesus' direct command (*Mark 6:13*). The power to cast out demons would be a predominant sign in the establishment of the early church (*Acts 5:16; 8:7; 16:16–18; 19:11–12*). Another evidence of the authority by which the followers of Christ would preach would be speaking "new languages," which did not occur until the day of Pentecost. At that time, the Holy Spirit descended on the disciples, and they spoke in "other languages" so that every person present "was startled to recognize his own dialect" (*Acts 2:4–6*). This sign would occur again some years later when the gospel message was preached to the Gentiles (*Acts 10:46–47; 19:6*). Still another sign that would demonstrate the power of God would be that His followers would be unaffected by snake bites or poison. There is only one biblical record of such an occurrence.

> [3]*Paul gathered a bundle of brushwood and put it on the fire. The heat forced a poisonous snake out of the brushwood. The snake bit Paul's hand and wouldn't let go.* [4]*When the people who lived on the island saw the snake hanging from his hand, they said to each other, "This man must be a murderer! He may have escaped from the sea, but justice won't let him live."*
>
> [5]*Paul shook the snake into the fire and wasn't harmed.* [6]*The people were waiting for him to swell up or suddenly drop dead. But after they had waited a long time and saw nothing unusual happen to him, they changed their minds and said he was a god. (Acts 28:3–6)*

While there are no scriptural accounts of anyone drinking poison without effect, there are some peripheral historical evidences of such events.[11] One such reference by early church historian Papias tells of a man named Barsabbas, possibly one of the candidates considered for apostleship (*Acts 1:23*), who drank a poisonous concoction and, by the grace of the Lord, received no harm.[12] However, in all records, whether biblical or supplementary, the disciple did not deliberately place himself in harm's way to exhibit this capability.[13] Rather, such events demonstrated God's power to protect His disciples in circumstances that would normally be fatal.

16:19 *After talking with the apostles, the Lord was taken to heaven, where God gave him the highest position.*

After these final instructions, Jesus ascended into heaven. He departed from their presence and assumed His assigned position at the right hand of God. Jesus' earthly ministry was completed. He came into the world for the specific purpose of redeeming humankind from the curse of sin through His own death on the cross. Jesus had told His disciples while debating with the members of the Sanhedrin, "The Lord said to my Lord: 'Take the highest position in heaven until I put your enemies under your control'" (*Mark 12:36*). Jesus clearly knew His rightful place with His Father. Even before His death, He knew His final appointment would return Him to the very throne from which He was sent into the world.

16:20 *The disciples spread the Good News everywhere. The Lord worked with them. He confirmed his word by the miraculous signs that accompanied it.*

Jesus' final instructions were fulfilled in the lives and words of His disciples. These were the same men who had been frightened and amazed by the many aspects of Jesus' power and control over all of the elements of the human experience. They had abandoned their Lord at the time of His betrayal and had struggled to believe that

Jesus had risen from the dead. However, filled with the Holy Spirit, they fulfilled God's purpose for their lives. They became powerful and dynamic witnesses to the power and glory of God shown to man in the life, death, and resurrection of Jesus, the eternally appointed Messiah. The message of God's kingdom was further endorsed by unmistakable signs, some of which are noted in verses seventeen and eighteen, which confirmed the authority by which the disciples preached. The church of Jesus Christ was born, and the world would never be the same.

Notes/Applications

Why would the eternal God lower Himself to enter the dimensions of time and space? How can we ever comprehend the great and timeless scope of His sacrifice? If there were one predominant theme weaving through the Gospel of Mark, it would be the journey from mental and spiritual stupor to a great spiritual awakening experienced by the many people who were touched by Jesus' ministry. Consistently and repeatedly, Mark comments on the reactions of Jesus' disciples to the actions and teachings of Jesus. Mark presents the evidence of Jesus' life, ministry, death, and resurrection. With this, we place the final piece of evidence in a long list of compelling proofs that Jesus is the Son of God. He is:

- The one prophesied by Old Testament writings
- The one prophesied by John the Baptizer
- The one ordained by God Himself
- The one Who conquers the temptations of Satan
- The one Who declares good news to the world
- The one Who is the authoritative teacher
- The one acknowledged by evil spirits to be the Messiah
- The one Who has authority over our physical realities
- The one Who has authority to forgive sins
- The one Who has authority over all the forces of nature
- The one Who has authority over life and death
- The one Whose true identity is revealed in the Transfiguration

- The one to conquer death and live forevermore

The burden of decision is now placed squarely on our shoulders. Do we embrace His matchless love, or do we disregard it as a mythical fabrication?

Those of us who have been called "out of darkness into his marvelous light" (1 Peter 2:9–10) can only respond with grateful, humbled hearts as the evidence of our Father's encompassing love washes over us. We raise our faces in joy and praise to our Redeemer as we look heavenward and behold His glory at the right hand of the Father. Our tongues cleave to the roofs of our mouths, and our words of gratitude seem completely inadequate. Nevertheless, in concluding a study in the Gospel of Mark, we are reminded of the overriding purpose for our lives in Christ—the Great Commission. Yes, Jesus saved us, but He saved us for a reason—not just that we might live with Him throughout eternity but also that the power of God's redemption might be made known to others by the evidence of His love in action through our lives.

TEXT NOTES

INTRODUCTION

1. William Hendrickson, *Exposition of the Gospel According to Mark,* of *New Testament Commentary* (Grand Rapids: Baker Books, 1975), 3.

2. William L. Lane, *The Gospel of Mark,* of *The New International Commentary on the New Testament* (Grand Rapids: Eerdmans Publishing Company, 1974), 2.

CHAPTER ONE

1. W. E. Vine, *Vine's Expository Dictionary of Old and New Testament Words* (Nashville: Thomas Nelson Publishers, 1997), 951–952.

2. George Ricker Berry, *Lexicon of Greek to English Interlinear New Testament (KJV)* (Grand Rapids: Word Publishing, 1981), 4.

3. Vine, *Vine's Expository Dictionary,* 925.

4. See Mark 1:36 in the *New American Standard Bible* (La Habra, California: The Lockman Foundation, 1960).

5. Vine, *Vine's Expository Dictionary,* 187.

CHAPTER TWO

1. Kenneth L. Barker and John R. Kohlenberger III, ed., *Zondervan NIV Bible Commentary*, vol. 2, New Testament (Grand Rapids: Zondervan Publishing House, 1994), 144.

2. William L. Lane, *The Gospel of Mark*, of *The New International Commentary on the New Testament* (Grand Rapids: Eerdmans Publishing Company, 1974), 109–110.

3. *New Geneva Study Bible*, ed. R. C. Sproul (Nashville: Thomas Nelson Publishers, 1995), 1565.

CHAPTER THREE

1. J. D. Douglas, ed., *New Bible Dictionary*, 2d ed. (Wheaton, Ill.: Tyndale House Publishers, 1962), 1074.

2. William L. Lane, *The Gospel of Mark*, of *The New International Commentary on the New Testament* (Grand Rapids: Eerdmans Publishing Company, 1974), 143.

3. John Gill, *Exposition of the Old and New Testaments*, vol. 7 (1810; reprint, Paris, Ark.: The Baptist Standard Bearer, 1989), 397.

4. "Christ a Redeemer and Friend," words by John Newton, *Olney Hymns* (London: W. Oliver, 1779). Public Domain.

CHAPTER FOUR

1. George Ricker Berry, *Greek to English Interlinear New Testament (KJV)* (Grand Rapids: Word Publishing, 1981), 100.

2. Charles F. Pfeiffer and Everett F. Harrison, *The Wycliffe Bible Commentary* (Chicago: Moody Press, 1962), 997.

3. Warren W. Wiersbe, *Wiersbe's Expository Outlines on the New Testament* (Colorado Springs: Victor Books, 1992), 114.

CHAPTER FIVE

1. *New Geneva Study Bible*, ed. R. C. Sproul (Nashville: Thomas Nelson Publishers, 1995), 1569.

2. John MacArthur, *MacArthur Study Bible* (Nashville: Thomas Nelson Bibles, 1997), 1467.

3. John Gill, *Exposition of the Old and New Testaments*, vol. 7 (1810; reprint, Paris, Ark.: The Baptist Standard Bearer, 1989), 405.

4. Warren W. Wiersbe, *Wiersbe's Expository Outlines on the New Testament* (Colorado Springs: Victor Books, 1992), 114.

5. William Hendriksen, *Mark*, of *New Testament Commentary* (Grand Rapids: Baker Books, 1975), 193–194.

6. William L. Lane, *The Gospel of Mark*, of *The New International Commentary on the New Testament* (Grand Rapids: Eerdmans Publishing Company, 1974), 196.

CHAPTER SIX

1. William Hendriksen, *Mark*, of *New Testament Commentary* (Grand Rapids: Baker Books, 1975), 227.

2. William L. Lane, *The Gospel of Mark*, of *The New International Commentary on the New Testament* (Grand Rapids: Eerdmans Publishing Company, 1974), 208–209.

3. *New Geneva Study Bible*, ed. R. C. Sproul (Nashville: Thomas Nelson Publishers, 1995), 1571.

4. John Gill, *Exposition of the Old and New Testaments*, vol. 7 (1810; reprint, Paris, Ark.: The Baptist Standard Bearer, 1989), 423.

5. Flavius Josephus, "Antiquities of the Jews," in *The Complete Works of Flavius Josephus*, trans. William Whiston (Grand Rapids: Kregel Publications, 1960), 383.

6. George Ricker Berry, *Greek to English Interlinear New Testament (KJV)* (Grand Rapids: Word Publishing, 1981), 106.

7. Gill, *Exposition of the Old and New Testaments*, 426.

8. Lane, *The Gospel of Mark*, 229.

9. John F. Walvoord and Roy B. Zuck, *Bible Knowledge Commentary* (Colorado Springs: Chariot Victor Publishing, 1983), 131.

10. John Calvin, "Commentary on the Gospel According to John," vol. 1, in vol. 17 of *Calvin's Commentaries*, trans. Thomas Myers (1843; reprint, Grand Rapids: Baker Books, 1999), 236.

11. Hendriksen, *Mark*, 259.

CHAPTER SEVEN

1. John Gill, *Exposition of the Old and New Testaments*, vol. 7 (1810; reprint, Paris, Ark.: The Baptist Standard Bearer, 1989), 429.

2. W. E. Vine, *Vine's Expository Dictionary of Old and New Testament Words* (Nashville: Thomas Nelson Publishers, 1997), 232.

3. William Hendriksen, *Mark*, of *New Testament Commentary* (Grand Rapids: Baker Books, 1975), 278–279.

4. John Calvin, "Harmony of the Evangelists: Matthew, Mark, and Luke," vol. 2, in vol. 16 of *Calvin's Commentaries*, trans. Thomas Myers (1843; reprint, Grand Rapids: Baker Books, 1999), 251.

5. George Ricker Berry, *Greek to English Interlinear New Testament (KJV)* (Grand Rapids: Word Publishing, 1981), 112.

6. Excerpt from "Hark! There Comes a Whisper" by Fanny Crosby, *Sacred Songs and Solos* (London: Morgan and Scott Ltd., late 19th century). Public Domain.

CHAPTER EIGHT

1. John F. Walvoord and Roy B. Zuck, *Bible Knowledge Commentary* (Colorado Springs: Chariot Victor Publishing, 1983), 137.

2. Walter A. Elwell, ed., *Baker Commentary on the Bible* (Grand Rapids: Baker Books, 1989), 780.

3. William Hendriksen, *Mark*, of *New Testament Commentary* (Grand Rapids: Baker Books, 1975), 316.

4. James Strong, *Greek Dictionary of the New Testament*, of *Strong's Exhaustive Concordance of the Bible* (Iowa Falls, Iowa: World Bible Publishers, 1986), 25.

5. Gerhard Friedrich, ed., *Theological Dictionary of the New Testament,* vol. 2 (Grand Rapids: Eerdmans Publishing Company, 1964–1976), 21.

6. William L. Lane, *The Gospel of Mark,* of *The New International Commentary on the New Testament* (Grand Rapids: Eerdmans Publishing Company, 1974), 304.

CHAPTER NINE

1. Matthew Henry, *Matthew Henry's Commentary on the Whole Bible* (Peabody, Mass.: Hendrickson Publishers, 1991), 1796; William L. Lane, *The Gospel of Mark,* of *The New International Commentary on the New Testament* (Grand Rapids: Eerdmans Publishing Company, 1974), 314; John Calvin, "Harmony of the Evangelists: Matthew, Mark, and Luke," vol. 2, in vol. 16 of *Calvin's Commentaries,* trans. Thomas Myers (1843; reprint, Grand Rapids: Baker Books, 1999), 307; Kenneth L. Barker and John R. Kohlenberger III, ed., *Zondervan NIV Bible Commentary,* Vol. 2, New Testament (Grand Rapids: Zondervan Publishing House, 1994), 169.

2. Walter A. Elwell, ed., *Baker Commentary on the Bible* (Grand Rapids: Baker Books, 1989), 783; William MacDonald, *Believer's Bible Commentary,* ed. Art Farstad (Nashville: Thomas Nelson Publishers, 1995), 1342.

3. William Hendriksen, *Mark,* of *New Testament Commentary* (Grand Rapids: Baker Books, 1975), 338.

4. Albert Barnes, *The Gospels,* of *Barnes' Notes on the New Testament* (1884; reprint, Grand Rapids: Baker Books, 2001), 176; Henry, *Matthew Henry's Commentary,* 1796.

5. John MacArthur, *MacArthur Study Bible* (Nashville: Thomas Nelson Bibles, 1997), 1478.

6. Excerpt from "O Wondrous Sight!" Words by Sarum Breviary (Venice: 1495) (Coelestis formam gloriae); translated from Latin to English by John M. Neale, 1851.

7. W. E. Vine, *Vine's Expository Dictionary of Old and New Testament Words* (Nashville: Thomas Nelson Publishers, 1997), 1019–1020.

8. Vine, *Vine's Expository Dictionary*, 1019.

9. John Calvin, "Commentary on the Book of the Prophet Isaiah," vol. 4, in vol. 8 of *Calvin's Commentaries*, trans. Thomas Myers (1843; reprint, Grand Rapids: Baker Books, 1999), 439; John Gill, *Exposition of the Old and New Testaments*, vol. 7 (1810; reprint, Paris, Ark.: The Baptist Standard Bearer, 1989), 452.

CHAPTER TEN

1. John F. Walvoord and Roy B. Zuck, *Bible Knowledge Commentary* (Colorado Springs: Chariot Victor Publishing, 1983), 148.

2. John Gill, *Exposition of the Old and New Testaments*, vol. 7 (1810; reprint, Paris, Ark.: The Baptist Standard Bearer, 1989), 454.

3. Flavius Josephus, "Antiquities of the Jews," in *The Complete Works of Flavius Josephus*, trans. William Whiston (Grand Rapids: Kregel Publications, 1960), 327.

4. John MacArthur, *MacArthur Study Bible* (Nashville: Thomas Nelson Bibles, 1997), 1482.

5. William L. Lane, *The Gospel of Mark*, of *The New International Commentary on the New Testament* (Grand Rapids: Eerdmans Publishing Company, 1974), 372.

6. John Calvin, "Harmony of the Evangelists: Matthew, Mark, and Luke," vol. 2, in vol. 16 of *Calvin's Commentaries*, trans. Thomas Myers (1843; reprint, Grand Rapids: Baker Books, 1999), 417–418.

CHAPTER ELEVEN

1. John Calvin, "Harmony of the Evangelists: Matthew, Mark, and Luke," vol. 2, in vol. 16 of *Calvin's Commentaries*, trans. Thomas Myers (1843; reprint, Grand Rapids: Baker Books, 1999), 447.

2. John Gill, *Exposition of the Old and New Testaments*, vol. 7 (1810; reprint, Paris, Ark.: The Baptist Standard Bearer, 1989), 234.

3. W. E. Vine, *Vine's Expository Dictionary of Old and New Testament Words* (Nashville: Thomas Nelson Publishers, 1997), 564.

4. Excerpt from "Through This Holy Week of Our Salvation," words by William H. Draper, *Hymns for the Holy Week*, 1898. Public Domain.

5. John MacArthur, *MacArthur Study Bible* (Nashville: Thomas Nelson Bibles, 1997), 1485–1486.

6. MacArthur, *MacArthur Study Bible*, 1486.

7. William L. Lane, *The Gospel of Mark*, of *The New International Commentary on the New Testament* (Grand Rapids: Eerdmans Publishing Company, 1974), 400–402; Matthew Henry, *Matthew Henry's Commentary on the Whole Bible* (Peabody, Mass.: Hendrickson Publishers, 1991), 1803.

8. Excerpt from "Why Did the Jews Proclaim Their Rage?" words by Isaac Watts, *The Psalms of David*, 1719. Public Domain.

CHAPTER TWELVE

1. William Hendriksen, *Mark*, of *New Testament Commentary* (Grand Rapids: Baker Books, 1975), 473.

2. J. D. M. Derrett, *Fresh Light on the Parable of the Wicked Vinedressers* (RIDA 3rd Ser. 10, 1963), 11–41.

3. John Gill, *Exposition of the Old and New Testaments*, vol. 7 (1810; reprint, Paris, Ark.: The Baptist Standard Bearer, 1989), 469.

4. Homer A. Kent, Jr., *Jerusalem to Rome: Studies in the Book of Acts* (Grand Rapids: Baker Book House Company, 1972), 169.

5. John MacArthur, *MacArthur Study Bible* (Nashville: Thomas Nelson Bibles, 1997), 1489.

6. *New Geneva Study Bible*, ed. R. C. Sproul (Nashville: Thomas Nelson Publishers, 1995), 374.

7. Gill, *Exposition of the Old and New Testaments*, 473.

CHAPTER THIRTEEN

1. Flavius Josephus, "Antiquities of the Jews," in *The Complete Works of Flavius Josephus*, trans. William Whiston (Grand Rapids: Kregel Publications, 1960), 334–335.

2. Cleon L. Rogers, Jr., and Cleon L. Rogers III, *The New Linguistic and Exegetical Key to the Greek New Testament* (Grand Rapids: Zondervan Publishing House, 1998), 96.

3. William Hendriksen, *Mark*, of *New Testament Commentary* (Grand Rapids: Baker Books, 1975), 517.

4. Josephus, *The Complete Works*, 320, 329–330.

5. Hendriksen, *Mark*, 520–521.

6. W. E. Vine, *Vine's Expository Dictionary of Old and New Testament Words* (Nashville: Thomas Nelson Publishers, 1997), 774.

7. John Calvin, "Harmony of the Evangelists: Matthew, Mark, and Luke," vol. 3, in vol. 17 of *Calvin's Commentaries*, trans. Thomas Myers (1843; reprint, Grand Rapids: Baker Books, 1999), 133–135.

8. William L. Lane, *The Gospel of Mark*, of *The New International Commentary on the New Testament* (Grand Rapids: Eerdmans Publishing Company, 1974), 466.

9. John Gill, *Exposition of the Old and New Testaments*, vol. 7 (1810; reprint, Paris, Ark.: The Baptist Standard Bearer, 1989), 476; Matthew Henry, *Matthew Henry's Commentary on the Whole Bible* (Peabody, Mass.: Hendrickson Publishers, 1991), 1808.

10. Practical Christianity Foundation, *Daniel: In God I Trust* (Holiday, Florida: Green Key Books, 2002), 181–187; Hendriksen, *Mark*, 525–526.

11. Gill, *Exposition of the Old and New Testaments*, 476; Henry, *Matthew Henry's Commentary*, 1808.

12. Josephus, *The Complete Works*, 580.

13. Gill, *Exposition of the Old and New Testaments*, 477.

14. "Come, Thou Long-Expected Jesus," words by Charles Wesley, *Hymns for the Nativity of Our Lord*, 1744. Public Domain.

15. R. C. Sproul, *The Last Days According to Jesus* (Grand Rapids: Baker Books, 1998), 65–68.

16. Gill, *Exposition of the Old and New Testaments*, 477.

17. Gleason L. Archer, *Encyclopedia of Bible Difficulties* (Grand Rapids: Zondervan Publishing House, 1982), 338–339; Rogers, Jr., and Rogers III, *The New Linguistic and Exegetical Key to the Greek New Testament*, 55; Hendriksen, *Mark*, 540.

CHAPTER FOURTEEN

1. Flavius Josephus, "Antiquities of the Jews," in *The Complete Works of Flavius Josephus*, trans. William Whiston (Grand Rapids: Kregel Publications, 1960), 368.

2. *New Geneva Study Bible*, ed. R. C. Sproul (Nashville: Thomas Nelson Publishers, 1995), 1591.

3. William Hendriksen, *Mark*, of *New Testament Commentary* (Grand Rapids: Baker Books, 1975), 558.

4. *Complete Jewish Bible*, trans. David H. Stern (Clarksville, Md.: Jewish New Testament Publications, 1998), 1282.

5. Hendriksen, *Mark*, 560.

6. William L. Lane, *The Gospel of Mark*, of *The New International Commentary on the New Testament* (Grand Rapids: Eerdmans Publishing Company, 1974), 497.

7. John MacArthur, *MacArthur Study Bible* (Nashville: Thomas Nelson Bibles, 1997), 1494.

8. Lane, *The Gospel of Mark*, 502.

9. John Calvin, "Harmony of the Evangelists: Matthew, Mark, and Luke," vol. 3, in vol. 17 of *Calvin's Commentaries*, trans. Thomas Myers (1843; reprint, Grand Rapids: Baker Books, 1999), 204.

10. G. F. MacLear, D. D., A *Classbook of New Testament History* (Grand Rapids: Eerdmans Publishing Company, 1962), 280–281.

11. MacLear, A *Classbook of New Testament History*, 280–281.

12. James M. Freeman, *The New Manners and Customs of the Bible*, ed. Harold J. Chadwick (North Brunswick, N.J.: Bridge-Logos Publishers, 1998), 477.

13. Hendriksen, *Mark*, 585.

14. Excerpt from " 'Tis Midnight, and on Olive's Brow," words by William B. Tappan, *Poems*, 1822. Public Domain.

15. William MacDonald, *Believer's Bible Commentary*, ed. Art Farstad (Nashville: Thomas Nelson Publishers, 1995), 1359–1360; Lane, *The Gospel of Mark*, 527; Kenneth L. Barker and John R. Kohlenberger III, ed., *Zondervan NIV Bible Commentary*, Vol. 2, New Testament (Grand Rapids: Zondervan Publishing House, 1994), 195.

16. MacArthur, *MacArthur Study Bible*, 1498.

17. Hendriksen, *Mark*, 585.

CHAPTER FIFTEEN

1. Flavius Josephus, "Antiquities of the Jews," in *The Complete Works of Flavius Josephus*, trans. William Whiston (Grand Rapids: Kregel Publications, 1960), 379.

2. J. B. Jackson, A *Dictionary of Scripture Proper Names* (Neptune, N.J.: Loizeaux Brothers, 1909), 15.

3. Josephus, *The Complete Works*, 580.

4. William Hendriksen, *Mark*, of *New Testament Commentary* (Grand Rapids: Baker Books, 1975), 640.

5. John F. Walvoord and Roy B. Zuck, *Bible Knowledge Commentary* (Colorado Springs: Chariot Victor Publishing, 1983), 186.

6. William L. Lane, *The Gospel of Mark*, of *The New International Commentary on the New Testament* (Grand Rapids: Eerdmans Publishing Company, 1974), 497.

7. Cleon L. Rogers, Jr., and Cleon L. Rogers III, *The New Linguistic and Exegetical Key to the Greek New Testament* (Grand Rapids: Zondervan Publishing House, 1998), 102.

8. James M. Freeman, *The New Manners and Customs of the Bible*, ed. Harold J. Chadwick (North Brunswick, N.J.: Bridge-Logos Publishers, 1998), 483–484.

9. W. E. Vine, *Vine's Expository Dictionary of Old and New Testament Words* (Nashville: Thomas Nelson Publishers, 1997), 250.

10. Walvoord and Zuck, *Bible Knowledge Commentary*, 187.

11. William MacDonald, *Believer's Bible Commentary*, ed. Art Farstad (Nashville: Thomas Nelson Publishers, 1995), 1362.

12. Charles F. Pfeiffer and Everett F. Harrison, *The Wycliffe Bible Commentary* (Chicago: Moody Press, 1962), 1023.

13. Kenneth L. Barker and John R. Kohlenberger III, ed., *Zondervan NIV Bible Commentary*, Vol. 2, New Testament (Grand Rapids: Zondervan Publishing House, 1994), 199.

14. Hendriksen, *Mark*, 649.

15. Lane, *The Gospel of Mark*, 564.

16. Walvoord and Zuck, *Bible Knowledge Commentary*, 188.

17. Walvoord and Zuck, *Bible Knowledge Commentary*, 188.

18. J. D. Douglas, ed., *New Bible Dictionary*, 2d ed. (Wheaton, Ill.: Tyndale House Publishers, 1962), 253–254.

19. Hendriksen, *Mark*, 651–652.

20. Freeman, *The New Manners and Customs of the Bible*, 488.

21. Lane, *The Gospel of Mark*, 568.

22. John Gill, *Exposition of the Old and New Testaments*, vol. 7 (1810; reprint, Paris, Ark.: The Baptist Standard Bearer, 1989), 363.

23. Gill, *Exposition of the Old and New Testaments*, 364.

24. Hendriksen, *Mark*, 663.

25. Walvoord and Zuck, *Bible Knowledge Commentary*, 189.

26. Freeman, *The New Manners and Customs of the Bible*, 488–489.

27. Gill, *Exposition of the Old and New Testaments*, 365.

28. Freeman, *The New Manners and Customs of the Bible*, 489–490.

29. "Throned Upon the Awful Tree," words by John Ellerton, 1875. Public Domain.

30. R. C. H. Lenski, *The Interpretation of St. Mark's Gospel*, of *Commentary on the New Testament* (Columbus: Wartburg Press, 1943), 727.

31. Matthew Henry, *Matthew Henry's Commentary on the Whole Bible* (Peabody, Mass.: Hendrickson Publishers, 1991), 1816.

32. *New Geneva Study Bible*, ed. R. C. Sproul (Nashville: Thomas Nelson Publishers, 1995), 1596.

33. Lane, *The Gospel of Mark*, 580.

34. "O Come and Mourn with Me a While," words by Frederick W. Faber, 1849. Public Domain.

CHAPTER SIXTEEN

1. William Hendriksen, *Mark*, of *New Testament Commentary* (Grand Rapids: Baker Books, 1975), 681.

2. W. A. Elwell, *Evangelical Dictionary of Biblical Theology*, electronic ed. (Baker Reference Library; Logos Library System. Grand Rapids: Baker Book House, 1996).

3. Hendriksen, *Mark*, 682–687.

4. William L. Lane, *The Gospel of Mark*, of *The New International Commentary on the New Testament* (Grand Rapids: Eerdmans Publishing Company, 1974), 601–603.

5. William MacDonald, *Believer's Bible Commentary*, ed. Art Farstad (Nashville: Thomas Nelson Publishers, 1995), 1363–1364.

6. John F. Walvoord and Roy B. Zuck, *Bible Knowledge Commentary* (Colorado Springs: Chariot Victor Publishing, 1983), 194.

7. Cleon L. Rogers, Jr., and Cleon L. Rogers III, *The New Linguistic and Exegetical Key to the Greek New Testament* (Grand Rapids: Zondervan Publishing House, 1998), 104.

8. W. E. Vine, *Vine's Expository Dictionary of Old and New Testament Words* (Nashville: Thomas Nelson Publishers, 1997), 993.

9. Homer A. Kent, Jr., *Jerusalem to Rome: Studies in the Book of Acts* (Grand Rapids: Baker Book House Company, 1972), 33–34.

10. John MacArthur, *MacArthur Study Bible* (Nashville: Thomas Nelson Bibles, 1997), 1502–1503.

11. R. C. H. Lenski, *The Interpretation of St. Mark's Gospel*, of *Commentary on the New Testament* (Columbus: Wartburg Press, 1943), 769–771.

12. John Gill, *Exposition of the Old and New Testaments*, vol. 7 (1810; reprint, Paris, Ark.: The Baptist Standard Bearer, 1989), 495–496.

13. Walvoord and Zuck, *Bible Knowledge Commentary*, 196.

Commentaries available from
PRACTICAL CHRISTIANITY FOUNDATION

DANIEL
In God I Trust

MARK
Jesus Christ, Love in Action

JOHN
The Word Made Flesh

THE GENERAL EPISTLES
A Practical Faith

REVELATION
Tribulation and Triumph

For more information, please visit www.greenkeybooks.com